The Adoption Triangle Revisited
A study of adoption, search and reunion experiences

A 80:

D0656187

Acknowledgements

First and foremost, we would like to acknowledge our great appreciation to all those birth mothers, adopted people, adoptive parents and birth fathers who responded to the study. Without them there would be no study. We are also very appreciative of the staff at The Children's Society Post Adoption and Care Team, based in Peckham, London, for their active involvement and continued support of the project. Their wealth of experience in the field of adoption and their advice, comments and guidance at every stage proved invaluable. Particular thanks go to:

Elizabeth Webb, Janet Smith, Rose Wallace, Erica Peltier, Jenny Setterington and Penny Whittingham.

We also greatly benefited from the knowledge, expertise and suggestions of the Advisory Group whose membership was made up of:

Cindy Downs, Monica Duck, Carol Edwards, Barry Luckock, Philly Morrall, Julia Ridgway, Jill Walker and Elizabeth Webb.

We are grateful to Louise Swift, statistician from the University of East Anglia, with whom we consulted when analysing some of the more complex data and to Deborah Cullen at BAAF for her assistance on the legislative framework. Editing suggestions made by Professor Malcolm Hill of the Glasgow Centre for the Child and Society and Shaila Shah from BAAF proved invaluable and greatly helped to give shape to the final text. We have been very fortunate in having the back-up services of dedicated administrative and secretarial staff including Danielle Sawyer, Margaret Grant and Rose Durey at BAAF (London); Linda Morris in Edinburgh; Ruth Timlett, Ann Stephens, Liz Hill, and Carole Crossley, administrators at The Children's Society; and Richard Baylis who volunteered his time to help send out the questionnaires.

We are especially indebted to our funders, The Nuffield Foundation, including the unwavering support of Sharon Witherspoon, its Assistant Director (Social Research and Innovation).

About the authors

John Triseliotis is Emeritus Professor at the University of Edinburgh. Alone, or with research colleagues, he has undertaken many studies on adoption, foster care and residential care and has authored, co-authored or edited over 20 books on the same themes.

Julia Feast is the Policy, Research and Development Consultant, BAAF. In the past she has managed The Children's Society's Post Adoption and Care: Counselling and Research Project, worked as a local authority social worker and Team Manager and as a Children's Guardian. She has written widely on the subject of adoption and has co-authored many books.

Fiona Kyle is a developmental psychologist. She is a Research Fellow in the Centre for Neuroscience in Education, Faculty of Education at the University of Cambridge. She holds a Ph.D. in Developmental Psychology.

Contents

person had searched or had been sought • Contact and its
impact on the relationship • Other impacts of contact • The
current closeness of the relationship • Current physical and
emotional health • Summary

Foreword

David Howe

Most adoption research, understandably, has concerned itself with the question of how adopted children fare with their new families. These adoption outcome studies rarely go beyond childhood. Rather belatedly, it wasn't until the 1980s that curiosity and concern were expressed about the fate of the birth mothers whose children were adopted. And oddly, the views and experiences of adopters themselves still remain relatively under-explored.

However, the gradual increase in the number of adult adopted people searching for and often achieving a reunion with one or more of their birth relatives has brought the three principal adoption parties together, if not always physically, then emotionally. These search and reunion events, often supported by counsellors, provided researchers with a rare opportunity to gain a long-term, adult-based perspective on the adoption experiences of adopted people, adopters and birth parents. Under the drive of one of the authors, Julia Feast, an initial study looked at the adoption, search and reunion experiences of a large number of adult adopted people. But this examined the view of only one of the main players. The second phase of the research, reported in this book, took the much more ambitious step and looked at the adoption, search and reunion experiences of all three members of the adoption triangle. The result is a unique and fascinating insight into a wide variety of adoption matters from the perspective of the three principal actors. Thus, we learn not only what adult adopted people have to say about being adopted and having contact with a birth relative, but we also hear the thoughts of birth mothers and fathers, and the children's adoptive parents.

Extraordinarily, the authors not only managed to survey over 300 adopted adults, birth mothers and adoptive parents, but within this population they found 34 instances where all three parties of the same triangle responded. Thus, we are given an intriguing account of each adoption and reunion story from the standpoint of the adopted adult, the birth mother and the adoptive parent. John Triseliotis, Julia Feast and Fiona Kyle are to be congratulated on not only taking outcome investigations to their logical, fully rounded and exquisite conclusion, but also accompanying us on an uplifting journey that helps us understand the complex pulls and pushes of nature and nurture as they play out in the lives of those who adopt, those who are adopted, and their genetic parents. For all those interested in the universal questions of who are we, where do we belong, to whom are we connected, to whom do we matter and who matters to us, and why, this is a book to be studied and savoured.

David Howe
Professor of Social Work
University of East Anglia
Norwich

April 2005

1 Historical and legislative developments on adoption, search and reunion

Background

The research reported here is mainly about the different perspectives of adopted people, their birth mothers and adoptive parents on adoption, search and reunion. It was carried out between 2000 and 2002. It builds on the earlier study by Howe and Feast, *Adoption: Search and Reunion*, which was published in 2000 by The Children's Society (republished by BAAF in 2004). While that study focused wholly on the perspectives of adopted people, this one takes matters further by identifying and assessing the impact of the search and reunion on all three members of the so-called "adoption triangle". To our knowledge this is the first systematic study that has brought together people in the same adoptive triad using sizeable samples. The study brings together the characteristics, views, experiences and perspectives of all three main parties affected by the adoption search and reunion process.

Adoption is a crucial long-term institution in virtually all societies but, unlike some others, in Western societies it has also come to be closely associated with secrecy. This secrecy was increasingly being challenged until new laws in England and Wales in 1975 led to the opening of the sealed records, thereby initiating a new period of greater openness. Similar legislation was later introduced in Northern Ireland in 1989 (Scotland has had an open records system since 1930, and also Finland from approximately the same time). Other countries were to follow with legislative changes that were broadly similar to those in England and Wales. An artefact of these changes was the emergence of studies monitoring the meaning and outcome of the search, contact and reunion experience mainly from the perspective of the adopted person. The secrecy permeating adoption policy and practice was not new as otherwise we would not have had the tragedy of Oedipus, which resulted from the failure of his adoptive parents to disclose the adoption. Even if it is a myth, myths often reflect social attitudes of the period. Other similar stories about the secrecy of origins, not necessarily with incest involved, abound not only in fiction but also in fact, including many adoptions legally contracted in the 20th century in the UK and elsewhere. Some other cultures keep adoption open from the start, but then often such adoptions have been, until recently, confined to adoption by relatives. Neither does full openness always lead to problem-free adoption. For example, birth family interference has been known to destabilise the adoption.

In the absence of adoption legislation until the early part of the 20th century, it is hard to say with any certainty how much openness existed in the mainly informal type of adoption that occurred in the past in the UK. From about the latter part of the 19th century until the first Adoption Act (England and Wales) 1926, a de-facto form of adoption emerged as an offshoot of long-term foster care. Long-term foster care itself was intro-duced by the Poor Law authorities, around the 1840s in Scotland and 1860s in England, mainly as a diversion from institutional care. Before the introduction of the Children Act 1948, the care of deprived children was closely linked to the operation of the Poor Law and the principles which underpinned it. As an example, when the quality of parental care and the child's perceived interests were seen to warrant it, children were kept apart from their parents with neither being aware of each other's whereabouts. Among other things, the idea that destitute parents or their children could have rights seemed a far-fetched notion at the time. Subsequently, the practice of limiting contact, or separating children and parents from each other, which operated within the workhouses, was extended to the boarding-out or foster care system. Even after World War II, parents had only limited access to their children in residential homes or in long-term foster homes. Its more recent equivalent is what came to be known as the "clean break" approach in the 1980s for older children moving to "permanent" foster care or adoption (Triseliotis, 1991).

As another example of the dominant ethos of the period, Dr Barnardo required foster parents to sign an undertaking not to allow personal or written communication between a foster child and their relatives, except with the written consent of the Director (Fratter, 1995). Possibly the ultimate in what came to be known as the "clean break" philosophy was the shipping, until the 1960s, of thousands of deprived children from Britain to Canada and Australia, 'not all of them orphans and not always with their parents' knowledge or consent'. Fratter added that the belief that the welfare of a deprived child was best served by his being prevented from having contact with his family – that their interests were in conflict – remained largely unchallenged (p. 4). Even today, where difficulties arise involving accommodated children, or when "permanence" is planned, the first casualty is often contact with members of the birth family.

Possibly the first systematic research to identify the importance of parental contact to children came over forty years ago from a study in long-term foster care (Weinstein, 1960). Among other things, the study found that the self-image and self-concept of children who were visited by their parents in foster homes were significantly higher than those who were not. Subsequent studies were to report similar findings. This contributed to a questioning of the "clean break" approach, which also occurred as a result of other social changes related at this time to adoption (Triseliotis, 1991).

Adoption and the public

By all accounts the idea of adoption was not a popular one during the early part of the 20th century and as a result, there was considerable opposition to adoption legislation (see Kornitzer, 1952). By 1952, though, Kornitzer referred to adoption as having become fashionable among the middle classes and being practised mainly as a solution to infertility and childlessness. What contributed to this change is difficult to tell but it could be the ushering in, at the end of World War II, of more optimistic notions about human nature and environmental influences. At the same time, and until about the early 1970s, adoption was largely confined to healthy infants with a "pedigree" background (Triseliotis and Russell, 1984).

The dominant thinking surrounding adoption in the early part of the 20th century appeared to be significantly influenced by ideas concerned with protection. The wish to make adoption more popular during and after the first World War, when non-marital births were described as soaring, was linked to the belief that people would be encouraged to adopt if there were guarantees of secrecy and anonymity in the proceedings. Alongside this also went the wish to protect children and birth mothers from the stigma of "illegitimacy", which by all accounts was most oppressive at the time. Successive Adoption Acts from 1926 to 1976 gave expression to this sentiment for protection through anonymity. It was also not until 1949 in England and Wales, and 1964 in Scotland, that adopted children could inherit from their adoptive parents. It was because of the inheritance provision that the Adoption (Scotland) Act 1930 provided that an adopted person, on reaching the age of 17 (now 16), could have access to their original birth records. This also made it possible, for those who wished to trace members of their birth family, to do so. When the right of inheritance from birth parents was abolished in 1964, this part of the legislation was retained making possible the study, *In Search of Origins* (Triseliotis, 1973), which led to the opening of the birth records in England and Wales and subsequently in many other countries. The beginnings of an understanding, though, of the importance of disclosing their status to adopted children, and later on of access to background genealogical information, must have emerged by the early 1950s because the Hurst Committee (Hurst Report, 1954) heard evidence then from a number of witnesses in England who:

> ... thought that the adopted person has a right to this information and expressed the view that it is not in the interests of adopted children to be permanently precluded from satisfying their natural curiosity (Para 201, p. 53).

Influenced by this evidence, the Committee recommended that adopted people in England and Wales aged 21 years and over should be able to apply to the court for a full copy of their Adoption Order, which would include details of their birth parent(s)' names. Previously such information could only be made available on application to a court and with proof of exceptional circumstances. The Committee's recommendation, however, was not legislated upon, nor was the recommendation that the application to adopt should include a pledge to tell the child of the adoption. The subsequent Act (The Adoption Act 1958) preferred to maintain the status quo. It was to be almost another twenty years before access to birth records was to be legislated for.

The advent of greater openness for adopted people

The appointment of the Houghton Committee in 1969 to look at adoption, among other childcare matters, coincided with a period of rapidly changing social attitudes about the family, sexual relationships and non-marital births. By this time, the birth of a non-marital child was beginning to be accepted without stigma being attached to the mother or the child, a process that was to accelerate within the next few decades. At the same time, improved social welfare services for single parents and the widespread availability of contraceptive devices and abortion meant that the number of infants for adoption was declining rapidly.

This was also a period of widespread social unrest about what were seen to be the injustices of the prevailing social systems in the Western World. Possibly the same ideas inspired action on the part of minorities to establish their distinctive rights, including adopted people who were now making the case for access to their original birth records. For example, in such countries as the USA and Australia, adopted people formed themselves into action groups to promote their right for access to birth records and other identifiable information. By the end of the late 1970s, mothers who had parted with children for adoption were also forming their own action groups for equivalent rights. In Australia, alliances were struck between adopted people and birth parents campaigning for changes in the legislation.

At the time of the Houghton Committee, evidence was beginning to emerge suggesting that the non-disclosure of adoption and/or the non-sharing of background genealogical information could lead to the adopted person's "bewilderment" and to a negative impact on their developing identity and sense of self (Schechter, 1960; Sants, 1964; McWhinnie, 1967). Perhaps influenced by this, one of the tasks the Houghton Committee set up for itself was to find out more about the subject of access to birth records and whether adopted people in England

and Wales should have a right of access similar to that in Scotland. To this effect, the Committee commissioned one of us (Triseliotis) to carry out a study in Scotland to evaluate the use made of access to birth records by adopted people.

The interim paper published by the Committee in 1970 did not appear convinced of the necessity of opening the birth records in England and Wales. While acknowledging the importance of disclosure, the paper re-iterated the need for anonymity to protect all the parties concerned from possible future problems. The Committee even contemplated recommending the abolition of the Scottish provision to bring it in line with England and Wales. The paper added:

> Greater openness about adoption does not, however, necessarily entail a knowledge of the actual names of the natural parents and other identifying information (Para, 231, p. 85).

In the meantime, Triseliotis' study was made available to the Committee before the publication of its final report in 1972. The report, later to be published under the title, *In Search of Origins* (Triseliotis, 1973), highlighted, among other things, the negative impact of secrecy and of the non-sharing of background genealogical information on the adopted person. The study also made links between this and the impact secrecy had on the adopted person's identity, feelings of self-worth, self-esteem and overall mental health. As an example, many of those searching had not been told about their adoption by their parents, but found out accidentally or from outside sources. Sometimes disclosure had been delayed until adult life, which was experienced as most traumatic, in some cases leading to an identity crisis for the adopted person. Even where the adopters disclosed the adoption early on, they had no informa-tion to pass on to the child because the adoption agencies had not given it to them.

Many adopted people in the study also came to feel that their parents appeared uncomfortable with the idea of adoption. Worse, some thought that their parents carried a sense of shame and conveyed the same view to them. This appeared to reinforce the experience of prejudice that many adopted people said they came across from others in the community, if they came to know that the person was adopted. In some instances, engagements and friendships were broken off when the other person or sometimes their family learnt that the individual was adopted. To avoid such negative reaction many adopted people, like their parents, avoided telling others that they were adopted.

The final report of the Houghton Committee, which was published in 1972, acknowledged the importance of telling a child that he or she is adopted and that at some stage in their life they would also need to know about their origins because it:

> ... helps the proper development of a sense of identity and urged that adopters be provided with relevant background information (Para 28, p. 8).

And later on:

> The weight of the evidence as a whole was in favour of free access to background information, and this accords with our wish to encourage greater openness about adoption. We take the view that on reaching the age of majority an adopted person should not be denied access to his original birth records (Para 303, p. 85).

The Houghton Committee's recommendation for a change in the law in England and Wales resulted in Section 26 of the Children Act 1975. Later it became Section 51 of the Adoption Act (England and Wales) 1976. In England and Wales, adopted people could now have access to their birth records on reaching the age of 18 (instead of 17 as it was then in Scotland). People adopted before 12 November 1975 were required to attend counselling interviews before they would be given information contained on their birth records (no such counselling was required in Scotland). However, if an adopted person already knew their original name, then they did not need to attend a counselling interview, because they would already have enough information to be able to obtain a copy of their original birth certificate.

The requirement for counselling was inserted in the Act largely to calm the anxieties and hostility of sections of the press, and of some Members of Parliament, who viewed access as the equivalent to opening Pandora's box. They were suggesting that this step would lead to vindictiveness and blackmail on the part of adopted people. Based on his findings, Triseliotis pre-empted this stereotyping of adopted people by saying:

The adoptees' quest for their origins was not a vindictive venture but an attempt to understand themselves and their situation better. The self-perception of us all is partly based on what our parents and ancestors have been, going back many generations. Adoptees, too, wish to base themselves not only on their adoptive parents, but also on what their original parents and forebears have been, going back many generations . . . no person should be cut off from his or her origins (Triseliotis, 1973, p. 166).

Since 1975, when access to birth records first became available, there have been many policy and practice developments in adoption, particularly over what information adoption agencies are willing to pass on to the adopted adult who seeks information about their origins and family background. Nowadays, most adoption agencies are willing to provide information from the adoption record including identifying information about the birth family, birth parents, siblings, grandparents, uncles and aunts. However, sharing information from adoption records has presented adoption practitioners with particular challenges as they struggle with the question: whose information is it? It is acknowledged that access to comprehensive information can help adopted people to gain a fuller sense of who they are. This means that they are in a better position to make informed decisions about their life, for example, to begin a search for relatives or be more aware of particular health issues that might be hereditary.

It is over a quarter of a century since the records have been opened in England and Wales and over 70 years in Scotland. A rough estimate suggests that around 550,000 adopted people in England, Wales and Scotland, or about 55 per cent of the total, have availed themselves of the opportunity to seek genealogical information from their records and/or establish contact with a birth relative, predominantly the mother. No cases have been reported so far of either blackmail or vindictiveness being displayed on the part of adopted people. The possibility of an adopted person becoming a blackmailer, exploitative or vindictive cannot be excluded, but then there are many non-adopted persons who are like that and no one is calling for them to be deprived of access to their birth records.

The rights of adopted people were further extended as a result of a ruling by the High Court (reported in *The Times*, 21 July 2001, p. 17) when it ruled in favour of an adopted person who was refused access to confidential information from agency records about her past (*Gunn-Russo v Nugent Care Society* and Secretary of State for Health [2001]). The judge ruled that the Society had not lawfully exercised the wide discretion it had under regulations to disclose material on an adoption.

It appeared that the right of adopted people for access to their birth records had been well established but, without warning, the Adoption and Children Bill (England and Wales), which went to Parliament in the autumn of 2001, made drastic proposals which would eventually have led to limitations on this right where birth parents required anonymity, except under certain strict rules. The basis for this recommendation was never made clear. The introduction to the Department of Health's memorandum of evidence, *Key Changes*, notes at point 3 that several of these changes have been made in response to evidence to the Select Committee. Yet NORCAP (a self-help organisation for adopted people and their parents) checked 129 written submissions of the evidence presented to the Select Committee and could find no submissions that called for clauses on the lines of those proposing the withdrawal of the right to access. Ironically, of the 129 submissions made, 104 were from birth relatives or organisations representing large numbers of birth relatives who were asking broadly for similar access facilities as adopted people (Memorandum from NORCAP).

Perhaps those who drafted the Bill had in mind the case of *Regina v Registrar-General ex parte Smith* (1990) 2 FLR 79 where there was a ruling that an adopted person does not have an absolute right to his or her birth certificate. John Smith, an adopted person, had been imprisoned for murder. He suffered recurrent bouts of psychotic illnesses. In 1999 he attacked and strangled his cellmate. He said he woke during the night and had thought he had seen his adoptive mother. There was no reference to his birth mother. In 1987, he applied for a copy of his original birth certificate and the Registrar-General decided on the grounds of public interest not to provide the information. It is worth noting that, when non-adopted children harass, attack or murder their birth parents, there is no call to take away everybody's right to know who gave birth to them. Possibly as a result of the weight of evidence to the House of Commons Special Standing Committee in the autumn of 2002, the Government withdrew the relevant clauses. However, and what could be considered as a backward step, the subsequent Adoption and Children Act 2002 introduced a new framework under which birth parents will be entitled to express a view about the release of confidential information.

Sections 54 and Sections 56–65 of the new Act describe the duties and powers that adoption agencies have in collecting and sharing information which is part of the adoption record. For future adoptions (those after the Act is implemented), identifying information about birth family members would not normally be given to the adopted person unless the person the information is about has given their permission. This has important implications for current family placement practice as adoption workers need to be aware, when gathering information about the family history and family members, that the people it concerns know that it exists so that they can give their permission for it to be passed on to the adopted adult should they seek such information in years to come. If this is not carried out prior to the adoption being made, it may later present challenges and particular dilemmas. Adoption agencies will now have to demonstrate that they have taken reasonable steps to obtain the views of the person that the information concerns before it is given to the adopted adult. Many years may have passed between the Adoption Order having been made and the adopted adult seeking information, so it may be a real challenge and a costly and time-consuming exercise for the adoption agency to take those reasonable steps before the information can be shared with the adopted person. It could also place an adopted person in a situation for which they are not yet ready. At present, adopted people usually have time and the option to digest the information they receive before taking the step to begin a search and make contact. For some people this can be a very short period, others may stop and start, still others may take years. Some adopted people decide not to search. As we go to press, we are still waiting for the Regulations and Guidance for the Adoption and Children Act 2002, and we are yet to see how much the adopted person's position in the search and reunion process will be altered by the new requirements. The new requirements may remove the adopted person's choice.

The position of the birth family

The position of birth parents and relatives in relation to contact after adoption has two aspects: first, in relation to contact after the adopted person reaches the age of 18 in England and Wales and 16 in Scotland; and second, the more recent development of continuing contact from the point of the making of the Adoption Order. The concern here is with the first type of contact. The Children Act 1975, which provided for access to birth records by adopted people, made no clear provision for birth parents or other relatives. Although an adopted person could take the initiative to seek out a birth relative, the opposite was not possible. It was a one-way process. Birth mothers did not even have the right to find out whether their child was alive or dead. The Act did place a responsibility on local authorities to establish and maintain within their area a service designed to meet the needs, in relation to adoption, of parents or guardians of children who had been adopted. It was not clear, however, whether the provision extended to the birth parents when they had lost their legal status as parents. Furthermore, the Act did not allow for the disclosure of identifiable information to the birth parents that theoretically, at least, could lead to the tracing of the adopted person.

Gradual but increasing pressure on the Department of Health to make it easier for birth relatives to have reciprocal access facilities, as those extended to the adopted person, resulted in a Department of Health (previously Department of Health and Social Security) Circular (LAC (84)3) in the form of guidance to the Adoption Agencies Regulations 1983. The Circular suggested giving birth parents information on the child's progress, without disclosing his or her new identity or whereabouts (LAC (84) 3 – Para 120). In the meantime, the impetus for further change was reinforced by new studies, this time concentrating on the impact of relinquishment on mothers who had parted with their children for adoption. Although the samples studied were not representative, they suggested that relinquishment was experienced as a very stressful and traumatic event and that many mothers were haunted by this for years to come. Parting with a child for adoption was found to involve intense feelings of loss, grief, anger and guilt that many mothers could not wish away. The stressful nature of the event was also said to give rise to physical and mental illness (Winkler and Keppel, 1984; Bouchier *et al*, 1991; Howe *et al*, 1992; Hughes and Logan, 1993. See also Chapter 2 for a brief review of these studies). It is for these reasons that, for many mothers parting with very young children for adoption today, there is often the possibility of continuing direct contact, a development that has received less attention in Britain than in some other countries, because most attention has been focused on children exiting care through adoption. Possibly because of these studies, Wells (1993) argued for total openness and so did Bouchier *et al* (1991). In contrast, Hughes and Logan (1993) claimed that many birth mothers themselves rejected outright the idea of full openness.

A further compromise regarding the birth parents' wish to search seemed to have been reached following the provision of the Children Act 1989 asking the Registrar General to operate an Adoption Contact Register for adopted adults and their birth relatives (Section 51A Adoption Act as inserted by Section 88, Schedule 10, Para 21 Children Act 1989). The purpose of the Register was to put adopted people and their birth parents or other relatives in touch with each other provided this was what they both wanted. In effect, contact can be arranged only when both sides have registered willingness to do so. However, while the introduction of the Register cannot prevent an adopted person from trying to locate a birth parent or relative through access to the original birth records, birth parents are in effect unlikely to be able to trace the adopted person since they have no right to information about his or her new identity. The Department of Health and Welsh Office consultative document on adoption (*Review of Adoption Law*, 1992) acknowledged a growing recognition of the need to involve birth parents in the adoption process in ways that facilitate contact, but no further action took place.

Between the establishment of the Adoption Contact Register in England and Wales in 1991 and the end of December 2004, the total number of registrations reached 38,525 of whom 27,346 (or 71 per cent) were adopted adults and 11,179 (or 29 per cent) birth relatives. During this period, a total of 912 (or 2.4 per cent) links were achieved between adopted people and birth relatives. Since 1989, when Northern Ireland established an Adoption Contact Register, until the end of December 2004, the number of people who had registered totalled 432. This figure is made up of 300 (or 69 per cent) adopted people and 132 (31 per cent) birth relatives and there have been seven (1.6 per cent) links. An equivalent Scottish Register held by Family Care in Edinburgh, was established in 1984. Between then and 2002 the number registering was 6,910 of whom 4,527 (or 66 per cent) were adopted people and 2,383 (or 34 per cent) birth relatives. Apparently fewer than 10 per cent of those registering were birth fathers. A very rough calculation suggests that over the whole period some 250–300 links were made, or around four per cent (private communication).

The ratio of adopted people to birth relatives registering is surprising, given the fact that adopted people, unlike birth relatives, have access rights to their original birth records. We already know that 75 per cent of non-searching adopted people were not aware of the Adoption Contact Register (Howe and Feast, 2000). Possible explanations are that fewer birth relatives are aware of the existence of the Register or that the urge for contact is far more pronounced among adopted people than birth relatives and greater among women than men. The low proportion of links achieved is possibly an endorsement of the legislative provision that allows adopted people to seek out birth relatives without having to rely solely on the Register.

Although the Register was a step forward, dissatisfaction still remained among birth relatives because it was seen as too constricting a device. Furthermore, adoption workers were uncertain of the limits of their power to arrange for possible meetings. Arguments were now being advanced that agencies, as part of their intermediary role, should be given wider discretion to be more proactive on behalf of birth parents and other relatives who sought contact. This pressure resulted in a new document prepared by The Children's Society on behalf of the Department of Health called *Intermediary Services for Birth Relatives: Practice guidelines* (2000). This provided guidance for adoption practitioners about how they might help birth parents and relatives who seek contact with an adopted person to do so. The Practice Guidelines encouraged adoption agencies to have a more sympathetic approach to birth relatives and to have a more proactive approach to providing intermediary services for birth relatives.

Subsequently the Adoption and Children Act 2002 (England and Wales) brought in a major change for birth relatives. For the first time the legislation recognised the needs of thousands of birth mothers (and other birth relatives too) who want to know how their adopted child, now adult, is and whether or not he or she would want to have contact. This major change was mainly due to the campaign by birth mothers and other adoption organisations. It was also due to the research evidence which showed that the majority of adopted adults who had been approached and informed of a birth relative's enquiry thought that they had a right to be informed, so that they could make their own decisions about how they wished to respond. Ninety per cent of the adopted people who were informed of a birth relative's interest went on to have some form of contact (Howe and Feast, 2000).

Section 98 of the Adoption and Children Act 2002 has made a provision that helps to address the needs of all adults affected by adoption. This section enables regulations to be made for the purpose of a) assisting adults adopted before the Act came into force to obtain information in relation to their adoption and b) facilitating contact between such persons and their relatives. This means that under Section 98 birth relatives will now have the legal right to ask a registered intermediary agency to provide an intermediary service so that contact can be made with their adopted relatives to let them know of their wish for contact. The new legislative framework is expected to be implemented sometime in 2005 and in two phases: firstly, the right will be given to birth relatives where the adoption took place before 1975 and later to birth relatives where the adoption took place after 1975. One of the reasons for this is that it is acknowledged that the children who have been placed for adoption during the past thirty years may have been adopted for very different reasons. For instance, they may have been removed from their family for reasons to do with maltreatment – physical, sexual and/or emotional abuse.

There is no statutory requirement for a voluntary agency or local authority to provide an intermediary service; however, they must direct the birth relative to an adoption support agency registered with the Commission for Social Care Inspection (CSCI) to provide intermediary services. The adoption agency that holds the adoption record will also be under an obligation to pass on any information in their possession about the adopted person and the adoptive family to the adoption support agency. This would include the adoptive name and such identifying information as will enable the adoption support agency to begin the task of locating the current whereabouts of the person being sought. The agency responsible for the adoption can, however, express their view about the birth relative's request for an intermediary service and provide any other information which they may feel has implications in the decision-making process to contact the adopted adult and his or her adoptive family.

In adoptions that were privately arranged, or in a situation where the identifying information has been destroyed or lost, the intermediary agency may apply to the Registrar General for the information he or she may hold which would enable the identity of an adopted person to be established.

An intermediary agency is prohibited from disclosing any information to the birth relative requesting an intermediary service without the expressed permission and informed consent of the adopted adult. Regulations and guidance are yet to be issued but they will provide the framework for intermediary agencies to provide intermediary services that aim to meet the needs of all those affected by adoption.

The Adoption Contact Register will continue and the main features of how it functions have been retained. However, there has been one significant change. The main purpose of the Adoption Contact Register when it was implemented in 1991 was to facilitate contact between adopted adults and their birth relatives, but now within Sections 80 and 81 of the 2002 Act, adopted adults and their birth relatives will have the facility to place a veto. They will now be able to register their wish for no contact.

The adopters

As already hinted at, until the 1970s, successive pieces of legislation aimed to protect adopters from possible interference from the birth family by trying to guarantee secrecy in the proceedings. As a first step, the information linking the adoption certificate with the original birth certificate was kept in a special register by the Registrar General and no adopted person had a right of access to it, except in Scotland. In England,

Wales and Northern Ireland, this could only be done on the approval of the courts, which was rarely given. The Acts of 1949 and 1950 and court rules that followed provided further protection for adopters by allowing them to remain anonymous during the court proceedings, which could make it difficult, if not impossible, for a birth parent to identify them (The Adoption of Children (County Court) Rules 1949, The Adoption of Children (Summary Jurisdiction) Rules 1949 and the Adoption of Children (High Court) Rules 1950). Inadvertently, perhaps, the secrecy encouraged by the legislation also influenced a significant number of adoptive parents not to disclose the adoption to the child and may also have contributed to the perceptions of the birth family as potentially intrusive, both emotionally and physically.

The reluctance to disclose adoption or share genealogical information about the child was related to a common view that the blood relationship was not important. To a large extent the biological connection was seen as irrelevant, encouraging also the belief that adoptive parenting was similar to biological parenting. Research had not yet taken place to show how significant this actually was to adopted people. Furthermore, some adoption agencies in the past, especially in the USA, avoided passing on genealogical background information about the birth family to the adopters. In this way, it was argued, adopters could honestly say to the child, or adopted adult asking questions, that they themselves did not know. Although research there was then non-existent, it would have been thought that the disclosure of adoption and the sharing of background information was not an empirical but an ethical issue. Telling the truth is also a judicial requirement.

As far back as 1952, Kornitzer had no doubt about the importance of telling children about adoption as early as possible, but she made no reference in her book to also giving them background and genealogical information. However, when a new edition of the book appeared in 1959 she devoted three chapters to telling, making reference also to the value of conveying to the child a positive image of his or her birth family and stressing the importance of truth and honesty. She also advised on the creation of a scrapbook to help show the child's personal background details about the birth parents and other relevant information. From her study of adoption outcomes, some ten years later, she found that, of

585 children in the sample, apparently one-quarter had not learnt (by the time they were five years old) of their adoption from their adoptive parents, or had learnt in some way that carried with it the risk of severe shock. Some still did not know that they had been adopted, at the time of interview (Kornitzer, 1968, p. 184). There appears to be much more openness between adoptive parents and their children now compared to the past, but an ongoing dialogue between the adopted person and their parents still presents problems for some (Craig, 1991). Apparently, a majority of calls that are made to the adoption helpline, Talkadoption, which is for adopted people under the age of 25, are from those who want more information about their background but do not feel able to talk about this desire with their adoptive parents (Greenwood and Foster, 2000). Similarly, and because of the diversity of lifestyles that have developed in the last thirty or so years, community attitudes appear much more accepting of different forms of parenting, including adoption, step-parenting and surrogate parenting.

Studies on search and reunions over the past thirty or so years have highlighted the kind of information that adopted people have wanted to enable them to construct aspects of their identity by integrating their biological and psychological families in their developing self. Since the 1970s, most adoption agencies have been using these insights in their preparation of prospective adopters. At least one study monitoring such preparations reported that most adopters had made good use of it (Craig, 1991). While everyone in this study disclosed adoption early, as recommended, and which was also confirmed by the adopted children who were interviewed in their late teens, a tiny minority of parents still found it difficult to share letters and photographs relating to the birth family. In keeping with the changing times, agencies now give adopters information on their child's background in writing and are prepared to entertain the possibility of continuing direct or indirect forms of contact between the child and members of their birth family. Children joining new families now usually have life story books, and sometimes videos, providing details and photographs about their background and adoption circumstances.

Openness in adoption

By the late 1970s, the adopted person's right of access to their birth records to aid their sense of generational continuity became more widely acceptable in this and many other countries. As a response to similar needs, "open" forms of adoption, with varying forms and degrees of ongoing contact between adoptive and birth families were also introduced in countries such as New Zealand in the early 1980s and subsequently in the USA. This mainly applied to infants, who formed the vast majority of adopted children. In the UK, openness, or what came to be known as post-adoption contact, took a different form and arose mainly from the different type of adoption pursued here, i.e. the concentration on older children with special needs who were moving from care to adoption. This new type of adoption in Britain initially introduced a new twist to the idea of openness, leading, in most cases, to the total severance of ties between younger and older children and their birth family. Although some of the older children involved were known to have emotional ties with a parent or birth relative, nevertheless a "clean break" policy of total severance was followed. Once placed for adoption, there was to be no further contact between the child and their birth family, irrespective of the strength of any existing emotional links. The fact that it might be in the interests of the child to maintain existing emotional links, went largely unrecognised until the topic was publicly aired (Triseliotis, 1985; Triseliotis, 1991). Subsequently, and possibly because of the publicity and the gradual emergence of several small-scale studies suggesting that face-to-face post-adoption contact was in the interests of some children, and that on the whole it was working well, by the mid–1990s, policy and practice began to change once again. As an example, one recent study (Lowe *et al*, 1999) found that, in 77 per cent of adoption placements made in England and Wales between 1992 and 1994, different forms of contact were agreed with a member of the birth family. A significant proportion of the arrangements involved face-to-face contact.

It is not the purpose to debate here the details of open adoption, or of post-adoption contact, but simply to illustrate the move from total secrecy to different levels of openness, with the aim of promoting generational continuity and at times, especially in the case of older children, maintaining other continuities such as relationships. Such forms of contact usually presuppose eventual acceptance of the adoption by birth family members, co-operation between the parties and the absence of acrimony and attempts at undermining the adoptive family. However, some agencies (known to one of us through the undertaking of private work) view a birth parent's contesting of the adoption as signifying resistance to it and preclude them from having any form of contact after the Adoption Order is granted. This is usually irrespective of the strength of the ties between parent and child. It must be recognised that every birth parent has the legal right to oppose, if they wish, the adoption of their child. Contact arrangements *after* the Adoption Order is granted should be a separate matter and the situation assessed on the parent's attitude at the time.

The future of adoption

Adoption as an institution has faced many challenges in Western-type societies over the years. In recent times, with improved economic and social conditions and the widespread availability of contraception and of abortion facilities, very few infants, compared to older children, are released for adoption. However, and in spite of assisted forms of reproduction made available to previously infertile couples, the need for infants to adopt has not declined; see, for example, the increase in the number of children adopted inter-country.

In the past, adoption offered a solution for infertile couples and also met the needs of birth mothers who were unable to keep the child born outside marriage. As single parenthood no longer has the social stigma it once had, very few babies need to be adopted. For many childless couples, it is no longer an available option to create a family. While this is true for infants, in Britain attention has turned to older children within the care system who cannot return to their birth families. At the same time, most other countries of Western Europe have moved in a big way towards intercountry adoption. Unlike Britain, a common characteristic of these countries is that they do not allow adoption against the wishes of birth parents mainly because it would sever continuities (Warman and Roberts, 2003). The USA and Canada have paid attention to both older children and to intercountry adoption. Another challenge has been the calls for the abolition of the institution of adoption and its substitution by other types of placement arrangements. These calls appear to have come about from a combination of factors such as the association of adoption with secrecy, leading to generational discontinuity from birth families, the sense of loss and rejection in many adopted people and the trauma for birth parents of losing a child to adoption. As an example, The Law Commission of New Zealand put forward the recommendation for abolishing the legal concept of adoption and replacing it with a modified version of guardianship that would recognise and confer the legal status of parenthood while also addressing custody and access (see Selwyn and Sturges, 2001). Policies in the State of Victoria in Australia have already moved in this direction, certainly in the case of older children (Marshall and McDonald, 2001). Calls for the abolition of adoption have also come from some individuals for whom adoption was an unhappy personal experience (see for example Robinson, 2000). While it is appropriate that these questions have been raised, the proponents of the abolition of adoption do not appear to appreciate the fact that the great majority of adopted people are satisfied with their experience of adoption or that a large majority of adoptions, across a range of measures, are very successful.

However, the face of adoption has changed significantly in the past few decades. Nowadays, children are mostly adopted from the care system after state intervention has established that they can no longer be looked after by their birth families. For some of these children and sibling groups, they will have been cared for by their birth relatives and whatever negative experiences they may have had, they may also have strong feelings and memories about their parents or family. Some of these children may say that they do not want to be adopted, although they need a new family. Alternative placement plans will include foster care. These may be planned as a long-term option or become a long-term option because no alternative is made available and a strong and enduring relationship can grow between the foster carers and the child. There is no consensus in the practitioner and research community about whether long-term fostering and guardianship can provide the long-term security of relationships and commitment a child needs through childhood and beyond. While there are many examples of children who grow to feel a part of their foster family and come to regard them as family in adulthood, the legal insecurity of foster care and the procedural requirements of local authority care can put both the relationships and the arrangements under severe strain. Whatever the intention or needs of the people concerned, these can then become a risk factor in the placement.

There are a number of complex interacting factors which make for a successful alternative family placement policy and practice. Unravelling these to provide one clear and unambiguous direction for every child or young person is probably not possible. It requires a sensitive and detailed understanding of children's needs and development, a realistic and timely plan, the proactive planning of a range of alternative placement options and ongoing support from a range of services for the child, the new carers and the birth family. There is no short cut to any of this and the long-term risks to children and young people of not providing this have become very clear over the years.

2 Literature review on search and reunion

Introduction

In this review of the research literature, frequent reference is made to the Howe and Feast study, *Adoption, Search and Reunion* (2000), on which the current study extensively builds. Whereas previous research focused on adopted people who had sought information or contact, what was novel about that study was its sample – which included a group of adopted people who had not initiated a search, but had been sought out by a birth relative, mainly the mother. The study then went on to compare the characteristics and experiences of those who had searched (seekers) with those who had been sought (non-searchers). It covered 394 searchers (87 per cent of those who had searched) and 78 non-searchers (68 per cent of those who had been approached on behalf of a birth relative).

Adopted people: search and reunion

In a recent literature review on search and reunion, Muller and Perry (2001) covered around one hundred studies on the subject conducted in different countries, but mostly in the USA. The authors acknowledged that some of the studies were not statistically generalisable, mainly because of their unrepresentative or small samples. Other problems also present themselves when trying to contrast outcomes from studies carried out in countries with different traditions and whose legal systems on the question of contact and reunions differ significantly from each other. In spite of this, there is also broad commonality in many of the findings, which adds to their credibility. Possibly the most contested issue in the field of search and reunion is "why adopted people search". In answer to this question, Muller and Perry (2001) summarised three theoretical models which emerged from their review of the research literature: (i) the psychopathological i.e. attributing adopted people's desire to search 'to some personal deficiency or to the malfunctioning of the adoptive family'; (ii) search as a normal process and as a developmental task that adopted persons must complete as part of their psychosocial development; and (iii) the explanation that places adoptive persons' search within the context of socio-cultural norms and expectations. These distinctions about motivation and purposes are exceedingly helpful to have, but while a proportion of those who search will fall into each of the three categories, others overlap, suggesting a more complex process (Rozenburg and Groze, 1997; Howe and Feast, 2000). Curiosity about backgrounds, why adoption, possible feelings of loss, rejection and guilt, along with the quality of the adoptive parenting, all appear to influence and permeate the lives of many adopted people in manifold ways.

It is widely accepted that adoption is bound by culture, customs, values, traditions, social, religious and other beliefs, all of which influence not only the adoption experience, but also if and when a search takes place. None of these influences are static and neither is the adoption experience. Some of the circumstances that motivated adopted people 30 to 40 years ago to search continue to be the same, but others have changed because the social context has changed too. For example, within the climate of secrecy that predominated in the past, and when the idea of a search was discouraged and frowned upon, it usually took a very highly motivated, determined and perhaps even driven person to set out on a quest. Not surprisingly, the proportion that searched then, for example, in Scotland where the records were always open, was very small, around 40 a year. In contrast, within the new climate of openness, the numbers of enquirers and searchers have shot up over the last 25 years. Whereas some of the few who were searching 30 to 40 years ago were driven by a very strong determination, now those who do not search are in danger of being labelled as "incomplete" or "frozen" personalities (see Haimes and Timms, 1985). However, supportive evidence for this is lacking.

Who searches?

A key question often being asked is how far there are similarities and differences between searchers and non-searchers. However, the two groups are not completely distinct. In the Howe and Feast (2000) study, while 47 per cent of non-searchers had never thought about searching,

42 per cent had. Those who would not have searched gave a number of reasons, including not wanting to hurt their adoptive parents, not knowing of the relatives' existence, not feeling a need, or fearing rejection. A small scale study by Stanway (1996/97) reported that adopted people faced with the prospect of being sought out by their birth parents felt the need for choice and to feel in control.

Gender: Several studies have compared the characteristics of "searchers" and "non-searchers". Searchers in Triseliotis' (1973) study were about equally split between men and women, but subsequent studies reported that roughly twice as many women as men have searched, allowing speculation that perhaps women are differently motivated from men (Gonyo and Watson, 1988; Pacheco and Eme, 1993; Howe and Feast, 2000). Among adopted people searching, women were also more likely than men to report an unhappy adoption experience and to report more identity problems (Sachdev, 1992; Pacheco and Eme, 1993). There is also the suggestion that stronger feelings are generated in women than in men by such events as marriage, pregnancy or childbirth, triggering the actual quest. With adoption having been seen, especially in the past, as a "single mother" predicament, perhaps it was to be expected that the most likely person to be sought was the mother (Triseliotis, 1973; Sachdev, 1992; Howe and Feast, 2000). It was also rare in the past for the child's birth certificate to name the father, even though this was somewhat more likely to be found in the adoption agencies' records. It is often only at the point when adopted people have access to this information that the birth father becomes a "real" person. Thoughts about searching for him may then become a possibility. The birth mother is also the more likely person to hold the information the adopted person is after, including the answer to the key question: 'why was I put up for adoption?'.

Age: Triseliotis (1973) found that half the searchers in his study were aged between 25 and 34 with 30 per cent being under 25 and the rest (21 per cent) over 34. Compared to these findings, some later studies reported fewer adopted people searching in early adulthood, i.e. under the age of 25, and more searching several years after legal entitlement, i.e. over the age of 35 (Pacheco and Eme, 1993; Sachdev, 1992). The average age of searchers in the Howe and Feast (2000) study was around 31 and there was almost no difference between searchers and non-searchers. Women, though, were more likely to start their search earlier than men.

Personal characteristics and experiences: In terms of biographical and adoptive family circumstances, the Howe and Feast (2000) study found few differences in such characteristics between searchers and non-searchers. However, studies have found non-searchers to have more positive self-concepts than searchers and to feel more positive about themselves and their adoptive families (Aumend and Barrett, 1984; Betrocci and Schechter, 1991; Howe and Feast, 2000); be less curious than searchers (Midford, 1987; Roche and Perlesz, 2000); or have higher levels of loyalty towards their adoptive family (Wegan, 1997; Howe and Feast, 2000). Two studies have also reported that, on average, searchers were found to have significantly lower scores on standardised measures of self-esteem and a less positive sense of identity; report poorer relationships with their adoptive parents; have less positive feelings about being adopted; and to have experienced more chronic stress (Sobol and Cardiff, 1983; Aumend and Barrett, 1984).

In the Howe and Feast (2000) study, significant differences in the rates of feeling 'happy, loved, and loving' were noted between searchers and non-searchers, with non-searchers more likely to describe their feelings, experiences and current relationships more positively. For example, these differences were reflected in the proportions of non-searchers who said they felt they "belonged" in their adoptive family, compared to the searchers. In addition, half of the searchers in the same study said they felt different to their adoptive family when they were growing up, compared to only 27 per cent of the non-searchers. The majority of both groups reported feeling happy but the percentage was higher in the non-searcher group. Almost two-thirds (65 per cent) of searchers, but 85 per cent of non-searchers, strongly agreed or agreed that they felt happy about being adopted. Similarly, 77 per cent of the searchers and 91 per cent of the non-searchers strongly agreed or agreed that they felt loved by their adoptive mothers.

With 53 per cent of searching adopted people evaluating their adoption experience as positive, the Howe and Feast study recognised that searchers were not a homogenous group but were made up of three distinctive sub-groups, which the authors described as 'integrated, differentiated and alienated'. The "integrated" searchers were positive about their adoption, did not feel different and felt they belonged. They were happy in their adoption but curious about their roots. The "differentiated" searchers felt they belonged but were different from their adoptive family. The total opposite to the integrated group were the "alienated" group (27 per cent) who felt that they were different and did not belong. They equally had questions about their roots, but added to this was the question of why they were given up for adoption. Overall, the small "alienated" group was much more likely to say that their adoption was not properly handled by their parents, that they did not feel they belonged or were loved within their adoptive families, and often had a greater need to develop a relationship with the birth relative. Since three-quarters were not categorised as alienated, it highlights the complexities behind the adopted person's motivations to search for birth relatives. The findings from the Howe and Feast study generally suggest that feeling ambivalent or negative about one's adoption might be one factor that motivates some people to search but it is not the only factor in the searching equation. Even though searchers are more likely than non-searchers to express negative views about their adoption, it still leaves over half the group describing their experience as a positive one.

Communication about adoption and searching: There are two "tellings" in adoption: The first concerns the disclosure of adoption to the adopted person and the second the disclosure of the search by the adopted person to their adoptive parents. Betrocci and Schechter (1991) found that non-searchers were told earlier about their adoption while Triseliotis (1973) reported that those searching for background information only were more likely to have been told early about their adoption compared to those searching also for reunions. However, Howe and Feast (2000) found no difference in the timing of telling about adoption between searchers and non-searchers. Grotevant and McRoy (1998) reported a positive association between fully disclosed adoption and adopters' feelings of empathy towards their children and birth parents. Turning to the second telling, half the adopted people in the Pacheco and Eme (1993) study and one-third in Sachdev's (1992) had not told their adoptive parents that they had started a search. In the Howe and Feast (2000) study, 71 per cent had told their adoptive mothers and 68 per cent their adoptive fathers. Only 21 per cent had not told anyone.

The decision and timing of the search – concerns and fears: Adopted people are reported to have a general basic need to find out more about their roots and why they were placed for adoption. They may also have been thinking about it for some time before acting. Several studies suggest that the onset of the search appears to be triggered by an event such as an emotional crisis, a loss, or a happy event, e.g. marriage, pregnancy, or the birth of a child (Triseliotis, 1973; Kowal and Schilling, 1985; Sachdev, 1989) but this was not found by Howe and Feast (2000). It has also been thought that searching reflected an adopted person's wish to hurt the birth mother for "abandonment" and the adopters for unsatisfactory parenting but evidence over the last thirty or so years suggests that, on the whole, adopted people neither wish to hurt others nor themselves. As far back as 1973, Triseliotis concluded from his interviews that the adopted person's 'quest for their origins was not a vindictive venture, but an attempt to understand themselves and their situation better' (p. 166). Howe and Feast (2000) also reached similar conclusions but another study reported that, while each demonstrated a considerable concern for the other parties' interests and feelings, at the same time they perceived the other party as being insensitive to their own feelings and needs (Sachdev, 1989). However, some caution is necessary because the triads in the latter study had not been matched.

What are adopted people looking for? Questions to which adopted people were found to be seeking answers have included: what is my biological and social history and heritage? What are my roots? Who do I look like? Who am I? Why was I given up for adoption and was I wanted and loved by my birth family? Some adopted people were looking for answers to practical questions, particularly a medical history or a combination of practical and personal information. At the same time, a proportion hoped that the search would lead to new relationships (McWhinnie, 1967; Triseliotis, 1973). Andersen (1988), writing from clinical and personal experience, commented that 'a fairly consistent reason adoptees give for searching is that they hope for a change in the way they experience themselves as people' (p. 623). Besides genealogical information, many of the questions posed and asked have to do with feelings of loss and rejection, but apparently they are not always expressed openly in this form. How exactly these twin feelings operate, and whether they can be ameliorated by the quality of the adoption and reunion experience, is not clear. Again, Andersen (1988, p. 19) wrote that the search 'is most funda-mentally an expression of the wish to undo the trauma of separation'. Another added that the resolution of the loss of an attachment figure requires cognitive acceptance of the loss that is linked to a satisfactory account of the causes of the loss (Weiss, 1988). Weiss went on to say that if the loss makes no sense (as is the case for many adopted people who do not know or understand why they were placed for adoption), there is an ongoing, nagging search for an explanation. Until this is done, recovery is apparently impeded. In a study of intercountry adoption, the main explanation offered for the higher levels of disturbance found among adopted adolescents was 'increasing concerns over their biological parent-age' and their 'sense of loss having once been abandoned' (Velrhurst, 2001, p. 139). Such feelings are not apparently inevitable. The Howe and Feast (2000) study found that only half the adopted people in their sample admitted to feelings of rejection by their birth family.

Why do some adopted people not search? Both the decision to search and the failure to search have been presented as "pathological". For example, the question was posed earlier of whether adopted people who do not search are "frozen" or have "incomplete" identities as some have suggested. One writer indirectly asserted this view by saying: 'Everyone identifies with the hero who must go forth into the world alone to search for his origins, but in the adoptee's case this is a literal quest. At times he feels that he too has a thousand faces, a thousand identities – and yet none' (Lifton, 1979, p. 29). More surprisingly, Haimes and Timms (1985) who studied only searchers, added that 'those adopted who do not make any enquiries at all as they reach adolescence and into adulthood are perhaps far from emotionally mature and stable . . .' (p. 83). In contrast, Howe and Feast (2000) concluded from their study, which included both searchers and non-searchers, that non-searchers were 'a more robust version of the integrated adoption experience type'. On the same subject, Gonyo and Watson (1988) referred to the adopted person's loyalty to the adoptive parents, of not wanting to disturb a birth parent, fearful of what they might find, and fear of failure. One writer taking a sociological perspective asserted that searching is associated with adopted people's feelings of stigma, the argument being that, in order to gain social acceptance, adopted people must neutralise their stigma through the search (March, 1995).

As already mentioned, Howe and Feast (2000) highlighted findings distinguishing between those who were classified as "alienated" and feeling "different" from the rest. Furthermore, they added that those who had been placed transracially were, perhaps understandably, much more likely to have felt different to their adoptive families when growing up and were also more likely than those placed in "same race" placements to be classified as "alienated" (45 to 29 per cent) or different (34 to 23 per cent) and less likely to be categorised as "integrated" (21 to 48 per cent) in terms of their adoption experience (p. 153). Almost a third (32 per cent) said they had been treated differently by their adoptive extended family compared to 17 per cent in "same race" placements. Rates of happiness with their adoption and evaluation of their adoption did not differ between "same race" and transracially placed, but only 56 per cent said they "belonged", compared to 71 per cent of those in "same race" placements. Three out of ten, compared to only 13 per cent of those in "same race" placements, also said that people in the community had treated them differently. Apparently nearly all black, Asian and mixed parentage children experienced racism on a regular basis during child-hood. The study goes on to claim that the presence of a permanent and solid core of self was sometimes missing from those placed transracially, e.g. they were not always certain of who they were.

The search and after
On making contact, between 7 to 15 per cent of adopted people are said to have experienced immediate rejection by birth relatives, mostly by the

mother (Sachdev, 1992; March, 1995; Howe and Feast, 2000). Some of these mothers may have changed their minds subsequently. However, according to adopted people, around three-quarters of the birth parents reacted positively at the first meeting, but 40 per cent of adopted people had negative feelings about the first meeting (Campbell *et al*, 1991; Pacheco and Eme, 1993; Stoneman *et al*, 1980). An important finding has been that initial reactions were not predictive of how the relationship would subsequently develop (Sachdev, 1992). The most common description of the relationship developed with the birth mother was that of friendship, with fewer than one-fifth describing it as a mother–child relationship (Stoneman *et al*, 1980; Kennard, 1991; Sachdev, 1992; Pacheco and Eme, 1993; March, 1995; Gladstone and Westhues, 1998). In two studies, a significant number of adopted people described the relationship as "distant", "tense" or "ambivalent", but they did not say how, if at all, it changed over time (Kennard, 1991; Gladstone and Westhues, 1998).

Of the 394 searchers in the Howe and Feast (2000) study, 274 (70 per cent) located a birth relative. Of these, 60 per cent found them within three months. Over nine out of ten then went on to have some form of direct, usually face-to-face, contact. Similarly, nine out of every ten of those approached by a birth relative also went on to have some kind of direct contact. Finding a birth mother also meant establishing contact with siblings, birth grandparents and the mother's birth relatives. Of those who found a birth relative, seven per cent suffered an outright rejection, the birth relative refusing any contact. Inevitably this left them feeling upset and hurt. Another nine per cent had the contact terminated within a year after only one or two contacts, which was again experienced by the adopted person as rejection. During the first year, two-thirds of searchers, and 59 per cent of those approached, had some kind of contact, either by letter, phone or meeting with their birth mother at least once a month in the first year. Compared to non-searchers, searchers were more likely to have face-to-face contact. Contact with a birth sibling or father was lower. The Howe and Feast (2000) study and others showed that over the years there is a small but steady decrease in the number of adopted people who maintain contact with their birth mother or that contact becomes very infrequent.

Apparently the emotional impact of reunion affected searchers and non-searchers differently. In the Howe and Feast (2000) study, 71 per cent of searchers evaluated the reunion as emotionally satisfying, but those who had evaluated their adoption negatively were more likely to report that their emotional outlook had worsened since the reunion, including feeling more angry. People who experienced their adoption positively also felt more positive about the reunion. Almost half of the searchers (46 per cent) and 30 per cent of the non-searchers said that their self-esteem had improved since contact. Those classified as "alienated" and "differentiated" were the most likely to benefit. A significant minority of searchers (11 per cent), compared to 24 per cent of non-searchers, felt that the reunion experience had been upsetting (Howe and Feast, 2000).

Reunions and relationships

Irrespective of the outcome of the search, most studies reported that on average over nine out of every ten adopted people who sought contact had no regrets (Triseliotis, 1973; Sachdev, 1989; Pacheco and Eme, 1993; Howe and Feast, 2000). From their survey of the research literature, Muller and Perry (2001) identified a range of factors that influence the development of a close relationship between adopted people and birth parents. They included: the two sides establishing clear boundaries regarding the involvement in each other's lives; adopted people having a close relationship to their adoptive parents who also supported the contact with the birth parent; adopted people having only minimal expectations regarding the future relationship with their birth parent; the two sides having similar lifestyles and compatible temperaments; birth parents being accepting of the adopted person's adoptive identity; and the birth parent's present family reacting posi-tively toward contact. A Canadian study reported that nearly all of the adopted people and birth parents were satisfied with the reunion experi-ence, but "mismatched" expectations resulted apparently in "serious problems" (Love, 1990). Pacheco and Eme (1993) reported that only 51 per cent of adopted people said that their need for emotional support from their birth parents had been satisfied. In contrast, Howe and Feast (2000) recorded that 71 per cent found the reunion emotionally satisfying. Three-fifths of searchers (61 per cent) compared to 44 per cent of non-searchers were also likely to say that they felt 'more complete as a person' since the reunion.

Reporting from their US study, Pacheco and Eme (1993) judged the reunion as positive in 86 per cent of cases. In an Australian study, 67 per cent of searchers and 83 per cent of 'found people' rated the experience as positive (Cowell et al, 1996). The reasons given were predominantly about being able to have a good relationship or having questions or expectations resolved positively (p. 1). All the adopted people indicated that the reunion had resulted in positive effects on their life, except for one searcher who had regretted it. The positive responses centred around 'completing their family' (p. 38). In yet another study, the more adopted people "blamed" their birth mothers for the relinquishment, the less positive apparently the contact experience (Rosenzweig-Smith, 1988). In the Pacheco and Eme (1993) study, 85 per cent of adopted people indicated that the reunion had improved their self-concept, 71 per cent their self-esteem, and 62 per cent their ability to relate to others. However, the majority of adopted people agreed that they gained more from meeting siblings than from meeting birth parents. In the end, 15 per cent did not have any contact with the birth family after the initial meeting and 14 per cent saw them annually or less often. Broadly similar figures were quoted by Sachdev (1992).

Adoptive parents and birth parents

Most studies on search and reunions have found that the majority of adopted people who established a long-term relationship with a birth mother still had their primary relationship with their adoptive parents. However, those who felt most comfortable with their adoptive family were those who had evaluated their adoption positively. For example, similar to Triseliotis' (1973) study, Howe and Feast (2000) reported that adopted people with happy, positive adoption experiences may simply be looking for information about their background and not another family relationship. However, if they were to meet their birth mother, they may discover that they have a lot in common and that they get on well together. Overall, a negative evaluation of the adoption experience made it more likely that the individual would remain in contact with their birth mother, but positive evaluation had no discernible effect, i.e. the adopted person was just as likely to remain in contact as not.

The general conclusion that can be drawn from the various studies is that blood and genes may bring the parties together, but they do not form relationships. Other attractions have to be present if contact is not to wane or cease altogether. Attributes such as looking alike, sharing intellectual and other interests, temperament, the impact of the adoptive experience and the absence of blame for being adopted can stimulate attraction and form the basis of a relationship which can prove long-standing. Even then, this is not usually done at the expense of the relationship with the adoptive family.

The birth family: relinquishment, search and reunion

It is still the case that, when it comes to evidence about the long-term impact of the relinquishment decision on birth parent(s), properly sampled studies are very hard to come by. Triseliotis *et al* (1997) briefly summarised what studies had to say on the subject of birth parents and relinquishment, noting also that parting with a child for adoption involved intense feelings of loss and grief, not dissimilar to other serious losses in life. Most birth mothers' continued preoccupation with the child is said to represent their unresolved feelings of loss (Millen and Roll, 1985), while another writer concluded from her summary of studies that birth parents experience 'profound and protracted grief reactions, depression and an enduring pre-occupation with a worry about the welfare of the child' (Brodzinsky, 1990, p. 304). Apparently many birth mothers also come to feel responsible for giving away their child, even if at the time they had no other choice. As a result they may look upon themselves as "unworthy", develop a very low opinion of themselves and a poor self-image with low self-esteem. For some, their sense of loss, far from diminishing with time, seemed to intensify and was particularly high at certain milestones, such as the child's birthdays or starting school. Similarly, Grotevant and McRoy (1998) reported that for all birth mothers, the child remained psychologically present, while Fravel *et al* (2000) explained this by saying that although the child is physically absent from the birth mother's life, he or she remains psychologically present in her mind. Weinreb and Murphy (1988) explained this preoccupation by saying that relinquishing mothers continue to have "parent-like" concerns for their children. It is also asserted that the stressful nature of the event, and the continued preoccupation with it, can give rise to physical and mental illness (Winkler and Keppel, 1984; Bouchier et al, 1991; Howe et al, 1992; Hughes and Logan, 1993; Wells, 1993).

Whether updated information about the child, open adoption and/or face-to-face post-adoption contact can help reduce feelings of loss and grief is still a matter for debate. Grotevant and McRoy (1998) asserted that some birth mothers still experienced grief reactions after seeing their children, but other studies reported that birth mothers who had contact with the adoptive family showed better resolution of their feelings than did mothers who never had such contact or had less open contact. Apparently the main benefit identified was seeing that the child was alright (Keppel, 1991; Dominick, 1988; Grotevant, 2000; Neil, 2000).

Search and reunion

The most likely birth relative to initiate a search is the mother (71 per cent) followed by a sibling (23 per cent) with only a few birth fathers. Studies have also reported that many of the mothers who sought contact linked it with the wish to reassure themselves that the child was well and to release feelings associated with the parting, that is, explaining to the child why they had to part with him or her, hoping that the child would understand and forgive. There was also the wish to share practical information about the respective families, hear about their child's adoption experiences or just see him or her (Post-Adoption Social Workers Group of New South Wales, 1988; Bouchier et al, 1991; Hughes and Logan, 1993). In the longer term, some birth mothers were hoping to keep in touch and be "friends", while at the same time, some did not want to intrude or "pretend" that they were taking the adoptive parents' place (Bouchier et al, 1991).

Not all birth mothers enquiring about their adopted children were seeking contact or a parent–child relationship (Hughes and Logan, 1993; Bouchier et al, 1991). The New Zealand experience also showed that, at the time of parting, only one in every five mothers registered wanting their children to trace them. The others placed a veto on any contact (see Network 2:1, Wellington, New Zealand, 1987). These women, however, parted with their children at a time when the stigma of non-marital births was disappearing and improved social services were available for single parents. Because of these developments they had more choices than being pressurised to part with their child.

After reunion

Face-to-face meetings appear to bring out contrasting feelings in many birth mothers. On the one hand, there is guilt, grief and anger towards themselves, or their own families and partners for not supporting them to keep the child, and on the other, relief and joy, and perhaps pride, at finding their birth child being well. It appears that birth mothers do not take a parental role in relation to the adopted person, but that of a 'friend of the family' (Rockel and Ryburn, 1988; Grotevant and McRoy, 1998). Depending also on how the child has turned out, there can be either gratitude or anger towards the adopters (Post-Adoption Social Workers' Group of New South Wales, 1988).

Birth fathers

If mothers parting with a child for adoption have in recent years received increased attention, birth fathers have hardly featured. Apart from their reported elusiveness, their non-inclusion in the adoption process is attributed to the negative attitudes held about them by adoption agencies and to general negative stereotyping (see also Garfinkel, 1967). Witney (2004) noted that voluntary agencies (before 1975) and social workers were often overworked and their prior concern was to find accommodation and care for the young women who found themselves unmarried and pregnant. They had little time to consider the child's original father. Pannor *et al* (1971) viewed the exclusion of the birth father from the decision about the child as largely denying his existence. Yet one US study reported that approximately half of the fathers interviewed had some involvement with the adoption procedure and most of these said that the adoption was due to their own non-readiness for fatherhood or that they felt adoption was in the best interests of the child. These respondents were approving of adoption. However, birth fathers who were excluded from the adoption

35

procedures and who said that adoption was arrived at because of external pressures, e.g. by family, doctors, lawyers or adoption agencies, were opposed to adoption. For this second group of fathers, exclusion appeared to be long lasting. The study went on to claim that the older a birth father had been at the child's birth, the more likely he was to hold a negative view of adoption. Relatively few said that having been a birth father had an impact on their current parenting function, but apparently those who felt excluded from the adoption process were two-and-a-half times as likely to have fathered additional children as those who had participated in the adoption (Deykin *et al*, 1988, p. 248). One of the fathers is quoted as saying:

No one thinks of the birth fathers! I hurt every day. I can't go any place without wondering. Every 15-year-old girl I see – I wonder is she my daughter? For the last 15 years I have been living in hell. I would do anything to find her.

A recent British study (Clapton, 2003) explored the experiences of 30 fathers who had been involved in giving up a child for adoption, the place of this experience in their lives and, where applicable, accounts of later-life contact with a child. The findings mirror the studies of birth mothers. For example, there was evidence of feelings of loss, and in some cases of grief, along with curiosity and concern about what had happened to the child. The fathers' exclusion from the decision-making process, and in some cases of seeing the mother and child, added to feelings of powerlessness. Apparently a large majority of the men reported the onset of acute distress in the weeks and months following the adoption. Many also said that the detrimental effects of adoption had contributed to disrupted relationships in their lives in the years following the adoption. One reported difference from the experiences of birth mothers was that their sense of loss included the loss of the relationship with the birth mother. The main motive of those seeking contact was for news of the child and his or her welfare and well-being. Witney (2004) has also reported similar findings. She concluded that 'the sample of men involved in unmarried pregnancies in the 1950s, 1960s and 1970s indicates that not all unmarried fathers are feckless, adoption was not a cut and dried process, and the original fathers may not all have walked away from the situation' (p. 60).

In contrast to the Deykin *et al* (1988) study quoted earlier, this one reported that there was some reluctance on the part of fathers to search, in order to avoid 'rocking the boat' for the child and their adoptive family. In the Howe and Feast (2000) study only three per cent of birth fathers had apparently initiated a search.

Adoptive parents: search and reunion

A question often being asked in relation to adoptive parents is how far their child's quest poses a threat, or is viewed as identity enhancing and life enriching for him or her. Largely qualitative evidence gives examples of a range of emotions adoptive parents are said to go through when their child shows an interest in searching or actually establishes contact with a member of their birth family. Even when they are pleased that their child has established contact, a sense of apprehension appears to permeate their experience. The two key feelings reported are fear of their child being hurt in the process, and fear of the loss of their child's love or even a complete rejection by the child (Post-Adoption Social Workers Group of New South Wales, 1988; Sachdev, 1992). It is further suggested that, of the three parties in the adoption triangle, adoptive parents have the least to gain from the search and particularly from reunions. It is also suggested that the search and contact can reactivate in adoptive parents the grief associated with not having had a child of their own. With most attention over the last thirty or so years being focused on adopted people and birth parents, adopters could easily feel left out and virtually powerless to influence events. As an example, the Post-Adoption Social Workers Group of New South Wales (1988) quoted one adoptive parent as saying:

So often we hear how natural mothers seek to find their adopted children and the despair and trauma they suffer. I wonder if anybody can appreciate the feelings of adoptive parents? The last twelve months have been devastating for my husband and me (p. 20).

In another study, adoptive parents' fears of losing their children were typified by the comment that 'there is no room for adoptive parents in search and reunion' (Valley *et al*, 1999).

The above responses are not difficult to understand. What appears to influence many adopters' reactions is the feeling that they are not in control. In South Australia, for example, adoption legislation was changed in 1988, with all adoption records being made available retrospectively to adopted people and birth parents, unless a five-year veto was placed by either the birth parent or adopted person requesting no contact with the searcher (Mann, 1998). It is claimed that in all this the adoptive parents found themselves to be mere spectators. Mann adds that, unlike adopted people who have written several accounts of their experience, adoptive parents have remained primarily silent. She goes on to assert that the 'shame and guilt that was so much part of the birth mother's experience in earlier decades is now appearing to be transferred to adoptive parents' (p. 50).

In a Canadian study, seven out of every ten adoptive parents were reported as strongly "agreeing" or "somewhat agreeing" with the idea of releasing identifying information to adopted people upon request. However, further "probe" questions revealed that their support at the theoretical level was underlain by apprehension and reservation when they were asked to consider it in relation to their own adopted children (Sachdev, 1989, p. 56). The adoptive parents wanted to be sure that the adopted person's decision was not motivated by 'vengeance or resentment' and, because of these fears, three-quarters of them wanted to have the right to exercise a veto before identifying information was released. While recognising that their child would have a natural curiosity about their biological parents, it was hoped that he or she would not have such a desire because they had provided them with a 'loving home' and with as much background information as they had. One adoptive parent is quoted as saying:

To be truthful, I would be devastated, but if it is something he has to do and he insists then I can't stop him (p. 58).

In the New South Wales study (1988) reported earlier, adoptive parents reacted differently to the news that their adopted child was seeking contact with a birth parent. Some actively supported a son or a daughter in their quest and were surprised to see that finding their birth mother did not "confuse" them nor that it was not the end of their relationship. Others felt let down when they realised that the search was going on behind their backs, even though they always told their children that, once 18, and if they wanted it, they would support them to contact a birth parent. Yet others were really glad that their son or daughter expanded their relationships through finding a birth relative. Although adopted people may find more peace in themselves after contact is established, some adoptive parents feel uncertain about their child's continued loyalty to them. Even successful endings apparently had their 'sad moments' (p. 26).

Based on accounts by adopted people, Pacheco and Eme (1993) found that only one-third of them were supported by their adoptive family in the search (Sachdev's figure was 36 per cent being "strongly supportive"). Furthermore, the majority said that contact did not affect the relationship with their adoptive parents and in some cases served to cement them further (Triseliotis, 1973; Depp, 1982; Rosenzweig-Smith, 1988; Pacheco and Eme, 1993; Howe and Feast, 2000).

Overall conclusions

It could be said that the studies in origins, search and reunion which took place over the last thirty years or so have provided the evidence about the importance of the biological connection in adoption. In other words, adopters can no longer pretend that adoption is no different from biological parenting. These studies carried the debate a number of steps further from Kirk's (1964) developed strategy about 'acknowledgement' versus 'rejection' of difference. It is the paradox of adoption that, while it works very well or well for the great majority of adopted people, this fact does not stop them from also wanting to know as much as possible about their adoption, antecedents and roots or to initiate relationships with members of their birth families. The two are not mutually exclusive even if there are differences between searchers and non-searchers.

Many questions still remain unanswered or only half answered by research. They include the relationship between receiving sufficient background information and initiating contact; or differences between searchers and those who never search. Although there is a fair amount of evidence to support the outcome as being positive, it also appears that searching and its aftermath are significantly influenced by the experience of growing up and the quality of the relationships within the adoptive home. Overall, we could conclude from the various studies that search and reunion confer benefits on the great majority of adopted people who set out to search or are found. The high levels of satisfaction reported among adopted people after undertaking the search suggests that openness is much more preferable to conjecture and fantasy. Most reunions appear to work well, but in a minority of cases there can be pain, disappointment and frustration.

The weight of the evidence is also on the side of those who found that there are significant qualitative differences between searchers and non-searchers. For example, levels of alienation and of feeling "different" within the adoptive home, were found to be significantly higher among searchers than non-searchers. However, a large proportion of searchers did not feel like this (73 per cent), and a proportion of non-searchers felt equally alienated and "different".

Available studies also report that many birth parents achieve more peace in themselves after establishing contact or reunions, although adoptive parents are said to have the least to gain. In the great majority of cases, the adoptive parents still remain the "real" parents for the adopted person. Awareness of this appears to be recognised by adopters but this cognitive acceptance does not stop emotional concerns about the adopted person being hurt or rejecting them. A key aim of this study is to identify more precisely the impact of the search and reunion experience, particularly on birth and adoptive parents.

3 The current study and methodology

Introduction

This chapter describes the aims and methodology of the current study and how and why it has been conducted in this way. Definitions of relevant terminology and an outline of the statistical analysis are also presented.

The central aim of the research was to provide a comprehensive picture of the adoption experience and the impact of the search and reunion process and its outcome on all three members of the adoption triangle. As explained in Chapter 2, this large-scale study was purposely designed to build upon and extend the findings from The Children's Society's study about adopted people's search for identity and reunion (Howe and Feast, 2000), by including the experiences of birth mothers and adoptive parents as well as the adopted people within the same triad and who originally took part in that study. Because the first part of the study concentrated on adopted people, the current part gives more prominence to the birth mothers and adoptive parents. While adopted people initiate the majority of searches and subsequent reunions, previous research concerning birth mothers has focused on the minority of birth mothers who had made enquiries or searched for the child they had placed for adoption many years ago. Therefore, little was known about the experiences of the majority of birth mothers who had not enquired or searched, but who were contacted by the adopted person. For this reason, the current study has included both searching and non-searching birth mothers and contrasts the experiences of the two groups.

Adoptive parents are also an integral part of the adoption, search and reunion process and experience and yet they appear to be a relatively forgotten group. A literature search revealed very few properly sampled studies of adoptive parents detailing their experiences and feelings when their sons or daughters made a decision and actually searched, either for background information or for contact and a reunion with birth relatives.

Much of our knowledge comes from research with adopted people rather than directly from the adoptive parents themselves or from samples of adopted people and adoptive parents who were not part of the same dyad.

Aims of the study

The principal aim of the research was to provide a comprehensive overview of the experiences and impact of the adoption, search and reunion process and outcome on all three members of the same adoption triad using sizeable samples. The specific aims for each group were:

Birth mothers
- To report the birth mothers' accounts and experiences from conception to approximately eight years after contact and reunion, including:
  - from pregnancy to parting with the child;
  - from parting to being sought or searching for their sons and daughters;
  - expectations of and initial reactions to the search;
  - the aftermath of the contact and reunion.
- To compare and contrast the circumstances and experiences of non-searching birth mothers who were sought by the adopted person with those mothers who searched for their sons and daughters.
- To compare and contrast matched dyads of birth mothers with their son/daughter on a range of shared experiences.

Adoptive parents
- To describe the experiences of adoptive parents throughout the adoption process, covering:
  - parenting the adopted person;
  - the quality of relationships with the adopted person during different stages;
  - the disclosure of adoption and sharing of background information;
  - the reaction to, and the experience of, the reunion and contact.
- To compare the experiences of adoptive parents whose child searched for their birth relatives with those whose child was contacted by birth relatives – mostly by the birth mothers.

- To compare and contrast matched dyads of adoptive parents with their son/daughter on a range of shared experiences.

Adopted people

- To update their contact situation since the Howe and Feast (2000) study.
- To report on their self-esteem, emotional health and possible sense of rejection and loss arising from the separation from their birth family.

Triadic experience

- To compare the matched perspectives of those in the adoption triangle on aspects of the search and reunion process and outcome within any one reunion.

Research design

A large-scale postal questionnaire was designed to obtain and report the experiences of birth mothers, adoptive parents and adopted people who had had a reunion. To avoid reporting the experiences of separate groups of adoptive parents and birth mothers, a matched-sample design was employed whereby the adopted person was pivotal. Only birth mothers and adoptive parents whose adopted child took part in the first study were included (Howe and Feast, 2000). By using related groups of birth mothers and adoptive parents, we ensured that the groups were reporting on the same experience and thereby different perspectives could be obtained of the same event. If unrelated samples of birth mothers and adoptive parents had participated, it would have been harder to attribute any differences between the groups to different perspectives as they would have been reflecting upon and describing different events. Six separate, yet related, groups of participants were identified and subsequently recruited:

1. Birth mothers who had searched for their birth child (seekers)
2. Birth mothers who had been contacted by their birth child (sought)
3. Adopted people who had searched for their birth relatives (searchers)
4. Adopted people who had been contacted by their birth relatives (non-searchers)
5. Adoptive parents of adopted people who had searched for their birth relatives

6. Adoptive parents of adopted people who had been contacted by their birth relatives.

Pilot study

A pilot study was conducted to ensure that the questionnaires were appropriate and easy to understand and complete. Respondents were asked to complete the questionnaires and also comment upon the design, relevance of questions and the ease with which the questions could be understood. We were particularly interested in whether the questionnaires were too lengthy. Social work practitioners from the Post Adoption Care Counselling and Research Project at The Children's Society provided lists of suitable pilot participants who were not drawn from the sample for the main study. The pilot questionnaires were completed and returned by thirteen adopted people, nine adoptive parents and nine birth mothers (representing both searching and non-searching parties). The comments were mostly favourable and it was decided not to shorten the question-naires as respondents reported that, although lengthy, this was necessary in order to elicit a comprehensive overview of the adoption, search and reunion process. Suggestions concerning the design of the questionnaires were incorporated wherever necessary. The data were analysed in order to check that the questionnaires were suitable to elicit responses. The pilot data are not included in the current account of the main study.

Recruitment of participants for the study

In the initial recruitment process, all the adopted people who had partici-pated in the Howe and Feast (2000) study were contacted and asked if they would be willing to participate in a further study. They were also asked to provide details of their birth parents and adoptive parents and whether they were willing for us to contact them. From this we generated a list of possible participants, all of whom were sent a questionnaire. A total of 480 questionnaires were sent out and 395 were completed and returned, resulting in a high overall response rate of 82 per cent. A further 41 (9 per cent) were returned uncompleted with varying reasons supplied for non-participation, including 'too long ago, cannot remember' and 'I do not want to open up old wounds'. A further one per cent of questionnaires were returned as the intended recipient had moved. Thus, in total, we heard back from 92 per cent of the intended recipients. It should be noted that we have no way of knowing how representative the current sample is of all the intended recipients.

Not all returned questionnaires were eventually included in the study. This was for three reasons. First, as one of the aims of the study was to look at the consequences of the reunion process, only parties who had had a reunion were included; the data from 14 respondents were excluded as a reunion had not yet taken place. Second, only adopted people whose birth mothers or adoptive parents had also returned a questionnaire were included in the study, resulting in the exclusion of 21 adopted people. However, there were 22 instances where we did retain the data of certain birth mothers and adoptive parents to increase the sample size for those chapters reporting their experiences, even though we did not have the adopted person's data and therefore we could not use them in the dyadic or triadic comparisons.

Third, for ease of calculation, it was decided to include the data from only one adoptive parent in each family. In order to maximise the number of respondents, all adoptive parents had been sent a questionnaire and given the option of completing one individually or returning a jointly completed one from them both as a couple. There were 34 instances where two individually completed questionnaires were received, one from the adoptive mother and one from the adoptive father. In these cases, only questionnaire data from the adoptive mother were included. A later analysis revealed that the excluded adoptive fathers' answers were almost identical to those of their wives.

Participants' characteristics

In the end, the data from 312 individuals were included in the study. Table 3.1 and Figure 3.1 show the number of individuals in each participant group. Out of the 126 adopted people who participated, 104 had initiated the search process (searchers) and the remaining 22 of them had been contacted by a member of their birth family (non-searchers). Likewise, out of the 93 birth mothers who took part, 32 of them had initiated the search for the adopted person (seekers) and 61 had been sought by the adopted person (sought). The adoptive parents were described as being adoptive parents of adopted people who were "searchers" (n = 77) and adoptive parents of those adopted people who were "non-searchers" (n = 16).

Table 3.1
Number of participants in each group

	Total number of respondents	Cases where the adopted person searched	Cases where the adopted person did not search
Adopted people (AA)	**126**	104	22
Birth mothers (BM)	**93**	61	32
Adoptive parents (AP)	**93**	77	16

Figure 3.1
Breakdown of participant groups

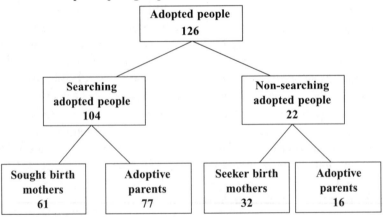

Out of the main sample, there were 78 instances in which both the birth mother and the adopted person had participated thus forming birth mother dyads. There were also 86 adoptive parent dyads consisting of the adoptive parent and the adopted person. Furthermore, within the dyads, there were 34 instances where all three parties had completed a questionnaire: the adopted person, the birth mother and the adoptive parent thus providing data about a triadic experience (see Table 3.2, Figure 3.2 and Figure 3.3).

Table 3.2
Dyadic and triadic relationships

	Total number of dyads/triads	Cases where the the adopted person searched	Cases where the adopted person did not search
Birth mother dyads	**78**	60	18
Adoptive parent dyads	**86**	71	15
Triads	**38**	27	11

Figure 3.2
Breakdown of dyadic relationships

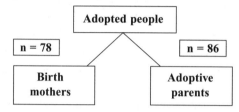

Figure 3.3
Breakdown of triadic relationships

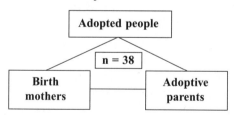

The questionnaires

The postal questionnaires were primarily designed to elicit quantitative data with space provided after most questions for respondents to expand upon their answers. There were also several open-ended questions to allow the respondents to describe their experiences qualitatively. One question-naire was devised for each group – birth mothers, adoptive parents and adopted people – covering issues and areas highlighted by practitioners and previous research. The questionnaires for birth mothers and adoptive parents were based upon the questionnaires for adopted people from Howe and Feast (2000) in order to allow direct comparisons to be made on several responses.

- The birth mothers' questionnaire contained 124 questions covering the pregnancy and adoption, the in-between years, the searching or being sought and the reunion and outcomes.
- The adoptive parents' questionnaire contained 104 questions covering their experience of the adoption itself, life before the reunion, their son/daughter searching or being sought, the reunion and outcomes.
- The adopted people were given a shorter updating questionnaire containing 55 questions. The purpose of this was to obtain updating information about contact (whether new contact had been made or existing contact had ceased) and other areas of interest not covered in the first study such as whether they felt a sense of rejection/loss, including the self-administered Goldberg (1972) General Health Questionnaire and the self-administered Rosenberg (1979) Self Esteem Questionnaire. To the best of our knowledge, the latter standardised questionnaire has not been used with adult adopted people. All three questionnaires contained a substantial amount of identical or similar questions to allow for dyadic and triadic comparisons to be made. To avoid question repetition, some data from the Howe and Feast (2000) study, for those adopted people participating in the current study, were used.

Most of the questionnaires were sent to participants over an eight-month period between May and December 2001. A handful of questionnaires were additionally sent out at the beginning of 2002. Each questionnaire was accompanied by an information leaflet and included a pre-paid addressed return envelope. The information leaflets were specifically designed for each group of participants. They provided information about the study and instructions about what to do if they did not wish to participate or required help completing the questionnaire or if they needed support with the emotions or feelings that ensued upon completing the questionnaire. All respondents were sent letters thanking them for their participation.

Birth fathers

After the data were collected for the main sample of adopted people, birth mothers and adoptive parents, it was decided to try and extend the scope of the study by including birth fathers. We identified 33 birth fathers of adopted people already participating in the study, which meant that they had all had a reunion. They were sent specially adapted questionnaires, based upon the birth mothers' questionnaires but with additional questions covering issues such as when and how they found out about the pregnancy, birth and subsequent adoption. Out of the 33 possible respondents, 15 birth fathers completed and returned a questionnaire, resulting in a comparatively low response rate of 45 per cent. We recognise that this can be a biased sample and caution is urged when interpreting the findings. Due to the relatively small sample size, only qualitative analysis was undertaken. For this reason, it was decided to include the birth fathers' analysis in a separate chapter, rather than as part of the main study. For all of the birth fathers, with the exception of one, the adopted person had initiated the contact. In 14 of the cases, we had the data from both the birth father and the matched adopted person, and in a further seven instances, we also had the data from the matched birth mother. The experiences of the birth fathers were presented alongside those of the matched birth mothers and adopted people.

Advisory group and ethical issues

An advisory group was established which was fairly representative of the people involved in the adoption, search and reunion process. It included several social work practitioners (both post-adoption workers and those involved with adoption placements), academics, a birth mother, an adoptive mother and an adopted person. The advisory group met on five separate occasions at regular intervals over the duration of the study. It provided a forum to discuss relevant topics, including the design of the study and ethical issues. Members were shown a first draft of the three questionnaires prior to the pilot study and they provided feedback on the wording of individual questions and on the overall content. The expertise of members of the advisory group ensured that the design of the study and the questionnaires was appropriate in order to realise the aims of the study.

The analysis

The central aim of the research was to examine and report on the adoption, search and reunion experiences of the birth mothers, adopted people and their adoptive parents. This involved describing each party's experiences as a group, examining any significant differences between the searching and non-searching respondents and looking for relationships and associations between variables. In those cases where we had the data from two or three of the members of the triangle, their answers were contrasted to identify similarities and differences, i.e. dyadic and triadic perspectives and experiences. The exercise was complex, partly due to the sheer quantity of data from three main samples, one for each member of the triad, and another six sub-samples, i.e. those who searched and those who were sought (and their adoptive parent) from each group. The data were essentially categorical, with some continuous variables. Much of the categorical data could also be treated as ordinal data due to the categories being ordered on a 5-point scale, representing the respondents' level of agreement (e.g. strongly agree, agree, mixed, disagree or strongly disagree) with a particular statement. Therefore, a variety of tests were employed depending upon which variables were being examined or compared. In the instances where there was a choice of tests, both tests were used to substantiate the results.

This study will not report on all significant differences found between the groups (such as searching vs. non-searching groups) as they were too numerous. Furthermore, to ensure that the findings of the study are accessible to a wide readership, only the level of significance has been reported to indicate a significant result rather than the detailed statistics. Readers may sometimes notice a discrepancy between the percentage values reported in the tables for each overall group in comparison to the values presented with the dyadic and triadic groups. This is due to the dyads and triads representing smaller, yet matched, and thus more reliable, sub-samples. Due to the comparatively small matched-sample sizes, levels of significance were only quoted when statistically robust. Owing to the number of samples and sub-samples, some repetition has been unavoidable.

Caution is also necessary in that, where a significant relationship between two variables is quoted, no assumptions are made about cause and effect as other unknown factors may have intervened and influenced the outcome. Equally, when significant differences are suggested between two groups, such as between searching and sought birth mothers, or searching and non-searching adopted people, it must be noted that not everyone in each of the respective groups is like that. The significance simply indicates that something is more likely to be found within one rather than the other group. It should also be remembered that only birth mothers, adopted people, and their respective adoptive parents who had had a reunion were sampled and so findings cannot be extrapolated to those parties where a reunion did not occur.

4 The pregnancy and parting with the child

A birth mother:

When I told my mother about the pregnancy, she was upset and it had to be kept secret. She was afraid of anyone finding out and the scandal that would break out. She refused to let me keep the baby. Her initial reaction did not change. I was allowed to tell no one and had to go away from home so no one would know. She was ashamed of me. I had no choice because no one would help or support me to keep the baby. On parting with the baby, my mother and boyfriend pretended that nothing had happened and wouldn't even talk about the baby. Just to be able to talk to someone . . . I had no choice. When I decided to keep the baby, the social workers in the Mother and Baby Home pressurised me and bullied me to give him up.

Before parting I felt very isolated and very sad. I wanted to keep him, but I couldn't, as I didn't have a place to live or any money. I felt trapped by other people's dictatorship and lack of help or support. I have never forgiven myself for having him adopted. Ever since he was born, I have felt guilt for not keeping him and if I'd been stronger, I could probably have kept him. After he went I felt like I had done the wrong thing. But I had no choice.

This chapter sets out the birth mothers' self-reported experiences from the stage of becoming pregnant to confinement and parting with the child. A total of 93 birth mothers' experiences were studied. This included both birth mothers who were sought by the adopted person (N = 61 or 66 per cent) and those who took the initiative to seek their son or daughter (N = 32 or 34 per cent). It will be recalled that birth mothers were far more likely to be sought out by the adopted person than to take the initiative to search. What could be seen as a low proportion of birth mothers seeking contact may be explained by the legal restrictions placed upon them and discussed in Chapter 1 along with the view reported by many mothers to this study that they felt they had no right. (This study did not cover birth mothers who rejected outright the adopted person's wish to establish contact.)

Age, marital status and social class of birth mothers

The average age of the mothers at the time of the study was 58 years. When they were first contacted by their son or daughter or made the first contact themselves, it had been an average of eight years earlier so they were, on average, 50 years old at the time. It could be claimed, therefore, that the post-contact period had been tested over a lengthy period of time. Most of the mothers fell into the 51–60 age group (Table 4.1). The age differences between sought and seeker mothers were not significant. Our group of mothers was much older in comparison to those featured in the Bouchier *et al* study (1991), but the latter had not yet been involved in a reunion and not all of them wanted to. Three-fifths (or 60 per cent) of the mothers in this study were married and almost one in ten were living with a partner. Around 15 per cent were single and 16 per cent separated or divorced. With one exception, all the birth mothers described themselves as white in origin; the one exception was an Asian mother. One of the white mothers was from South Africa and all the others from the UK.

Table 4.1
Present age group of birth mothers

Age group	Sought mothers %	Seeker mothers %	All %
41–50	12	9	11
51–60	54	69	59
Over 60	34	22	30
Total	100	100	100

Sought birth mothers N = 61; Seeker birth mothers N = 32

At the time of the study, the great majority of mothers were in non-manual jobs (74 per cent) such as secretarial and clerical, with a significant number in managerial and professional occupations, including nurses, teachers and social workers. The rest were in manual and semi-skilled or unskilled jobs such as sale assistants, home helps, telephonists or housekeepers. The proportion of all women classified in professional, semi-professional and non-manual occupations was high and almost twice the national average. Our explanation for the high proportion of mothers in non-manual occupations, supported by other evidence, is that in the 1950s and 1960s, when the majority of these mothers parted with their child, it was the implicit practice of hospital social workers to refer women in broadly non-manual occupations to voluntary adoption agencies, where the current study took place, and the rest to local authority children's departments, as they were known at the time (see Triseliotis, 1970; Triseliotis and Russell, 1984).

The pregnancy and the reactions of those around the birth mother

Almost half the birth mothers (48 per cent) were under the age of 20 at the time they gave birth to their child, with one out of every ten being 16 or under. Almost 40 per cent were aged between 20–24 and the rest (13 per cent) 25 years or over (Table 4.2). There were no significant differences between sought and seeker mothers. The average period between the child's adoption and contact was 25 years. Becoming pregnant outside marriage had filled many of these mothers with feelings of shame, embarrassment, guilt and confusion about what to do. Their parents, far from providing relief and support, had added to these feelings.

Table 4.2
Age of birth mothers at the birth of their child

Age group	%
14–16	11
17–19	37
20–24	39
25–29	10
30–39	3
Total	100

N = 91 (missing 2)

Birth fathers in Clapton's (2003) study reported experiencing broadly similar feelings.

The way mothers responded to the question of how family members and friends had reacted to news of the pregnancy, and subsequently to their confinement and relinquishment of the child, suggested strong, continuing and vivid memories of the event. Most of these mothers had become pregnant in the 1950s and early 1960s, when social attitudes towards pregnancy outside marriage were still very censorious, resulting in heavy stigma both for the mother and the child. A change in attitudes did not begin to emerge until the late 1960s, too late for these mothers to benefit. Contraceptives were also not widely available then, as now, and the Abortion Act 1967 had not yet come into effect. Neither did the social security system provide the income benefits that might have enabled a single mother to keep her child, even against the wishes of those around her.

Three out of ten mothers had told their family and friends about the pregnancy voluntarily, but a similar proportion felt they had to tell because they needed support. Around one in eight (12 per cent) had not told, while in the remaining cases, relatives and friends came to know as the pregnancy progressed. The parents were the most likely people to be told (88 per cent), followed closely behind by the father of the child (84 per cent), then a friend (73 per cent), a sister (49 per cent) and finally, a brother (39 per cent). Unsurprisingly perhaps for that period, seven out ten parents had reacted to the news of the pregnancy with dismay, shock and upset and wanting it to be kept secret and concealed. The least shocked and upset were friends, followed by the child's father (see Table 4.3). No significant differences were found between the reactions of the parents of sought and seeker birth mothers, except that a higher percentage of seeker mothers reported that their mothers had been upset when they found out about the pregnancy (p = 0.021).

Parents had not wanted others to know about the pregnancy because of the shame and embarrassment it would bring to the family. The extent of the prevailing stigma is illustrated by the example of one doctor who apparently refused to see the mother because she was bearing a non-marital child. Typical comments attributed to parents by both sought and seeker mothers included: 'they felt horrified'; 'betrayed'; 'wanted me to

Table 4.3

All the initial reactions of those around the birth mother when they learnt about the pregnancy

Reaction	Mother* %	Father %	Siblings %	Child's father %	Friends %
Shocked	68	69	49	31	16
Upset	72	63	28	19	9
Supportive	35	32	49	21	82
Understanding	15	15	42	21	58
Helpful	22	18	31	13	67
Rejection	5	4	–	37	–
Keep it secret	60	62	15	22	2

*Sought mothers N = 52 (missing 9) Seeker mothers N = 26 (missing 6)
Note: In this and other tables where reference is made to *all,* as different from *main* answers, multiple answers could be offered.

be hidden away'; 'angry and blaming me'; 'disgusted with me' or 'shocked' and 'dismayed'.

One birth mother had been so 'scared' of her parents' reaction that she lied, saying she had been raped. Sometimes there had been anger and tears, with the pregnant woman being blamed and made to feel 'bad' or 'wicked'. Total rejection came only from a handful of parents, though many mothers interpreted the withholding of emotional support and being sent 'away', mainly to a mother and baby home, as having been rejected. The following are just two of many graphic examples about the parents' reactions:

I had committed the gravest sin. My father wrote to say how upset and outraged my mother was and that I was not to come home.

My baby, they told me, would have bad blood. In their days I would have been hounded out of the village. I was terrified.

Some parents had gone to great lengths to conceal their daughter's pregnancy and a lot of effort and emotion must have gone into keeping the secret. In one case, and because the mother would often weep out of grief, outsiders were told by a parent that it was because she had 'the flu'.

One father would only allow his daughter out after dark so as not to be seen, and another viewed the pregnancy as an 'invasion' of his home, though apparently he was working in another part of the country and rarely went home. A practical step in keeping the pregnancy secret was sending the mother to a mother and baby home. A typical comment by some mothers was that it was made clear to them that 'there was no way I could have stayed at home'. If the mother lived in another part of the country at the time, the message to her was to not return home until after confinement and the child's adoption. A reminder that one of the key reasons why successive Adoption Acts from 1926 to the late 1970s provided for total secrecy was, it was said, to "protect" the mother and the child from the stigma of a non-marital birth. It would be wrong, therefore, to assume that the mothers were total victims of their family's machinations because mothers too wanted to avoid the stigma and largely complied with the arrangements.

In spite of their initial reaction, a third of parents were said to have been 'supportive' and a few 'helpful' and 'understanding'. Occasionally, one or both parents would rally round and be supportive in helping with hospital arrangements or with the adoption, but also being careful that it remained secret. Some of the parents were supportive and understanding from the start or after their initial reaction. Some parents' disappointment had to do with their daughter spoiling her educational opportunities, career or general future prospects, but nevertheless went on to be supportive: 'upset initially, but supportive' or 'they were shocked but helpful'. Although a number of parents would have liked to see their daughter marry the child's father to make it "respectable", there was no unusual pressure on her to do so. Occasionally a parent would advise the mother not to rush into marrying, because 'she might come to regret it later'. As one of these mothers explained: 'My family were all very supportive, particularly my mother'.

Irrespective of whether parents were initially hostile or supportive, almost 80 per cent of them were said not to have changed as the pregnancy progressed. Those who were supportive, even if shocked and upset at the start, on the whole continued to be so and very few of those who were hostile at the start became more understanding and supportive later. While many of the birth mothers' own mothers had been fearful of the damage to the family's reputation if the news broke out, a minority were said to have wanted to be more supportive, but carried little influence or power against the wishes of their husbands. This need not come as a surprise considering the imbalance of power and control between men and women in marital relationships at the time. One father was said to be unable to accept it even now when he was nearing the age of 80. Some typical comments of continuing hostility included: 'I went to live with friends and never saw or had any help from my family'; 'I tried to talk to my parents after returning home for the confinement but they refused to talk'; 'My parents were adamant about not willing to discuss options'; or 'The secrecy aspect never changed and the lies became "agreed stories" '.

Compared to parents, siblings were less likely to be shocked or upset or wanting to keep the matter secret. They also proved more supportive, understanding and helpful. No sibling was quoted as being rejecting in their attitude. Brothers were said to have reacted by being more under-standing compared to sisters. Friends proved to be the least likely to be shocked or upset.

Emotional and practical support

Because of the importance attached by studies to the availability of emotional support during pregnancy and immediately after relinquish-ment, mothers were first asked to indicate how much emotional support they had received when they told about the pregnancy. Again, most emotional support had come from friends (65 per cent) and the least from the child's father and the parents (Figure 4.1). Compared to sought mothers, those searching reported receiving significantly less emotional support when they told their mothers ($p = 0.029$) and relatives ($p = 0.006$) about the pregnancy. For example, over 50 per cent of seeker mothers said they had had no emotional support compared to only 29 per cent of sought ones.

Only a minority of birth mothers (under a third) said they had received a lot or enough emotional support from their mothers or fathers. In such cases, there was reference to a 'loving' mother and in a few cases, support from both parents. One or two referred to having had 'love' from their

Figure 4.1

Emotional support received when told about the pregnancy

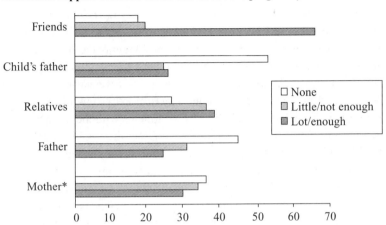

Total N= 77; *Sought mothers N = 51 (missing 10); Seeker mothers N = 26 (missing 6)

parents, but not 'understanding'. The emotional support from the child's father was as low as that from the parents. Occasionally, emotional support would come from an older sibling, a grandparent, or a relative. The main experience, though, was of parents who were experienced as 'frozen' or 'non-loving' and as being more concerned for their own reputation than the mother's feelings. Overall, and because the pregnancy was not often talked about, or was 'a no go area', most parents were experienced as not making themselves emotionally available to their daughter. Secrecy and concealment also imposed the withholding of positive feelings, because to do otherwise would be to legitimise the pregnancy. A not unusual comment by some mothers was:

As the pregnancy was not talked about, there was no support also.

Furthermore, because many parents had decided that the child would be adopted, the problem, they felt, was resolved and there was no need for any further reference to the pregnancy or to attend to emotional needs. It was perhaps to be expected that those parents who reacted angrily to the pregnancy also largely withheld emotional support. The pattern reported for emotional support was repeated when it came to practical support. Only 43 per cent of mothers said they had had a lot or enough practical support from their mother and 19 per cent from the child's father. In contrast, 61 per cent of friends were said to have provided a lot or enough practical support. As already mentioned, it was mostly friends who would rally round to offer both practical and emotional support. Parents who were emotionally supportive were also more likely to help with practical arrangements. Practical help came mainly in the form of attending ante-natal clinic appointments with the mother being accompanied there by her own mother; a father driving his daughter to the hospital; the occasional purchase of clothing for the baby; or paying for the mother's board and lodging. 'Totally' supportive or 'loving' parents who helped to make practical arrangements were few but appreciated. Parents who were experienced as being 'emotionally un-available' but who offered practical support, had their motives questioned. Some mothers described them as 'selfish', such as when parents made arrangements for them to enter a mother and baby home or move to another town. Being sent 'away' was generally perceived as 'being got rid of' because of the fear of neighbours finding out about the pregnancy. As one respondent put it:

My parents supported me for their own ends and not for myself.

Nor did birth mothers say that they had had financial support from any other source, e.g. charities or government agencies. The extensive use of mother and baby homes at the time is illustrated by the fact that over half of mothers (53 per cent) said that they had stayed in one during their pregnancy. Another quarter stayed at home, almost a fifth (18 per cent) with relatives or friends, and the rest (8 per cent) in a bed-sit or other similar type of accommodation. Although some staff in mother and baby homes were said to have been understanding and supportive, the overall atmosphere was reported as having been one of 'condemna-tion' because they were seen as having 'sinned' and should have felt 'ashamed' of themselves. There was also the belief that, if staff were condemnatory, this would act as deterrent to a further non-marital pregnancy.

Occasional practical support and understanding had also come from some doctors and the church. Besides emotional support in the form of listening and understanding, practical support in the form of money and/ or accommodation was also offered. It was not unusual for a friend's family to put up the mother until the birth and the adoption arrangements were over. Some mothers commented that friends had been more supportive than family, or 'my friends wanted me to be near them because of my parents' reaction'. The following are typical examples:

My friend's family were totally supportive, letting me stay with them and welcoming the baby until he was adopted.

My friend's family did all they could to be supportive but of course they could not replace my own family and I felt extremely rejected.

The child's birth

For these mothers, decisions about contact with their baby from birth onwards were taken out of their control, thus reinforcing existing feelings of powerlessness. With one exception, all the birth mothers had been "allowed" to see their baby, but for five per cent, there was no more contact after that. Over a third had been able to care for their child for up to three weeks and a broadly similar proportion for up to six weeks. The rest had more time with their child (23 per cent). One birth mother had been allowed to look at the baby only for a few minutes but not hold her. Almost three-fifths said they had been given no choice as to whether to breast or bottle-feed their baby and the great majority (71 per cent) had been encouraged to bottle-feed. Some recognised that the motives may have been well meant to prevent them from getting too attached to the baby and suffering more pain, but they thought that it was a decision that they, and not others, should have been allowed to make. A few had experienced hospital staff as being equally censorious as their parents, adding that the main interest was to get their signature consenting to the child's adoption. This, some added, only doubled their 'sense of isolation because nobody had any sympathy left for a sinner'.

Relationship with the child's father

Almost three-fifths of the birth mothers referred to the child's father as 'a boy friend' or sometimes a 'fiancé', but a third of the relationships were described as 'casual' or 'short-term' and in five per cent of the cases, the child was described as being the result of rape. In Witney's (2004) study, a similar percentage of birth fathers said that they had been in a steady/long-term relationship with the mother of their child. It could not therefore be claimed that these were mostly casual relationships. Nor was the image true that, at the time, most mothers giving birth to a non-marital child were involved "in one night stands". Mothers in this study also claimed to have told 84 per cent of the child's fathers about the pregnancy and that two-thirds of them were aware of the child's birth. A quarter of the fathers had seen the baby shortly after birth and almost three out of every ten fathers had seen the baby before he or she went for adoption. Double the proportion of seeker, rather than sought, mothers also reported that the child's father had seen the baby. In Clapton's (2003) study, 87 per cent of fathers reported that they knew of the birth at the time and 50 per cent had seen and held their baby (this high proportion could reflect the self-selected nature of the sample).

While less likely to be upset or shocked, like the mothers' families, nevertheless birth fathers in this study were reported by their child's mother to have proved to be the least helpful and least supportive. Furthermore, a significant number dropped out of the mother's life or 'panicked' about what to do. Almost two-fifths showed outright rejection and only a minority (around a fifth) were perceived as supportive, under-standing and helpful. Of 37 (40 per cent) fathers who had known about the baby and been consulted, 33 had agreed with the adoption plan. The majority, however, had not been consulted. Around a fifth of both sought and seeker mothers continued the relationship with the child's father and nine (or 9 per cent) of them married him.

Overall, the birth mothers' comments on the support provided to them by the child's father were very mixed. While a small number of fathers were reported as having been emotionally supportive throughout, or as wanting to be supportive, they were also said not to have known how to go about it. A few wanted to marry the mother, and a handful did so after the baby was adopted. In other cases the mother, her parents or the boyfriend's parents did not want the marriage. As one mother put it:

My boyfriend was doing his National Service then but he was not allowed any more contact with me by my parents because they did not think he was suitable.

Many fathers, being young, were said to have taken fright or moved out of the mother's and the child's life altogether. In some cases, the relationship had been ended before the pregnancy was known; in others, after the fathers learnt about it; and in others still, after the birth of the child. Some fathers did not want to have anything to do with the pregnancy either because they wanted to continue with their studies, had a new girlfriend or did not want their families to know. A couple of them suggested termination and those already married did not, on the whole, want to know; in a few cases, a father offered some money. In contrast to this, mothers again stressed the emotional and practical support they had had from friends and occasionally from an aunt or uncle. A handful of birth fathers who had come from overseas either did not want it to be known or had already left the country. One or two suggested that mother and baby went with them to their country, but the mothers had rejected the idea.

The ethnic origins of four per cent of the fathers were said to be different from that of the mother, but none of the mothers said that the father's ethnic background had influenced their decision over the adoption, adding that others had made the decision on their behalf anyway. One or two wondered, however, what kind of life their child would have had considering the racism they themselves had suffered because they had been associating with a person from a different ethnic background.

Influences in reaching a decision

For the birth mothers, the main factors that had influenced the adoption decision were mostly external rather than personal. When birth mothers were asked why they thought their child had been adopted, chief among *all* the reasons offered, and perhaps not unexpectedly, were that of being single (82 per cent) followed by the lack of financial resources (78 per cent), and over half said they had had nowhere to live (Table 4.4). When the main reasons were singled out, the picture changed, with parental wishes being the dominant factor influencing the parting decision (35 per cent), followed by social pressures (26 per cent), i.e. the associated stigma, and the lack of practical support (21 per cent). However, almost a fifth of mothers (18 per cent) said this was their own decision. Besides societal attitudes and parental pressures, these mothers had to reckon also with the inadequacy of the social security provision at the time.

As one of them said:

Even now when I see women who have been enabled by the state to bring up a child/children alone, I feel quite bitter that there was no help for me.

Housing shortages were far more severe than now and childminding and nursery facilities were only just beginning to be seen as a necessity to offer mothers more personal choices. Personal pressures appeared to operate only in a small proportion of cases, such as the mother wanting to continue with her studies or employment or lacking confidence in her parenting abilities. A small number expressed envy, and some anger, at the current provision for single mothers, which had been denied them.

Table 4.4
All and main reasons for parting with the child

Reason	All reasons %	Main reason* %
Single status	82	
Parental wishes	62	35
Social pressures	53	26
Personal choice	28	18
Too young, studying, working	12	–
No finance	78	21
Nowhere to live	52	–
Child in care of Social Services	8	–
Total		100

*Sought mothers N = 56 (missing 5); Seeker mothers N = 28 (missing 4)

Although true when seen in the context of that period, it is also possible that some mothers were retrospectively rationalising the adoption decision to lessen the burden of guilt they felt.

Pressurised into adoption?

In answer to the question of whether they had felt pressurised into adoption, two-thirds said 'yes'. A fifth said 'no' and the rest (13 per cent) were uncertain (Figure 4.2). Most of the pressure had come from parents and was reinforced by staff in mother and baby homes and hospitals. Although a higher proportion of seeker mothers said they had been pressurised, the difference did not amount to full significance. Looking at the responses in another way, two-thirds of mothers did not think they had been offered any choice at the time. Over eight out of every ten mothers had reached the adoption decision, or had the decision reached for them, before the birth of the child. This would fit with studies in the 1960s charting the decision-making process of mothers giving birth to non-marital children (see Yelloly, 1965).

Figure 4.2
Did mothers feel pressurised into adoption?

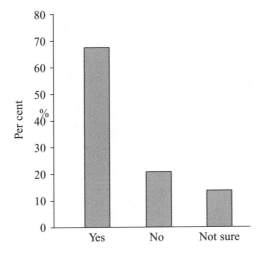

N = 92 (missing 1)

Compared to sought mothers, seekers were somewhat more likely to say that they had come under pressure to part with the child, but it did not reach full statistical significance. Sometimes the pressures would be unspoken or subtle and come from one or both parents. Many birth mothers said that they had become aware from early on that their own preferences did not matter and that they had to do 'as they were told'. The combination of lack of emotional and practical support was aptly summarised by one of them:

> No understanding, no support, no job, no money, nowhere to live. I was terrified.

Other mothers came to feel that their parents and professionals had 'colluded' in pressurising them, each one repeating that it was 'best for the child', that it would be 'selfish to do otherwise' or parents and social worker saying 'the baby deserved better'. A minority (20 per cent) explicitly said that the decision was entirely their own because of their own pressures. There was a kind of acknowledgement that they were not yet ready for parenthood or had to consider their long-term future: 'I loved him but I knew I could not care for him'.

Emotional support when parting with the child

The pattern of emotional support that was offered to the birth mother following the birth and relinquishment was broadly similar to that offered to her when she first told about the pregnancy. If anything, it was now reduced further (Table 4.5). Again, it was mostly friends who had stood by the mother. The most unsupportive was the child's father (71 per cent), followed by the mother's father (68 per cent), relatives (58 per cent) and mothers (55 per cent) (Table 4.5). Broadly the same parents who had withheld emotional support during pregnancy did the same at parting. Compared to sought mothers, seekers were more likely to report receiving less emotional support from either parent (mother $p = 0.05$; father $p = 0.020$).

Lack of emotional support and denial of the birth often persisted in the years that followed. Any mention of the child was apparently incidental and the fact that the family had experienced a major loss went largely unacknowledged. Open grieving, some mothers added, was not possible:

'It all had to be done quietly'. It was also reported that many families, including some mothers, were relieved when it was all over, without the secret having been revealed. A not unusual comment was that, once the child was adopted, the problem had been solved. As one mother put it:

> My parents wanted to pretend it never happened.

And another:

> I was absolutely gutted, so unhappy and isolated because I had no one to talk to when I went home. The moment I got home my father put his arms round me and said, 'now you must forget everything that happened and get on with your life. We will never speak of it again.' And he never did.

In a minority of cases, a parent, mostly the mother, was perceived as 'empathising', or 'trying to understand' and even showing distress. However, several respondents likened their parents' attitude to that of an 'ostrich' and others said that 'nobody seemed to care' about their feelings or thought that they might 'need support'. Another respondent felt at the time that it was her 'against the rest of the world'. A few others were prepared to say that perhaps they had been too 'self-contained' or 'too independent', making themselves inaccessible to those wanting to help. One of them explained: 'As I tended to keep my

Table 4.5

How much emotional support mothers said they had at the parting with the child

Amount	Mother* %	Father %	Relatives %	Child's father %	Friends %
Lot/enough	21 (30)	18 (25)	18 (38)	16 (25)	55 (65)
Little/not enough	24 (34)	15 (31)	24 (36)	13 (24)	19 (19)
None	55 (36)	68 (44)	58 (26)	71 (51)	26 (16)
Total	100	101	100	100	100

*Sought mothers N = 51 (missing 10); Seeker mothers N = 27 (missing 5)
Note: Numbers in brackets refer to emotional support offered when the mother told about the pregnancy.

feelings to myself, I don't think my partner or friends felt I needed emotional support'.

Overall, some three-quarters of respondents would have liked more support at all stages, and 'someone to talk to', but there had been none. As a result of the denial and secrecy, many mothers said they had felt 'alone' and 'extremely isolated'. A few claimed that the events led to them having a 'breakdown' or being depressed for a long time later. The sense of distress and vulnerability arising from the experience at different stages, along with feelings of isolation 'as if nobody cared', was summed up by one mother with the words:

I have never felt so lost and abandoned before or since. This is the very first time I was asked about my feelings.

Feelings before parting and soon after adoption

There was little difference in the type and strength of feelings experienced by most mothers before and soon after parting. These are shown in the composite tables below (Table 4.6). Topping the list for all feelings was grief and sadness, followed by unhappiness, powerlessness, isolation, guilt, depression, anxiety, worry, confusion and, least likely, anger. Compared to sought mothers, seekers were more likely to say they had felt worried about their child ($p = 0.024$) and more of them had felt sad and depressed after the parting. However, those who were relieved increased from 20 per cent before the parting to 32 per cent afterwards. There were no significant changes between the pre- and post-parting periods in the strength of the main, as different from all, feelings that dominated the birth mothers' experience. As already mentioned, more mothers now felt relieved, and fewer felt confused and bewildered, at the post-parting period mainly because the matter was over. More puzzling is that only four per cent reported feeling angry. Considering the pressures many said they came under, it is perhaps surprising that many more did not feel like this. A possible explanation is that the anger was suppressed or became intense grief. Furthermore, they appeared to accept that it was their fault and that they were to blame. For most mothers, both before and after adoption, there was sadness, isolation, powerlessness, feeling like they were in 'a bad dream', 'absolutely gutted', 'loss and bereavement', 'completely and utterly desolate', 'confused, depressed and lonely', 'sick and helpless', 'numb', 'as if the world had come to an end' or 'cried myself to sleep'. 'I felt,' one woman reported, 'that it was me versus the world. I had no friends left. Even my family abandoned me. I'm glad that times have changed'. And another: 'Numbness – severe depression. Major loss feelings – like part of me had been amputated'.

Alongside these intense feelings of loss and sadness, the thought or belief that it was 'best' for their child went some way to reduce the pain. They were told, and they largely came to believe it, that the baby was going to a 'good' or 'loving home' or would have 'a happy life'. Many had 'convinced' themselves that it was best for the child, thus helping to assuage some of the guilt arising from not being able to take on responsibility for their child. It is not surprising, as will be seen from the next chapter, that a key reason for why mothers wanted to establish contact

Table 4.6

All and the *main* birth mothers' feelings before parting with the child and soon after adoption

Feeling	All feelings %		Main feelings %
Sadness/grief	85	Powerless/isolated	41
Unhappy	73	Sad/unhappy/depressed	40
Powerless	69	Relieved/content/happy	15
Isolated	61	Confused/bewildered	6
Depressed	59	Angry	4
Anxious	55	Worried about child	4
Worried	55		100
Confused	54		
Angry	43		
Bewildered	35		
Relieved	26		
Content and happy	6		

1. Total of all feelings N = 91; Sought mothers N = 59 (missing 6); Seeker mothers N = 32
2. Total of main feelings N = 84; Sought mothers N = 55 (missing 6); Seeker mothers N = 29 (missing 3)

was to see whether the child was doing well and was happy. Finding that their child was 'doing well' would, to some extent, justify the parting to themselves and help lower the intensity of the guilt and sadness felt. A typical comment was:

A loss, but happy that she will have a nice family and brothers. All the things I could not give her.

The relief experienced by a significant proportion of mothers was mostly ascribed to 'the whole thing being over' and looking for some peace of mind after months of unrelenting pressures, described by some as a 'nightmarish' period. While many of the feelings such as sadness and powerlessness were in relation to themselves, worry and anxiety were in respect of the child and his or her future.

The offer of counselling

Birth mothers were asked how much formal counselling they had been offered or received during pregnancy, at confinement or soon after and by whom. Any form of counselling in those decades would mostly have come from moral welfare workers attached to adoption agencies and mother and baby homes or perhaps welfare workers or medical social workers attached to hospital maternity units and more exceptionally a psychiatrist. From our knowledge and writings of the period, moral welfare workers were likely to put the emphasis on the "sin" that the mother had committed, thus reinforcing the kind of condemnatory attitudes mothers had already come across. Over three-quarters of birth mothers claimed to have had no counselling. Just over a fifth said they had a lot or a little, either during pregnancy, at confinement or soon after. While a few said they would have liked the help of a counsellor, a similar proportion had wanted to put the whole experience behind them and get on with their lives by 'shutting out' the experience or trying to avoid appearing 'weak'.

Changes and continuity in the birth mothers' feelings about the adoption decision

Even though the great majority of birth mothers did not want to own or accept the decision as theirs, four out of every five said they had 'decided' on adoption before confinement. For almost half there was no change of mind, but well over a third said that their feelings changed after the child's birth, even though the adoption went ahead. Irrespective of whether or not their feelings changed, a significant number recalled how difficult it proved to keep to the original decision once the child was born. One of them, echoing the views of some others, said she had had the urge to take the baby and run away. A change of mind seemed more likely by those who had fed, bathed and changed the baby over a few weeks. Others observed that, although their feelings had changed, they knew there was nothing to be done, because the same circumstances and conditions still prevailed both at home and outside. The minority of birth mothers who said that from the start the adoption was their own decision, continued to believe that it was the right thing to do, had 'never doubted it' and did not want to allow themselves to waver.

Summary

Most of the birth mothers featuring in this study gave birth to their child, and parted with them, in the 1950s and 1960s when harsh attitudes, along with shame and stigma, surrounded non-marital births. As a result, and to maintain the secret, many birth mothers and their families built elaborate stories and fictions to disguise the pregnancy and birth, with many of them being sent to mother and baby homes or to another part of the country in order to conceal the pregnancy. It is not surprising, perhaps, that many came to feel that it had not been their decision to part with their child and suggested that it was taken out of their control. A significant minority, however, were clear that the decision had been theirs. Because of the stigma and the absence of emotional support and understanding from the immediate family, or the child's father, and because the decision had been taken out of their hands, the great majority also came to feel lonely, isolated, abandoned, vulnerable, powerless and largely victims. Equally, some of their parents had found themselves torn between the wish to be supportive and the fear of shame. Furthermore, and because the pregnancy had become a taboo subject, it could not be talked about within the family and so no emotional support could be made available either.

Some doctors, nurses and other professionals, e.g. moral welfare workers, were said to have shared the parents' and society's censorious attitudes, reinforcing both the shame and the concealment of the pregnancy and birth. They, too, were said to withhold emotional support and saw adoption as resolving all the concerns and also providing the child with a 'good home'. This meant that birth mothers were again deprived of opportunities to express their intense grief and feelings of loss. Mander's (1995) study lends support to their accounts regarding the judgemental attitudes of some medical professionals. Although it is recognised that retrospective accounts can be coloured by new experiences and the new social climate, nevertheless, given that because so many mothers spoke in similar terms, it must be accepted that this is how they perceived their experiences during a period of intense stress. Finally, compared to sought mothers, seekers were more likely to report that their parents were more upset when they found out about the pregnancy and that they received less emotional support from them. Most support (for those who did not get it from their families) came mainly from friends, flat-mates and, somewhat less so, from siblings. Compared to sought mothers, seekers were more likely to feel worried about the child.

5 Life without the child and attitudes to the legal position

Birth mother:
Ever since the parting, I have lived with a feeling of loss and guilt. I have never forgiven myself or ever will, for doing the wrong thing by having him adopted. This affected my marriage to his father and hence I ended up divorcing him. I believe I let my child down.

The previous chapter outlined the birth mothers' reported experiences from the stage of becoming pregnant to parting with the child. This chapter charts the in-between years from adoption to being sought or setting out to seek their sons and daughters, along with perspectives on contact and the law.

The adoption decision

Looking back, seven out of every ten birth mothers said that, in spite of all the pressures they had experienced, adoption was still the correct decision at the time. Almost a fifth (18 per cent) did not think so and the rest (12 per cent) were unsure. Those mothers who said that it was the right decision repeated mainly what they had said before the adoption took place, i.e. that they had little or no family or external support, felt they had little to offer the child, were young and immature or that adoption allowed them to get on with their lives. One mother had, in fact, reclaimed her son from the prospective adopters soon after the placement was made, but returned him after a few days because she could not get the support she needed to look after him. Those who had found, after contact, that their son or daughter was doing well, quoted it as an additional justification for the parting: 'From my daughter's point of view, it was the right decision'. In contrast, a few mothers, especially seekers, were still angry because the prevailing circumstances had prevented them from keeping their child. One of them described adoption as 'cruel and as an isolating

73

experience'. Another said that nobody could convince her that adoption was 'the right decision'. More angrily, a third described it as: 'nothing short of obscene to force a mother to give up her baby'.

The effects over the years of parting with the child

When birth mothers were asked about all the effects on them of the parting, over the years, the sense of loss and sadness were high (90 per cent) followed by guilt (79 per cent), the pressure to continue keeping the secret (64 per cent) and inability to get over the decision (36 per cent) (Table 5.1). Turning to the main feelings, for two-fifths it was the sense of loss and sadness, followed by having to keep the secret, guilt, inability to get on with life, inability to get over it and health problems. There was sadness, crying, loss of self-esteem and, in two cases a suicide attempt. Compared to sought mothers, seekers were more likely to say that, during the in-between years, they were unable to get over the adoption, felt worried ($p = 0.01$), anxious ($p = 0.024$), had poorer physical health ($p < 0.001$), poorer mental health ($p = 0.005$), took to alcohol ($p = 0.16$) and had persistent low self-esteem, all attributed to the adoption. While no cause and effect relationship can be inferred, nevertheless these statistical correlations suggest that, compared to sought mothers, seekers had been far more distressed during this period. In other words, loss/sadness topped the list as part of all and main feelings. Far from disappearing, these feelings seemed to become a permanent feature of their lives: 'overwhelming', 'never a day went by without thinking about her' or 'no use trying to run away from them'. Memories would at times bring tears because of the intensity of the feelings experienced, which were said to be 'relentless'. One of them characteristically remarked: 'Nothing can possibly describe the hell of losing a child this way'. And another:

> I tried to run away from the pain but the pain was always with me. Always wondered what happened to my son. Cried a lot. Felt like a victim. I was angry with my mother.

Feeling that they had to keep the secret and not being able to talk to others about their emotions, as different from just the adoption, some mothers referred to themselves as 'bottled up', 'suppressed' or 'blocked' over the years until contact was made.

Table 5.1
All **and the** *main* **effects of the parting decision on birth mothers over the years**

Effect	All effects %	Main effects %
Loss/sadness	90	40
Guilt	79	17
Keeping the secret	64	19
Unable to get on with life	49	–
Low self-esteem	40	7
Unabe to get over it	39	–
Depression	37	–
Blocked it out	29	–
Poor physical and mental health	24	7
Alcoholism	3	–
No negative effects	8	10
Total		100

*Sought mothers N = 56 (missing 5); Seeker mothers N =30 (missing 2)

While guilt closely overlapped with sadness and loss, a significant number of mothers were also able to distinguish between guilt and other feelings. The guilt was mainly associated with what they perceived as their rejection of their child and wondering if their child would judge them harshly for that. Some guilt also arose from their compliance with the adoption decision and for not putting up a better fight at the time. Nor surprisingly, many of them longed to explain why. If one of the key questions that the adopted person asks is 'why was I adopted?' a key answer for mothers was to explain themselves and answer the question: 'why did I let him/her be adopted?'. Some reported that the thought 'preyed' on their mind or that the guilt was constant and could not be wished away. The 'relentlessness' of the guilt, as one put it, led to more sadness and more depression. Guilt also led to greater anxiety about the child's welfare and greater worry about the quality of the adoptive placement. For the majority, the negative feelings associated with the adoption kept coming back. Although they had to get on with their lives, this was accompanied by recurrent memories of the lost child. As one of them put it:

I thought of her every day, but it hasn't stopped me having a life.

Ability to make relationships

Seven out of every ten mothers did not think that the adoption experience had affected their capacity to form new relationships. Getting married and having other children, along with making new relationships, were events singled out as having had a big positive impact on their lives and going some way, in their view, to lessen the negative effects of parting. Some of these mothers stressed that the parting had made them even more determined to sustain future relationships. However, around one out of every seven (14 per cent) reported that parting with their child had affected, in some way or other, their ability to form new relationships. While no cause and effect can be demonstrated, among those who felt affected by the parting decision in this way, some referred to being afraid of close relationships, or that it had negatively affected relationships within their marriage and even within a second marriage. A few made a conscious effort to avoid being hurt by avoiding making new relationships.

Most mothers (71 per cent) did not think that parting with their child had affected their decision to have other children, but just under a fifth said it had. The great majority had given birth to two more children after the adoption, but for one out of seven, the adopted one had been their only child. Around eight per cent had at least one other child adopted and one mother and her husband had adopted a non-related child. Many explained that they badly wanted to have a child that they could keep and parent: 'All I wanted' said one 'was to have a baby that I could keep'; another was 'desperate' to have her own child but this time keep it; yet another was desperate to have a child to 'call my own'. While some admitted to wanting to have another child 'to replace' the lost one, a similar proportion wanted to avoid a child of the same sex as it would only remind them of the pain they had gone through. A handful were honest enough to say that they did not feel very maternal. Several were put off by the parting experience from having any more children, and a similar number were 'frightened' that someone would come and take this child away too.

Similarly, the majority of mothers (62 per cent) did not think that parting with their child for adoption affected the quality of their relationship with their other children. If anything, they said, they came to view the new child as 'special' or it made them more determined to give their other children 'all the love and care' they were unable to give to the adopted one. However, two-fifths said that parting with one child had definitely, or possibly, affected their relationship with their other children – this was mainly in the form of spoiling them because of the earlier feelings of guilt and wanting to make amends. Some admitted that this was largely for their own, rather than their children's, benefit.

Thoughts about the child

The birth mothers reported almost always thinking about the now adopted child, but particularly during the first year and at anniversaries. Birthdays (91 per cent) followed by Christmas (78 per cent) were the most likely times during which mothers thought about their child. The kinds of thoughts were wide-ranging and the principal ones are set out in Table 5.2. Most common were thoughts of whether the child was happy, followed by whether the adoption had been successful. Other thoughts (but not main ones) were about the child's personality, what he or she looked like, whether the child felt rejected or not, or if he or she would like to meet and perhaps have a relationship.

Table 5.2
All **and** *main* **thoughts about the child**

Thoughts	All %	Main %
Whether happy and well	98	52
Was the adoption successful?	95	27
What he/she looks like/personality	82	7
Does he/she feel rejected?	67	1
Would he/she like to meet/form a relationship?	62	4
Is he/she alive or dead?	59	9
All		100

N = 93

Birth mothers used many graphic phrases and sentences to describe their thoughts during this 'worrying' period thus: 'is he well?', 'is she happy?', 'is he well cared for?', 'does he hate me?', 'do they love him?', 'what does he look like?', 'would she like to meet?', 'would he like a relationship?' Some mothers explained that, before the Children Act of 1975, which provided that adopted people could have access to their birth record under certain conditions, they did not even think about the possibility of a meeting because they knew that adoption was final. Surprisingly, whether the child felt rejected hardly featured as a main thought even though one of the main expectations on meeting was to explain why. Other typical comments included:

> *I spent my time looking into prams and wondering what she looked like. Birthdays and Christmas were worse.*

Although many mothers tried to get on with their lives, they still continued to wonder 'what had happened to him', 'what she looked like', 'was he happy?'

Current practice expects adoption agencies not only to give full information to the birth family about the adopters, but also to maintain letterbox contact to help keep mother and child well informed about each other (see Triseliotis *et al*, 1997). In this study, only around one out of every seven mothers said they had a lot or enough information (14 per cent) on the adoptive family before or after parting. Some three-fifths (59 per cent) had a little or not enough information and the rest (27 per cent) had none. Only one birth mother reported that she had met the adopters before the adoption. Around 40 per cent would have liked to have met them, but a fifth would not. The others were not sure. No mother reported any continued indirect forms of contact either.

Other associated thoughts had to do with possible harm falling on the child and even death through illness (see also Bouchier *et al*, 1991; Mander, 1995).

Important differences were also noted between seeker and sought mothers. Significantly more seeker, than sought, mothers had wondered if the child were alive or dead ($p = 0.016$), were curious to know what he or she looked like ($p = 0.025$), and had speculated whether her son or daughter would like to hear from them ($p = 0.006$) or would want to meet them (p = 0.013). When it came to feelings, seeker mothers again were significantly more likely to be more worried than sought ones (p = 0.011) or feel more anxious about their child's well-being (p = 0.024).

Sharing the adoption secret

By the time of contact, eight out of every ten mothers had spoken to someone else about the adoption. Many also reported that it had been a big burden to carry the adoption secret for so many years. On the whole, husbands/partners had been told either before or after the marriage or partnership, but in a number of cases husbands/partners did not come to know until after contact had been made. All seeker mothers had told their husbands/partners compared with only 75 per cent of sought ones. One mother did not tell her first husband about it but did tell the second. Almost half of sought mothers (46 per cent) and 16 per cent of seekers had not told their other children or husbands/partners about the adopted child until told that their son or daughter was seeking them or just before the point of contact. A typical comment was that they had told their other children 'only after my son contacted me'. Although over a quarter of those who told them did so when the children were young, others waited for a significant event such as when expecting a child, when a child started school, became of age or if there was a family bereavement. Friends were more likely to know than family members.

A number of mothers distinguished between speaking about the adoption and discussing their feelings surrounding the experience. Others remarked that there was no one that they felt they could discuss it with until much later in life: 'I never spoke about it for 37 years,' said one. A small number who did not discuss it with anyone felt that it was either 'a secret that had to be kept' or that 'it had nothing to do with others'. However, a handful would talk about it 'to anyone who would listen'. For many, talking about it also meant being reminded of the pain of parting and they preferred to 'block it out'. Significantly more seekers than sought mothers had spoken about the adoption to others over the years (p = 0.003) and were also more likely to have told their other children earlier (p = 0.033).

Physical and mental health

We focused on health because previous studies, notably Winkler and Van Keppel (1984) and Logan (1996) found that mental health issues had featured largely in their studies. The question of health in this study was approached in two ways. Questions were asked about the birth mothers' current physical health and also about their mental health at three different stages: before the pregnancy, from adoption to contact, and currently.

Current physical health

Almost nine out of every ten birth mothers rated their current physical health as very good or good and the rest (11 per cent) as mostly poor. Glendinning (2002) suggested that around nine per cent of women in the age group 45–64 reported their physical health as poor, in other words, similar to our sample who were broadly in the same age group or slightly older. Almost a third of mothers had not visited their doctor in the last six months (31 per cent) but a fifth had done so four or more times (17 per cent). Seeker, as opposed to sought, birth mothers had paid more visits to their doctor in the six months (p = 0.029) prior to this study.

Mental health

Only three per cent of birth mothers reported that they had been diagnosed with mental health problems prior to the pregnancy or parting with the child, two of them having had hospital treatment for their condition. However, following the parting with their child, 24 per cent reported that they had been diagnosed and treated for mental health problems (see Table 5.3). Half of these reported going into hospital.

Table 5.3
Birth mothers diagnosed and treated for mental health problems

No mental health problems *%*	*Mental health problems* *%*	*Total* *%*
76	24	100

All mothers N = 93

Compared to sought mothers, seekers in this study were three times more likely to have had a psychiatric diagnosis (sought = 15 per cent; seekers = 50 per cent; p = 0.005) with half of them again being treated as inpatients. The majority of mothers reported that clinical depression was the main problem and two of them had made suicide attempts. These findings again support previous ones suggesting that searching mothers had been more severely affected by the loss of their child and hence felt the need to atone for the loss. Clinical depression affects about one in 20 British adults at any one time, and 22 per cent will suffer from it during some time in their lives. The Scottish NOP Survey (2002) quoted earlier reported that 26 per cent of women aged 35–54 (not shown for older age groups) had, at some point, been told by a doctor or other professional that they had a specific mental health problem in the form of depression. It could therefore be argued that the overall sample of birth mothers, with the exception of searching ones, was well within the norm. The data suggest that, although most mothers experienced sadness, unhappiness and stress, this did not always reach levels meriting a psychiatric diagnosis, except mostly in the case of searching mothers. The difference between the current study and other studies that found significantly higher levels of mental health problems, mostly depression, is that the previous samples were biased towards searching or enquiring mothers. For example, Logan (1996) reported that, of a small sample of 28 mothers who had relinquished children for adoption and had recently approached an adoption agency for help relating to contact and other issues, 11 (or 39 per cent) had been diagnosed by a doctor as having 'mental health problems'. Broadly similar findings were reported by Winkler and Keppel (1984) and Bouchier *et al* (1991). These are significantly higher figures compared to those found by this study and lend support to the view that birth mothers who approach agencies are not representative of all birth mothers who have relinquished children for adoption (Figure 5.1). It cannot be inferred that because these mothers, mostly seekers, developed psychiatric problems between parting with the child and contact, the parting per se was responsible for the problems. Unknown factors may have intervened in their lives to cause these problems, even though they were also more likely than other mothers to say that they had received less emotional support during the

Figure 5.1

Diagnosis and treatment for mental health problems

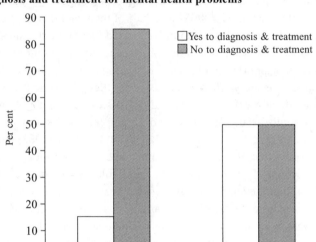

Sought mothers N = 60 (missing 1)   Seeker mothers N = 32

various stages from the pregnancy to the parting with the child and cited parental pressure as the main reason for the adoption.

Irrespective of the probable source of their mental health problems, most of the mothers in this study linked their psychiatric problems to the parting. These included: 'bouts of depression', 'depressive tendencies', 'depression from the separation of my child', 'long-term depression and sleepless nights', 'breakdown, depression', 'depression, anxiety and panic attacks', 'general depression and lack of self-esteem', 'serious episodes of depression', and 'had a breakdown'.

One mother said:

Bad bouts of depression requiring hospitalisation. Attempted suicide, ECT. Now on lithium – made a good difference. But nobody related my being an unmarried mother in 1964 to my depression, being alone and isolated.

Birth mothers who reported past mental health problems, mostly seeker mothers, also reported receiving less emotional support from their mother (p = 0.034) and even less from relatives (p = 0.024) when told of the pregnancy. They were also more likely to say that they would have liked more emotional support during the pregnancy (p = 0.015), around the child's birth (p = 0.011) and after parting with the child for adoption (p = 0.025). Many mothers reported not being able to talk to their parents about their feelings, but seeker mothers were again more likely to say that they did not receive adequate emotional support from their families and that they would have liked more. One of the key findings of the Brown and Harris (1978) study was the linking between depression in women and the absence in their lives of a confidant.

Those with mental health problems were more likely to cite parental pressure as the main reason for the adoption (p = 0.007), and this was more prevalent among seeking than sought mothers (p = 0.016). Mental health problems were much less likely to be reported by birth mothers who said that the adoption decision had been a personal choice. Although the numbers were small, mothers with mental health problems had received more counselling during the pregnancy than those who did not report such problems (p = 0.046), suggesting that counselling made no difference, possibly because they presented more deep-seated psychological problems.

Turning to the mothers' current emotional health after contact, the study scored their self-reported ratings on the Goldberg General Health Questionnaire (GHQ) (Goldberg, 1972). This is a screening test which 'detects inability to carry out normal functions, and the appearance of new and distressing phenomena'. The lower the scores, the better the emotional health of the subjects (Goldberg and Williams, 1988), although it is not a diagnostic tool. In relation to birth mothers who parted with children for adoption, the 20 questions GHQ was originally used by Winkler and Keppel (1984) and later Bouchier et al (1991). In the present study, and based on the GHQ, the majority of mothers (77 per cent) reported that they had good emotional health over the past few weeks prior to completing the questionnaire. Thirteen per cent declared scores of 4–9, indicating that they were experiencing moderate difficulties, while another 10 per cent scored 10–15 points suggesting severe emotional problems (Table 5.4). There were no significant differences between seeking and non-seeking mothers. The proportion of mothers in this study who scored no problems at all was much higher than those found by Bouchier *et al*'s study (58 to 22 per cent). When it came to serious problems the proportions were about the same. The finding, however, of significant differences with Bouchier *et al*'s (1991) study could be explained by the fact that the mothers in that study were seekers or were making enquiries and had not yet had contact with their children. The differences found also point to the possible positive impact of contact and reunion, particularly on seeking mothers.

Table 5.4
Current state of emotional health

GHQ Score	This study %	Bouchier et al (1991) %
0	58	22
1–3	19	48
4–9	13	19
10–15	10	11
Total	100	100

N = 91 (missing 2)

Health problems and the adoption

The majority of birth mothers (70 per cent) said that they could not ascribe any health problems they had to the adoption, but one in eight (12 per cent) did, with the remaining 18 per cent being uncertain. The majority also implied that although parting with their child was 'sad', 'distressing', 'painful' and 'hard' at the time, nevertheless they coped or gradually got over it by mostly concentrating on their new family. Some stress experienced arose from other sources such as the behaviours of a son or daughter, marital problems, financial issues or other external factors. The following is a typical comment from mothers in this group:

I never recovered from the whole dreadful affair. Something, which for most is natural, wanted and beautiful, for me, was a living nightmare.

The only way to survive was to put up a wall, which of course was dangerous to my mental well-being.

Compared to sought mothers, seekers, were more likely to attribute their health problems to the adoption (p = 0.002). Those who made connections referred to treatment they had received, mainly for depression or anxiety.

Knowledge of the legal position

Almost two-thirds of all mothers were aware of changes in the law in 1975 giving certain rights to adopted people in England and Wales to have access to their birth records and establish contact, if they wished. The rest were not. There were no significant differences between seeker and sought mothers in terms of whether they knew about the 1975 Act or not, but unlike sought mothers, seeker ones were less likely to worry about its possible impact on them. In spite of this awareness and the desire of most to establish contact, few had decided to search or place their names on the Adoption Contact Register. As seen later, they advanced a number of ethical and practical reservations about doing so.

Figure 5.2 summarises the birth mothers' main reactions to the legal changes. Over two-thirds said they were pleased about the change but

Figure 5.2
The mothers' main reaction to the Children Act 1975

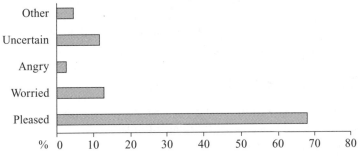

N = 59 (Above table includes only those who were aware of the Children Act 1975.)

85

one in seven (14 per cent) were worried and three per cent angry. However, seeker mothers were more likely to be positive in their initial reaction to the law than non-seekers (p = 0.010).

The Adoption Contact Register

Whilst a number of birth mothers had always hoped that their son or daughter would try to contact them on reaching adulthood, only just over half of them (54 per cent) had heard of the Adoption Contact Register, which could help bring them together. Far more seeker (81 per cent) than sought mothers (40 per cent) knew about its existence (p < 0.001). Some mothers who did not know about the Register had tried to find ways of letting their son or daughter know that they were looking for them. Of birth mothers who knew about the Register, 38 per cent of sought mothers had entered their name compared with 54 per cent of seeker mothers. The latter were also far more likely to be involved with groups such as NORCAP or had already been in touch with The Children's Society to try to find possible ways of establishing contact. Birth mothers who knew about the Register (54 per cent), but did not enter their name, gave a number of explanations for not doing so, mainly wanting to leave the initiative to their child: 'I wanted him to contact me first', or 'I felt if my child wanted to look me up it was up to him'. Behind some of these comments was also the fear of rejection or disappointment. As one of them put it: 'I was afraid because of the pain of disappointment or if he didn't want to know me'. Some felt they had no right to 'intrude' in their child's life or 'upset the adoptive parents'. One of several mothers who were angry about the changes in the law remarked: 'I wished for no contact and was very angry when I was contacted – though I recognise my daughter's right to find out about me.'

Rights for birth relatives

When it came to the issue of whether mothers thought that birth relatives should have the right to obtain identifying information about the adopted person once aged 18 and over, answers were divided (Figure 5.3). Almost two-fifths said 'yes' (38 per cent), over a fifth 'no' (22 per cent) but another two-fifths (40 per cent) were uncertain. Double the proportion of seeker, than sought, mothers were in favour of the proposal (p = 0.032).

Figure 5.3
Should birth relatives have rights of access?

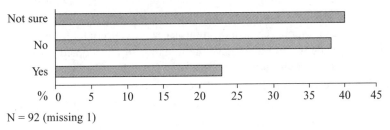

N = 92 (missing 1)

A similar question asked in Bouchier *et al*'s (1991) study of mothers who had not yet had contact but wished it, produced almost double the amount of support for such a right compared to this study, but that sample again was made up of searching or enquiring mothers. Only seven per cent in that study were uncertain compared to 40 per cent in this. Those mothers who said 'yes' in this study mainly thought that it would help: 'to end years and years of yearning and emptiness', 'because not knowing is the worst thing' or 'to let the child know that I still care'. One mother commented:

I feel it is a monstrous situation that a woman who has brought a child into the world should be left without any further knowledge of that child – all she has is a big black hole.

For some mothers it would be an opportunity for the child to know that they 'still cared', that adoption need not be an 'amputation', to learn how each one had 'got on in life' or for the son or daughter to find out more about their roots, medical information, etc. Seeker mothers were more emphatic when signifying their approval for access, viewing it as an equivalent right to that of the adopted person: 'Not knowing is the worst thing'; 'the law as it stands is archaic'; 'just to achieve peace of mind'. Irrespective of whether mothers were for or against the idea, many had wanted to be considerate and sensitive to the feelings of the adoptive parents too. One of them put it like this:

We are the MOTHERS that gave birth. I don't want to take the place of the adoptive mother. I feel we have the right, though, to explain in our own words WHY!

Some of those who believed that birth relatives should have the right to obtain identifying information, and many of those who were uncertain, still stressed that the primary consideration would have to be what was seen to be best for the child, indicating also some concern for the adoptive parents. They would rather leave the initiative to the adopted person to decide: 'it is up to the adopted person' or 'if the adopted person wants it'.

Of those who were opposed (22 per cent) to the idea, some said that it should be left 'entirely' to the adopted person or that, having given up the child, mothers had no right to 'invade their child's privacy' or seek them out in case it caused them and their parents unhappiness. More poignantly, a sought mother said:

Having agreed to adoption, they relinquished those rights and they should not be given the opportunity to possibly disrupt the adopted person's life. It must be his choice.

Most of those who were uncertain (40 per cent) felt that the decision should be left to the adopted person, stressing, at the same time, that each case could be different and that it could turn problematic if the adopted person did not wish it. Only making information available was more acceptable. One person stressed that birth families should not have an automatic right, but be subject to 'a thorough background check' and that the adopted person should have consented to contact. Even though most mothers were often longing for contact, they also tried to display what they thought was a balanced approach between their need to know and have contact and the interests of their sons and daughters and that of the adopters.

Should all adopted people be encouraged to search?

When the question was asked whether all adopted people should be encouraged to have contact with their birth relatives, opinion was evenly divided between those who said 'yes' (43 per cent) and those who wanted to remain neutral (45 per cent). Another 12 per cent disagreed. Strangely, perhaps, there was no significant difference between sought and seeker birth mothers. Irrespective of whether birth mothers were in favour of encouraging contact, or neutral, in their opinion, and possibly because most of them felt they had been *deprived* of choice in the past, many were now anxious to stress choice for their son or daughter. As some said: 'It should be up to the individual to make up their own mind'; 'everyone should have choice'; 'they should never feel pressurised'; 'it must be the adopted child's decision'; 'only if they want it'; 'people have a right to privacy'; 'it has to be their own choice'; 'the opportunity should be there'.

Several mentioned encouragement but not pressure and a similar proportion referred to the circumstances of each party that had to be considered. Of those opposed, there was concern that it might cause upset or that it could cause pain if it did not go smoothly. In this respect, the comments of seeker mothers did not differ from those of sought ones, especially in wishing to give choice and consideration to the adopted person.

Should there be no adoption in society?

Because of some calls for the abolition of adoption, all members of the adoption triangle were asked whether, in their view, there should be no adoption in society. In spite of most birth mothers' reported distress and unhappiness at parting with their child, almost three-quarters (73 per cent) were opposed to the idea of not having adoption. One out of ten strongly agreed with doing away with it and another 17 per cent remained neutral (Table 5.5). Seeker mothers were more strongly in favour of the statement

Table 5.5
Should there be no adoption in our society?

Level of agreement	Sought mothers %	Seeker mothers %	All mothers %
Strongly agree/agree	11	9	10
Neutral	11	28	17
Disagree	79	63	73
Total	101	100	100

N = 89 (missing 4)

'there should be no adoption in society' than non-searching ones were (p = 0.018).

Possibly influenced by how they thought their son or daughter fared in adoption, three-quarters extolled the benefits of adoption: 'excellent'; 'marvellous'; 'wonderful'; 'adopters have given many children a very happy life'; 'the children found a caring and stable family'; 'better than abortion'; 'wonderful for unwanted children to have a chance in life'; 'adoption is an excellent answer to some children's problems and also for couples who long to have a child'.

It was of particular interest to note not only the emphasis that sought mothers placed on children having a right to a stable family, but many seeker mothers too said the same. One seeker mother said that a lot of children, including her own, 'have had a better life'; another 'I can think of no better alternative than to try to provide parents and a loving and secure home for children without these things'. As others also put it: 'Wonderful – unwanted children given a chance in life. It brings so much happiness also to people who cannot have children'.

Some mothers went further by stressing the right of each child to have a family: 'It is the right of every child to have a loving home with long stability'.

Many said that the emphasis would have to be on what is best for the child and that adoption fulfilled this expectation. Some placed particular emphasis on children who 'do not have a safe and loving home/parent', or the child that was 'abused' or grossly 'neglected'. A few also thought of people who cannot have children and in this respect adoption could be mutually beneficial. A rhetorical question asked by many was 'what is the alternative?' with some answering it and saying 'an orphanage?', which they did not find acceptable.

Of those opposed to adoption (10 per cent), some made comments such as 'if there was no adoption I would have brought up my child'. Another stressed that although adoption is 'very necessary', because of strict social conventions, it is 'absurd and wrong'. Still another, while saying that there would 'always be a need for adoption', felt that the kind of pressure she was submitted to should be 'illegal'. Other comments from this group included: 'never having got over the adoption', 'it causes too many problems and is not good for anyone'.

Summary

The period between parting with the child and contact proved to be an unhappy and distressing one for the great majority of birth mothers. Even the minority who said that they managed to "block it off" and carry on with their lives found that they could not entirely escape from what had happened. The dominant feelings experienced during this period had to do with grief arising from the sense of loss and guilt associated with the perceived "rejection" of their child. Similarly, the main thoughts that birth mothers had over the years were closely linked to the fate of their child, that is, whether he or she was well and whether the adoption had worked out well and their child was happy. If things were going well with the adoption and their child, this appeared to go some way to lift part of the grief and its associated guilt. Additional thoughts focused on what their child looked like, if the child felt rejected or would like to meet and perhaps form a relationship. Although most mothers did not think that adoption had affected their capacity to make new relationships or have other children, a significant proportion did not tell their other children or husband/partner about the adopted child until they learnt that their child was seeking them or just before contact. In this respect, seeker mothers were more likely to have done so than sought ones.

While only an insignificant proportion of birth mothers had been diagnosed with a mental health problem before adoption (3 per cent), in the time between the parting and contact, 24 per cent had a psychiatric diagnosis mainly for depression, with half of them having had inpatient treatment. Seeker mothers were far more likely to have been diagnosed with mental health problems than sought ones. Equally significantly, a greater number of seeker mothers said that they had paid more visits to their doctor in the last six months and attributed many of their physical and mental health problems over the years to the adoption. Those with emotional and mental health problems, particularly seeker mothers, were also more likely to say that they had received less emotional support during the various stages from the pregnancy to the parting with the child. Similarly, they would cite parental pressure as the main reason for the adoption. Poor mental health was less likely to be reported by mothers who said that adoption had been their personal choice. Those with mental health problems were also more likely as a group to have received counselling during the pregnancy.

A number of significant differences were found between sought and seeker mothers. Compared to sought mothers, seekers were more likely to:

- have poorer mental health;
- be unable to get over the adoption;
- wonder what the child looked like;
- wonder whether the child was well and happy or alive or dead;
- ponder whether he or she would like to hear from them or meet;
- react with less worry about the provisions of the 1975 Act providing for access to adopted adults;
- know about the existence of the Adoption Contact Register;
- favour the proposal for access to the adopted person by members of the birth family;
- support the statement that there should be no adoption in society.

Overall, seeker mothers had been affected more severely by the loss of the child and possibly felt the need to repair the loss more than non-seekers did.

6 Being sought and seeking

Sought mother:

I hoped he had a happy and full life. If he wanted to meet me and possibly get to know me and include me in his life, then it had to be totally his decision.

Seeker mother:

I didn't enter my name in the Contact Register because I didn't know about it. I believe birth relatives should have the right to obtain identifying information about their child once they have reached 18 years old, because children who have been adopted often want to contact birth parents. I needed to know that he was well and happy. I have always thought about my baby and I had to know if he was alright. Once I decided to contact him, my main fear was that he would refuse to see me especially if he had felt rejected.

The two previous chapters reported on the birth mothers' experiences from the pregnancy to the parting with the child and from the parting to the search. This one explores the reactions of birth mothers on hearing that they were being sought and the reasons given by seeker mothers for why they set out to find their child. Birth mothers were just as likely to be searching for a daughter as a son.

Sought birth mothers

Seven out of every ten birth mothers were contacted on behalf of their son or daughter by the adoption agency that had placed their child. In 12 per cent of these cases, contact was through an intermediary such as NORCAP. In almost a fifth of cases (18 per cent) their child made direct contact. In one case, it was the adoptive mother who made the contact by getting in touch with the birth mother's mother.

It was to be expected that, on hearing that their sons and daughters were seeking them, birth mothers reacted with a mixture of feelings ranging from excitement to happiness, but accompanied also by a fair amount of anxiety. For example, around three-quarters expressed excitement and pleasure and an equal proportion expressed nervousness. Although most sought mothers welcomed the contact, a minority of around eight per cent would have wanted to have more control over the decision which had been taken away from them by the adopted person having taken the initiative (Table 6.1).

Table 6.1

All and the *main* reactions of birth mothers on hearing that their son or daughter was searching for them

Reactions	All %	Main* %
Excited/pleased/happy	76	48
Nervous	76	13
Surprised/shocked	59	21
Worried/frightened	36	16
Fear of upsetting others	34	–
Uncertain	29	–
Understanding	20	–
Hurt	7	–
Angry	5	–
Hostile	3	–
Other	10	2
Total		100

N = 56 (missing 5)

Excitement and pleasure

The main response of almost half of sought birth mothers was one of considerable excitement and pleasure when they heard that their son or daughter was looking for them. They used words and phrases such as: 'over the moon'; 'overjoyed'; 'ecstatically happy'; 'elated'; 'thrilled'; 'pleased'; 'happy'; 'longing for it'; 'it's something I always hoped for'; 'thrilled and excited' or 'like winning the pools'. The following is a typical comment:

Absolutely over the moon when I learned that she wanted to make contact with me. I'd been hoping she would write from when she was young.

Shock, worry, nervousness and fear

Some of the nervousness, anxiety and fear had mainly to do with whether their child would like them or blame them for the "rejection" or how to tell other members of the family who did not know. One described her feelings when the phone rang and someone at the other end said 'I think you may be my mother' as leaving her in a state of shock. Part of the worry and anxiety expressed by some of these and other mothers was how to tell their other children or husbands/partners about the adopted person, having concealed it from them so far (46 per cent of sought mothers and 16 per cent of seekers had not yet told their other children or husbands/partners about the adopted child until after they were informed that their child was seeking them or just before the point of contact). It should also be recalled that several continued to keep the secret even after contact. Like some others, one of those who had not spoken to her children or partner about it said:

Fearful because my daughters and partner had no knowledge that I had had a child.

And another:

My husband of 23 years knew nothing about my having a child adopted.

Another mother, although regretful for having lied to her husband in the past, did not think she could bring herself to tell him at this late stage. Yet another reported how unprepared she found herself for the 'turmoil' that was to occur in her family. Some of the nervousness experienced also had to do with how their child would react on meeting them, e.g. whether he or she would like them, express bitterness arising from feelings of "rejection", or with contact not working out and dashing their hopes and expectations. As one of many said:

Absolutely delighted but also scared and nervous. Afraid she wouldn't like me and would blame me for giving her away. Wouldn't know what to talk about.

Anger

Real anger was exceptional, although a handful of birth mothers felt very angry and disturbed, mainly for losing control over the decision. For some, their anger had to do with the inevitable difficulties of having to tell their other children about it. On the whole, these mothers would have preferred to 'let sleeping dogs lie'. One felt a mixture of emotions including: 'confused, upset, lonely, depressed, and invaded'. Another was even angrier, viewing contact as a threat to her family life and 'as a betrayal to my other children'. Several felt bitter towards the adoption agency for allowing it to happen, thus breaking its previous promise of confidentiality. Nevertheless, the great majority of mothers, even though feeling anxious and fearful, were pleased that they had been contacted because it had been their long-held hope that this might happen one day.

Change of reactions

Birth mothers were about equally split between those who said that their initial reaction changed and those who said that it did not. Most commonly, a change resulted when reactions from a spouse or children turned out to be more positive than feared.

Most family members were said to have reacted positively when told about the adopted person and contact. Sometimes they offered words of caution such as: not to 'set your hopes too high' or that it could turn out to be 'a dark horse'. There was no doubt, though, about the reported happiness for the mother: 'happy for me'; 'surprise, joy and excitement'; 'thrilled'; 'very pleased and interested' or 'everyone thought it was lovely'. Most husbands/partners were also reported to have responded positively, saying they were 'happy' for her, 'extremely supportive', 'pleased' or 'excited' or 'wanting to meet him'.

However, for a few mothers, the change in reaction was in the opposite direction when the original elation was spoiled by the reaction of their husbands/partners or their other children. While a few were 'quietly hostile', others were concerned about the impact on their children. One husband told his wife that she need not respond and several others were very concerned that their wives might be hurt in the process. One candidly admitted to feeling left out because all the others 'had a common bond which he did not have'. As a result he did not want their children to know.

Typical reactions before and after contact

Initial reaction by mothers	Later comments by same mothers
• Nervous as to how we would get on.	⇒ We had nothing to worry about.
• Absolutely delighted but scared and nervous whether she would like me.	⇒ We got along really well and seem to have settled into a mutually enjoyable relationship.
• Fear because my daughters and partner didn't know that I had had a child.	⇒ When I told them, everyone was thrilled to bits for me, and my girls were thrilled to have a brother.
• Initial delight and excitement but also worry she would blame me for rejecting her.	⇒ I need not have worried. The fear of rejection did not come true.
• Uncertain because my husband knew nothing of my daughter's existence.	⇒ Unhappily I have to keep this a continuing secret from my husband, which is sad.
• I wanted to see her but was afraid she wouldn't like me and would blame me for giving her away.	⇒ The strong emotions I felt initially gave way to uncertainty. I didn't know what she wanted or who I was . . . She talked about her parents – so who was I? I found it very difficult.

On the whole, children were said to have been mostly pleased and even 'thrilled', but in a few cases there was also wariness, jealousy and even anger.

Four out of every five sought mothers immediately, or after a brief consideration, agreed to have contact. The rest took more time. Some mothers said that they had never thought of 'refusing', adding that it would have been 'emotionally cruel' to do so or that 'it was the natural thing to do'. Others saw it as a 'debt' to their children to see them because they deserved some answers about why they had been placed for adoption and about their 'real' family. The wish for contact had been present in most of these mothers' minds for many years and contact was therefore the realisation of their long-held desire that they would one day meet or have a 'dream come true'. Apart from having waited for so long, the other main reasons for agreeing to have contact were to see what their son or daughter looked like, how he or she had turned out, whether they had a good adoption and the need to explain why they had been adopted. A significant number believed that their child had a right to know why he or she was given up for adoption. One mother commented that she was desperate 'to fill the hole' in her heart that had been there for 30 plus years. In the end, however, seven per cent changed their minds and decided not to have contact.

Why sought mothers had not searched

Two-fifths of sought birth mothers said that they had previously thought about searching, but over half (54 per cent) had not. Top of *all* the reasons (Table 6.2) given for not searching was their view that it was not their right to do so, and that any initiative would have to come from their child (71 per cent). When only the *main* reasons were considered, the major one to emerge was again the belief that it was not their right to do so (59 per cent): 'Did not think I had a legal right'; 'I thought it was not allowed'; 'not aware I could'. Waiting for the adopted person to take the initiative also lessened the fear some mothers had that their sons and daughters might still be angry and reject their approach. One mother remarked that, although she was 'desperate' to have her daughter back into her life, it was her daughter's life that had been affected and therefore it would be her decision. Another explained:

I think I was afraid of what she would think of me, but above all I was terrified I had done the wrong thing, thinking she needed a 'real' family.

Another 46 per cent of these birth mothers said that they did not know how to search. One of them observed that, whenever she tried, she came to 'a dead end' and was told to wait instead for her daughter to get in touch. Almost two-fifths (39 per cent) made no effort to establish contact because others, mainly members of their new family, did not know about the adoption. One mother told how she had started a new life and her new family knew nothing about the child or the adoption. As a result:

The experience was closed off in a corner of my mind, almost unreal, as though it had never happened.

Overall, the majority of these mothers' responses pointed to a lack of entitlement and fear about the reaction of their son or daughter. To varying degrees they had accepted the inevitability of lost contact and left it largely to the adopted person to make the first step. As a result, the resumption of links was on the whole reactive but usually a pleasant surprise, even though often permeated by a fair amount of anxiety.

Table 6.2
All and *main* reasons for why sought birth mothers did not search

Sought birth mothers	All reasons %	Main reasons* %
Not my right	71	59
Did not know how to search	46	22
Fear of rejection	39	6
People close to me not aware of adoption	39	10
Blocked it out	23	–
Inhibited by legal reasons	21	–
Afraid of finding something unpleasant	15	–
Did not want complications	15	–
Wait until time was right	10	–
Not enough time or money	8	4
Did not want contact	4	
Total		101

*N = 56 (missing 10)

Seeker mothers

Around nine out of every ten seeker birth mothers made their approach to the adopted person or the adoptive family through the agency that had placed their child. Only seven per cent made an approach directly or through an intermediary. For around a third, the adopted person was located within a month and for almost two-fifths, between one and six months; for the rest it took over six months. While almost all the mothers were nervous and many worried about what they might find, these feelings went alongside those of excitement at the prospect of meeting their son or daughter after so many years. Nevertheless, half of them continued to be worried and fearful at the prospect of finding out something terrible, being rejected, not being wanted, not being liked, or upsetting their child or the adoptive family. For some, the longing clashed with ethical concerns such as whether they had a right to search, but unlike sought mothers, their strong desire to find their sons and daughters overcame the ethical considerations. These seeker mothers offered two main explanations for why they set out to search. Almost all of them wanted to know how their child was doing and whether he or she was well and had a happy adoption. Typical comments included: 'To know whether my daughter was fine'; 'whether physically alright'; 'to know that he was OK'; or 'just to know if she was alive and happy'.

These mothers took the initiative to establish contact, often prompted by an unwillingness to see this 'devastating' loss as final. Adoption, for them, especially at the time they had parted with their children, was a form of death because the possibility of future contact was negligible. As a result it would only be thought natural if it led to searching behaviour on the part of some parents, something found in cases of actual death, to help alleviate the grieving, anxiety and guilt (see Bowlby, 1980; Parkes, 1986; Stroebe and Stroebe, 1987). In these mothers' cases, and unlike actual bereavement, the child was alive somewhere. They could not, perhaps, give up or fully mourn a child who was still alive and yet they could not be with them. Their second explanation had mainly to do with the seeking of some form of expiation from their sons and daughters by explaining to them why they had been adopted and let them know that they were not forgotten or rejected and were still loved.

Although for all birth mothers the idea of searching and finding their adopted sons and daughters was present ever since the parting, the actual search was sometimes triggered by an important event in their lives. It could be a wedding, a pregnancy, the birth of a child, death in the family or being under pressure from a partner or one of their other children. For many seeker mothers, the timing of the search was inherently connected with when they became aware that there was a kind of legal loophole for doing so: 'the law allowed it now'; 'only now realised I could search'; 'a lot of press coverage about availability'; 'watching a TV programme'. Several felt encouraged by the reaction of their family when told about the adoption. A few others realised that they were getting older and time was not on their side. Some had also consciously planned to give their son or daughter time to reach a specific age, e.g. 18 or 25 and that, if they did not get in touch by then, they would then take the initiative.

Expectations of contact

It was thought that, when considering initial expectations, there would be some disparity between seeker and sought mothers. While seeker mothers would have formulated certain expectations before embarking on their quest, sought ones, because of the surprise element, would be at a disadvantage. However, over the years, and as seen in the previous chapter, all mothers had formulated thoughts about their child and many nurtured hopes of a possible future meeting. As a result, no differences were found between the expectations of sought and seeker mothers. Equally, their thoughts about the child, as set out in the previous chapter, coincided closely with their expectations of contact, which are set out below.

Table 6.3 shows that, when considering *all* expectations, nine out of every ten mothers wanted to have news of their child and hear whether they were well and happy. Almost eight out of every ten also wanted to see what he or she looked like, and about a similar proportion to explain reasons for the parting. In addition, six out of every ten were hoping to develop a relationship. The anxiety, worry and guilt that most mothers felt over the years could only be lessened, in their view, by the knowledge of the child being and doing well and of having had a good adoption. Finding that it had been like that would greatly add to their 'pleasure'

Table 6.3
Birth mothers' *all* and *main* expectations of contact

Type of expectations	All expectations %	Main expectations %
Know whether he/she is well & happy	94	42
Have news of him/her	86	25
See what he/she looks like	79	4
Explain why the parting	77	15
Hope for a relationship	59	14
Total		100

Sought mothers N = 56 (missing 5); Seeker mothers N = 29 (missing 3) and 'happiness' and go a long way to justify the parting decision. Other explanations included the wish to tell their son or daughter that he or she had never been forgotten over the years, was loved and never rejected. The following is a typical explanation:

> I wanted to explain why I couldn't keep her, say sorry and tell her how much I had loved her. Say that adoption has always been a regret, that she was not rejected and had always been loved.

Summary

Most sought mothers were both excited and elated at the news that their sons and daughters were trying to establish contact with them. Seeker mothers felt similarly at the prospect of doing so soon. A handful of sought mothers felt that control had been taken out of their hands and their privacy invaded, but there was no evidence that they were unduly inconvenienced by the approach. We can presume that the seven per cent who refused contact had similar reasons but did not yield to the request for contact. Neither was there evidence that seeker mothers were careless and insensitive in their search. Although a minority of sought mothers had previously initiated unsuccessful searches themselves, the majority had held back feeling they had no right to do so, were afraid that their sons or daughters might reject them, or they might upset the adoptive family. Seeker mothers entertained similar concerns but their strong desire to establish contact eventually overcame other considerations.

The dominant expectation had to do with the wish to find out whether their sons and daughters were well and had a good adoption. This was followed by the wish to explain why they had been adopted and tell them how much they loved them and that they were not forgotten or rejected. Knowing that their child was well and had a good adoption, along with being able to explain to them why the parting had occurred, appeared to do away with some of the guilt arising from the parting. Although forming a relationship was part of their expectations, it did not hold centre stage before contact took place, although searching mothers stressed it more than sought ones.

For both sought and seeker mothers, the excitement and pleasure of seeing their sons and daughters was also tempered by considerable anxiety, worry, and sometimes fear, that they might hear that he or she did not have a good adoption, or be blamed for the parting or that their son or daughter might not like them. A minority were also worried about the reaction of their husband or other children, because some of them did not know about the adoption. As will be shown in later chapters, most of these anxieties did not materialise. Seeker mothers were more likely to express heightened fears of their child not having been happy, whereas sought ones were more concerned with whether they would get on with their sons and daughter and be liked by him or her.

7 Birth mothers and contact

Birth mother:

I used to think that if she had a good and happy life, it perhaps justified the past. I wanted to say sorry and say also how much I loved her. My biggest fear was that, if she had been unhappy, it would add to my feelings of guilt.

The three previous chapters have reported on the birth mothers' experiences from the pregnancy to the parting with the child, the in-between years up to the point of contact and their reactions on hearing that they were being sought and why some of them set out to search for their child. This chapter examines the mothers' perspectives on how contact evolved. For the most part, data are presented from mothers as a whole but noting differences when these occurred between seeker and sought mothers.

Fears about contact

The previous chapter has shown that the news that their sons and daughters were searching for them was received by most birth mothers with considerable excitement and pleasure but also tempered with some anxiety, worry and perhaps fears about contact. When it came to their fears about contact, the predominant one was finding out that their son or daughter had been unhappy. Other fears had to do with their child not liking them or being angry because of their having parted with them (Table 7.1). At the same time, they were also concerned about making things difficult for their child's family and, to a lesser extent, for their own family. When it came to the *main* initial fears, as separate from *all*, well over a third of mothers (36 per cent) were afraid mother and child might not like each other. This was followed by those who were afraid of finding that their child had not been happy (23 per cent) or the impact contact would have on their family (22 per cent). The fear that their son or daughter might be angry with them accounted for 13 per cent (Table 7.1). Seeker mothers' main fear was likely to be that the adopted person had been unhappy, whereas sought mothers were more concerned with whether they would get on and whether the adopted adult would like them, possibly because of the parting (p = 0.026). A few birth mothers feared rejection simply because of what they looked like and some commented that the adopted person might find them too old compared to younger women. At the same time, as will be seen later, several adoptive mothers were expressing fears of losing their child to the mother who was a 'younger woman'.

Overall, the pre-contact fears did not materialise and proved unfounded. Mothers were pleased to hear that their sons or daughters were doing well and had harboured no angry feelings towards them for the parting. Some commented that, even if they had never established contact, it was a kind of 'bonus' to know that their son or daughter was alive and doing well.

Table 7.1

All and main initial fears about contact expressed by both sought and seeker mothers

Type of fears	All fears %	Main fears* %
Finding he/she had been unhappy	77	23
Not being liked	68	36
Being angry with mother	64	13
Making it difficult for adoptive child's family	63	–
Not getting on	56	–
Overwhelmed by emotion	36	6
Making it difficult for birth family	35	22
Not liking him/her	24	–
He/she may want more than I can offer	24	–
Total		100

N = 83 (missing 10)

Establishing contact and frequency of contact

Because of different forms of contact, their fluidity and overlaps, and the fact that some birth mothers could be somewhat inconsistent in what they said, percentages given should be seen as approximate, although reliable. In the majority of cases, initial contact was established by letter (71 per cent), followed by phone (19 per cent) or face-to-face (10 per cent). Mostly intermediaries negotiated the initial approach. After that, a usual first step was the use of the telephone and the exchange of letters to give each other time to think things over and pave the way for the next move. In a few cases the period was protracted, involving mainly adopted people sought by their mothers. At the time of the study, two-thirds of all the mothers had had either direct or indirect contact with the adopted person for over five years and a quarter from between two to five years. When it came to only face-to-face or direct contact, almost half of mothers had had contact for over five years and more than a quarter from between two to five years. On average, around 40 per cent of these had eight years of face-to-face contact. Only four per cent of mothers had not yet established any form of contact and 17 per cent had not had any face-to-face contact (Figure 7.1).

Initial meetings could take place in a coffee shop, the adopted person's home, the birth mother's or a sibling's home: 'initially lunch at her flat'; 'visits to each others' home'; or 'she invited me to meet her partner and daughter at their place'. More typical, and depending on distance, was a mixture of indirect forms of contact interspersed with face-to-face ones. For example, there was reference to organising other members of the family along with telephone calls in-between. One birth mother discovered that she and her son were living in the same town:

> When I first had contact with my son, he was living in the same town and I saw him regularly. When he moved, contact was less frequent, mainly by phone.

Figure 7.1
Length of face-to-face contact

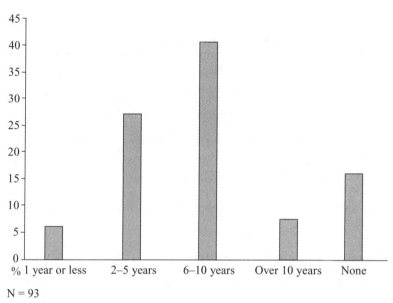

N = 93

Frequency of indirect and direct contact during the first year

Table 7.2 sets out the frequency of both direct and indirect forms of contact between mothers and their sons or daughters during the first year. Apart from six per cent of mothers who had no form of contact with their child in the first year, three out of every five (60 per cent) had indirect forms of contact monthly and the rest at other intervals. When it came to direct contact, almost a fifth (19 per cent) had no direct contact but two out of every five had at least three or four meetings during the first year, with another 30 per cent having met once or twice. Four per cent said that they only met once and not again. Compared to searching mothers, sought ones were likely to report more frequent contact, both direct and indirect, during the first year (direct: p = 0.009; indirect p = 0.003). Compared to sought mothers, seekers had significantly less frequent forms of contact during the same period (p = 0.009). This was mainly because adopted people were more cautious or less keen to commit themselves; for example, some would fail to phone or write after having said they would.

Table 7.2

Frequency of indirect and face-to-face contact during the *first year*

Type	None	At least weekly	At least monthly	Every 3–4 months	Once or twice	Not after first contact	All
	%	%	%	%	%	%	%
Indirect	6	26	35	18	10	5	100
Face-to-face	19	8	11	21	30	11	100

N = 85 (missing 8)

*7 per cent said they or their children lived abroad, thus making direct contact very difficult or very infrequent.

Current frequency of contact

Data on initial and subsequent contact showed that, in most cases, a steady pattern had been maintained in the frequency of contact and it was still quite high at the time of the study. Around one in every seven birth mothers (13 per cent) who had initially established contact no longer had any form of contact with their sons and daughters. However, over half (56 per cent) had indirect contact at least monthly and another 21 per cent had indirect contact every 3–4 months (Table 7.3). Leaving aside those who lost contact altogether, the pattern of contact, at least indirect contact, remained the same as reported in the first year. Some 30 per cent of mothers reported that they no longer had face-to-face contact, but five per cent had contact at least weekly, 11 per cent monthly, 18 per cent every 3–4 months and the rest at greater intervals. Overall, of those who still had face-to-face contact, 33 per cent had at least three or four meetings a year. Seven per cent said that they or their child lived in another country, making direct contact difficult or very episodic (see Table 7.2). As with the first year of contact, sought mothers reported significantly more frequent current direct and indirect forms of contact in comparison to seekers (p = 0.005). Birth mothers also differed significantly in the main reasons they gave for contact having stopped or become reduced. Sought mothers more frequently cited distance while with seekers it mainly had to do with the adopted person's wishes (p < 0.001).

Table 7.3
Current frequency of indirect and face-to-face contact

Type	None	At least weekly	At least monthly	Every 3–4 months	Once or twice a year	All
	%	%	%	%	%	%
Indirect	14	23	33	21	10	101
Face-to-face	30	5	11	18	37	101

N = 88 (missing 5)

The frequency of direct contact, both in the first year and subsequently, was largely determined by the distance separating them, especially for sought mothers. Thus some mothers could have very frequent direct contact while for others it was occasional. Some mothers described contact as regular, weekly, fortnightly or monthly. In between there could be telephone calls, birthday or Christmas cards or letters. Many sought and seeker mothers reported happy and satisfying meetings: 'lovely'; 'very intense and happy'; 'spending time together and getting to know each other'; 'we hit it off right away'.

A small number of mothers would frequently child-mind for their son or daughter. While some reported that contact with the adopted person was not any less frequent than with their own children, a minority reported that it was. Two-thirds of mothers were happy with the current level of contact but one-third were not. The latter were to be found mostly amongst the seekers. The most common response by both sought and seeker mothers for being satisfied was that they were 'lucky' or 'glad' to have any form of contact at all. Many had come to believe that they would never see their son or daughter again and establishing contact was therefore a real bonus for them.

What limited the frequency of contact

There was a strong wish on the part of a significant number of mothers to see more of their children but distance, the adopted person's wishes and/ or family commitments limited contact. Others were happy to go along with how things were, not wishing to cause 'trouble'. In over half the cases, distance from each other, both within the country or intercountry, was the main reason given by birth mothers for why contact was not as frequent as desired. Periodically, either one or the other would visit and spend time together. However, in another 17 per cent of cases, less frequent contact was attributed to the adopted person's family commitments and in a further 12 per cent it was reported that the adopted person did not want to see much of them (see Table 7.4). It is, perhaps, understandable if some mothers rationalised it when they said they wanted to give their child 'space' or they recognised their child's commitments to their immediate family. As one of them explained: 'I don't want to be too involved and am happy to go along with whatever he wants'.

As already mentioned, significantly more seeker than sought mothers reported that contact had stopped and that their son or daughter either did not want to see them at all or not much. Explanations varied from what mothers perceived to be the state of their relationship to what appeared to be face-saving ones. For example, one mother reported that her son simply did not wish to have any more contact; another that her

Table 7.4
Birth mothers' view of what currently limited the level of contact

Reason	%
Distance	54
His/her family commitments	17
Does not want to see too much of me	12
No bars to contact	5
I do not want to see my birth child	4
Upsets adoptive parent	2
Other	7
Total	101

N = 86 (missing 7)

daughter's husband was objecting; and a third that her daughter had too busy a life. One mother said with some resignation, but with no apparent bitterness:

I feel that we both have the answers and I can accept her choice that we cease contact. I am now at peace with the past.

Cessation of contact

Caution is again urged when considering exact percentages about continued face-to-face contact because of the fluidity of relationships and occasionally confusing information about direct and indirect contact. As a general guide, we can accept that 30 per cent of face-to-face contact had ceased over the years. Significantly more seeker than sought mothers stated that the adopted person did not want to see them (p = 0.033). In the majority of cases, contact was stopped at the initiative of the adopted person, especially in the case of seeker mothers. In the remaining cases, it was either by mutual agreement or the mother's decision. The main reasons given were arguments and so-called inability to cope with the reunion. Typical comments included: 'she felt unable to cope and asked for contact to stop'; 'he met a new girl friend and rejected me'; 'it may be because her parents are upset about contact'; or 'she informed that she didn't want any more contact at the moment'. One mother said: 'I wrote after a long silence but she did not reply'. And another, 'it may have to do with her parents being upset and not really needing me in her life, even as distant'. In yet another case, a birth mother ceased contact because of her feeling that the adoptive mother wanted to be part of her family.

When birth mothers were asked what factors encourage the continuation of contact, common responses were:

- it has to feel comfortable;
- they must have a lot in common or compatibility;
- they should connect at a deep level;
- the son or daughter has to show that they are glad to see you;
- mothers being caring and sensitive to their son or daughter's feelings;
- mothers not making too many demands.

111

Seeker mothers put much emphasis on contact 'feeling comfortable'. As already seen, more of them had lost contact or had less frequent contact and there were suggestions that when they had, it did not always feel comfortable. When contact eventually came to a halt, it did not come as a surprise because the signs were building up. The developing pattern was of decreasing frequency, contact becoming indirect and then stopping altogether.

Parent, friend or stranger

Birth mothers were asked to say how they reacted to their son or daughter when they first met and how these feelings had changed over time. Some caution is necessary when interpreting the findings outlined in Table 7.5 because they are based mainly on closed questions, with a minority based upon open-ended ones.

Almost half reported to having felt 'like a friend' or variations on that theme. Only around 20 per cent professed to have felt 'like a parent' from the start, implying, at times, 'love at first sight'. Over a quarter, however, reported having felt like a 'stranger'. After a number of years of ongoing contact, the proportion of those who came to feel like a parent went up to 24 per cent, but still the predominant feeling was that of a friend. The majority of those who initially felt like strangers now came to feel like a friend/relative or parent/friend. Both parties had been initially struck by physical resemblances and sometimes by similarities in mannerisms, temperament, outlook and demeanour. There were no significant differences in how sought and seeker mothers described the relationship when they first had contact and over time. A seeker mother summarised how her feelings had evolved:

When I first met my daughter I did not really feel like a parent, more like a big sister or close friend. Now I feel more like a mum to her as I have got to know her, but she does not call me mum. I realise that her mother is her adoptive mother and I would not want her to be hurt. Overall, I have not only found my daughter, I also have two beautiful grandchildren.

Table 7.5

How birth mothers with face-to-face contact described the initial and later main feeling towards their son or daughter

Initial description*	%	After ongoing contact[†]	%
Like a parent	22	Like a parent	24
Like a friend/relative	29	Like a friend/relative	50
Like a parent/friend	17	Like a parent/friend	14
Like a stranger	28	Like a stranger/distant	3
Uncertain	5	Uncertain	9
Total	101	Total	100

*N = 66 (missing 27) [†]N = 79 (missing 14)
Note: some caution is needed in interpreting this table because it is based on an interpretation of both quantitative and qualitative data.

Those like a mother/parent

A significant number of mothers said that the initial relationship had felt like that of a mother or of a 'mum' or 'parent', sometimes described as being very intense; or that 'bonding' was immediate; or as if 'we had known each other for years'. Typical comments included: 'I felt like her mother from the second I first saw her'. Some added that the relationship was so intense and close from the moment they first met that it was difficult to put an exact name to it: 'Incredible bonding even on an initial meeting'. A seeker mother added:

> *An amazing connection in that physically she looked like me, and we were on the same wavelength emotionally. Maybe this is like a parent–daughter.*

Some birth mothers may have felt like a parent, but this was not always reciprocated. One mother explained that she may have felt like a 'mum' but her daughter does not call her 'mum' because she says her 'mum' is her adoptive mother. Another compared what she felt for the adopted person with her feelings for her other children and remarked:

> *We have the most enormous affection for each other. At the same time it is not the same kind of love I feel for my other children brought up by me.*

Those like a friend or relative

Around a third of birth mothers said that initially they had felt like a friend or relative to their son or daughter: 'close friends'; 'close friend with a very special bond'; 'like a relative than mother bond'; or 'not like a parent, more like a big sister or close friend'. One of them remarked that she had grieved for a baby long gone and now an adult, but she was 'treasuring' the friendship. Sometimes it could be a mixture of feelings such as being both like a mother and a friend. 'All rolled into one', said one mother, with another adding:

> Close friends with a very special bond – elation – completion. Total delight. These feelings did not change over time we are mother and son.

One explanation of why some mothers still perceived themselves as 'friends' was the presence of the adoptive parent(s).

Those like a stranger

As seen in Table 7.5, a significant number (28 per cent) initially felt like 'a stranger' to their son or daughter, some explaining it as being due to the lapse of such a long time and the absence of any contact in-between. Others used the word 'unreal' or even felt guilty for not responding in a parent-like way. With more contact, most of these came to feel 'like a friend' or 'relative'. Where exceptionally a sense of strangeness persisted, it was accompanied by guilt and feeling it was their fault that they could not connect.

Current closeness to the adopted person

Of those who had continuing direct contact, almost three-quarters (74 per cent) described the relationship as very close or close, 15 per cent as mixed and the rest, 12 per cent, as not very close or not close at all (Figure 7.2). There was no difference in closeness between seeker and sought mothers.

Figure 7.2
Level of closeness with the adopted person

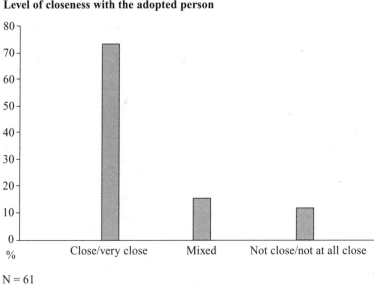

N = 61

Contact between birth mothers and adoptive parents

Three-fifths (60 per cent) of birth mothers declared that, from the start of contact, they were 'very keen or keen' to meet with their sons or daughters' adoptive family, although three out of every ten were not. One out of every ten definitely tried to avoid contact. Forty per cent of the birth mothers eventually had contact with their child's adoptive parents; 32 per cent of the total sample had face-to-face contact. While significantly more seeker than sought mothers initiated contact with the adoptive parents, sought ones were more likely to have met face-to-face, mostly at the initiative of the adopted person (p = 0.020). Before and after direct contact, there were letters, cards or a telephone conversation. In two-thirds of the cases, it was the son or daughter who initiated contact; in over a quarter the birth mother herself; and in six per cent the adoptive family. On the whole, adopted people who had been sought were less keen to introduce their birth mothers to their adoptive parents.

Sought and seeker mothers gave broadly similar explanations for wanting or not wanting to meet their sons and daughters' adoptive family. These ranged from those who did not want to upset the adoptive family to those who were keen to meet them to thank them or to express 'gratitude' for rearing their child:

I would like to thank them for taking her and loving her for me. I would love to meet them.

A significant number of birth mothers had sensed that either the adoptive parents or their child or both would not welcome contact. For some, this was a disappointment but for others, a relief because they were uncertain how they would come across to their child's parents. A repeated concern by a sizeable proportion of birth mothers was not to do anything that might upset the adoptive family. Some said: 'I didn't feel I should impose on them'; 'I would not want to invade their privacy'; or 'I wouldn't like to hurt them'. One mother, however, was against contact because she could not face the fact that the adoptive mother:

. . . had him for 33 years and knows all his baby ways, teeth, crawling, walking, etc., first school days, marriage, all the things I have missed out on.

Another felt bitter because, after having met the adoptive father, he had not told his wife about the meeting, 'in order not to upset her', perpetuating, in this mother's view, the "secret". The adoptive mother apparently found out only by accident and was deeply hurt.

Meetings were often anticipated with some anxiety by birth mothers and occasionally with 'awe'. They were not aware that the adopters, as we shall see in Chapter 12, were equally apprehensive. Birth mothers were uncertain of how contact would develop or how they should present themselves. For some, memories of the stigma and condemnation that they had experienced as a result of the pregnancy resurfaced and they feared that the adopters might look upon them in the same way. Others felt it was the "final chapter" and that they had to face up to it. Words and phrases used included: 'Ashamed and very in awe of these people'; 'nervousness to start with but comfortable'; 'worried but extremely grateful'; 'apprehensive'; or simply 'nervous but had to do it'. Finding common interests was viewed as essential to help sustain contact. Most of those who had met the adoptive parents had only praise for them: 'I need not have worried,' said one of these mothers, because 'she made me feel very comfortable, as if I have known her all my daughter's life'. Feeling 'comfortable' increased the chance of keeping in touch.

Continued contact or sustained relationships with the adoptive family depended largely on initial reactions, especially how much they liked each other and the part played by the adopted person, e.g. whether encouraging, distanced, the age gap and interests. A frequent response was keeping in touch every now and then: 'I have a lot of respect for them – but a sustained relationship is a bit hard because basically, other than our son, we have very little in common'. A few others continued to keep in touch through a card at Christmas. Several said that they came to feel jealous or envious of the adoptive parents who had experienced their children right through from childhood and beyond:

> They showed me photos of him growing up and I probably felt jealous. They had something I did not.

Over time, around 40 per cent of contacts between birth mothers and adopters had stopped mostly because of lack of common interest and with a few saying that, once in contact with her son or daughter, there was no point in continuing. However, a fifth said that their feelings towards the adopters had changed. The change could be in either direction – feeling even more positive about them or the opposite. One of a number said: 'looking down on me, wanted thanks all the time for what they did, or to say that the adoption worked out very well'. Nevertheless, it was mainly the attitude and interest of the adopted person which largely influenced the continuation or cessation of contact. Lasting relationships reported between birth mothers and adopters were very few.

Summary

The birth mothers' main fear before contact was of finding that their sons and daughters had had an unhappy adoption and/or of not being liked by them, mainly because of the parting or their appearance. Some form of contact was nearly always established and, in the great majority of cases, it involved face to face contact. Much of the contact was sustained over an average of eight years and 86 per cent still had at least indirect contact with 70 per cent having face-to-face contact. Excluding those with no contact, over half had had face-to-face contact at least once every 3–4 months and the rest less frequently. Contact takes a variety of forms and it can also be fluid and changeable. Distance was the main limiting factor followed well behind by their son's or daughter's circumstances or their expressed wish for less or more intensive contact. With the exception of those cases where the birth mother declined to see the adopted person, the latter largely dictated the pattern of contact. Overall, we can accept that, for around seven out of every ten birth mothers frequent or infrequent direct contact was likely to be maintained. In this respect, contact stood the test of an average eight years and was still continuing.

Significant differences noted between sought and seeker birth mothers included:

- The main fear of seekers was that the adopted person had been unhappy, whereas sought mothers were more concerned with whether they would get on and whether their son or daughter would like them or not. The main explanation for this difference is that seeker mothers appeared to feel greater guilt over the adoption decision.
- Compared to seekers, sought mothers were likely to report more frequent direct and indirect contact both in the first year and currently. Sought mothers were also more likely to report that contact felt comfortable.
- In two-thirds of cases, contact was stopped at the initiative of the adopted person and it was more likely to involve seeker than sought mothers.
- Sought mothers were more likely to cite distance as an explanation for less frequent contact, whereas seekers reported that the adopted person was not keen to see them.

8 Birth mothers reviewing contact

Birth mother:

My fears and worries were dispelled on meeting him. I instantly felt a great love and affinity with him and it was obvious he was a well-adjusted, intelligent, considerate family man. An incredible closeness developed between us from the moment we first met. But I am also reminded that he has an adoptive family and they are very close. Meeting him has definitely helped me with all the feelings that surrounded the adoption. I now know that I made the right decision and I no longer worry about his well-being.

The four previous chapters described the births mothers' experiences from the pregnancy to the parting with the child, the in-between years up to the point of contact, their reactions on hearing that they were being sought and why some of them set out to search for their child and their views on contact. This chapter provides an overview of contact from the mothers' perspective.

How contact impacted on the mothers' feelings over the adoption

Among other things, Chapter 5 reported on the mothers' feelings about the adoption over the years. This included the sense of loss, guilt and depression arising from the parting decision, worry about the child's well-being, and the stress of having to keep the secret. Three-quarters now reported that contact had proved helpful or very helpful in dealing with these feelings (Table 8.1). However, approximately one out of every ten (12 per cent) said they were not sure and seven per cent that it had had no effect. Hardly anyone (2%) said that contact had been unhelpful, even if it didn't turn out entirely as they would have liked. The 40 per cent who reported a sense of loss were more likely to say that they had found contact

helped more with feelings surrounding the adoption than the others
(p = 0.044).

Table 8.1
How contact impacted on the mothers' feelings over the adoption

V. helpful	Helpful	Not sure	Unhelpful or v. unhelpful	No effect or non-applicable	Total
%	%	%	%	%	%
53	22	12	2	11	100

N = 85 (missing 8)

For most mothers, contact provided relief or reassurance about a number
of strong negative feelings and thoughts that had persisted with them
for years. Feelings and thoughts of loss, guilt and worry, which had
haunted them for years, had now been largely neutralised and thus had
lost their hold on them. There was relief to find that their child was
well, had had a happy childhood and did not blame them for the parting.
Compared to their feelings in the past, they now felt 'overjoyed'; 'at
peace with the past'; 'total relief'; 'something positive out of the
nightmare'; 'a huge burden was lifted'; 'laid the guilt to rest'; 'pride at
meeting such a wonderful person'. Others said: 'I am really happy';
'the large gap in my life has now closed up'; 'our family has now been
completed'; 'final chapter in a long 18 years of worry and upset'; and
'it does feel so good not to carry this "dark secret" about any more'. A
number of mothers referred to the experience as one of 'healing'. Other
typical examples included:

> I don't feel guilty now that I know she's been happy and has had a
> good life.

> It feels like I got myself back. The covert depression is no longer there.
> I feel much more content with life.

Many mothers used contact as an opportunity to explain to their sons and
daughters the reasons why they had parted with them and to let them
know that they loved them and often thought of them. Hearing their
adopted children say they that did not "blame" them added to the relief of

many mothers. For the small number who said it had been their decision to part with their child, contact and seeing their child doing well reassured them that they had made the right decision: One recalled 'Great happiness in finding this accomplished adult'.

' A handful were still feeling angry or bitter about the original parting: 'still feel guilty about giving her away'; 'it was a major mistake'; 'it still makes me feel bad'; and 'I still feel the guilt and shame'. Another typical comment was:

> *I still regret what I had to do. Giving up your own flesh and blood is the hardest thing in the world to do, even though it was the right thing to do at the time.*

How positive was contact for all three parties?

In nine out of ten cases, birth mothers were certain that contact had proved beneficial to themselves (Table 8.2). Almost four-fifths said the same about their child. When it came to the adoptive parents, though, only a quarter of birth mothers said that contact had been positive for the adoptive parents. There was also continued concern from some about the adopters' feelings, recognition that some of them possibly found contact hard and a wish not to do anything that might prove hurtful or upsetting. As one of them put it: 'If I thought she [adoptive mother] was suffering by our contact, I would be very sorry'. Overall, mothers came to view

Table 8.2

Do you feel that the contact experience has been positive for yourself, your child and the adoptive family?

Level	Yourself* %	Your child %	Adoptive parents %
Very positive/positive	89	78	25
Not sure	8	20	49
Very negative/negative	1	3	13
No effect	2	–	7
Deceased/unaware of contact	–	–	7
Total	100	101	101

*N = 88 (missing 5)

121

themselves as the main beneficiaries of contact followed by the adopted person, and far behind them, the adopters. In this respect they appeared to support a common view that adoptive parents could feel left out. The predominant view among mothers was that contact had proved 'positive', 'beneficial' or 'satisfying', especially to themselves and their child. The reason for this included 'completeness' or 'it answered my worries and has helped my daughter'. As another put it:

> For my child and myself this contact represents the missing link in our lives, the chance to feel completeness.

Contact and life changes

Almost two-thirds of mothers (64%) said that their life had been 'enhanced' since they made contact with their child, with almost a third (32%) saying that there was no change; only a tiny proportion (4%) said that it had deteriorated (Figure 8.1).

Figure 8.1
Life changes since contact was established

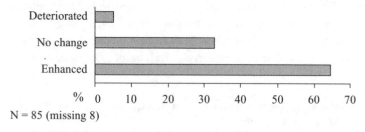

N = 85 (missing 8)

According to almost two-thirds of the mothers, contact appeared to be addressing the kind of concerns and anxieties that they had had over the years and, with a few exceptions, was viewed as beneficial. The change for the great majority appeared to be a personal and intrinsic one. Contact with their child and finding them to be 'doing well', 'being wonderful', 'thoughtful, kind and loving' were the decisive factors for these mothers. It made them, they said, do away with the 'guilt' or 'the worry' or made them 'feel better', 'relieved', 'happier', or 'at peace with themselves'. Like many adopted people who talked about 'completing the jigsaw of their lives' through contact, a few mothers now said the same, i.e. 'I feel that the final piece of the jigsaw has been put in place'; 'I feel more complete'; and 'like I got myself back'. The following is another typical comment:

All the pain I had about the adoption has gone out of the window since I have met my son.

The one-third of mothers who said that contact had made no difference to them added that they had carried on 'as usual'; 'as normal'; 'same lifestyle but more content'; and 'life goes on in the same way'. One of them remarked:

'No change' sounds rather negative but 'enhanced' is not exactly how I would put it either. It is good to know her, to be in touch but my life has not really changed. It has just completed the jigsaw, so to speak.

The four per cent who said that things got worse mainly felt like this due to the contact not having gone well for themselves or their families, such as the adopted person not wanting any more contact or a husband or child reacting negatively to contact.

Being sought or seeking

Almost all sought mothers (93 per cent) and all seeker ones expressed pleasure and satisfaction from being sought by their sons and daughters or for having searched for them (Table 8.3). One mother, who said that contact had caused her 'intense pain and grief', was still pleased about it. Irrespective of their initial reactions to contact, only one mother currently felt unhappy about being contacted and another six per cent had mixed feelings about it. The mixed feelings had to do mainly with the complications that the contact had introduced into their families. Even so, only a couple of these mothers wished that contact had not taken place. Seeker mothers, too, were glad they had sought out their son or daughter and established contact, describing their reactions as: 'ecstatic'; 'overjoyed'; 'I cannot think of anything that could have pleased me more'. One referred to the joy it brought to all members of her family. For another it had been the force that was driving her in the search:

*It feels like I got myself back – the covert depression is no longer there.
I feel much more content with life.*

Table 8.3
How glad are you now that your son or daughter sought you out?

Very pleased/pleased	Mixed	Not pleased	All
93%	6%	1%	100

N = 88 (missing 5)

Expectations of contact

Asked to say whether their initial expectations of contact had been met or
not, almost three-quarters of mothers said that they had been met either
very well or well (74 per cent). Almost a fifth (17 per cent) said that they
had mixed feelings about it or were uncertain. Only eight per cent said
that their expectations were not well met or not at all met (Figure 8.2).
Besides the benefits identified earlier, the added bonus for many mothers
was having continued contact and a relationship.

The mixed feelings or reservations of some of the 17 per cent of
mothers had to do with the 'chemistry', as one of them put it, not working
out. The view of these mothers, who mostly continued having indirect
contact, was that there was something missing, possibly because they had
not parented their child to create 'a context' or 'a depth' in the relationship.
One mother found herself feeling 'a parent and stranger' at the same time.
Most of the negative comments (8 per cent), i.e. where expectations had
not been met at all, were because the relationship had not progressed as
expected. One mother observed that, although the beginning of contact
had been what she had expected of it, she was 'disappointed and upset'
that the continuation of the relationship 'was not successful'. Like others,
one said:

*I am disappointed that I no longer have contact but do not regret the
contact in any way.*

Figure 8.2
How well the mothers' initial expectations were met

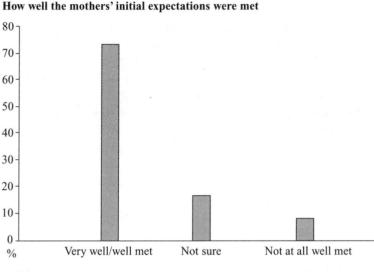

N = 86 (missing 7)

Contact and how it affected the birth mothers' relationship with their families

Almost half the birth mothers reported no change in the relationships within their families following contact with their son or daughter (Table 8.4). A similar proportion said it had led to an improvement and in only around one out of ten cases had contact led to strains within the birth mothers' families or to the deterioration of relationships. In effect, three times more relationships were said to have been enhanced than to have deteriorated. In this respect, no significant differences were found between sought and seeker mothers. In nine of the cases the mother had married the adopted person's father but, while the majority of them had been delighted with the news, a couple of fathers felt differently and later refused to see the adopted person. One husband, who was also the birth father of the adopted person, was said to have found it too hard to cope with his son's contact and another refused contact outright. The mothers' explanation was that they were still feeling guilty for not having supported her enough at the time to avoid

125

adoption. A handful of half-siblings also refused to have any contact but some of them came round to it eventually.

General reactions, though, were favourable, such as 'all love her [adopted person]'; 'just fitted in'; 'my family are very happy for me'; 'we are all happier knowing the jigsaw is complete'; 'my step-son and step-daughter enjoy having a sister'; 'my other children feel more complete knowing their lost sibling'. Many mothers reported that contact had helped to lift the 'burden' and 'depression' they had carried over the years, adding that they were now feeling much better in themselves and were also better wives and better mothers to their other children. A not unusual comment was:

I no longer get times of sadness and depression so my relationship with my husband has obviously improved. The other children simply accept him [adopted son] as part of the family.

Although family relationships were said, on the whole, to have been enhanced as a result of contact, in some cases jealousy and rivalry emerged because of the attention paid by the mother to the adopted person leading to 'tensions'. This happened not only with some of the other children but apparently more so with some husbands/partners. Birth mothers reported that some of the latter said they felt excluded from this 'cosy' relationship, and it even took one of them six years before he came to terms with the existence of his wife's child. Three mothers found their marriages were threatened or one of their other children walked out as a result. One of them remarked that, because of the appearance of the adopted person, she had ongoing 'pain' for her other children and a few referred to the 'strain' contact had introduced into the family. The following is one of a number of comments indicating difficulties:

My husband was not happy that I made contact with my daughter, he did not take to her. My son was the only person who liked her out of the family and has kept in contact with her.

Unsurprisingly, perhaps, the tensions were more pronounced within those families where the birth mother had not previously told them about the adoption:

My other son and daughter suffer enormous jealousy and cannot understand why I never told them. They feel betrayed and let down.

Table 8.4

How contact with their son or daughter affected relationships with their spouses and other children

Effect	Husband/partner %	Children %
Enhanced	19	31
Deteriorated/strained	13	11
No change	45	48
Not applicable	23	11
Total	100	101

N = 78 (missing 15 or not relevant)

Contact and stress

Although nine out of every ten mothers were pleased that they had established contact with their son or daughter, nevertheless over a quarter experienced contact, when compared to other major life events, as having been 'extremely stressful' and over a third as having been moderately so (Table 8.5). What was stressful about it was the anxiety about how their adopted child would react to them, what the child thought of the parting, and also concerns over developing a relationship. The impact on their other family was also part of the stress.

Table 8.5

Contact and stress as experienced by sought and seeker birth mothers

Level of stress	Sought mothers %	Seeker mothers %	All mothers %
Not at all stressful	40	25	35
Moderately stressful	38	39	38
Extremely stressful	22	36	27
Total	100	100	100

N = 86 (missing 7); Sought mothers N = 61 (missing 3); Seeker mothers N = 28 (missing 4)

127

Overall view of the outcome of contact

Table 8.6 summarises how the birth mothers came to view the overall outcome of contact. These are their responses to a set of statements.

Between 40–60 per cent of birth mothers said that their emotional life, self-esteem, ability to relate to others and feel relaxed had all improved since contact. Correspondingly, 22 per cent said that they had felt unchanged and for five per cent, their emotional outlook had worsened. No birth mother said she wished she had never met her son or daughter. Turning to the quality of the experience, 94 per cent felt that contact had been a positive experience, and 86 per cent felt satisfied about the outcome of contact. When it came to levels of contact and quality of relationships, 69 per cent were content with the current level of contact and 71 per cent with their current relationship with their son or daughter. At the same time, 59 per cent would have liked more contact. Around one out of every ten (11 per cent) said that they felt disappointed by their first contact and another 10 per cent felt angrier since contact. A third of mothers found it hard to cope with the intensity of the feelings aroused by contact and 21 per cent came to feel confused about their feelings for their son or daughter. Half of them were certain that their sons and daughters were just like them but one out of every ten reported feeling like a stranger to their son or daughter, with a similar proportion being uncertain. (There is a slight disparity in the proportion who said they felt like a stranger to their son or daughter when answering a similar question in Chapter 7. This time the proportion went up from 3 to 10 per cent.)

One of the key questions that the study set out to answer was whether contact had helped birth mothers to cope better with past feelings of loss, guilt and worry which were all connected with the adoption decision. Looking at the overall picture, almost all of them reported that they had been pleased that their sons and daughters had established contact or that they had searched for their child, and 94 per cent described the experience as positive. Only eight per cent said that their expectations of contact had not been met. Only one birth mother said that she wished she had not established contact or had not met her child. Other key benefits identified by the mothers included satisfaction; relief and being at peace with themselves; no more guilt and sadness; improved emotional outlook;

Table 8.6

Overall review of the outcome of contact

Statement	Strongly agree/ agree %	Uncertain %	Strongly disagree/ disagree %
(a) I am happy with my current level of contact with my son or daughter*	69	13	19
(b) I would like more contact with my son/daughter	59	21	20
(c) I am satisfied with my current relationshipwith my/daughter	71	13	17
(d) I feel I can relate better to people because of my contact	38	30	32
(e) I felt disappointed with my first contact with my son/daughter	11	4	85
(f) My emotional outlook has improved since the contact	60	20	21
(g) My emotional outlook has worsened since the contact	5	8	87
(h) Overall I feel the contact has been a positive experience	94	2	4
(i) My self-esteem has improved since contact	45	23	32
(j) My family's reaction to my contact has been positive	86	8	6
(k) I wish I had not met my son/daughter	–	–	100
(l) I feel more relaxed since I have had contact with my son/daughter	64	15	22
(m) I feel unchanged since the contact	22	8	70
(n) I feel angrier since the contact	10	8	82
(o) Overall I feel satisfied with the outcome of the contact	86	4	10
(p) I feel a stranger with my son/ daughter	10	10	81
(q) My son/daughter is just like me	50	31	19
(r) I feel confused about my feelings for my son/daughter	21	10	69
(s) I found it hard to cope with the intensity of my feelings	33	14	53

*N = 80 (missing 13)

improved self-esteem; enhanced life since contact and the end of confused feelings about their sons and daughters. On the more objective GHQ score which measured current emotional health, birth mothers came out well. On the whole, birth mothers were happy and content with any amount of contact they had even if it had not continued. Those who had reported experiencing intense feelings of loss between the adoption and contact appeared to benefit most from contact and reunion.

Finally, Figure 8.3 illustrates the change of the dominant feelings and thoughts for birth mothers over the four stages. Overall, high levels of satisfaction and contentment replaced the sadness, guilt, fears and anxieties that were a characteristic of the pre-contact period.

Figure 8.3
Birth mothers' dominant feelings and thoughts at different stages

	Stage 1 *Pregnancy to parting*	*Stage 2* *From adoption to the search*	*Stage 3* *Seeking and being sought*	*Stage 4* *Post- contact*
Shame/stigma	Yes	√	Only partly	N
Guilt	Yes	√	√	N
Rejection/isolation	Yes	√	√	N
Loss/sadness/grief	Yes	√	√	N
Anxiety/worry (about child)	Yes	√	√	N
Keeping the secret	Yes	√	√	N
Does he/she feels rejected?	Yes	√	√	N
Curiosity	Yes	√	√	N
Would he/she like to meet?	Yes			
Excitement/pleasure		√	√	N
Fear of being hurt or hurting	N/A	N/A	√	N
Anxiety about hearing bad news	N/A	N/A	√	N
Improved emotional outlook	No	No	No	N
Improved self-esteem		No	No	N
At peace with self	No	No	No	N
New relationships formed	N/A	N/A	N/A	N

Symbols: √ = present ; N = not present
N/A = not applicable

Summary

Almost all birth mothers said that they had been pleased that their sons and daughters had established contact with them or that they had searched for their child, and three-quarters reported that their expectations of contact had been well or very well met, with only eight per cent saying 'not at all'. At the same time, over a quarter experienced the process of contact as having been 'extremely stressful' in comparison with other major life events. There were no significant differences between sought and seeker birth mothers in whether they thought their lives had changed since the contact, whether they were pleased about being sought/searching, whether their initial expectations had been met or about the severity of the stress in comparison to other major life events or in any of the review outcomes.

For around 90 per cent of birth mothers, contact and reunion was a happy and satisfying experience. However, a group of 12 per cent (N = 11), including sought and seeker birth mothers, were dissatisfied on at least three variables, i.e. they wanted more contact, felt disappointed with contact and found it hard to cope with the intensity of their feelings. Six per cent (N = 6) were dissatisfied on five variables: unhappy with contact, dissatisfied with the relationship with their sons or daughters, wanted more contact, found it hard to cope with the intensity of the feelings aroused by contact, and not satisfied with the overall outcome.

Having outlined the birth mothers' reactions and perspectives, the book will now move on to those of their sons and daughters.

9 Growing up adopted

Adopted person:
Had a wonderful mother [adoptive] and experienced few feelings of rejection or loss connected with my birth family, but meeting my birth mother and being told the reasons for being put up for adoption did help.

Introduction

The outcome of adoption from the adopted person's perspective has been the centre of attention of most studies undertaken in this field over the last fifty or so years. Some studies have been of a follow-up type, others retrospective and some longitudinal. The gist of the studies is that around seven out of every ten adopted people appear to do well or very well by being adopted, another ten to 15 per cent fall in the intermediate category and the rest are more dissatisfied (see especially Jaffee and Fanshell, 1970; Bohman, 1970; Raynor, 1980; Triseliotis and Russell, 1984). Because some themes about the growing-up years from the perspective of the adopted person were examined by the first part of the study (Howe and Feast, 2000) this one mostly concentrates on some new areas. In the Howe and Feast (2000) study, significant differences in the rates of feeling 'happy, loved, and loving' were noted between searchers and non-searchers, with non-searchers more likely to describe their feelings, experiences and current relationships more positively. For example, these differences were reflected in the proportions of non-searchers who said that they felt they 'belonged' in their adoptive family, compared to the searchers. In addition, half of the searchers in the same study said they felt different to their adoptive family when they were growing up, compared to only 27 per cent of non-searchers. The majority of both groups reported feeling happy but the percentage was higher in the non-searcher group. Almost two-thirds (65 per cent) of searchers, but 85 per cent of non-searchers, strongly agreed or agreed that they felt happy about being adopted. Similarly, 77 per cent of searchers and 91 per cent of non-searchers strongly agreed or agreed that they felt loved by their adoptive mothers. A small "alienated" group was much more likely to say that their adoption had not been properly handled by their parents, that they did not feel they belonged or were loved within their adoptive families and often had a greater need to develop a relationship with the birth relative. However, three-quarters were not categorised as alienated. This chapter overall reports on findings about the adopted persons' growing-up years and the closeness of relationships with the adoptive parents and the wider adoptive family. Particular attention was paid to emotional health, self-esteem and possible feelings of rejection and loss experienced by adopted people as a result of being parted from their birth family.

Gender, place in the family, age and social class

Of the 126 adopted people featuring in the study, 45 (36 per cent) were male and 81 (64 per cent) female; 22 (17 per cent) were sought by their birth mothers and the rest were searchers. The majority of searchers were female but birth mothers were just as likely to be searching for a son as for a daughter. Only 16 per cent of adopted people grew up as only children without siblings. Almost half of the adopters (45 per cent) had one or more birth children and around a third had adopted other children. Reflecting the policy and practice of the period, nine out of every ten had been placed with their adoptive families when under the age of 18 months. Their average age at contact with birth relatives was 29 (Std 7.4) and when completing this questionnaire, 37 (Std 6.4). In effect, around eight years had elapsed between initial contact and the time they participated in this study.

There were no significant differences in age between male and female searchers and non-searchers. Using the Registrar General's social class classification of occupations, almost half the adopted people were classified in social classes I and II, i.e. professional and managerial, which included occupations such as company managers, teachers, lecturers and nurses. Another 28 per cent were in non-manual occupations (social class III) and employed mainly in secretarial and administrative posts, 17 per cent held skilled manual occupations (social class III) and the remaining seven per cent were grouped in social classes IV and V (semi-skilled and unskilled) (Table 9.1). What these percentages show is the very high proportion (76 per cent) of adopted people employed in non-manual type occupations, which is well above that found in the general population. Differences between male and female adopted people were not significant. However, while 81 per cent of searchers were classified as holding non-manual occupations, only 53 per cent of non-searchers were similarly classified (p = 0.016).

Table 9.1
Social class classification by occupation*

Class	I&II Prof. & Managerial	III Non-Manual	III Manual	IV&V Semi-skilled & Unskilled	All
%	48 (25)	28 (22)	17 (24)	7 (24)	100 (95)^

N = 98 (missing 28)
*Note: The classification is based on the Registrar General's 1981 classification. The difference in the total percentage represents those in the armed forces.
^Numbers in brackets refer to the general population.

Closeness to adoptive parents

Over eight out of ten adopted people (84 per cent) rated their relationship with their adoptive parents during childhood as having been very close or close, with one out of ten rating it as not close or not at all close. The rest referred to it as mixed (Table 9.2). No significant difference emerged between searchers and those sought by their birth mothers. As possibly expected, the closeness of the relationship fell sharply in adolescence. It went up in adulthood, but it never regained the level achieved in childhood. While some adopted people attributed the change to preoccupations with their adoption, others did not want to single out their adoption as the cause. In the absence of findings about how close to their parents non-adopted people feel, we cannot be certain whether the changes in adolescence are the same. The sharp fall in closeness during adolescence could at least be partly attributed to heightened awareness among them about the meaning of adoption and the sense of rejection and loss involved at a time when they are trying to develop a coherent narrative about themselves as adopted. However, the sharp fall could also be attributed to the general desire of adolescents and teenagers to establish their separateness by distancing themselves from their parents. In doing so, some appeared to use their adoption around which to organise their separateness.

Around two-fifths (41 per cent) of adopted people whose closeness to their adoptive parents remained constant between adolescence and adulthood were more likely to have better emotional health (p = 0.013) and a significantly higher self-esteem (p = 0.022). What is of equal interest is that it was females with mostly lower self-esteem and poorer emotional health whose closeness to their adoptive parents increased between adolescence and adulthood. Adolescence proved to be a particularly unsettling experience for females than males. For example, 71 per cent of adopted males reported close or very close relationships with their parents during adolescence compared to only 38 per cent of females.

Table 9.2

The adopted person's perception of their closeness to their adoptive mother and father at different stages

Closeness	Early childhood*		Adolescence[†]		Before contact[††]	
	Mother	Father	Mother	Father	Mother	Father
	%	%	%	%	%	%
Very close/close	84	77	49	51	67	67
Mixed	7	15	25	26	18	18
Not very close/						
Not at all close/	10	8	25	23	15	15
Total	101	100	99	100	100	100

*N = 124 (missing 2); [†]N = 124 (missing 2); [††]N = 119 (missing 7)

Adopted people, both as children, adolescents and adults, reported similar levels of closeness to both their adoptive mothers and fathers. In other words, closeness to the one was highly associated with closeness to the other (p < 0.001). Because of this association, closeness and other variables are quoted either in respect of the adoptive mother or simply adoptive parents. The presence of birth children in the family did not affect closeness. Closeness to adoptive parents both in childhood and currently was significantly associated with self-esteem (childhood $p = 0.001$; currently $p = 0.002$). In effect, the greater the reported closeness to the adoptive parents, the higher also the self-esteem of the adopted person.

Close to very close relationships: Many of those describing close or very close or close relationships with their adoptive mothers and fathers would add how they conveyed to them a sense of 'security' and 'belonging'. Others said that they had connected 'at a very deep level', that they could not imagine 'being closer to anyone else', or that they were 'real' parents. A father could be described as 'a powerful role model', 'a marvellous man' or as 'strict but fair'. The following is a more typical comment:
No reason to feel anything but loved and secure.

One out of ten had lost their adoptive fathers by the time of the study but only two had lost their mothers. Some fathers had died before the adopted person was 16. One person who lost his father at the age of 15 remarked:
I was closer to him than anyone. The only man I trusted. He was my friend as well as my dad.

Mixed or distant relationships: Depending on the stage they were reporting, between 16 and 33 per cent of adopted people referred to mixed feelings, not very close or even distant relationships with their parents in childhood, adolescence or in adult life. It was also the view of a small number (10 per cent) that they never really came to feel close to their adoptive mothers or to have bonded. They may have felt 'loved but not close' as one said. This small minority attributed it mostly to their mothers being 'distant' or 'closed emotionally', or 'she saw it as her duty to parent'. More rarely, some said that they had not connected with either parent. Some added that they themselves did not like 'cuddles', wanted to stay 'aloof' or 'felt different' or like 'outsiders'. One of them said:
Never bonded emotionally. They made sure I wanted for nothing, but failed to meet my emotional needs.

The small percentage (10 per cent) who described the adoptive mothers in the above terms does not support the generalised comment made by Modell (1994) from her US study that the adopted people in her sample described the adoptive mother as 'selfish and stingy . . . rigid, material-istic, emotionally cold, and unsexual – or sexually unproductive, and not exactly a real parent' (p. 228). In her study they portrayed the birth mothers as 'good and generous'. This very likely reflects a high level of bias in her self-selected sample.

The teenage years were singled out by many as the ones of 'rebellion', 'angst', 'doubts' or 'kicking out at authority'. Many of them returned to closer relationships later on but a significant proportion did not return to the kind of closeness they had felt in childhood. Some attributed their attitudes and behaviours during adolescence to being adopted, but later came to realise that this was not the case. As one of them put it: 'I tended then to attribute attitudes towards being adopted. Looking back I realise that in adolescence I probably was more sensitive.' Again typical comments for this period included:

I wasn't close to any of my adoptive family as an adolescent, but as I have got older our relationship has improved tremendously.

The minority who reported more mixed or distant relationships in adult life, and before contact was established (as different from childhood and adolescence), again explained it as being mainly due to the lack of closeness, no shared interests or to 'emotional distance'. A few who had felt distant from their mothers also remarked that they had never been close to their fathers: 'nothing in common'; 'no love lost'; 'distant'; 'authoritarian'. A young woman came to feel 'repulsed and angry' because her father tried to interfere with her sexually. This was the only instance of sexual abuse reported to the study.

Closeness of relationships with siblings and other adoptive relatives

Most adopted people described close and inclusive relationships with other members of the adoptive family. The closest were with grandparents (72 per cent), but significantly lower levels of closeness to siblings and

137

aunts/uncles (54 per cent) were reported (Table 9.3). With regard to siblings, the disaffected said they had 'nothing in common'; 'never got on well'; or 'we drifted apart'. In contrast, others commented that nobody could replace a sister or a brother and referred to lasting relationships. No comparisons could again be made with sibling relationships within the general population as no such studies are known to us.

Table 9.3
Adopted person's closeness of relationship with siblings, grandparents and aunts/uncles while growing up

Closeness	Siblings* %	Grandparents[†] %	Aunts and uncles[††] %
Very close/close	54	72	54
Mixed	30	16	22
Not very close/not at all	16	12	24
Total	100	100	100

*N = 116 (missing 10); [†]N = 117 (missing 9); [††]N = 116 (missing 10).

The main criticism of around one out of every five adopted people was that they did not feel they were included or fitted in with the extended family. As one of them put it: 'I always felt that I was not really related to them – isolated'. Those who said that other members of the family treated them differently were also more likely to report feeling rejected by their birth family ($p = 0.017$). Although numbers who felt like this were small, adopted people of a minority ethnic background (and adopted trans-racially) were more likely to say that they were not loved unconditionally by the extended family, had not felt part of the family, and failed to develop a sense of belonging to the wider family. A few viewed themselves as having been used as a 'therapeutic tool', or 'to make a statement' or as one of them put it: 'accepted only if I moulded myself into a white, obedient, undemonstrative, unemotional, not too intelligent, unassertive, subservient, grateful female'. Another one who established contact remarked that he now had two families but:

> ... neither of which gives me the feeling of love and acceptance that I so crave. I feel more like an orphan than ever.

Surprisingly, perhaps, closer relationships were reported with grand-parents, with seven out of every ten describing them as close or very close. While several adopted people of minority ethnic origin experienced grandparents as not approving of them, for the great majority grandparents proved a source of satisfactory and more enduring relationships. Some went out of their way to point out that:

My grandparents never gave a hint we could be different by being adopted.

Table 9.4 presents the views of adopted people on three variables which were singled out during the first part of the study (Howe and Feast, 2000), i.e. whether they were happy about being adopted, whether they felt loved by their adoptive mother and whether they had developed a sense of belonging within the adoptive family. Seven out of ten reported they felt happy about being adopted and had developed a sense of belonging to their adoptive parents; 86 per cent felt loved by their adoptive mother. Significantly fewer women than men were likely to say that they agreed or strongly agreed that they belonged to their adoptive families ($p = 0.006$).

Table 9.4

Whether the adopted person was happy about being adopted, felt loved and developed a sense of belonging*

Views	Happy being adopted* %	Loved by mother[†] %	Sense of belonging[††] %
Agree/strongly agree	73	86	73
Uncertain	18	4	9
Disagree/strongly disagree	10	10	17
Total	101	100	99

* N = 120 (missing 6); [†]N = 124 (missing 2); [††]N = 124 (missing 2).

Ethnic origin

Of the whole sample, twelve (10 per cent) described themselves as of different ethnicity, meaning black and/or of mixed heritage or Asian. It would be dangerous to draw too many conclusions from this small number, but some differences from the rest of the sample are set out below. In the first place, the majority thought that their difference in ethnicity did affect them and that ethnic identity and culture became an issue for them. For example, their reported current closeness to their adoptive mothers was below that of the rest of the sample (58 compared with 73 per cent). It is not that they felt altogether unhappy about their adoption but they came to feel different from others and ask questions of themselves about who they were. The experiences that stood out for this small group were the knowledge that they were different; the racism they suffered, mainly at school; not being fully accepted by the extended family or not fitting in with those around them; and at times feeling misunderstood. Talking about the experience of racism, some attributed it to being brought up mainly in white areas, or that it took place mainly at school. One of them remarked:

> *I knew I wasn't the same as I stuck out. I had racial taunts at school, even from my sister – but we were young. They were a very white British family, I couldn't be like them.*

One woman explained:

> *Racially I felt 'apart' as they're white. I got bullied at school about my race and I didn't trust that my adoptive parents really believed I was of equal status to their natural children.*

Some emphasis was also placed on wanting to find out and know more about their cultural background to help firm up their identity, described as 'wanting to know why I was brown' or 'deal with the vacuum'. Others made similar points in slightly different ways. 'To me,' said one, 'it [identity] was a problem as I wondered about myself'. And another, 'I tried to fit in but it was hard because he [father] looked so different'. Some of them added how different it felt after they had moved to more ethnically mixed neighbourhoods:

I didn't have close friends until I was a teenager when we moved to a place with another black family and I had a black teacher. It made me feel more comfortable with other people who were like me.

A handful, while acknowledging that they felt loved in their families, put the emphasis on simply feeling 'different', but not because of their ethnicity or colour. Their explanations were similar to those of others who came to feel rejected by their birth family. As they put it: 'Just knowing that my mother and father were not my natural parents made me feel different'; or 'looking at life very differently from them and still do'; or 'no physical likeness, personality different, interests very different'. Another knew that her adoptive parents meant well but she could not force herself to be something she was not.

Emotional health

Like birth mothers and adoptive parents, adopted people also completed the Goldberg General Health Questionnaire (GHQ) (Goldberg, 1972). Based on the GHQ, the adopted person's assessment of their emotional health showed 74 per cent of them as having low scores, i.e. good emotional health (0–3). Scores of 4–9 were scored by 12 per cent, indicating moderate difficulties. Finally, another 14 per cent scored 10–15 points, suggesting more severe emotional problems (Table 9.5). Overall, one out of every four was shown to have medium to more serious emotional problems. These cannot be contrasted with other studies because we are not aware of any that have used the GHQ for this group. The older the adopted person, the lower the GHQ score or the better their emotional health ($p = 0.021$). Women were more likely than men to report a higher level of emotional problems ($p = 0.031$). The poorer the adopted person's emotional health, the lower also their reported self-esteem ($p < 0.001$). In contrast, the better their emotional health, the happier they felt about being adopted ($p = 0.029$) and the more they felt they belonged in the adoptive family ($p = 0.015$). Significantly higher emotional problems were declared by adopted people who thought that being adopted had affected their ability to make relationships, their marriage, general well-being, education and career. Although our numbers were small, non-searchers were less likely to feel the adoption had had such negative effects. (Levels of significance for each area ranged from $p = 0.01$ to $p < 0.001$.)

Table 9.5
Current state of emotional health

GHQ Score	%
0	57
1–3	17
4–9	12
10–15	14
Total	100

N = 125 (missing 1)

In response to the question about whether any health problems they had were related to their adoption experience, two-thirds were certain that they were not, one out of every six thought they were (16 per cent), and the rest (18 per cent) were not sure. Some of those who were not sure about the connection said that it was impossible to separate the adoption experience from their life experiences, including their emotional health. 'It is always', as one of them put it, 'at the back of one's mind'. The majority explained most of their emotional problems as arising from work, family pressures, and depression following the loss or illness of a loved one or marriage difficulties. 'It was tempting', one of them said, 'to attribute problems to the adoption experience but probably not accurate'. Those adopted people who thought that their health problems were un-related to their adoption were more likely to score better on emotional health ($p = 0.001$) and report higher levels of self-esteem ($p < 0.001$). Also, the closer the reported relationship to the adoptive mother, the less likely was the adopted person to link any emotional health problems to the adoption ($p = 0.018$).

The minority of adopted people (16 per cent) who associated their emotional problems with the adoption experience talked of depression, 'lack of confidence', 'insecurity', 'emotional instability', 'ups and downs', 'continued insecurity', 'mental angst', 'prone to melancholy' or as experiencing 'guilt' from disloyalty towards the adoptive parents because of the search and contact. Their problems were mainly around their upbringing or stress arising from contact. Those who attributed the problems to being adopted referred to emotional distancing from their parents, being treated differently from birth children and by the wider family, or being of a minority ethnic background. There was reference to 'non-nurturing experiences', 'unhappiness' and 'never fitted in'. For example, one described his adoptive family as 'dysfunctional' and another said his adoptive mother would not have passed today's adoption criteria, adding:

If I had a happier adoption I might have been different.

A few perceived the breakdown of a relationship or depression following bereavement as related to the original rejection by their birth family, and in a number of cases emotional problems were definitely linked to the search and contact. Several others said that feelings of 'rejection' and 'abandonment' were reinforced when a birth mother refused or ceased contact, e.g. feeling 'very depressed at the second rejection' or 'nobody to send a card to'. The contact process could also lead to anxiety, depression or 'emotional upheaval'.

. . . stress/anxiety symptoms, depression due to the difficulties I was experiencing with my birth mother.

There was also the occasional person who attributed their emotional problems to a feeling of having let down their adoptive parents or being 'disloyal' because of having established contact with a birth parent. One of them reported:

I have suffered mentally. I continually fight my 'guilt' feelings of causing my parents pain in tracing my mum, but I had to do it. She offered me more love than I'd ever experienced in my life and I needed that. I needed to feel wanted and that I was worth something – my birth mum makes me feel that way, my parents never did. I know they love me but they can't show it. A simple 'I love you' would be worth more.

143

Self-esteem evaluation

Because the literature on adoption suggests that being adopted may affect how people view themselves and also their self-esteem, use was made of the Rosenberg (1979) Self-esteem Questionnaire to test this out. An earlier work (Rosenberg, 1965, p. 31) explained 'high self-esteem' as meaning that the individual respected themselves, considered themselves worthy, not better than others but definitely not worse, did not feel he or she is the ultimate in perfection but, on the contrary, recognises their limitations and expects to grow and improve. Rosenberg explained 'low self-esteem' as implying 'self-rejection, self-dissatisfaction, self-contempt. The individual lacks respect for the self he observes. The self-picture is disagreeable, and he wishes it were otherwise'.

Figure 9.1 shows that almost three-quarters of adopted people were rated as having from medium to high self-esteem and the rest (26 per cent) low. Although proportionately more searchers than non-searchers were rated as having low self-esteem, this did not reach full statistical

Figure 9.1
The Rosenberg self-esteem evaluation

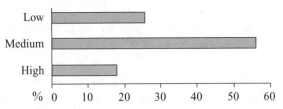

N = 126

significance. The higher the self-esteem, the fewer emotional problems scored on the GHQ ($p < 0.001$); the happier they felt with being adopted ($p = 0.003$); the closer their current relationship to their adoptive mother ($p = 0.004$) and father ($p = 0.002$); the more they felt loved by their adoptive parents ($p = 0.001$); the more they felt they belonged in the adoptive family ($p < 0.001$); and the more they said they loved their adoptive parents (mother $p = 0.008$; father $p = 0.001$). These findings would support the view that self-esteem, like emotional health, is related to the quality of the adoptive relationships and experience.

144

Sense of rejection and loss

Sense of rejection

The possible sense of rejection and loss felt by adopted people because their birth parent(s) parted with them has been occupying centre stage in the adoption research and theoretical literature for some thirty years and possibly more (see Triseliotis, 1973). However it is put, adoption implies that the biological family rejected or abandoned the adopted person. In a recent study of intercountry adoption, the main explanation offered for higher levels of disturbance found among adopted adolescents was 'increasing concerns over their biological parentage' and their 'sense of loss having once been abandoned' (Velhurst, 2001, p. 139). Around two out of every five (39 per cent) adopted people in this study said they came to feel always or sometimes rejected in childhood but this went up to 51 per cent in adolescence before returning to the childhood levels (Figure 9.2). What was different in adolescence was that 30 per cent always felt like this, which was 10 per cent more than before. The finding gives more credence to the view that, by adolescence, the adopted person becomes much more aware of their adoptive status and its meaning, resulting in intensified feelings about their adoption. There were strong associations between those who felt rejected in childhood, adolescence and adulthood (p < 0.001). In other words, for the majority who felt like this, the sense of rejection was felt throughout their lives up to the contact stage, and for a few, beyond. A number of them who felt strongly about their rejection stressed how unwanted they came to feel by one's 'own blood', how it made them feel worthless, 'unworthy to keep' or as if 'discarded', 'made/born but not been wanted' or that every time they experienced rejection in life, 'it triggered unconscious unworthiness and felt very painful'. Another one commented:

> . . . being told that the only reason I was not aborted was due to my birth mother's anxiety for her own health!

And another:

> Rejection became ingrained in me from early on and it was difficult to get rid of it. The knowledge that your own did not want you.

Although our numbers of non-searchers were small, nevertheless, significantly fewer non-searchers, than searchers, reported feeling rejected at any stage. Overall, current closeness to adoptive parents related to feelings of rejection in adolescence and strength of rejection in adulthood and adolescence. In other words, higher levels of closeness to adoptive parents suggested lower levels of rejection felt (p = 0.006). Equally, the closer the adopted person's reported current relationship to the adoptive parents, the less likely it was for them to have felt rejected by their birth family. Those who felt rejected were also more likely to report that they were less happy about being adopted (p = 0.021), less comfortable talking about their adoption to outsiders (p = 0.008), and that they did not belong (p = 0.027). The less rejection adopted people felt during childhood the higher also their current self-esteem (childhood p = 0.04).

Figure 9.2
Adopted people's sense of rejection from having been given up by their birth parents

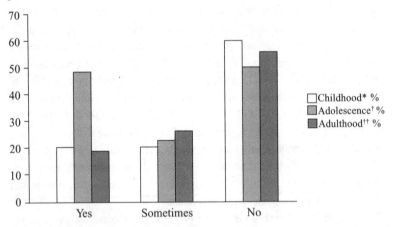

*N = 122 (missing 4); [†]N = 125 (missing 1); [††]N = 124 (missing 2).

Strength of the rejection
Of adopted people who felt rejected, or sometimes rejected, 67 per cent came to feel it most strongly in adolescence, followed by childhood and then adulthood (Table 9.6). Adopted people who felt loved by

their adoptive parents were less likely to feel strongly rejected (mother p = 0.008; father p = 0.013). Overall, as the closeness to the adoptive parents increased, so the strength of the felt rejection decreased. Similarly, the higher the adopted person's self-esteem, the more likely a weaker sense of rejection in childhood (p = 0.042).

Table 9.6
Strength of felt rejection during different stages

Strength	Childhood* %	Adolescence[†] %	Adulthood[††] %
Very strong/strong	54	67	44
Mixed	27	29	36
Not very strong or not strong at all	20	4	20
Total	101	100	100

*N = 41(missing 9); [†]N = 49 (missing 15); [††]N = 45 (missing 12)

What helped to lessen these feelings

The main factor that helped to lessen feelings of 'rejection', or perhaps not cause them to develop at all, was the love of the adoptive parents. It has already been noted that the closer the relationship with the adoptive parents and the more adopted people felt loved by them, the less likely it was that such feelings would develop or, if developed, would be weak. What the overall findings suggest is that the quality of the adoption experience can go a very long way to reduce feelings of rejection and, as will be seen later, those of loss too. There was no doubting, however, where adopted people put the emphasis for the lessening of such feelings: they made many references 'to the love and support of my adoptive family'; 'time and love from adoptive parents'; 'made to feel wanted by my adoptive parents'; 'wonderful adoptive parents'; 'a close and loving family and friends'. Sometimes it was a combination of a number of things such as:

Adoptive mum's love for me. Access to background papers on natural family and adoption (all papers mum had I had free access to from young age). Knowledge that I would trace when I was 18.

147

Others explained that it also helped when their adoptive parents encouraged them to consider the feelings of their birth mother and to try to understand her position at the time. For one person of mixed ethnicity, feelings of rejection were lessened as he grew older and understood how difficult it must have been for a young white woman to have a black child in the1950s.

What contributed to the increase of such feelings
If the quality of the adoption experience helped to lessen feelings of rejection, the opposite was equally true, even though it only happened in a very small proportion of cases. Some typical comments were: 'felt like a cuckoo in the nest'; 'no close relationship'; 'not emotionally nurtured'; 'not getting enough mothering from my adoptive mother'; and 'being told I should be grateful for having been adopted'. Others remarked:

My mother [adoptive] never seemed to be satisfied with me, my appearance or attitudes. I was being made aware that I was not biologically hers.

During arguments when growing up my sisters would say, 'You don't belong in this family'.

If feelings of rejection were lessened by being given background information and explanations which helped the adopted person to understand 'why adoption', not knowing and not talking about adoption had the opposite effect. If it was not spoken about, it strengthened the feelings of rejection and conveyed that it was something 'to be ashamed of' and undermining to their 'self-esteem'. Some typical comments included: 'adoption not being talked about'; 'not being able to talk about my birth family to anybody'; and 'adoption being a taboo subject'.

It was also suggested that feelings of rejection or loss could be re-experienced as a result of a new rejection or the loss of people who were important to them. The explanation being that it was like a scar that could be re-opened. The impact of other rejections was described as 'triggering unconscious unworthiness'; 'opening the wound of earlier rejection'; 'continuing to feel unwanted'; and ' being unworthy of love'.

Sense of loss

One writer recently reported that the search 'is most fundamentally an expression of the wish to undo the trauma of separation' (Anderson, 1988 p. 19). Another added that the resolution of the loss of an attachment figure requires cognitive acceptance of the loss that is linked to a satisfactory account of the causes of the loss (Weiss, 1988). Weiss went on to say that, if the loss makes no sense (as is the case for many adopted people who do not know or understand why they were placed for adoption), there is then an ongoing, nagging search for an explanation. Until this is done, recovery is apparently impeded. While the sense of rejection seems more obvious, i.e. having being 'discarded', or 'abandoned' by your own, that of loss is somewhat less so and possibly more subtle, hence adopted people in this study found it less easy to define. They could only describe what it felt like with some saying that they missed growing up with a birth parent to experience the parent–child relationship. Others described the loss as 'a void'; 'a gap'; 'always wondering what might have been'; 'something missing' or as one of them put it, 'just at a deep level something missing'. Others added, 'no one to tell me what it was like giving birth to me'; 'loss and absence was a most powerful emotion for me'; 'the thought of having no blood relations'; and 'what I thought I never had'. Another commented:

> *The sense of loss is like a hole in your body which can never be repaired, only sometimes you feel OK.*

As with the sense of rejection, a sense of loss was experienced by almost two-fifths in childhood (37 per cent), over half (55 per cent) in adolescence and almost half in adulthood (48 per cent) (Table 9.7). As mentioned earlier these were largely the same people who also felt rejected. In effect, a sense of rejection and a sense of loss went mostly, but not always, hand-in-hand. Like the sense of rejection, those sought were less likely to have experienced feelings of loss in childhood (p = 0.002). On the whole, what was found about the sense of rejection, both statistically and qualitatively, was repeated when it came to the sense of loss, including the levels of significance. As a result, this section is presented briefly. As again with those who felt rejected, adopted people who felt a loss in adulthood had less close relationships with their parents, were significantly less happy

149

about being adopted, felt less loved by their adoptive parents and did not feel that they fully belonged. They were also found to have lower self-esteem and more likely to report that being adopted had affected them in making relationships, their marriage, their well-being, their education, and their career. Many others who came to feel rejected or carried a sense of loss did not feel in the ways described above, but they were more likely to.

Table 9.7

Sense of loss experienced by adopted people at different stages and before contact

Sense of loss	In childhood* %	In adolescence[†] %	In adulthood[††] %
Yes	20	27	24
Sometimes	17	28	24
No	63	45	51
Total	100	100	99

*N = 123 (missing 3); [†]N = 124 (missing 2); [††]N = 122 (missing 4)

Strength of sense of loss

Of those who felt a sense of loss, between 42 and 54 per cent, depending on the stage, felt it very strongly or strongly. The worst period seemed to be in adulthood. The weaker the reported sense of loss in childhood, the more likely was the adopted person to report feeling happier in the adoptive home (p = 0.021) and that they belonged (p = 0.007). The weaker the sense of loss and rejection felt in childhood, the weaker also the motivation to search and the more positively they viewed the overall contact outcome. The figures also suggest that the strength of loss was not as strong as that of rejection during childhood and adolescence, but it was about the same in adulthood, i.e. just over half. At the same time, one out of five adopted people felt loss and rejection at all times.

Table 9.8
Strength of loss felt during different stages

Strength	Childhood* %	Adolescence[†] %	Adulthood[††] %
Very strong/strong	42	46	54
Mixed	34	27	30
Not very strong or not strong at all	24	27	15
Total	100	100	99

*N = 41(missing 5); [†]N = 49 (missing 16); [††]N = 45 (missing 14)

What helped to lessen these feelings

As with the sense of rejection, when it came to that of loss, it was again the quality of the adoption experience that apparently helped to lessen its impact, i.e. 'affection from my parents'; 'the experience of being nurtured'; 'wanted'; 'feeling loved'; 'feeling safe in my adoptive family'; 'time and attention from adoptive parents'; and feeling 'a great set of adoptive parents meant no loss felt'. The following is a typical comment linking the quality of the adoptive relationship with no or weak feelings of loss:

> *Thinking of my wonderful parents and the unconditional love they showed me.*

As with rejection, husbands, wives, partners, and a good marriage came in for praise for conveying love and acceptance. What also helped was looking forward to when they would be 18 and able to search and find the birth mother they were at times dreaming about:

> *It was feelings of missing her – even though I'd never known her. To lessen feelings I would fantasise, daydream about what she was like.*

What contributed to an increase of such feelings ·

What contributed to an increase in the sense of loss was the poor quality of the adoption experience, along with not knowing enough about the circumstances of their adoption or why they had been adopted, knowing little or nothing about the birth parents, what happened to them, or what they looked like. It is not surprising, therefore, that there was considerable overlap between those who felt rejected and those who felt a sense of loss. As a result, some of the same comments about the absence of love and affection, lack of emotional nurturing, and missing something within the adoptive home, were repeated. As with rejection, new losses, such as through bereavement or break up of relationships, contributed to an increase in the sense of loss. For adopted people of minority ethnic background, it was mainly the not fitting in and 'not looking anything like my adoptive family' that mattered:

> My adopted family represented my white world and there seemed a big hole where my brown world should be.

The impact of adoption

Between 58 and 76 per cent of adopted people were certain that their adoption had not negatively affected them in forming relationships, their marriage, well-being, education and career but the rest felt it had in one way or another (Table 9.9). The majority who thought it had not affected them used comments such as: 'never a problem'; 'always felt comfortable with my adoption'; 'I am not aware of any negative effects'; 'I can't see that has made a difference'; and 'no negative feelings'. The next chapter shows that those who felt that their adoption did not affect these areas of their lives were also more likely to report closer relationships with their parents in adult life. In contrast, those who said that they had been negatively affected were also more likely to declare less closeness. Those who said that their adoption did affect them in the above areas of their lives concentrated their explanations on not having felt close to their adoptive parents and lacking in confidence and self-esteem, carrying feelings of inadequacy, having problems with personal relationships and even after contact, continuing to carry feelings of rejection and loss. As one of them put it:

> Feeling deep down in your very core that you are unlovable and unwanted affects every part of your life.

Table 9.9
Has being adopted affected negatively your life in any of the following areas?

	Making relationships* %	Marriage %	Well-being %	Education %	Career %
Yes	26	28	23	15	16
No	60	58	67	75	76
Unsure	14	14	11	10	9
Total	100	100	101	100	101

*N = 121 (missing 5)

Summary

Over eight out of ten adopted people (84 per cent) reported having developed close or very close relationships with their adoptive parents during childhood. There were no differences in closeness with mother or father. The closeness dropped significantly in adolescence, but partly recovered in adulthood to around two-thirds feeling this way. The same proportion (around two-thirds) also felt happy about being adopted, felt loved by their adoptive mother and felt they had developed a sense of belonging. Those who felt like this in these areas were mostly the same people. The next closest relationship to parents was with grandparents followed by siblings, but only just over half declared a close relationship with them. The closer the adopted people felt to their parents, the more openly their adoption was also discussed, the more they said they felt they belonged, the more complete they felt as people, the higher their self-esteem and the better their emotional health.

The levels of positive outcomes were somewhat depressed by the view of a small but significant group who either felt that they and their parents had not properly attached and/or that they were treated differently compared to birth children and/or by the extended family. Adolescence proved significantly more unsettling for females than males. Children of minority ethnic background, although few in the sample, were mostly in this group and were the most dissatisfied. The experience that stood out for this small group was the racism they came across, mainly at school, and their

153

awareness that they were different from, or not fitting in with, those around them, and not having been accepted by some members of the wider adoptive family.

Severe emotional problems were recorded for 14 per cent of adopted people, with women declaring more problems than men. Nearly twice as many women (26 per cent) rated their self-esteem as low. There was a significant overlap between low self-esteem and severity of emotional problems. Those with better emotional health and higher levels of self-esteem were also more likely to report closer relationships with their adoptive parents, feeling happier for having been adopted and having developed a stronger sense of belonging. They were also more likely to say that they did not carry a sense of rejection or loss and that adoption did not affect their capacity to make relationships, their marriage, general well-being, education or career. The findings suggest that self-esteem and good emotional health are related to the quality of the adoptive relationships and experience.

While the sense of rejection by the birth family and feelings of loss were not inevitable, almost half of the adopted people, either always felt this way or sometimes, came to feel like this at some stage in their lives. Those who felt rejected were roughly the same people who also felt a sense of loss. For a significant number, feelings of rejection and loss were felt very strongly. A fifth of all adopted people felt strong rejection and loss at all stages in their lives or at least up to the contact stage. Significantly, fewer non-searchers than searchers reported such feelings at some stages, but the closer the relationship to the adoptive parents, the less likely they were to have experienced feelings of rejection and loss. Over 70 per cent of adopted people also reported that their adoption did not affect many areas of their lives such as making relationships, their marriage, general well-being, education and career.

10 Adopted people and contact

Adopted person:
I was very close to my adoptive mother and my adoptive father. Being close does not describe my feelings. I now also have an ongoing relationship with my birth family. Overall I feel more confident, have a higher self-esteem and my life in general has been enhanced.

This chapter charts the adopted person's establishment of contact with members of their birth family, providing an overview of contact outcomes after an average of eight years since it was established. It also relates the outcome of contact to the experiences of growing-up and to the adopted person's current general well-being. In essence, this chapter tries to answer the question of whether contact contributes to the adopted person's general well-being.

Strength of motivation to search

Of adopted people who initiated the search, over three-quarters (77 per cent) said that they were strongly or very strongly motivated to do so. Only five per cent said their motivation was not strong or not at all strong. The rest had mixed feelings about it (18 per cent). Wrobel *et al* (1996) reported in their study that the more curious children were about their origins, the lower their self-esteem, especially boys. The present study was not in a position to administer before and after self-esteem question-naires, and therefore it is not in a position to comment on self-esteem before and after contact and reunion. However, no association was found between strength of motivation and low self-esteem as scored well after contact had been established. The study did find that strong feelings of loss appeared to increase the motivation for contact. Searchers who felt a "strong" or "very strong" motivation reported that their main motive for searching was to obtain background information, rather than seeking a relationship, stressing that it was something they 'needed to know'. Other typical comments included: 'I needed to know the truth'; 'find out why put up for adoption'; 'wanted answers'; 'very keen to make contact'; 'needed to know where I came from and my family medical history'. Others referred to a kind of obsession that drove them on, whatever the time or cost. Several sounded more 'desperate', as they put it, to find out more by establishing contact. The minority who were not strongly motivated, or had mixed feelings about it, were mainly not sure they were doing the right thing because of their loyalty to their adoptive parents. Once the process started, though, they were as keen to proceed as others. One of them remarked that 'it was too good an opportunity to miss'. Adopted people who had not told their parents beforehand about the search mostly said that they did not want to upset them or to appear 'disloyal'. One of them remarked: 'I love them dearly and I didn't want to hurt them'. Another one asserted that, by not telling his parents, he came to value them more. However, a minority referred to initial strains because of their adoptive parents' anxieties about contact leading to loss of control of the situation. In most cases, the tensions were reported as having been 'ironed out'. Some found themselves reassuring their parents and telling them how important they still were to them.

Establishing contact

As expected, the most likely person that adopted people had direct face-to-face contact with was the birth mother (81 per cent) followed by half-siblings (74 per cent) and grandparents (47 per cent). A third had direct contact with a birth father (Figure 10.1). Of the 12 adopted people from a minority ethnic background, eight established direct contact with their birth mother, two indirect contact, and in the case of the remaining two, their mothers were deceased. Between a quarter and a fifth of adopted adults established direct contact with at least an aunt or uncle, in addition to the parent. A few contacts were also established with other relatives such as cousins and nephews. The majority of contacts with fathers followed from contact with mothers. In the case of siblings or half-siblings, direct contact was established with some but not others, or dropped with one but maintained with another.

Figure 10.1
Face-to-face contact with members of the birth family

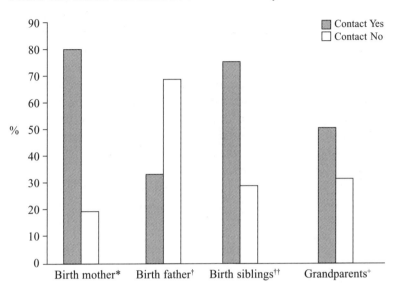

*N = 126 (8 birth mothers deceased); †N = 117 (missing 18 of which 9 deceased;
††N = 121 (missing 5); +N = 112 (missing 40 mostly deceased)

Initial expectations of contact

The connection between the search and the strong desire of many adopted people to find out more about their background, their family and medical history, and about their heritage has been known for sometime now (McWhinnie, 1967; Triseliotis, 1973). At the time of those studies there was a more clear-cut difference between those looking for background information and those also wanting to meet a birth relative. Over the years, and once the idea of searching received public approval, searching for information and for physical contact have become almost, but not entirely, synonymous. Although expectations overlapped extensively, when asked about their main one, almost two-fifths (37 per cent) of adopted people in this study wanted to establish roots and find out why they had been adopted (Table 10.1). Just over a quarter (27 per cent) wanted to see what the parent looked like and a fifth (20 per cent) to have news of them. Finally, 16 per cent hoped also to establish a relationship. With regard to all expectations, 90 per cent mentioned their wish to see what the parent looked like and 72 per cent to establish roots and find out why they had been adopted. Establishing a relationship was mentioned by 66 per cent. Underlying most of these expectations was the seeking of information to satisfy both curiosity and complex personal and social needs, which had mostly to do with identity and self-esteem. Establishing a relationship was only mentioned by 16 per cent as a *main* expectation. There were no significant differences in expectations or wishes between those of seekers and those sought. One of them summarised the multiplicity of expectations as follows:

> I did not necessarily want a relationship but to know why it had happened, whom I looked like, family history, illness, etc. I did not imagine birth relatives as people, more as a source of information.

Table 10.1
Adopted people's main expectations of contact

Expectations	Main expectations* %
Establish roots and find out why I was adopted	37
See what they looked like	27
To have news of them and whether they are well	20
Establish a relationship	16
Total	100

*N = 106 (missing 20)

Establish roots and why adopted

As Table 10.1 shows, the main expectation (37 per cent) of adopted adults in this study was finding out why they had been put up for adoption and to obtain background information. As other studies have also found, a key question for most adopted people is to know where they came from and find an answer to the question: 'who am I?' As many of them put it: 'fill in the gaps in my background'; 'complete the jigsaw of my life';

'find the real me'. Alone or overlapping was the question of 'why was I put up for adoption' and wanting to understand the reasons behind it. Being brought up in a largely different social context within which birth parents have more choices, it was difficult for some to comprehend how any mother would give up her child. Fathers were hardly mentioned. Some would add that they were not looking for a relationship or emotional attachment, but simply to know 'why'. As one of them put it, 'knowing would help me understand myself better'. They came to view this as a big gap in their understanding of themselves and their adoption. Others asked 'why me', 'why, why' or 'I want to hear it from the horse's mouth why'. Another typical comment was:

I would never have given away my daughter.

Some thirty years ago, Triseliotis (1973) made the comment that behind the wish of adopted people to know 'why adoption?' was a meta wish to know whether they were loved or not. Some, but not all, made a direct connection between wanting to know 'why' and whether they were loved and wanted by their own. Others thought it to be implicit. Some adopted people in this study were aware that the answers might turn out to be unpalatable or painful, but they still wanted to know. Not knowing meant that some carried images, mostly negative ones, that later proved to be quite or totally incorrect. Had they not found out, some reported they would have been carrying them throughout life. There were few instances of abandonment, incest or rape, but as the study focused on those who had established contact perhaps it did not come across the worst cases.

What they looked like

Nine out of every 10 adopted people mentioned wanting to know what the birth relative(s) looked like as one of a number of expectations and over a quarter gave it as their main one. It seemed important to them in terms of physical identity and as a way of placing themselves: 'see what they looked like'; 'desperate to see people who resembled me'; 'who do I look like?'; 'who am I?'; 'discover who I was like'; 'finding somebody who looked like me'. The following is a typical comment from this group:

There is and always has been a burning desire to see what my birth parents look like – to see someone who looks like me.

Having news and hearing if well

Having news of birth relatives and knowing that they were well, while also letting them see that they were well themselves, featured as the main expectation for 20 per cent of adopted people: seeing that the birth family 'were alright'; 'to see that especially my mother is well'; 'for them to know that I am happy and well'; that 'I'm OK' or 'that she made a good decision'.

Establishing a relationship

Although establishing a relationship was not at the forefront of the main expectations, many hoped that if everything worked out well it might follow. As will be seen later, a much higher proportion did develop relationships, but this largely followed after contact and having had the opportunity of getting to know birth relatives as people rather than as ideas. It might also have felt too disloyal to their adoptive parents to declare the establishment of a relationship as a primary initial expectation. A few stressed that they were not looking for a relationship, but only to have answers to the question 'why', what the relatives looked like, and to have background information and a family medical history. Others kept a more open mind, with one of them adding: 'a relationship would be the icing on the cake'. However, one of them remarked that he 'needed his mother back'. Along with the excitement about the prospect of meeting a birth parent or relative, there was also uncertainty, nervousness and the fear of hurting or being hurt: uncertainty had mainly to do with what they might find, nervousness to do with how to handle the situation, in particular a face-to-face meeting, and fear of hurting their adoptive parents or experiencing further rejection themselves.

Length of contact

For between 51 and 72 per cent of adopted people, after establishing contact with a birth family member, this had continued for five or more years. The contact with birth fathers was shorter, which reflects the fact that contact with them was established at a later stage rather than there being a higher dropout rate. Those who established contact with a father mostly learnt about him after meeting the mother and other birth relatives. Sibling contact appeared to be the most enduring (Table 10.2).

Table 10.2
Length of face-to-face contact with different birth relatives

Length	One yr or less %	2–4 years %	5 years + %	All %
Mother*	13	21	65	99
Father	19	30	51	100
Sibling	9	20	72	101
Grandparent	8	30	63	101
Aunt/uncles etc.	13	21	67	101

*98 (missing 28 because it does not include those who lost contact)

Frequency of contact

Most contact occurred a few times per year (Table 10.3). Leaving aside those cases where direct contact had stopped, the most frequent pattern of face-to-face contact with a birth mother was taking place once or twice a year. For another 39 per cent, it took place monthly or 3–4 times a year. Contact with siblings appeared fairly frequent, with almost half declaring contact monthly or 3–4 times a year (45 per cent). Contact with birth fathers was reported as being more frequent than with birth mothers but the small number of birth fathers means that a shift of one could affect the percentage disproportionately (N = 20). The most common pattern of direct contact with grandparents was once or twice a year. Adopted people in the sample group also kept contact with 38 other birth relatives, mostly aunts and uncles. The most common pattern of contact between them was once or twice a year or on special occasions. Main reasons quoted for not having more frequent contact was distance and a cooling off of the relationship. The latter was more likely to happen in relation to searching than sought mothers.

Table 10.3

Frequency of face-to-face contact for those who had contact for over a year

	B. Mother* *(N65)*	*B. Father* *(N20)*	*Siblings* *(N64)*	*Grandparents* *(N30)*
Frequency*	*%*	*%*	*%*	*%*
Mostly monthly	17	15	9	2
3–4 times a year	22	35	36	17
1–2 times a year	48	25	43	60
Special occasions	14	25	11	20
Total	101	100	99	99

What the relationship with the birth mother resembled

Adopted people who had face-to-face contact with their birth mother or father for over a year were asked to describe what the relationship was like at the start and currently. Their answers are set out in Figure 10.2. The most typical description to emerge for both stages was that of a friend or relative. The proportion of those who perceived it as of a parental type went up from 21 per cent initially to 24 per cent currently. Around a quarter described it as 'distant' or 'like a stranger' at the start but the proportion went down to a fifth currently. Those who described their birth mother's relationship with them as that of a 'parent' also reported a significantly less close relationship with their adoptive mother (p = 0.016)

Mostly as a birth parent

Almost a quarter (24 per cent) of adopted people had no doubt that the relationship they had developed was like a parent–child one. They would say that of 'mother and son'; 'father'; 'like that of a mother'; or 'definitely a mother'. Others wanted to stress both the parental and friendship aspect but with the emphasis on the parent–offspring relationship: 'a mixture of parent and friend'; 'mother and daughter but also friend'; 'son and mother but also friend'; or 'mother and best friend'. A handful referred to the relationship with their birth mother as being 'more natural' or 'more real', than that with the adoptive family. As one of them put it:

> *I never knew what love I had missed out on until I met her and my brothers.*

Figure 10.2

Description of initial and current face-to-face relationship with birth mother*

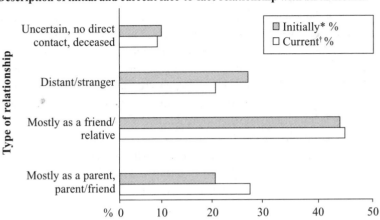

*N = 86 (missing 30); †N = 116 (missing 10)
Note: Some caution is needed when considering this graph because it is based on an analysis of both quantitative and qualitative material.

In contrast, many others were keen to stress the difference between their two mothers, adding that the adoptive mother was the only mother or 'she [birth mother] will never take the place of adopted mum'; 'very close family member but not a mother'; or 'I don't have with her the complete familiarity I have with my adoptive mother'. A more typical comment from this group:

> *Birth mother always be my real mum but will never take the place of my adoptive mum.*

Friend, parent or relative

Around half of adopted people were certain that their relationship to their birth mother was that of a friend or 'a distant friend or relative or long lost relative'; 'definitely a friend'; 'it is a friendship'; 'mother like an aunt, father like a friend'; or 'close female friend'. A more typical comment:

> *My relationship with my birth mother is one of friendship. I don't feel there could ever be a mother–daughter relationship.*

Distant/stranger

Almost a fifth of the adopted people said that the relationship was very distant or they were feeling like strangers to their birth parent, suggesting that the relationship did not go any further. The lack of a rearing experience and of common interests, or the perception of the other person as having "problems" contributed to the distancing. There was a suggestion that the longevity of these relationships was in doubt. In a number of cases there was a clash of expectations, such as the adopted person usually wanting mainly friendship or information and the parent wanting a parent–child relationship. As one of them put it:

> *I felt very uncomfortable because my birth mother wants a mother–daughter relationship whereas I want something more like a friendship as I have had a mother [my adoptive mother].*

The lack of shared experiences and memories was often quoted as a barrier to going back to a parent–child relationship. One of them remarked that, while having respect for his birth father for providing him the key to his heritage, nevertheless he was neither his emotional father nor his friend.

Current contact position

Currently, seven out of ten adopted people (70 per cent) continued to have some form of direct contact with a member of their birth family (Table 10.4). In another 12 per cent of cases, past face-to-face contact now became indirect. Previous indirect forms of contact largely continued in the same manner but in 10 per cent of cases they were discontinued.

Table 10.4
How contact stands currently

Face-to-face continues	It became indirect	Indirect continues	Indirect ceased	Other
70%	12%	6%	10%	2%

N = 126

Contact ceased

Between the time of establishing direct contact and the present, contact had ceased with almost a third of birth mothers and over two-fifths of birth fathers, almost a fifth of grandparents and over a quarter involving at least one sibling. No significant differences emerged between searching and sought adopted people. The surprising thing about continued face-to-face contact was the low level of reported lost contact with grandparents. It was the lowest when compared to other family members. Keeping in touch appeared more durable with grandparents than any other members of the birth family, irrespective of how close the relationship was reported to be.

Figure10.3
Face-to-face contact ceased

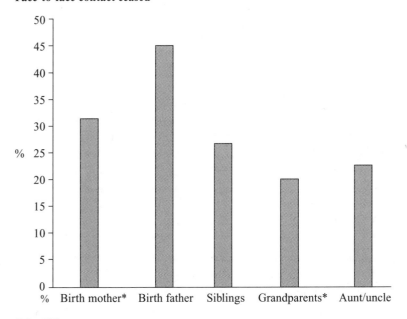

*N = 126
Note: 3% of birth mothers deceased between establishing direct contact and now; also 5% of birth fathers and 24% of grandparents. These were excluded from this graph.

165

Why contact ceased

When face-to-face or indirect contact ceased, it would mostly be at the initiative of the adopted person and less often that of the birth parent. Often the decision was mutual, and a relief to both, but not openly discussed. With both sides bringing some strong feelings from the past, it may not seem surprising that contact in some 30 per cent of cases came to an end either early or in later years. It would be unlikely that feelings from the past, the guilt associated with the parting on the part of the mother, and the rejection and loss felt by around half of adopted people would not have an impact on the development or end of the relationship. However, most explanations offered by adopted people focused mainly on the failure to establish mutually satisfying relationships. As we saw from a previous chapter, birth mothers mostly attributed the end of contact to the adopted person. Many of the reasons given by adopted people included not having things in common, no real connection, not liking each other, perceiving the birth relative as having personal or family problems, apathy or contact stopping at the relative's initiative sometimes simply by not responding, or contact causing upset to a member of the adoptive family. There were occasional comments such as 'lots of anger about', 'guilt' or 'not reconciling with the past'. On occasions, contact was also said to have simply lapsed either out of apathy or saying they should meet 'sometime' but never doing so. Some of them said: 'not suited'; 'not a big priority'; 'not being motivated'; or 'never enough time' to start all over. This was perhaps another way of saying that there was not much in common between the parties, but without closing the door altogether.

We agreed contact if and when necessary and it simply hasn't been necessary.

As already mentioned, incompatibility or lack of common ground or getting upset during meetings or not being understood, were some of the main reasons offered by adopted people for why contact with the birth mother had stopped. Typical explanations included being different and living very different lives or difficulties arising in the relationship. Perception of the birth mother as someone who had personal problems and making the relationship unrewarding was another key reason, as the following examples show: 'She [birth mother] was mixed up'; 'neurotic'; 'emotionally unstable'; or 'contact was causing me more upset than benefit'. One mother threatened to have no more contact if the adopted person contacted a sibling. Another adopted person remarked about his birth mother:

She was very neurotic and blamed me for her life . . . we might be connected by blood but we are not alike.

Contact was sometimes perceived as causing problems within the birth mother's family, mostly for the mother's husband/partner, e.g. 'her husband didn't like the idea of me turning up' or 'her husband was making life difficult for her because she was seeing me'. A particularly frank comment:

I don't see birth mother because of her husband. Don't see birth father because I don't like him.

On several occasions, however, direct contact was stopped because it was said to be causing upset to the birth mothers. One birth mother threatened to go to court if the adopted person persisted and another forbade the adopted person to ever contact her or her children. More rarely, contact was said to have caused problems for the adopted person's family, such as interference by the birth mother in the running of the family, wanting the children to address her as "grandmother" or being jealous of the adoptive mother.

Stopping contact with the birth father

Broadly similar reasons were given for stopping contact with a birth father as with a birth mother, i.e. 'just didn't get on'; 'I did not like him'; 'had nothing in common'; 'father refused responsibility for me'; or 'he has his own family commitments'. Several said that once their curiosity was satisfied there was no point in continuing. More candidly, one of them remarked: 'No further room for each other in our lives'. The opposite could equally be true, i.e. the birth father not being interested or contact not being 'convenient' because of his family responsibilities. One adopted person tried to re-establish contact some years later, but the birth father was not interested.

Stopping contact with other birth relatives

Again, broadly similar explanations were offered for why contact with a sibling stopped, e.g. 'no real connection'; 'no common interest'; 'just met once. No desire to see them again and vice versa'. One adopted person gave up contact with the sister because 'her letters seemed bitter, angry and confrontational'. It was not unusual for contact with one sibling to stop but continue with another.

Fluidity of relationships

Relationships being fluid, it was not unusual in a handful of cases for adopted people to say that they stopped contact at one time, but resumed it after a period or that they were planning to. This could mostly happen after falling out with a member of the birth parent's other family. The adopted person or the birth relative moving abroad, or to a distant part of the country, could also signal the end of the face-to-face relationship, but in most such cases indirect forms of contact continued, including by email. Moving to Australia, New Zealand or the USA was not uncommon and both sides expected to meet again at some future date.

Closeness of current relationships with birth family members

For adopted people with face-to-face contact, the closest relationship was with siblings (69 per cent), followed by birth mother (63 per cent), then birth father (55 per cent) and finally grandparents (45 per cent) (Table 10.5). The closer the adopted person's current relationship to their birth mother, the more pleased they were that they had searched or had been sought ($p < 0.001$); the more likely they were to say that their initial expectations had been met ($p < 0.001$); the more positive they rated the overall contact experience ($p < 0.001$); the more relaxed they came to feel after contact ($p = 0.008$); the more secure ($p = 0.007$) and the more complete ($p = 0.002$); and the more likely to report that their self-esteem had improved since contact ($p = 0.002$). Relationships with siblings were particularly valued because they appeared to generate high levels of affinity. Unlike meeting a parent, there was less of a generation gap and a sibling could also tell the adopted person more about the parent. The relationship was also uncomplicated by the baggage of the past.

Table 10.5
Closeness of the relationship now

Closeness	Birth mother* %	Birth father %	Siblings %	Grandparents %
Very close/close	63	55	69	45
Mixed	19	15	15	23
Not very close/not at all close	18	30	15	32
Total	100	100	99	100

*N = 62 (missing 36)

Benefits derived from contact

Half of the adopted people in the sample said that they derived many benefits from having had contact with their birth parent (Figure 10.4). Only three per cent reported having had no benefits at all, with the rest (46 per cent) saying that they had some. One of them added that among the benefits was the realisation that 'blood does not tie you to someone'. There were no significant differences between searchers and non-searchers. A range of benefits were identified and although difficult to separate because of overlaps, a number of groupings emerged and are

Figure 10.4
Benefits derived from having had contact with a birth parent

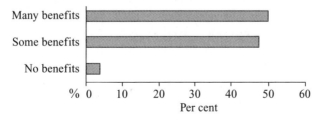

N = 122 (missing 4)

summarised below. Not surprisingly, the benefits reflected the kinds of expectations adopted people had before establishing contact.

Specific benefits of contact

Personal benefits

Adopted people reported many personal benefits to have come out of contact, by making reference to 'psychological development'; 'personal satisfaction'; 'forming relationships'; 'developing a sense of self'; 'grew as a person'; 'knowing myself'; 'found my soul'; 'feeling less emotional baggage to carry'; 'feeling wanted and honoured for what I am'; or as another one put it:

> Mental well-being, closeness, sense of identity ... an endless list of positive things.

Many adopted people did not think that because of these gains they should not have been adopted. Several remarked that had they been brought up by their mother, or any other birth family members, they would not have been the person they were. One who said that he felt he was missing something by not being brought up by his birth family, said he came to appreciate his adoptive family more after contact.

Genealogical and identity issues

Confirming previous studies (McWhinnie, 1967; Triseliotis, 1973; Howe and Feast, 2000), a significant number of adopted people put the emphasis on the benefits which arose from contact in terms of genealogical, historical and biographical terms and linked them to identity issues. Typical comments included: 'completing my self'; 'piece of puzzle found'; 'complete and secure'; 'feel whole'; 'knowing my roots'; 'a chapter of my life that can now be closed'; 'completed my history, 'discovering my identity'; 'now I feel I have some roots'; ' or 'the puzzle is complete'. All these appeared to be identity enhancing and provided answers to the question 'who am I', establishing who they were, 'a sense of identity, closeness and mental-well being', 'gaining confidence – feeling complete' or simply 'discovered my identity'. The following is a typical comment:

Sense of identity of knowing who you are and where you come from, getting answers.

Associated with the above benefits was also the view, expressed by some, that they had now 'completed the jigsaw' and could move on with their lives without being pre-occupied with the past and its gaps: 'I know where I come from and can move on now'; 'I closed an unfinished chapter'; 'have a much better understanding of who I am'. Gains for the few black and minority ethnic people featuring in the sample were similar as those of others:

Contact has given me a sense of self and cultural identity.

Knowing why given up

Knowing why they had been adopted was a major expectation for many in relation to searching, and contact offered them the opportunity to find out directly from their mothers and sometimes from other birth relatives. Most of them were satisfied with what they heard and there were hardly any recriminations. As one of them said: 'she told me why she had no choice at the time and it was OK for me'. Satisfaction was also gained from learning 'that she did not want to give me up'; 'I now know why and who'; 'finding I was loved'; 'knowing she cared'; and 'knowing why I was adopted'. There was satisfaction in being able to tell a mother that they did not resent her for giving them up and also letting her know that they were well and had a happy adoption. However, a handful also expressed some regrets, feeling that they should never have been parted from their birth families, more so after they learnt that another sibling had remained.

Developing new relationships

For a great number of adopted people other benefits from contact were associated with the relationship or friendship with a birth mother, father or other relative, which evolved over time. Where the relationship lasted, there was no doubting the great satisfaction felt by adopted people. More importantly, most of them stressed that the new relationships were not at the expense of those with their adoptive parents, but simply additional, and 'enriched' their lives. There were numerous positive comments and the following is only a small selection: 'very pleased with the relationship'; 'she's all and more than I could have expected'; 'no barriers to the friendship I have with my mother'; 'an extended family for my children'; and 'I see her every other day, talk to her by phone on the days I don't see her, we are very close'. Another added:

> I have had a relationship with my birth mother for six years, which has grown stronger during the last three.

Physical recognition

A large number of adopted people reported that contact had resulted in them being able now to recognise family resemblances after having seen what a parent or birth relative looked like. Some commented that seeing likeness in their mothers and recognising themselves in her, or in a sibling, gave them an enhanced sense of who they were. One added that in the past, 'I would search in a crowd looking for someone who looked like me but no longer'.

Knowing they are well

It was the hope of some two-thirds of adopted people that through contact they would find out about the welfare and well-being of their birth relatives and in the great majority of cases there was satisfaction after finding that they were well. Although it was understandable, as shown in a previous chapter, that one of the main concerns of birth mothers before contact was to know how well and happy the adopted person had been, it was not anticipated that so many adopted people would also feel the same about their birth relatives. The concern possibly arose not so much out of guilt, but from the realisation that parting with a child for adoption could not have been easy for their parents.

Medical history

At some point in their lives most people are very likely to see a doctor or go to hospital with a complaint or the more pleasurable event of giving birth. Inevitably, they will be asked about their family history and some will admit that they do not know. In our sample, some adopted people reported that they felt embarrassed when unable to answer simple questions about their family's medical history. As a result, an appreciable number mentioned the importance of learning about their medical history and whether there were any hereditary diseases in the family or not.

Benefits derived from contact with other relatives

When it came to identifying benefits derived from contact with other birth family members, there was special reference to the pleasure felt from meeting half-siblings and, for two people, full siblings. There was no mistaking the pleasure many said they experienced on meeting a half-sister, a niece, a brother or a grandparent. Siblings, along with aunts and uncles, proved to be a rich source of background information, especially when the birth mother or father was either dead or not available. One of them remarked how his sister was able to tell him a lot about their mother who had passed away. Another received photos of his mother who had died. For these and others, relationships also followed: 'being introduced to two delightful half-sisters was not only good for me but also for them'; 'am developing a close relationship with my half-sister'; 'I now have the sister I never had'. However, some 16 per cent reported no benefits from establishing contact with siblings, finding that their interests and outlook were dissimilar.

The fact that almost all adopted people identified one or more benefits should not detract from the fact that, for those whose birth relatives refused or terminated contact, there was more pain and disillusionment, a point to be discussed later. A small number, while being glad of the benefits derived from contact, also commented on the upheaval they went through and that the benefits were achieved at a personal cost or proved unsettling and traumatic. One added that she felt caught between the two different 'cultures' and outlooks of her birth and adoptive families because they were so different.

For whom contact was a positive experience

Most of the benefits of contact, as perceived by the sample of adopted people, were for themselves (85 per cent), followed by their birth relative(s) (69 per cent), while their adoptive parents (36 per cent) were well behind (Table 10.6). The more positive they rated the overall contact

173

experience for themselves, the closer also their current relationship to their birth parents, the less rejected they felt for having been given up for adoption, the less they felt a sense of loss, the higher their self-esteem, the fewer emotional problems they scored on the GHQ, and the more likely to report that, after contact, their self-esteem had improved, they felt more relaxed and more secure (levels of significance in all these areas ranged from p = 0.022 to p < 0.001).

Table 10.6
For whom was the experience of contact positive: self, birth relative(s) or the adoptive parents?

Level	Adopted person* %	Birth relative(s) %	Adoptive parents %
Very positive/positive	85	69	36
Not sure	9	23	28
Very negative/negative	5	6	17
No effect	1	2	8
Deceased/unaware of contact	–	–	12
Total	100	100	101

*N = 122 (missing 4)

The 85 per cent of adopted people who said that the experience was positive for themselves gave similar explanations as before about the benefits they derived from contact. They again used comments such as: enriched, pleased, very positive or happy. Only a minority had either mixed feelings or were negative about it, attributed mainly to unsatisfactory relationships and lack of common interests. Possibly the most disillusioned was one person who said that his adoptive parents had been 'hurt' by the experience and that his birth mother wished she had 'stayed away'.

The adoptive parents were singled out by their adopted sons or daughters as the one of the three parties who benefited least from contact (36 per cent). Although the majority of adoptive parents were supportive of contact, either from the start or afterwards, adopted people who perceived some resistance in their attitude thought that they did not perhaps benefit as much as themselves or their birth mothers. Comments included: 'mother felt threatened and jealous'; 'unsettled and angry about my contact'; 'she felt left out'; 'we don't talk about it really'; 'my parents were not too keen' and other similar comments. A more extreme example was the adoptive mother who was said to have felt:

> *. . . betrayed and that what she had done over the years was worthless. She felt my birth mother didn't deserve to have a relationship with me.*

Some adopted people sensed that, even when their parents were very supportive, when it came to actual face-to-face contact, the latter still felt threatened or anxious about the long-term outcome and a fear of being 'deserted' for the new family.

Almost seven out of ten adopted adults perceived their birth mothers as having benefited from contact, compared to 85 per cent of themselves. Many reported that it had been 'good for the birth mother'; 'positive experience for the birth mother'; 'both of us gained something'; 'wonderful for her'. Some comments encapsulated how contact was perceived as being more positive for them rather than for the birth mother but perhaps raised unnecessary anxieties for their adoptive parents:

> *Excellent for birth mother, good for myself. I think that my adoptive parents have an underlying feeling that they will lose me as my birth relationship develops.*

Adopted people of minority ethnic background

Twelve adopted people in the sample described themselves as being black or from a minority ethnic background. Of these, eight had established direct contact and two indirect. At the time of the study only three (25 per cent) were still in direct contact with their birth mother and one reported a close relationship. Where contact had been only indirect, it had ceased. What these small numbers suggest is that contact between adopted adults of minority ethnic background and their birth mother was less enduring compared to the rest of the sample. These small numbers could suggest that adopted people of minority ethnic background, and.

who grew up in all white households, were rather alienated from both their white and black/minority ethnic families or cultures.

Satisfaction with the present level of contact

Seven out of ten adopted people said they were happy with the present level of contact, but the rest were not. Searchers were somewhat less happy compared to non-searchers. However, in the remaining cases (30 per cent), contact had stopped either at the initiative of the birth parent(s) or the adopted person. Those who were happy with the present level of contact felt so because things were working out well between them and their birth relatives. Satisfaction was associated with the relationship or 'friendship' continuing, even if sometimes they could not see each other more frequently. The higher the adopted person's self-esteem, the more likely they were to say that they were happy with the current level of contact (p = 0.012). If the birth family had taken the initiative to stop, the adopted person could be 'disappointed', 'upset' or 'feel very rejected'. One or two hoped to try again, while several said that that was the end. Rejection, however, could come from either side. For example, a number of adopted people made it clear that it was their decision to stop contact or keep it simply at the level of birthday and Christmas cards. A few added that they did not even feel the need for contact now. The reasons were similar to those referred to earlier, mainly incompatibility in interests and outlook. If some regretted the distance between themselves and a birth relative, at least one of them was glad about it. Another one remarked that he had his life and they (birth family) had theirs and it was time to get on. In yet another case, contact was stopped by mutual agreement. The adopted person remarked:

> *Contact was mutually ended without any final good-byes. I do feel uneasy that any of my birth family may want to try and get in touch again because I'm happy with the family I have.*

What happened to the feelings of rejection and loss?

As can be seen from Table 10.7, between half and two-thirds of adopted people who, before contact, were experiencing feelings of rejection and loss said that following contact these either disappeared or lessened. For about a quarter they remained the same and for between 6 and 17 per cent they got worse. There were no significant differences between searchers and non-searchers. Adopted people who reported that feelings of rejection and loss disappeared or lessened after contact, reported also feeling significantly closer to the adoptive mother than those who reported that the feelings remained the same or worsened (p = 0.031).

Table 10.7
The feelings of rejection and loss after contact

Feelings	Disappeared/ lessened %	Remained the same %	Worsened %	Total %
Rejection*	55	28	17	100
Loss[†]	68	26	6	100

*N = 71 (missing 55); [†]N = 69 (missing 57)
This table is based solely on these who said they had experienced feelings of rejection and loss.

Disappeared/lessened

Adopted people said that contact with a birth parent or relative seemed to remove or significantly lessen any feelings of rejection. This came about either through finding from letters or through direct contact why they had been given up and by the kind of reception they had received from members of their birth family. Learning about the mother's circumstances at the time, such as that she had 'no choice', had been 'pressurised' or had had the decision 'taken away from her', seemed to satisfy them. Others reported that it had helped to meet their birth mother and hear from her why they had been adopted:

> *My birth mother reaffirmed everything my adoptive parents had said and also hearing how tormented and hurt she was and what an impossible decision she had to make – not taken lightly and has suffered ever since.*

One of those who previously felt rejected and that part of him was missing remarked:

It is strange that I felt whole again, as if some limb or part of me had been missing. I felt a sense of belonging and that I would actually be OK.

Those whose sense of loss seemed to disappear or lessen attributed it mainly to meeting a parent, learning more about themselves and the birth family's circumstances and/or hearing that they had been loved and wanted. Typical comments included: 'finding the missing piece'; 'learning about my birth and seeing the likeness between mother and daughter'; 'talking to her about the circumstances of the adoption'; 'filling the gap in my life'; 'many questions answered, loss gone'; and 'simply relieved to find that birth relatives were safe and well'. Meeting the birth parent and finding out what they looked or were like and knowing why they were given up seemed to satisfy many in this group.

No difference

Of those who originally felt rejected, 28 per cent said that contact had made no difference to their sense of rejection. One of them remarked that although explanations were offered for why they had been 'given up', nevertheless 'at the end of the day I was still rejected'. Another added, 'I still at times have a great fear of being abandoned'. And a third observed:

The feelings are still there, though I understand them better perhaps. Understanding feelings though does not make them hurt any less.

As with those who experienced a sense of rejection, a significant proportion of those carrying feelings of loss qualified the benefits from contact, stressing that the sense of loss can decrease but never disappear. They made illustrative comments such as: 'more understanding but the feeling is still there'; 'you can't wipe out 30 years of feelings'; or 'it was good to meet them but it is not a healing experience'. And another one:

I haven't worked through all my fears and especially around 'loss and abandonment'.

A greater number of adopted people said that following contact their feelings of rejection worsened than their feelings of loss did, mainly because of second rejections they experienced from birth relatives who ceased contact or did not want to meet them. Some 'felt angry and rejected for a second time'; 'felt rejected when she did not reply to my letters'; or simply 'my feelings [of rejection] get stronger as the contact gets less'. Anger was more likely to arise where the adopted person found the parent's explanation for 'why adoption' not satisfactory. In one case the adopted person realised that the reasons given by her birth mother did not tie up with those given her by her adoptive mother, and she believed the latter's version. Another found the birth mother's explanation 'selfish':

> She did [give me up] because if she had kept me she would have no social life. She didn't want to be tied down.

How pleased now with having searched?

Four out of five adopted people in our sample were very pleased or pleased that they had searched or had been sought, but almost a fifth had mixed feelings about it. The rest (2 per cent) were not at all pleased (Figure 10.5).

Figure 10.5
Reaction to having searched or been sought

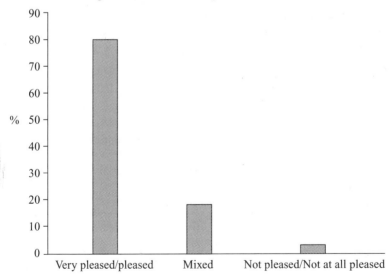

N = 125 (Missing 1)

179

The more pleased the adopted person was about searching or being sought, the closer the current relationship with their birth mother (p = 0.005). Also, the more pleased they felt about having searched or been sought, the higher their self-esteem (p = 0.032).

The vast majority who were pleased had no doubt that searching, and even being sought, was the right thing. Far from having regrets, they were very pleased about it. As some of them put it: 'I needed to do it'; 'pleased that at last it happened'; 'it had to be done'; and 'best thing in the world'. The mixed or negative reactions came from those who experienced rejection, were disappointed about the quality of the new relationship or resented the new demands made on them. One described the outcome as 'a total disaster'.

The meeting of expectations

Three-quarters of adopted people (75 per cent) reported that their initial expectations or wishes were very well or well met (Table 10.8). Only six per cent said the opposite, with almost a fifth (19 per cent) seeing the outcome as mixed. Somewhat more non-searchers than searchers reported that their wishes were met, but the difference did not reach full statistical significance. Asked to say how their answers compared to how they felt a year ago, just over three-fifths said it remained the same (76 per cent), one out of every seven described it as better (15 per cent), and the remaining as worse or not certain (9 per cent). Adopted people who said their expectations had been met reported closer current relationships to their birth parents (p < 0.001) and higher self-esteem (p = 0.005). Expectations were less likely to have been met for those who, prior to contact, carried strong feelings of rejection by their birth families (p = 0.006).

Table 10.8
How well the expectations of adopted people were met

Very well/well %	Mixed %	No or not at all %	Total %
75	19	6	100

N = 119 (missing 7)

As with their reaction to the search, expectations were met for so many because, they said, they were able to obtain more genealogical information, find out more about why they had been adopted, learn more about themselves, put a face on themselves, having had many gaps filled plus the forming of relationships in the majority of cases. (To avoid repetition see earlier comments under benefits from contact.) The main disappointment, which gave rise to mixed feelings about contact, or to outright frustration and sometimes distress, focused again around issues such as the non-fulfilment of the expectation for a closer relationship or that a birth parent or relative would not welcome contact. Others were disappointed that what they found did not live up to their expectations or that they could not obtain more background information, mainly on the birth father's side. The rejection of further contact came as a big disappointment, especially after building up hopes over many years. In one case, an adopted person wished contact had not taken place because he could have continued imagining what it would be like.

Relationships with adoptive parents after contact

This part of the study examined the impact of contact on the relationship because, as will be seen in a later chapter, a significant proportion of adoptive parents were initially apprehensive about it. Compared to the time when adopted people had started the search, just over half of them said that their relationship with their adoptive family remained the same. One-third said that it was enhanced, with the remaining 14 per cent saying that it had deteriorated (Table 10.9). There were no significant differences between searchers and sought. However, the closer adopted people felt to their adoptive mother before contact, the more likely they were to say that they became even closer after contact (p = 0.004). Those who had felt rejected by their birth families in childhood were more likely to report an enhanced relationship with their adoptive parents after contact than those who had not (p = 0.030). Of course, most of those who had not felt rejected already had a good relationship with their adoptive family.

Table 10.9

Changes in the adopted adults' relationship with their adoptive family since they had searched or had been sought

No change	Enhanced	Deteriorated	All
53%	33%	14%	100

N = 122 (missing 4)

The majority (53 per cent) of the sample who said that the relationship did not change explained that they already had a good relationship with the adoptive parents before contact and it continued like that afterwards. As some of them said: 'good as ever'; 'they were always my family and continue to be my family; 'it would never change because I love them very much'; and 'it made me appreciate them more'. In many cases, they added, their parents had supported or actively helped them in the search. One of them, like some others, made reference to the emotional turmoil that can result from the search and contact, adding: 'Nobody can ever replace my adoptive parents'. And another:

I have gone through incredible emotions. My respect and love for them [adoptive parents] is something I will never lose.

In a significant number of cases, and irrespective of the final outcome, strains did develop between parents and children because of the search and contact but these were mostly resolved, more so after the parents realised that the search and contact were not leading to the loss of their son or daughter. However, as some adopted people observed, the experience proved very stressful for a parent, or it was a difficult time or the parents came under strain. As one of them put it:

They were under great strain during search and initial contact with birth parents. This made me feel, and still does now, a lot closer to them.

The one-third who said that the relationship with their adoptive family had been enhanced as a result of the search and contact made many enthusiastic comments. They reported that contact had brought them closer together now than before, made them realise what they have in them, learnt to appreciate them more, or 'brought them closer with more love for them'. The following was one of a number of typical comments:

Contact has helped to confirm the strength of feeling and relationship I have with my parents.

A small minority (14 per cent) said that the relationship had deteriorated partially or completely, mainly because of the reaction of the adoptive parents to the search and contact, or that the adopted person had been "disowned" for a period or found it hard to talk to them about their birth family. One parent could not understand how and why their son wanted to get in touch with the mother 'who gave him up', while another adopted person observed that her parents disliked her birth family and declined to meet them. It was her view that they perceived them as a threat. Another one made reference to being "disowned" at one stage by her parents and a second had changed his surname to that of the birth family. Yet another said:

I came to realise how awful my adoptive family was after I found members of my birth family.

There was evidence of strains and some distancing between these adopted people and their parents. However, these tensions were already present and contact had simply exacerbated them.

Asked to say whether meeting their birth relatives had diminished their feelings for their adoptive parents, 97 per cent said 'no'. The very high level of 'no' meant that no statistical associations could be carried out. Even the few who had said that the relationship with their parents had deteriorated after contact maintained that their feelings for them had not changed. Most respondents were at pains to say that nothing had changed in their relationship towards their adoptive parents: 'if anything we were brought closer together'; 'respect them more'; 'my feelings have grown'; 'still very close'; 'love them very much'; 'glad I grew up where I did'; and 'nobody can ever replace my adoptive parents'. Other typical comments included:

I love my [adoptive] mum and dad very much. I wouldn't have become the person I am today without them. I'm absolutely sure of that now that I've traced so I'm very grateful to them.

Current relationships with the adoptive parents

When it came to relationships with their adoptive parents after contact, the closeness was rated at about the same level as before contact (Table 10.10). Again, there was hardly any difference in closeness towards adoptive mothers and fathers with seven out of ten describing their relationship as close or very close. Closeness with siblings and other relatives was rated significantly lower.

Table 10.10

Adopted person's *post-contact* relationship with their adoptive parents and other relatives

Closeness	Mother* %	Father %	Siblings %	Grandparents %	Aunts/ uncles %
Very close/close	73	71	51	68	43
Mixed	19	16	28	11	26
Not close/not at all	8	13	21	21	31
Total	100	100	100	100	100

*N = 124 (missing 2)
Note: At the time of the study 14% of mothers, 33% of fathers, 3% of siblings and 69% of grandparents were deceased.

Significantly higher levels of closeness after contact were reported by adopted people who had felt loved by their parents, whose adoption had been more openly discussed at home ($p = 0.009$) and who had not carried a strong sense of rejection or loss through different stages of their lives. The closer the current relationship with their adoptive parents, the happier they felt about being adopted and the more they felt they belonged. Current closeness to their adoptive parents was also associated with adopted people saying that being adopted had not affected them in any of the following areas of life: making relationships, their marriage, their well-being, their education, or their career. The closer also the post-contact relationship with the adoptive parents, the fewer emotional health problems were likely to be scored on the GHQ and the higher the adopted person's self-esteem. The opposite was also true, that is, if they reported weak or distant relationships with their adoptive parents. Levels of significance in all these variables ranged from p = 0.023 to p < 0.001.

The Adoption Contact Register, rights and adoption as an institution

The aim of this part of the study was to elicit the experiences of adopted people, some of the principles of contact and also the place of adoption in society.

The Adoption Contact Register

Two-thirds of adopted people reported that they knew about the existence of the Adoption Contact Register, but three-quarters of non-searchers had not heard about it. Some of those who had not known about it found out after they had established contact through the adoption agency or after a birth relative had contacted them. Of those who knew about the Register, three out of ten had entered their names. Some had chosen not to register out of fear of losing the initiative or losing control. They wanted to have the initiative and have time to think things over, or seek advice about how to 'cope' with developments: 'wanted to be in charge' or 'very worried that I would have nobody to help me cope if a match was found'. In one case it took ten years before the parent had also registered and contact was established. Another had refused to pay the fee to register, saying it was 'a right to know'.

Rights of birth relatives

Almost one-third of adopted people (31 per cent) were in favour of birth relatives (including birth parents) having the right to obtain identifying information about the adopted person, once she had reached the age of 18. Almost two-fifths (38 per cent) said 'no' and the rest (31 per cent) were not sure. One of those who had sought out his mother said:

I have very grave concerns about this proposal. I feel that this is an area where the ball needs to remain firmly in the court of the adopted person.

Others stressed that the child's family were now the adopters, and not the birth parents. One of them added that the birth parent had effectively

185

'waived' all rights to the child and went on to say: 'It is the right only of the adopted person to seek information. Contact registers, however, are a wonderful thing.' Contrary to expectation, 43 per cent of those who had been sought by a birth relative were supportive of the idea. As one of them put it: 'Why not? I would like to know that my mother could contact me if she wanted to.'

Encouraging adopted people to have contact with birth relatives

In answer to the question of whether all adopted people should be encouraged to have contact with birth relatives, there was an equal split between those who agreed (27 per cent) and those who opposed the idea (27 per cent). The majority, almost half (46 per cent), were not sure. There were no differences between searchers and sought. Of those who disagreed or were unsure, many took exception to the idea that any one should exercise any pressure on them. They felt not only the word 'encouraged' was too strong, but also stressed that contact is a matter for the individual to decide and not for others to do so on their behalf. Possibly emphasising that adopted people should not be treated as children, especially in adult life, they put stress on 'choice': 'it is a matter for the individual'; or that 'no one should feel they ought to because it happens to be the done thing'. Typical comments included:

It should be their choice, not pressed upon them.

Surely it is up to the individual as to how much contact they would have. If you want contact you will have it, if you don't you won't.

Of those who agreed, and quoting from their own experience, they stressed that contact could lead to benefits for the adopted person and the birth relative. One of those sought commented: 'I agree it's a good thing as it's worked for me'. A searcher stressed that 'encouragement' needs to be preceded with 'respect for the adopted person's place in dealing with the issue'.

No more adoption?

The question of whether adoption should continue to exist as an institution was asked because it has recently surfaced in a number of contexts, including the occasional autobiographical account by a birth mother or adopted person who had a negative experience (see, for example, Robinson 2000; and the proposal by the Law Commission of New Zealand for abolishing the legal concept of adoption and replacing it with a modified version of guardianship, Selwyn and Sturges, 2001). Policies in the State of Victoria in Australia have already moved in this direction, certainly in the case of older children (Marshall and McDonald, 2001). Similarly, most Western European countries do not allow adoption without parental consent. Nine out of ten adopted people disagreed or disagreed strongly that there should be no adoption in society. Only four per cent supported the idea, with another seven per cent remaining neutral.

Figure 10.6
Should there be no adoption in society?

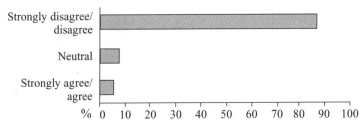

N = 124 (missing 2)

The vast majority who were in favour of adoption, referred either to their own satisfactory experience or to the 'plight' of children growing up in institutions. Besides stressing that adoption is 'an essential part of our society', there was emphasis on the need of some children to have 'a family to call their own'. Others referred to their own experience, making comments such as 'better upbringing than I would have received from my birth mother'; 'a wonderful childhood'; 'it opened doors for me that would not have existed'; 'fantastic opportunity'. Some others commented:

I have had 18 superb years growing up in a loving family – no children's home could ever replicate that.

Adoption benefited my family and me enormously.

Adoption gives hope to some, a better life chance and love to others and of course a great deal of love and happiness.

Emphasis was also placed on the security offered by a 'stable and loving family'; the provision of 'a more stable start in life'; 'opportunity to be brought up in a loving family environment'; 'a lifeline for both children and parents'; 'chance of a normal family life'; and 'I would have hated to be brought up in an institution'. The following is a more extensive and typical comment: 'In our present society there has to be every means possible to help unwanted, accidental, unloved children. Adoption is the answer.' Another one said:

Well, I wouldn't have wanted to grow up in a children's home – would you?

The few qualifications made were mainly about supporting birth families to bring up their child if this is what they want and are capable of, making certain that adoption is properly carried out, and that detailed background information is passed on to the adopters to share with the child in subsequent years:

It depends on circumstances and the reasoning behind the application – if it takes a child away from danger, e.g. abuse of any kind, then this can only benefit the child if nobody else.

Unfortunately, adoption is a part of life, for whatever reason. I believe it should be conducted professionally because of its sensitive nature.

One woman spoke bitterly about the sexual abuse by her adoptive father, but still said that there was a place for adoption instead of children growing up in institutions:

Abuse, both sexual and physical are rife, and mentally and psychologically it is very difficult for children living with "strangers" . . , My adoptive parents continually reminded me what I would have been

had they not adopted me. Who knows? One is always made to feel
grateful, i.e. love is not unconditional in the adoptive family.

Summary

The main expectation of both searchers and the small group of non-searchers was to obtain background genealogical information, find out why they were 'put up' for adoption, followed by wanting to see what birth relatives looked like, whether they were well and, finally perhaps establish a relationship. Along with the excitement about the prospect of meeting a birth parent or relative, there was also uncertainty, nervousness and the fear of hurting or being hurt. After an average of eight years, 78 per cent were still in some form of contact with a birth relative, with around seven out of ten having continued to have face-to-face contact with their birth mother.

Almost three out of ten came to look upon the birth mother as a parent but rather more (52 per cent) viewed her as a friend or friend/relative. For the remaining 18 per cent, the relationship was either distant or the birth mother felt like a stranger. Almost two-thirds described close or very close relationships with their birth mother, only slightly below those reported with adoptive parents (72 per cent). Contact had ceased in around 30 per cent of cases because of incompatible interests, different outlooks, poor relationships, the birth parent's personal problems, rejection by a birth parent (mostly the mother) which on occasions was brought about because it had caused problems mainly within the birth mother's family, or rejection by the adopted person. Adopted people were more likely to lose contact with a searching than sought birth parent.

Half of adopted people reported that they had derived 'many' benefits from contact with another 46 per cent saying they had derived 'some'. Only four per cent reported none. Eight out of ten were pleased that they had searched or had been sought, and for three-quarters their expectations had been very well or well met. The more pleased the adopted person was with searching or being sought, the closer the current relationship with their adoptive parents and the birth mother, and the higher their self-esteem and emotional health. Contact was perceived as having been most beneficial to themselves, then their birth mother and, well behind, the adoptive parents. Also, 97 per cent indicated that meeting their birth relatives made no difference to their feelings for their adoptive parents.

More commonly, close relationships were reported with both the adoptive parents and with the birth family. A sense of belonging and being loved by the adopters correlated with closer relationships with the birth mother, higher levels of self-esteem, better emotional health, an improved outlook following contact, the overall contact experience having been more positive, coming to feel more secure and more relaxed, satisfaction with the present level of contact, expectations having been met, the absence or reduction of feelings of rejection and loss, and areas of their lives such as making relationships, marriage, education, well-being and career not having been affected by their adoptive status. There were indications that non-searchers were more likely to report such feelings.

Where contact had been established, feelings of rejection and loss, if present, were said to have either disappeared or lessened for the majority of adopted people. However, for about a quarter of the sample, contact was said to have made no difference. Those who carried strong feelings of rejection and loss were also more likely than the rest to rate the overall contact experience as less positive and to report that their emotional outlook had worsened since contact.

A persistent proportion of between 10 to 20 per cent of adopted people reported that feelings of rejection and loss continued and also that being adopted had affected their marriage, well-being, education, career and the making of relationships. Broadly the same group reported lower self-esteem and poor emotional health and were less likely to be satisfied with the outcome of contact or to say that their expectations of contact had been met. The same group was also more likely to give negative answers when evaluating outcome questions about being adopted or about the contact and reunion experience. Low self-esteem and poor emotional health impacted on a number of outcome variables, and the other way around was equally true, depending on the variable.

11 Parenting the adopted child

Adoptive parent:
Having adopted filled the gap in our lives. He grew up knowing he was adopted. The teen years were trying but he grew out of it. We have seen him grow up and thrive and we now have grandchildren.

Introduction

Attention in this and the subsequent two chapters turns to the viewpoint of the adopters about parenting the adopted child, their reactions to the search and reunion, and how it fitted in with the overall adoptive experience. Ninety-three adoptive parents participated in this study. Over three-quarters of the questionnaires (79 per cent) were completed by adoptive mothers, 14 per cent by both parents and the remaining eight per cent by adoptive fathers. No important differences were apparent between the replies from fathers and mothers.

Characteristics

All adopters described themselves as white European. About two-thirds were between 50 and 70 years old at the time of the study. Around a third were over 70, with one out of ten being over 80. Their mean current age was 68 years (Std 8.5) and at the time their child had searched or had been sought, they had been 59 years old (Std 9.2). Therefore, this sample provides insights into adopters at a later stage in life than most other studies. Three-quarters of those responding described themselves as married and a quarter as single or widowed. In 16 per cent of the families, the adopted person was the only child. Almost half (45 per cent) also had birth children. Some children had been born after the adoption. Four out of five children (80 per cent) had been placed with the adopters when under the age of one, with another nine per cent being from 12–18 months and the rest (11 per cent) over 18 months old. In other words, nine out of ten children had been placed when aged 18 months and under. The children's age group at placement is similar to the Registrar General's official statistics for non-related adoptions at the time.

This was the period when the emphasis was on placing the "perfect" child, meaning very young and of "good stock" with the "perfect" couple, meaning middle class (see Triseliotis and Russell, 1984). Today's domestic adoption involves mostly "looked after" children who are significantly older, display behavioural or emotional problems, and/or have disabilities. Unlike the past, the appeal now is for adopters of any background wishing to offer a home to a child rather than provide a child for a home.

Social class of adopters

Three out of five adopters (59 per cent) were classified in the two upper social classes I and II, over a third were in non-manual occupations and seven per cent in manual ones. None were classified as semi-skilled or unskilled (Figure 11.1). Compared to the general population, the adoptive

Figure 11.1
Social class of adopters by occupational classification*

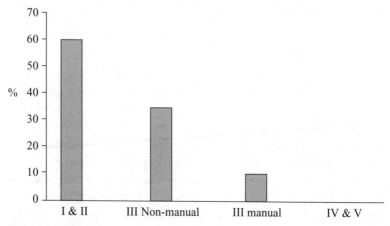

N = 56 (missing 37)
*The social class of adopters should be taken only as a rough guide because it was based on the occupation of either the male or female adopter and many women did not declare outside employment.

parents were over-represented in social classes I and II (professional, semi-professional and managerial). As already mentioned, this reflected the predominantly middle-class bias of adoption policy and practice in the 1950s and 1960s when these parents adopted. It was mainly after 1975, with the need for adoption of older and "special needs" children, and the availability of adoption allowances, that those in manual occupations came to feature as adopters in greater proportions (see Triseliotis, 1970; Triseliotis and Russell, 1984; Hill *et al*, 1989).

Why adoption

As perhaps expected, around 60 per cent of adopters said that they came to adoption because they wanted to create a family, with the rest wanting to enlarge it. There is no shortage of writings, contributed mostly by clinicians with a psychoanalytic orientation, reporting on the range of feelings that are usually experienced by couples that happen to be infertile. These can include sadness, depression, loss, or even envy and anger. Envy and anger are a minority response, but nevertheless present, such as when seeing friends and relatives being able to have children, but not themselves. Depending on culture and social attitudes, there can also be shame and guilt. Because of this, it is argued that, in the context of adoption, infertility could act as a stress factor when parenting the adopted child.

Family creators

The wish to create a family was the most common motivating factor to emerge, some adding that they could not be a 'family' without children, or that the coming of the children made them feel like a 'family'. Childlessness arising from infertility in one or both partners, or low sperm count, were the most common reasons given for their infertility. Being told they could not have children, or after having a number of miscarriages, they had been advised to seek other ways of creating a family: 'After four years of trying we decided to apply to The Children's Society and were accepted'. In the minds of most adopters the idea of family was closely associated with having children. Not being able to reach such fulfillment was experienced as a heavy blow, 'squashing' their expectations of having a 'family'. Many of them felt 'sad', 'devastated', 'deeply upset', 'very disappointed', 'grief and sadness', 'unhappy' or 'absolutely heartbroken'. Other typical comments included: 'Disorientation, frustration, anger, sense of loss'; or 'grief, sadness – sense of loss, failure and devastation'.

Hardly anyone expressed feelings of shame or anger, but more likely some envy because they felt that acquaintances could give birth to any number of children they wanted 'without having to go through so many hoops'.

Enlarging their family

A quarter of adopters who were not infertile had wanted to adopt because of their wish to enlarge their family. This group had at least one birth child but had been told either not to risk another pregnancy, or that another conception would not be possible. Adoption seemed to them the obvious way to give expression to their wish to parent more children. A common response from this group was:

> We had planned on having more children, but a miscarriage and subsequent hysterectomy prevented this – we knew that many children were in need of homes.

What happened to feelings about childlessness

It is often assumed that the sadness, disappointment and feelings of 'loss' arising from not giving birth to children will persist into the foreseeable future and can negatively affect the way the adopted child is parented. In this study, 79 per cent of adopters who could not have children claimed no long-term effects. The current emotional health of adopters who had been childless, as scored on the General Health Questionnaire, did not differ from that of adopters who had birth children. They attributed the disappearance of such feelings to having created a family by adoption and added that adoption 'totally' took the regret away or that the children 'did it' or took the disappointment away. Typical comments included: 'having our adopted children'; 'having adopted two lovely boys'; 'over the moon and have always felt he was mine although he was not a birth child'. Others referred to their adopted children as having been 'delight-ful', 'wonderful' or a 'real gift'. The implication of most explanations was that adoption had proved a great healer. Creating or expanding a family by adoption was seen as being as legitimate as having your own. As one of them explained: 'Adopting B and S fully met my need for children and gave my life a purpose to meet their needs as best as I could'. Another one observed:

> The feelings did not persist because we decided that adoption was the right way for us and had no regrets. Our two children [adopted] were our pride and joy and much loved.

For a significant group of parents (21 per cent), feelings of sadness still persisted. These parents were less likely to feel close to the child in infancy ($p = 0.016$), early childhood ($p = 0.001$) and adolescence ($p = 0.023$). However, there were no differences in closeness before or after contact or in current relationships between those who felt their feelings of sadness persisted and those whose feelings disappeared. One of them explained that, because they felt marriage was about having children, the sense of loss had remained with them. Others described how they missed 'the birth process'; 'the actual giving of birth'; or having a 'blood' relationship. Nevertheless, they insisted that in spite of still having some regrets, adoption had proved very fulfilling. One adoptive mother remarked that she had always felt strongly about having missed the birth process, but felt it more intensely when her children were giving birth to their own children.

Ethnicity

Twelve of the adopters indicated that the ethnicity of their child was different to their own and many of these children were black. Several adopters said they had wanted to adopt a "mixed race" or black child either because they thought this was where the need was greatest, or because they had already adopted another such child. Reflecting wider attitudes of the period, one of them reported: 'we felt that it was more important for the child to grow up in a loving home than to be left in an institution'. However, another adopter commented that, with today's much greater awareness about the importance of 'culture and ethnicity', they might not have adopted a black child. Yet another added how they underestimated the complexity of transracial adoption, having initially thought that love would be enough:

At the time of the adoption I thought love would be enough to give S. security and the environment to blossom and grow in. I had no concept of the complexities of race and identity and how inadequate my own experience of life was to be able to help her.

The majority of these parents reported that their immediate and extended family had welcomed their child. Several already had older children which, they said, had made it much easier for the new one to blend in. Only two families said that ethnicity had an effect on their immediate family and in three cases on the extended family. The immediate family had been affected mainly by the 'glares or silences of strangers' and feeling the need to explain to visitors that their children were adopted to avoid possible 'confusion'. Because of the visible differences, some parents said they had felt more anxious to repeat to their children that they loved them and so did the extended family. Three of the 12 families reported that some grandparents had found it hard to fully accept the children or regard them as grandchildren. One set of adopters had felt 'betrayed' by the attitude of the grandparents and another became aware that their daughter sensed, from early on, that the paternal grandmother did not accept her. After that they tried not to visit to avoid hurting the child. One girl had explicitly told her parents how difficult she found it to feel that she 'belonged in the family'.

When it came to how ethnicity exactly had affected the children, four families identified difficulties, but added 'nothing too serious'. The problems had emerged mostly at school with other children calling them names, teasing them, or not allowing them to play with the playground equipment. There were several examples, however, where it was said that ancillary and teaching staff had also picked on the children for being different.

M. and P. both suffered sustained racism from schoolmates, dinner staff and P. unconscious racism from teachers.

Several parents had recognised how difficult it was for a black child to grow up in an all white community and because of this, they said, they doubled their efforts to make them feel extra secure at home and to shield them from racism and discrimination. A couple of other parents added that they had made a conscious decision from the start to send their child to a more multi-ethnic school to make them feel more comfortable. Another remarked that having been a family with children of 'various' minority ethnic backgrounds, and their children having gone to school where there were other similar children, there had been no problems about fitting in. Nevertheless, some said, this could not disguise their anguish and anxiety knowing that their children could suffer from racism. As one of them put it:

My heart was wrenched apart at the racism and rejection that they suffered.

Another family expressed both pain and guilt saying:

. . . not being able to help S. in the most difficult problem of her life, i.e. not really being able to enter into the pain and confusion of feeling British, but being perceived as Indian and being rejected by both communities.

This parent went on to say that she could feel some of the pain but she had no answer or experience of how to help her daughter. This and other parents who adopted transracially had done so at a time when there was little or no know-how or preparation of how they might have acted to help their children cope with prejudice and discrimination. It would not have removed the problem, but it could have helped to reduce its impact. As mentioned in an earlier chapter, adopted people of minority ethnic background confirmed their parents' views that they had experienced difficulties because they looked different, and more so than their parents had realised.

Telling and talking about adoption

In the past, the timing of the adoption disclosure and the amount of background information passed on were thought to be closely associated with whether to search or not and with the searching behaviour. Triseliotis (1973) found that only 16 per cent of those searching more than 30 years ago had been told about their adoption by the age of six and hardly any genealogical information had been shared with them. Because of the policies and practices of the period, the adoptive parents themselves were hardly given any such information to pass on to the child. In 1964, Kirk postulated the view that open communication in adoption signified that adopters were 'acknowledging the difference' which in turn enhanced their relationship with the adopted child. In contrast, 'rejection of difference' would tend to disturb that relationship since it would probably inhibit the adoptive parents' 'capacity for empathy with the special problems that only the adoptee experiences' (p. 9). The subsequent studies in origin, over a hundred, confirmed Kirk's proposition about the importance of acknowledging the difference instead of denying it.

Just under nine out of ten parents in this study (86 per cent) said they had disclosed the adoption when their child was four or under. The rest told mostly after that age. More interestingly, 96 per cent said it had been the right time to tell. We can assume that by the 1960s and early 1970s, when most of these adoptions took place, the secrecy that was widespread before that period was gradually being replaced by increasing openness. Similarly, almost all the adopters said that they had found it either 'very easy' or 'easy' to tell, giving examples of how easy it proved to be. Only one couple said they had found it difficult. Because of the high proportion who told early, it was difficult to undertake tests of significance between different variables. The great majority told or read to their children recommended stories or made up stories from the child's life and how he or she had come to them. Some would also try to explain the adoption, even though they knew that the child could not yet understand. In a few cases, a parent had shared the photograph of a birth parent or read from a letter left by the birth parent:

> Sometimes, when D. was not too well he would sit on my knee for a cuddle and say tell me my story.

Other typical comments included: telling the child that he/she was 'special' and 'chosen'; 'it's no good hiding the truth'; 'told as soon as able to understand'; 'not to feel shocked if it came suddenly'; 'intro-ducing the word adoption as a term of endearment'; 'not to tell would have lost his trust in us'; 'always believed in being honest'; 'it came naturally'. Another typical comment:

> Having told her from the time she was in her cot there was never any dramatic "telling" time.

The dominant reasoning behind the disclosure was about being truthful and not keeping any secrets. A number of them added that 'with the truth you cannot go wrong'. The danger of the child finding out from outside sources was always in the minds of some parents and they wanted to pre-empt it. Others stressed the importance of the child growing up and feeling they always knew and that there were no surprises. There was less reference in the explanations to recognition of the importance of the biological connection but perhaps it was implied. At the time, of course, when these parents were faced with the challenge of telling or not, the studies confirming Kirk's (1964) proposition had not yet taken place.

The period between the child being 3–5 years old, and certainly before the child started school, appeared to be the most favoured period for telling. A number of parents also made the point that their children knew the word "adopted", even though they could not understand or explain its meaning till later years. While a few of them could not remember having had any special preparation from the adoption agency, most could remember two pieces of advice: 'Tell early' or 'tell as soon as the child is able to understand'. Some could also remember having been told to 'repeat' the telling. The suggestions given appeared to leave room for flexibility asking adopters to tell when they thought it was 'the right time' or the child 'could understand'.

The representative strongly recommended we tell him as soon as we thought he would understand and then remind him again from time to time.

Table 11.1
Age of the *adopted person* when their parents told them that they were adopted

		%
Always known/	< = 4 year	86
	> = 5 years	12
Cannot remember		2
Total		100

N = 93

Sharing information and talking about adoption

Almost all adopters (97 per cent) said they had felt comfortable with talking about adoption to their child and 89 per cent that they did not find it difficult to share background information with their son or daughter about their adoption. The remainder reported having felt like that 'sometimes'. No evidence was found that, following the initial disclosure, the great majority of parents experienced discomfort when talking about adoption with their child. Most of them (76 per cent) said that they tried to share what background information they had on the birth family, viewing it as their duty, or as the child's right to know, or as the best policy to follow. While the background information made available to them had often been brief and inadequate, they had tried to pass it on either in stages, depending on the child's age and the type of information it was, and a minority waited for the child to ask. Sometimes information given proved later on to have been incorrect, including in one case having been told that the birth mother had died in hospital. The period when these parents adopted was still one of considerable secrecy and it was not yet the practice of adoption agencies to obtain and share detailed background information, including photographs or videos. Also, open adoption and post-adoption direct or indirect contact had not yet emerged as shifts in policy and practice. Reflecting the practice of the period, only one couple had met a birth parent before the adoption. Ten per cent would have liked to, but half said they would not; the remaining two-fifths had been uncertain.

The teenage years were usually a popular time for sharing more information. Almost a quarter of parents did not think they had passed enough information to their child or could not be certain that they had. One out of ten had found some information about the child's background difficult to pass on. For example, one parent had avoided sharing the distressing information that a birth mother became disabled following a failed suicide attempt, though it was unclear whether this was connected with the parting decision. This information was later shared when the daughter was 18 and 'able to cope'.

Gradually gave S. all the information we had except one, that her mother was paralysed after she tried to kill herself by jumping from a bridge . . . I felt this was too big a grief to put upon a child until she began to search about her past.

However, 70 per cent of parents said that their child had been open to discussing adoption, one out of ten thought he or she had been reluctant and almost a fifth were uncertain. What was described as 'a lack of interest' on the part of the child made it difficult for a minority of them, they said, to continue the explanations. Such reluctance could be present from early on or after a certain age. Typical comments by these parents included: 'he did not seem interested in pursuing the matter by asking questions'; 'would turn away and not listen'; 'looked positively distressed'; 'there was no real interest shown by her after the age of seven'. These parents' dilemma was how much to persist and 'overload' or appear to 'batter' the child in the face of apparent resistance or give up and wait until asked, which is what many of them in this group did.

Although the great majority of parents would bring up the subject of adoption frequently or periodically, a minority would not raise it and waited instead for the child to ask. A significant number said they would answer questions only 'if asked'. One parent reported that, after telling their three-year-old about his adoption, he apparently said 'he didn't want to be that thing'. After that they had decided not to mention it for a while, and they never brought themselves round to doing so until their son found his adoption papers. Yet another family did not remind their daughter because they wanted her to feel 'part of the family'. There were similarities to what was found some 30 years ago, except that the proportion of parents who were waiting for the child to ask was now much smaller (Triseliotis, 1973). Although telling and explaining appear to have entered the consciousness of most adoptive parents, nevertheless there was a small group of around 10 to 20 per cent who had found it hard to make it a process or take the initiative of periodically re-introducing the subject.

The most difficult question faced by one couple was when their daughter asked them why they had changed her name from the one given her by her birth mother. Another family did not know how to explain that their child's birth grandfather did not want him at home because of being black. A difficulty experienced by a handful of others was when a child would pick up a comment from someone outside and come home asking whether their birth parent(s) wanted them or not. On the whole, though, most adopters had gone to great lengths to tell their children that it was circumstances that had made their birth parents part with them and not that they had not loved them. They tried to explain about poverty, disability, stigma and general inability to cope, but being both honest and understanding about the birth parents' circumstances, it was sometimes difficult, some implied, because the two did not always sit comfortably together. As a result, adopters would have liked much more detailed background information on such matters as reasons for the adoption, the father's background, members of the extended family, the birth parent(s)' temperament, talents and hobbies, photographs of birth relatives and so on. Information on the medical background of the child, including the father, emerged as a dominant requirement, but in general these parents stressed the need for more and better quality information.

According to the parents, around two-thirds of adopted people would talk about their birth family during different stages of their life (Table 11.2). Those who were said to talk a lot increased from under 10 per cent in childhood and adolescence to 24 per cent in adulthood. At the other end, the proportion of those who never, or rarely referred to the subject, dropped from 36 per cent in childhood to 13 per cent in adulthood. On the whole adopted people, either as children or as adults, would talk only periodically about their birth family to their parents or siblings. More often the initiative had to come from the parents. If adopted people raised the subject, it would mostly be after reading a story, viewing a TV programme, something said at school or on a birthday. Any talk would mostly be in the form of wondering what a parent looked like, who the birth child took after, if there were any siblings or what interests they might have. In this study, the more the child spoke about their birth relatives in adolescence, the better the emotional health of the adopters as scored on the General Health Questionnaire (p = 0.006).

Overall, adopters identified around a fifth of their sons or daughters as being 'very' or 'mildly' reluctant to talk about their adoption and/or birth family. A common explanation was that the topic was rarely raised and never seemed very important to their child. Many of them did not see it as 'reluctance' but as lack of interest, attributing it mainly to the very good relationship they had. They would say it was because he or she was very

Table 11.2
Extent to which the adopted person talked about their birth family

Period	A lot %	Sometimes %	Never %	All %
Childhood	5	60	36	101
Adolescence	8	69	23	100
Adulthood	24	64	13	101

N = 84 (missing 9)

happy all along, 'happy and well adjusted, no need', or that once they knew about their adoption, the subject was no longer important to them. A few thought that perhaps their child's reluctance to talk was because they had not wanted to 'hurt' them, even though they would have welcomed it. Several attributed the lack of interest to their child's strong wish to be *their* child. Commenting on their son, who eventually searched, one parent said: 'he seemed very happy and content with us as his family'. In the case of a sought daughter, the parent reported that:

She always said she was completely happy with her "mum and dad" and had no desire to trace.

Why a small proportion of adopted children, and later as adults, do not talk or ask questions about their adoption is not fully clear. Possible explanations are that the children sense some kind of discomfort in their parents' approach that puts them off from asking questions; fear being seen as disloyal; feel a strong desire to feel at one with the adopting family; feel possible fear of being separated or rejected; or carry strong internalised feelings of anger about the loss and rejection arising from being given up for adoption in the first place.

Telling others about adoption

Only four per cent of adoptive parents said they had found it difficult telling other people that their child was adopted. For the rest it had posed no problem and no unusual emotional blocks were experienced when telling others. Nevertheless, even among those who said they had been open and uninhibited about it, a significant minority stressed that they had not mentioned adoption 'to anyone where it seemed not called for', or had done so 'only when it had to go on forms'; 'when necessary'; or 'I carefully chose those I told'. It was also the view, among a number of adopters, that once the child grew up it was up to them whom to tell. Although one family told relatives and friends of the adoption, eventually they moved house to 'where no one knew of her adoption until she was old enough to tell her friends'. Telling others indiscriminately, as several adopters pointed out, would involve being also asked personal questions, which were private. As another one put it:

If my children were white I would not have necessarily told people they were adopted unless they needed to know.

There were two main reservations for not telling others, apart from relatives and friends. Some adopters saw this as information private to themselves and their child, but would tell 'if necessary' or 'if outsiders needed to know', but not go round informing everyone. One couple's view for not telling anyone came about after their child was being difficult at school and the teacher was reported to have said: 'you never know how adopted children will turn out'. Many adopters also felt that after a certain age it was up to their children to decide whom they would like to share this personal information with. Those who had adopted black children or those from a minority ethnic background appeared to be going the opposite way, that is, making even greater efforts to explain in order to avoid, as some put it, possible misunderstanding. On the whole, a significant number of adopters preferred to be selective about whom they told. Strange as it may seem now, by all accounts at the time that these families adopted, and for a number of years later, being adopted, and possibly being a child of divorce, carried a fair amount of stigma and discrimination, as shown by Triseliotis (1973).

The extended family

Nine out of ten adopters reported that the extended family had fully accepted their children. The rest veered between those who said 'sometimes' and two families who said that they had not. The overall view, however, was that the extended families had fully accepted their adopted son or daughter and gained a lot of pleasure from them. The children were, on the whole, treated as being 'birth children'; were 'never made to feel different'; 'delighted grandparents'; and that 'all four grandparents treated all their grandchildren equally'. A minority of parents, however, made the point that 30 to 40 years ago there was less understanding about adoption and like strangers, some family members too, had found it 'difficult to accept'. Initial reservations by a number of grandparents were dissipated once the adoption had been finalised and the children were said to have been accepted and loved 'dearly', or that a close 'bond' ultimately developed between them and the child. This did not apparently stop a number of grandparents, or other relatives, from making comments about the child not being 'of their own flesh and blood'.

Closeness to the adopted person

Almost all adopters reported having had no difficulty getting close to their child during childhood, with 99 per cent reporting very close or close relationships (Table 11.3). The great majority of children were under 18 months old at the time they were placed with the adopters, which would have helped with bonding and attachments. However, by adolescence the closeness of the relationship fell to 65 per cent. Although a later chapter will show that the closeness recovered by adulthood, it never reached the childhood levels. Equally, almost nine out of ten adopters (89 per cent) said that their child had been responsive or very responsive to them during his or her childhood, with the rest saying that the responses had been mixed or the child had not been very responsive. There were strong positive associations between the overall adoption experience and reported closeness to their adopted child during different stages. In other words, the higher the satisfaction with the adoption experience, the greater the reported closeness to the adopted person (early childhood $p = 0.042$; adolescence $p < 0.001$).

Adolescence, however, was reported to have been a low point for about a third of adoptive families. They described the relationship then as mixed or not close. As one of them rhetorically put it: 'have you tried adolescence?' Others made comments such as: 'she was a nightmare'; 'adolescence is not easy either for daughters or parents'; or 'I think in

Table 11.3

Past and current levels of closeness reported by adopters to their sons and daughters

Level of closeness	Childhood* %	Adolescence %
Very close, close	99	65
Mixed	1	25
Not very close or not at all	–	10
Total	100	100

*N = 90 (missing 3)

adolescence her feelings for us became confused'. A few parents linked difficulties in adolescence with the adopted person's wish to become more independent and a few others with adoption and identity. Certainly the teenage years had proved to be the most troublesome period, even though the parents did not think this was because their son or daughter was adopted. (An earlier chapter showed that adopted people also rated the closeness of their relationship to their parents during adolescence as significantly lower than it was in childhood.) Although there was under-standing that their son or daughter was perhaps trying to establish 'their identity' during their teenage years, there was equal frustration when the child had not been able to share their pre-occupations or anxieties. In a couple of cases, the parents more explicitly said that their child had not been able to come to terms with the fact of being adopted or of having been 'rejected' by their own family.

Those parents who said that the feelings they experienced after finding out they could not have children had *persisted*, rated their closeness to their adolescent child to be not as close in comparison to those whose feelings had not persisted (p = 0.023). Adoptive parents who rated their emotional health on the GHQ as non-problematic also felt closer to their adolescent child (p = 0.030). Although no comparable British figures are known to us referring to the relationship between adolescents in the general population and their families, part of the explanation could be that by adolescence there is a much fuller understanding about the meaning of adoption and possibly greater pre-occupation with it (see also

Brodzinsky, 1984). However, one US study reported that, 'contrary to theoretical expectation, when normative populations of adolescent adoptees and nonadoptees were compared along the dimension of identity formation, no significant differences emerged' (Stein and Hoopes, 1985, p. 62).

Of those adopters who had birth children, over eight out of ten (87 per cent) found the relationship with their adopted children similar to that with their own, but the remaining (13 per cent) claimed that it was 'different' meaning of a different nature, rather than qualitatively so. Almost all adopters were anxious to stress that they were all 'our children', 'all treated in the same way', and 'no difference' with the following being a typical comment:

They are all my children. I love them but they are all different.

The parents who said that there were differences between parenting their birth and adopted children wanted to stress that, while each child was treated as 'family', nevertheless the relationship could not be exactly the same. This was because, they explained, the children had different needs, dissimilar traits, or different personalities. Some stressed that each child's unique character had created a different type of relationship, especially as the children grew older. One of them explained: 'The same in principle but differently according to their needs and traits'. More interestingly, several others, while saying that they loved all their children 'just as much', said they had found it easier to understand their birth children, because they were more like themselves, that it had been easier to predict their behaviour or as one of them reported: 'you know your children in a way you don't know your adopted child'. In contrast, a handful of adopters disclosed that they came to feel closer to their adopted than to their birth child, because of their different personalities and responses. Others were conscious of unavoidably, perhaps, having made bigger efforts with their adopted child to make certain that no differences were experienced by them. For parents who had children born to them after the adoption, there was a kind of wish to explain or make up for this to the adopted child.

The overall adoption experience

Almost all adopters (94 per cent) rated their overall experience of adoption as very positive or positive (Figure 11.2). They described their overall experience as: 'brought us great joy'; 'wonderful to be a family'; 'would do it all over again'; 'adoption provided the family we couldn't have'; 'grateful for the experience'; or 'couldn't imagine life without her'. As one of them explained:

> Our children have brought us great happiness and our lives would have been empty without them.

A significant minority tempered their comments by highlighting also 'anxieties' and 'sorrows' or adding that it 'wasn't all plain sailing' but one adopter was certain that they would not have had their birth daughter if they had not adopted first.

As perhaps expected, there were strong positive associations between the overall adoption experience and reported closeness to the adopted person at different stages. The overall description of the adoption experience was also more likely to be positive if adopters felt that their son or daughter was 'just like them' (p = 0.021). Raynor (1980) also reported from her retrospective study that a sense of similarity appeared to strengthen the relationship.

Figure 11.2
The overall adoption experience

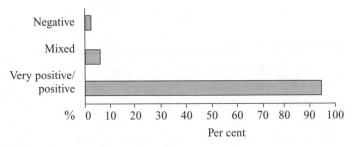

N = 93

The positives of adoption

Adopters identified a number of distinct positives about the overall adoption experience, including being a family and the joy of parenting, seeing children grow up and do well, continued relationships and having grandchildren. One of the many similar positive remarks was: 'Having the fun of bringing up a family, giving us a real purpose, life would be empty without them'. The sense of being a family continued for many of them through becoming grandparents, which they felt added to the completeness.

Being a family and the joy of parenting

If one of the main reasons for adopting was to create a family in order to feel 'complete', it was perhaps to be expected that having a child now fulfilled that expectation. In addition, considerable pleasure was derived from parenting their children, watching them grow up or from having been given an 'aim' in life. Repeated words and phrases included: 'complete'; 'pleasure and happiness'; 'fun and happiness'; 'given us a future we could not have had'; the fun of bringing up a family'; 'a wonderful experience'; 'fuller life'; and 'they brought a lot of love'. As one of them explained: 'I can't imagine what our life would have been like without the children!' And another:

> We would have had a childless marriage and missed all the joys, frustrations, laughter and tears of family life.

Seeing them do well

There was considerable pride when adopters were describing the 'joy' of watching their children grow up to being teenagers and then adults, do well in life and have their own family. As one of them explained: 'Watching them grow up into adulthood was a voyage of discovery'. A previous chapter noted similar satisfaction expressed by birth mothers after meeting their respective children and finding them looking and doing well.

Being supportive and continued relationships

A new dimension to the adoption experience, not covered by most previous studies, because they talked to adopters at an earlier stage in their lives, were the benefits of the long-term relationship. Many adopters emphasised the continued positive relationships they had with their adopted children and the support and friendship that had developed between them or the 'growing love and friendship'. There was added satisfaction that, when some faced illness or disability, their children had rallied round being supportive and showing that they cared. As one of them put it 'she is always there for me'. Like some other parents, one father remarked:

> She was a great support to me when her mother [my wife] died. She continues to be very close to me even though I am remarried and live abroad.

Equally, many parents living in the same vicinity as their children would undertake the childminding of their grandchildren or take them to or meet them from school or join them in other activities.

The downside of adoption

Besides the usual problems of bringing up children, especially adolescents, most parents could recall no other difficulties and the main response was that they had 'none'. Some compared their adopted children to children born to other members of their wider family, adding that any difficulties were not dissimilar. Even though this was now a long time in the past, when talking about the downside to adoption, a significant number referred to the pre-adoption waiting period and the anxieties associated with it. There was also the frustration of not having enough background information on the child and their family, while those who adopted transracially expressed frustration about the racial prejudice they experienced, some coming from close relatives. Some had been aware that their son or daughter was possibly suffering psychologically because adoption also involved rejection and loss and a struggle to establish a sense of self. One of them explained that:

> Knowing that ultimately the child is left with the problem of coming to terms with being adopted, I can't imagine how it must feel to 'lose' a part of yourself.

A significant number expressed the kind of guilt that many non-adoptive parents also come to feel – that of wishing they had been better parents. As some of them put it, they wished they had the same opportunity again to avoid making the same mistakes and do better. When difficult behaviours manifested in a child, the first thought was whether or not they had provided enough love or understanding and that perhaps a birth parent would have done better. Some had also wondered whether with an adopted child it is not, perhaps, as easy to understand fully their anxieties, preoccupations, likes, dislikes or talents to respond to them better. Another small group wondered whether their child's poorer academic achievements, 'willfulness', or their 'undesirable' traits were inherited from their parents, with several adding that perhaps in the end 'nature' had prevailed over 'nurture'. Several who perceived themselves as 'laid back' and 'quiet' had not been able to understand or cope with the exuberance of their child, attributing it to genetic factors. In the end, most parents had taken an optimistic view, not wanting to exaggerate difficulties and describing most of these as being part of the growing-up process. Only a handful cited possible anxiety and worry about their child wanting one day to search for their birth parent(s) as being a downside of adoption. This did not preclude an underlying fear of either their child or themselves being hurt in the process, but it did not appear to dominate their thoughts during the childhood years.

The meeting of expectations

When asked if the experience of adoption was as expected, most of the sample were keen to stress that they had no specific expectations, had no idea what to expect or they had wanted 'to take things as they came'. Just over three-quarters (76 per cent) said that their expectations had been met, almost a fifth (19 per cent) rated it as 'mixed', with the remaining five per cent saying they had not been met (Figure 11.3). Those parents who said that their experience of adoption had been as they expected it were also more likely to describe the overall experience as positive in comparison to those who said their experiences had not been as expected or had been mixed ($p = 0.001$).

Most adopters were glad, they said, to have a 'son' or 'daughter' or be a 'family' and that was 'good enough' for them. A couple admitted to having hoped that adoption would bring them 'happiness' and it had. While several had been somewhat worried beforehand that they might not be able to love the child, they soon discovered that their anxieties had been baseless. A minority made reference to some difficulties but these had not come as a surprise or were not enough to have put them off adoption. They were aware that non-adoptive families had their 'ups and downs'. One said: 'we didn't expect it to be plain sailing and it wasn't . . . but there were tremendous rewards'. Another added that:

> Despite upsets and many mistakes I'm glad it took place – I am very fortunate to have such a wonderful daughter.

Those who expressed mixed feelings (19 per cent) were split evenly between those who were mostly referring to the administrative procedures of adopting and the rest to the adoption experience per se. The latter gave a number of explanations as to why they had mixed feelings or even said that their expectations had not been met. There was reference to adoption proving 'harder or more difficult than expected', or to the 'naivete' of

Figure 11.3
The meeting of expectations

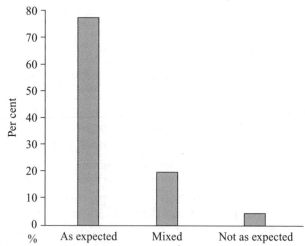

N = 88 (missing 5)

thinking that love would be enough or having had, perhaps, 'too simplistic a view of adoption at the start'. A handful were more disappointed, such as one family who said the adopted person did not want to identify with them and their family, another who could not get close to their adopted daughter, and a third who said they had years of worrying because of a 'wayward' daughter. Two or three others referred to non-anticipated difficulties after adopting a child of minority ethnic background, with one of them adding: 'I had not anticipated the stress that the racial differences would bring or how inadequately I was prepared for this'.

Overall review of relationships

Table 11.4 sets out the adopters' review of their relationship with their son or daughter over the years. Between 90 and almost 100 per cent looked upon this as having been very positive or positive. Only a few said that they were uncertain and hardly anyone else reported that the relationship was negative. (These high levels of satisfaction made internal computations impossible to carry out.)

Table 11.4
The adopters' review of their relationship with their son or daughter

Statement	Strongly agree/agree %	Uncertain %	Strongly disagree/ disagree %	All %
I feel happy about having adopted	97	3	–	100
I feel loved by my adopted son or daughter	94	5	1	100
I love my son or daughter	99	1	–	100
My son or daughter feels he/she belongs to the family	92	4	3	99

N = 92 (missing 1)

213

Physical and emotional health

Physical health

Almost nine out of ten adopters described their current physical health as good to excellent (89 per cent) and the rest as poor or very poor. A third of them had not visited their family doctor in the last six months, but 10 per cent had done so four or more times. In spite of their age, and compared to birth mothers, adoptive parents seemed to have made fewer visits to their family doctors in the last six months, but more than their sons or daughters.

Emotional health

Based on the GHQ, the adopters' score of their emotional health at the time of reporting to the study showed that 87 per cent of them had low scores, suggesting good emotional health, with 10 per cent scoring between 4–9, indicating moderate emotional difficulties. Another three per cent scored 10–15 points, suggesting more severe emotional problems (Table 11.5). On the whole, these adopters could be described as emotionally very healthy people. (This is discussed more fully in the next chapter.) A handful, however, referred to having experienced intense stress after they had realised that the adopted person was searching for their birth relatives or because a son or daughter was experiencing problems. Asked whether any health problems they had experienced were related to the adoption experience, the predominant response was that they were not.

Table 11.5
Current state of emotional health

GHQ Score	%
0	71
1–3	16
4–9	10
10–15	3

N = 90 (missing 3)

Impact of other life events besides adoption

Asked about the impact on them of other life events besides adoption, marriage, the birth of a child and close relationships were the most positive experiences (Table 11.6). Surprisingly, perhaps, only four per cent had experienced a divorce. As perhaps expected, death of a close relative had the most negative impact followed by health problems and then the inability to have children.

Table 11.6
Impact of other life events on adopters

Life event	Positive	Negative	No effect	Not Appl.	All
Marriage	96	–	4	–	100
Death of close relative	36	44	13	7	100
Health problems	18	26	32	25	101
Birth of other children	46	4	–	50	100
Inability to have children	10	17	27	47	101
Close relationships	80	1	13	5	99
Divorce	4	4	–	92	100
Career/employment	64	1	11	24	100

N = 84 (missing 9)

Summary

Most of the adopters came from professional, semi-professional and managerial backgrounds. In spite of being on average in their late sixties, they reported very good levels of physical and emotional health. Around a fifth of those who had adopted as a way of creating a family still carried lingering feelings about being unable to conceive and/or give birth to a child. However, there was no significant difference in the emotional health of adopters who had given birth to children and those who had not.

While most parents had continued to refer to adoption and share background information with the adopted child/person, a persistent proportion of between 10 and 20 per cent had delayed telling or the sharing of background information, waiting for the child to ask. Between a quarter and a third of adopted people were said never to have talked about their adoption, either in childhood or adolescence, but the proportion fell to 13 per cent in adulthood. There was evidence that the more frequent the discussion about adoption within the family, the better the emotional health of the adopters. Adoptive parents acknowledged that, on the whole, the few minority ethnic children featuring in the sample were less likely to be accepted either by the outside community or occasionally by members of the extended family.

Almost 100 per cent felt happy about having adopted and a similar proportion said they loved their child; 94 per cent felt loved by their son or daughter; and 92 per cent were certain that their son or daughter felt they belonged. Other positives had to do with creating a family; the joys of parenting; seeing their children do well; finding them supportive in later life; and the joy of having grandchildren. The biggest benefit of adoption, voiced by eight out of ten adopters, was that it had eclipsed feelings of loss resulting from not being able to have children. However, feelings of sadness persisted for over a fifth and these appeared to have negatively affected their closeness to their adopted child in infancy, early childhood and adolescence. These feelings had no impact during adulthood and after contact, possibly having lost their hold by then.

12 The adoptive parents' reactions to the search

Adoptive mother:
She wanted roots and security, to know her true identity. She did not always talk much about it, which I found hard. It changed after she got the first papers from the adoption agency. I was worried she might be disappointed, that she might be hurt, that she might be opening a can of worms.

Introduction

This chapter describes how adoptive parents in the study reacted to their son's or daughter's news about the search or when told that they were being sought by members of their birth family. How adoptive parents come to view their child's quest to find out more about their roots and members of their birth family has been receiving increasing attention since the opening of the adoption records and the advent of more open forms of adoption. Leaving aside Scotland, Finland and Israel, where there has been legislative provision for access to records for some time, in most other countries where the law was changed after the 1970s, there was often reported to be strong opposition from adoptive parents' groups. While some showed understanding because they perceived it as identity enhancing for their child, others felt threatened, angry and confused about the move. The fear of losing their child to the birth family and a general feeling of no longer being in control appeared to permeate the thoughts of many parents, including those who might have been well disposed to the idea (Post-Adoption Social Workers Group of New South Wales, 1988; Sachdev, 1992). Two writers commented that the adoptive parents were the least satisfied party because personally they stood to gain the least from the outcome (McMillan and Hamilton, 1992, p. 15). Howe (1996) too made the point that adoption policy and practice had shifted attention to children and their birth families to the virtual exclusion of any concern about the feelings and experiences of adopters.

Expectations from the search

When answering this question, expectations and reasons for the search were not too clearly distinguished by the adoptive parents and the answers overlapped extensively. Almost two out of every five parents (38 per cent) reported that their sons' and daughters' expectations had to do with satisfying their curiosity through obtaining background information and also seeing what the parent looked like. A similar proportion placed the emphasis on their child seeking answers to the question of 'why given up', the wish to establish their 'roots' and/or 'to complete their identity'. The need for a medical history was stressed by about one out of ten and a similar proportion said that they did not know what the adopted person was after. Only three per cent linked the search at the outset to a possible wish, on the part of the adopted person, to establish a relationship with a birth parent (Table 12.1). In many respects, the expectations quoted were not too dissimilar from those reported by adopted people, except that the latter had placed more emphasis on the possibility of developing new relationships. On the whole, these parents were recognising that the biological connection appeared important to their children. The trigger for the search, they reported, could be a new relationship, expecting or giving birth to a child, the breaking up of a relationship or loss through death or illness: 'when she discovered she was expecting'; or 'at the birth of her daughter'; or 'when she had children of her own she wanted to learn about her own origins'. In other cases, no specific event could be linked to it.

Table 12.1
Main expectations of contact as perceived by the adoptive parents

Expectations	%
Why given up, identity and roots	38
General curiosity/information/appearance	38
Medical history	9
Bereavement	4
Establishing a relationship	3
Don't know	9
Total	101

N = 90 (missing 3)

Curiosity, background information and physical appearance

Like adopted people, a significant proportion of adoptive parents had linked the expectations of their sons' and daughters' search to simple curiosity and to the gathering of background information. As some said: 'to satisfy natural curiosity'; 'natural instinct'; or 'learn more about her background'. Great emphasis was also placed on the adopted person wanting to see what the birth relative looked like or, as some of them put it, to 'recognise' themselves in the birth relative. They had expected the adopted person to come to understand themselves better from seeing what a parent or a sibling looked like: 'see what she looked like'; 'find out whom she resembled'; 'a deep desire to know who she looked like'; 'what traits he might find in his own child'; 'find out who their children were taking after'; or simply 'just to look at her natural parent'. A number of adoptive parents were satisfied, or appeared to believe, that there was nothing more to the search than curiosity. As one of them remarked:

Beyond satisfying her curiosity I am not sure that she had any other expectations.

According to the adoptive parents, birth and death appeared to trigger the wish to search as illustrated by a number of examples. Some adopters referred to the expected or actual birth of their son's or daughter's child as having given rise to curiosity, especially about the physical appearance of birth family members, or the wish for their child eventually to establish connections with birth family members. Access to medical history became important especially to expectant mothers who found themselves not knowing what to say when asked about their medical history. For others, it was after the child's birth: 'when her children were born and she had to fill in forms about family history'. The death of an adoptive parent was also said to generate the search for "something" because the adoptive person was 'badly missing' him. In another case, the search had followed the death of the adoptive father and the birth of the adopted person's child. One adoptive mother remarked that the search had been triggered after her husband died and her daughter came to feel 'that she was nobody'. In a case that suggested the separation of the adoptive parents, the adoptive mother reported that her son had been:

. . . let down by his father and perhaps felt that his birth father would be there for him.

Roots, identity and why given up

It should not, perhaps, come as a surprise that so many adopters recognised the importance of roots and identity in their son's and daughter's life. By the time of the search, the topic had been aired so often by the media that adoptive parents could not fail to link it to their child's situation. As a result, many of them came to view the search as the finding of answers to some key questions, and looked upon it as identity enhancing for the adopted person. The expectation was that background information obtained either from records and/or directly from a birth relative would make it possible for the adopted person to 'find their roots'; 'complete themselves'; 'establish their identity'; 'find their true self'; 'understand their origins'; or 'fill the hole in her life'.

. . . the need to know who she was, who she looked like, where she fitted and where she belonged.

Closely associated with the theme of roots and identity, many parents added the wish of the adopted person to find an answer to the question of 'why placed' or 'given up' for adoption and the circumstances surrounding it. A number of adopters again showed insight and awareness that the acquisition of such information by their sons and daughters could strengthen their sense of self-worth and self-esteem. They also knew that their son or daughter wanted to hear that he or she had been loved and had not been rejected by a birth parent. As noted before, a birth parent keeping one child, but not the adopted one, could increase the sense of rejection (Triseliotis, 1973). One adoptive parent explained that it made her daughter 'wonder how her birth mother could have given her away when she was so desperate to keep her son'.

Establishing relationships

As already mentioned, very few references were made by parents to the possibility that the adopted person might hope to develop an ongoing relationship with a birth parent, although a few referred to a friendship developing such as 'to be able to treat her mother as a friend'. Others added that their sons or daughters went out of their way to reassure them that they were not looking for parental figures but that 'it would be nice if they could become friends with a birth relative'.

The adopters' awareness about the search

Just as when adopters had to decide if, when and how, to reveal the "secret" of adoption, the situation appeared now to be reversed in that it was the adopted person who was in control of the "secret". One study found that adopted people whose parents were open to discussing adoption with them, and had an ongoing dialogue on the subject, were themselves more likely to share their search activity with them (Lichtenstein, 1996). The age at which adopted people told their parents about their desire to search and/or contact birth relatives varied. The most likely time was between the ages of 18 and 25 (Table 12.2).

Table 12.2
Age at which adopted people told their parents of their decision to search

	Under 18	*18–25*	*26–35*	*Over 35*	*All*
%	15	41	32	12	100

N = 74 (missing 3)

The number of adoptive parents in the sample whose children had sought contact was 77. Over two-thirds of them (68 per cent) said they had always been aware that their child was thinking about tracing their birth relative(s), with one in six (17 per cent) saying they were not. The rest were either unsure or reported that the adopted person was uninterested until then. Similarly, over a quarter of them had known about the actual search well beforehand, while around half (51 per cent) were told before

Table 12.3
When the adopted person told his or her parents about the search

Per cent	*Always known*	*Before search/contact*	*After contact*	*All*
%	26	51	23	100

N = 74 (missing 4)

contact was made and a further 23 per cent after contact had been established (Table 12.3). Adoptive parents who had always known or at least known before contact were also more positive about the search/ contact experience than those who were told after contact (p = 0.045).

Those adopters who said they had always known about the search (26 per cent) indicated that the reason it had not come as a surprise was either because they often spoke about it or their child had in the past made reference to that possibility. They had indicated to their child that they would be willing to help with the search in any way they could. A few had been cautious, saying that although they knew about their son's or daughter's interest in searching, they had wanted to leave it to him or her to ask for assistance. As one said:

I had always told him I would help him trace his birth mother if ever he wanted it.

Half of the adopters had been told either just before the search started or before contact. This took two main forms: either asking the parents for their opinion and even approval, or informing them of their intention. Either way, many of them had also asked their parents if they would mind or they would feel hurt. As one parent put it:

She discussed it with us before she started making contact. Went ahead with my blessing – I always said I would help her if she ever wanted to trace her family.

Those adopted people who left the telling until after the search had started, but before actual contact, were mostly informing their parents rather than asking for their approval. The following is a typical comment:

He asked us beforehand whether we would mind him contacting his birth mother and we said we did not. After their meeting he kept us informed.

A significant number of adopted people (23 per cent) had chosen to tell their parents after meeting a birth parent or relative. A usual explanation for the delay was to avoid distressing, upsetting or worrying their parents. Some possibly carried an element of both guilt and anxiety for the delay because they were said to have been relieved after telling or relieved to know that the parents were not upset or distressed. While some told their parents face-to-face, others preferred to phone and/or write simply to say that they had found a birth mother, brother or a sister. One parent recalled how they had always tried to avoid influencing their son to search, until he told them he had already established contact. However, another only heard about it, and the actual contact, after receiving a telephone call from the birth mother's husband. Several others had felt disappointed or hurt about not being told in advance, e.g. feeling 'shock that he had done it without referring to us'. Instead of face-to-face talk, the phone had often been used as a kind of third person to announce they were about to search or that they had already done so. A couple of parents remarked that the adopted person had appeared to find it easier to handle telling by phoning or writing. Even when parents had known beforehand about the search and/or contact, it had not stopped them from feeling 'sick', 'anxious', or 'worried'. In one case, the son had told his father and sister but not his mother, in order not to upset her.

Strength of motivation

Over three-quarters of adopters (78 per cent) described their son's or daughter's motivation to search as having been 'very strong' or 'strong' or that he/she was 'very keen' to do so. Only a handful said it was not very strong, with 13 per cent describing it as mixed. With few exceptions, very strong motivation to search was mainly viewed by the adopters as arising out of the adopted person's character. A number spoke about their son's or daughter's 'determination' to see something through or that, once having made up their mind, nothing would stop them. As one parent explained, 'she is the type of person who would not give up easily'. Several were described as having been 'frantic' or 'desperate' to find out more about themselves and only a small number were said to have been rather ambivalent or 'indecisive'.

Initial reaction to the search

The parents' reaction to their son's and daughter's search varied, with the great majority saying that they had wanted to be and had been supportive (80 per cent), understanding (74 per cent) and pleased (48 per cent), but also nervous (37 per cent), worried (27 per cent) or surprised (15 per cent) (Table 12.4). Being supportive, understanding and pleased did not rule out also being nervous and worried at the same time. When asked about their main reaction, broadly the same pattern emerged as with all reactions. Over half said they had tried to be understanding and supportive with 15 per cent saying that they had been happy and pleased. Surprisingly perhaps, those parents whose main initial reaction to the search/approach was to be frightened, worried, or nervous, rated the overall experience of adoption as more positive than those reporting other reactions (p = 0.044). Such a reaction did not necessarily arise from deep insecurity, but mostly from concern about the adopted person. One of them observed that possibly what she had needed was reassurance that it would be totally successful, but nobody could give that. Although the sub-sample of parents of non-searchers was small (N = 16), half of them said they had been surprised when they heard their son or daughter was being sought by a birth relative and a quarter of them had worried about it.

Overall, adoptive parents expressed two types of concerns: the first had to do with their son or daughter getting hurt in the process, e.g. being rejected; the second related to the impact of the search on themselves through the possible 'loss' of their child. Sometimes both concerns went hand-in-hand. Parents of those sought tended to feel more concerned, feeling that it was not perhaps the right time and/or that it was all too sudden. There was again a strong suggestion that those whose children had been sought were both more concerned and more annoyed, with some adding that the adopted person was not ready or prepared. Several referred to the adopted person as having been 'overwhelmed' emotionally or the experience having been overpowering or perhaps that the birth mother had acted without enough consideration about the impact of what she was doing. In an earlier chapter, it was shown that some adopted people who had been sought felt equally annoyed that the decision had been taken away from them. However, the parents also reported that in most cases it had all worked out well in the end.

The adopted person being hurt

There was no mistaking the concern expressed on the part of many adopters that their sons and daughters might be hurt in the process of

Table 12.4
Adoptive parents' *all* and *main* reactions to the search

Reactions	All %		Main %
Supportive	80	Understanding/supportive	59
Understanding	74	Frightened/worried/hurt/nervous	16
Pleased	48	Pleased/happy/excited	15
Nervous	37	Surprised	8
Worried	27	Other (uncertain, angry, upset)	2
Surprised	15	Total	100
Excited	16		
Uncertain	12		
Frightened	11		
Hurt	10		
Upset	4		
Hostile	–		
Angry	–		
Other	13		

N = 77 (The number refers only to adoptive parents of those who searched)

searching. Their main fear was that the adopted person might not be able to cope with a negative outcome. Often repeated phrases included: being hurt and disillusioned, disappointed and hurt by a negative response, his mother not wanting to see him, or being rejected again. Occasionally the concern was about upset that could follow from what their son or daughter might find. Others had shown some concern for the birth parent, saying that they might have moved on in life and perhaps had a new family, and being sought could prove unsettling. Most of the concern, though, was around the fear of a new 'rejection'. A typical comment voiced by many was that their child 'might be hurt by a negative response from his birth mother'. Without ascribing malevolence to the birth family, much concern was about what was referred to as a 'kind of second form of rejection' after the initial parting. One parent explained:

I was worried she might feel rejected, as she had felt rejected as a baby, so it would be a double rejection.

Loss

A significant number of adopters had felt threatened and afraid that contact could result in the 'loss' of the child they had nurtured over the years. There was fear of losing their child's love or losing contact with them, their child getting attached to a birth parent, or facing conflicting loyalties in relationships. As if one relationship would be at the expense of another, the main worry was about losing their sons and daughters to the birth mother. The following example, one of a number, illustrates a mixture of concerns on behalf of both the adopted person and themselves:

> The fear that he might be 'rejected' again and let down, but also the worry that he might go off and join his original family.

Some adoptive mothers had made unfavourable comparisons between themselves, as older people, and the birth mothers, younger and therefore possibly more attractive. One of them had feared that her daughter might look upon her as an 'old hag' after meeting her birth mother. Another remarked that she had been concerned that the birth mother might appeal to her daughter more than herself because she was ten years younger – a reminder from an earlier chapter that some birth mothers were also worried that their sons and daughters might not like their looks.

Passing on information to those sought

A number of the initial approaches to those *sought* by their birth mothers had been made to the adopters, with the request to let their sons and daughters know. With few exceptions, most of the parents had passed on the information, but a handful had kept it for some time before doing so. The majority had been understanding and sympathetic towards the birth mother's desire to establish contact, or knew or thought that their son or daughter would be happy to establish contact. As one of them put it: 'If I had given up a baby, I would like to know what had happened to him'. Others, however, had been sceptical or more hostile, fearful about their child being hurt, but also viewing the approach as an intrusion, or as being 'wrong' or that it came as 'a shock'. One father, whose wife had died two years earlier, took seven months before he could bring himself to tell his daughter that her birth mother was searching for her. He had also been concerned about how his adopted son would react knowing that his birth mother had not done the same. A handful had felt let down by the change in the legislation in 1975 and the developments that came about as a consequence: 'They had changed all the rules and moved the goal-posts – of course we were angry'. Another observed that:

After over 30 years of happy family life with him, it seemed almost like an intrusion into that life.

What happened to the concerns?

Table 12.5 shows that in 45 per cent of cases the adopters' concerns, highlighted above, were said to have changed partly or substantially for the better. In a broadly similar proportion they remained unchanged. Remaining "unchanged" did not mean that they were worried, because around half had no serious concerns from the start. Many of the fears and worries anticipated at the start – mainly rejection of the adopted person by the birth family or the fear of the adopted person rejecting their parents – had not materialised.

Table 12.5
Did initial concerns change over time?

Per cent	Changed	Unchanged	Changed partly	All
%	45	38	18	101

N = 77 (The number refers only to adoptive parents of those who searched.)

With some exceptions, adopters stressed that they were now satisfied about the way things had turned out for their sons and daughters, such as finding a mother, a blood brother, half-sister, or a grandparent, and more importantly that they had been received well:

Our nervousness was overcome when he was well received by his birth sister and natural father.

However, the fear that the adopted person might be 'hurt', 'rejected' or 'let down' was realised in around a fifth of cases. Parents referred to the adopted person suffering 'rejection' and themselves having to provide comfort and support. For some, the emotions evoked by the search were said to be 'too strong' or 'overpowering' mostly for their son or daughter, but also for themselves: 'he suffered when his birth mother refused to meet him'. And another:

We needed to offer a great deal of support as his natural mother again let him down and would not meet him.

On the whole, parents who had been initially approached by the adoption agency and informed of a birth mother's wish to pass on information to their son or daughter, changed their attitude after meeting with her, or on finding that members of the birth family were 'nice' people. They had been equally surprised to find that the birth family was 'very receptive and welcoming'. Possibly the biggest relief was the discovery that the search and contact had not affected the adoptive relationship, and in a significant number of cases it was said to have enhanced it. Many felt relief when they realised that they need not have worried because they were not going to lose their child. Many added that they had not lost her or him and were still 'mum and dad'. 'Our concerns', as one parent put it, 'that he would leave us were groundless – he is even more "sure" he is ours after the experience'. Another added:

We now know that our relationship with our daughter is stronger than ever.

A handful reported that contact had not only demonstrated their child's attachment to them, and that they were still the parents, but in some cases strengthened it, with one parent saying that all along they had been confident that the affection and devotion to their daughter would be able to weather any storm. Another had been reassured by her daughter: 'Don't worry. I know where I belong.' Although there were a number of exceptions, on the whole, adopters were mostly pleased on behalf of their sons and daughters, and for themselves, that things ended well or successfully for the great majority.

To what extent were parents involved in the search

A significant proportion (69 per cent) of adoptive parents had not become involved with the search either because they did not see the need or because they learnt about it too late. However, those who became actively involved reported fewer emotional problems on the GHQ (p = 0.004). The main explanation offered by those who knew about the coming search but were not actively involved was that their son or daughter was old enough, and mostly living away from home, and therefore capable of doing this themselves: 'she was capable of going ahead' or 'she was old enough to conduct her own business'. Others indicated that their sons or daughters were very independently minded and would have liked to do it themselves. One parent added:

> Our daughter was very firm that it was something that she must do by herself and declined my help.

Almost a third of parents who had always known that their son or daughter might search or those who had been told in advance actively helped in the search. Many were pleased to have been asked and a few were flattered. One parent had flatly refused to be involved because she felt 'threatened' by the process. Many parents either 'actively' helped to search for the original birth certificate or accompanied the adopted person to the adoption society that had arranged the adoption. A number of them helped to search birth/death and marriage records, the electoral roll and telephone directories nationwide to find the birth family. A few parents indicated that they went through the 'whole process', including participation in interviews at the Adoption Society and they came to learn the various stages. One confessed that although she had felt 'sick at heart' on learning that her daughter wanted to trace her birth mother, she still offered to help.

Impact of the search on the adoptive relationship

Seven out of ten adopters (70 per cent) reported that the relationship with their sons and daughters remained unchanged as a result of the search and reunion, but for the rest it had been 'enhanced' (Figure 12.1). Most of those who said the relationship remained unchanged, or that it had no impact, stressed that it was always good and it remained so. A few added that they never felt threatened by the search because they had always felt safe and their relationship 'remained as strong as ever' or that the adopted person's extra family made no difference to their relationship. One parent said that their son:

> . . . *no longer wonders about a mythical mother and father figure. He has met them both and made his peace with them. He is even surer that he wants to be 'ours'.*

Figure 12.1
Relationship with adopted person following search/contact

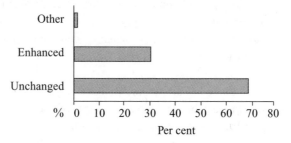

N = 90 (missing 3)

A big gain identified by three out of ten adopters was the discovery that the search had in fact enhanced their relationship with their son or daughter: 'strengthened'; 'enhanced'; feeling more appreciated'; 'brought us closer'; or 'she no longer believes that blood is thicker than water'. A not unusual comment was that the bonds that had bound them were tighter now because their son or daughter felt they 'truly' belonged to their adoptive family. 'Our daughter,' said one, 'feels very much closer to us and often tells us she is so glad we adopted her'. Where a son or daughter had suffered rejection by a birth relative, adoptive parents stepped in to offer extra support or 'share the sadness' which helped to further cement the relationship. As one of them put it, 'supporting and listening to her has brought us closer'. Above all, adopters had been particularly pleased to discover that they were still the parents and that their earlier fears had been 'groundless'.

Current frequency of contact between adopters and the adopted person

Almost nine out of ten adopters reported that they had some form of weekly direct or indirect contact with their son or daughter. For the rest, contact was mostly once every month. No one reported that there was no contact (Table 12.6). The British Social Attitudes Survey 13th Report (McLone *et al*, 1996) found that nearly three in four parents speak to their son or daughter at least once a week, which would suggest that adoptive parents are perhaps more frequently in touch with their children than the general population. Nine out of ten adopters said that they were happy about the frequency of contact, but the rest would have liked more. There were comments that contact 'couldn't be better'; 'I see her as much as I want'; 'I just love it'; or 'contact is like a breath of spring'. Contact could be face-to-face and/or involve frequent telephone calls or other forms of communication. There were no instances of adopters who said they had altogether lost face-to-face contact with their son or daughter or who indicated estrangement between them. A handful, however, suggested that either they themselves or the adopted person did not want to see too much of each other.

Table 12.6
Current frequency of contact with son or daughter

At least weekly %	At least monthly %	3–4 times a month %	Special occasions %	All %
87	10	2	1	100

N = 92 (missing 1)

Around a quarter of parents also claimed to have at least daily or weekly direct contact with the adopted person. (If those children who were abroad or at a distance were excluded, the percentage would be much higher.) Apart from a handful of adopted people still living with their parents, the rest in this group lived in the vicinity, mostly with their families, thus making frequent meetings possible: 'daily'; '3–4 times a week'; 'we are very lucky that she lives so near'; 'comes to a meal once a week'; 'at least weekly'; or 'we regularly spend Sunday evening with them'. In several cases a child living nearby was caring for a sick parent or visiting daily to make certain they were alright. In other cases a parent was babysitting or childminding or ferrying a child to and from school daily. As one of them explained:

> She lives only 10 minutes away from where we live. We see her most days when we look after our grandson while she goes to work.

And another:

> We visit for all four children's birthdays and attend school sports days, plays, etc. Two of the children at a time stay with us each school holiday or half-term. We always spend Christmas with them.

What limits more frequent contact

Distance was the most common explanation given for why contact was not more frequent for some. Possibly reflecting the experience of other families in the community, contact for those at a distance would be restricted to mostly indirect forms of communication with occasional visits and meetings (Table 12.7). Some 18 per cent of adopted people lived abroad, which made direct contact with their parents difficult. As expected, there were regular indirect forms of communication and periodically one or the other would travel to visit. The following was a typical example: 'by telephone about every two weeks. J. and family also visit me when we manage to arrange it'. Nevertheless, a small minority of parents (9 per cent) said they would have liked either more face-to-face or telephone contact. While trying to be understanding of their son's or daughter's busy life and family commitments, they would also add that 'it would be nice to see her more often' or 'have more telephone calls', but at the same time they knew their children 'were always there' should they need them. Turning to how contact between the adopted person and his or her birth family had affected their own frequency of contact, almost all adopters (96 per cent) said it had made no difference. The rest reported that it had either increased or came back to normal.

Table 12.7

What limits the frequency of contact between adopters and the adopted person?

	Distance	No limits	Not enough time	Other	All
%	49	23	23	5	100

N = 80 (missing 13)

Summary

Over two-thirds of adopters said that they had always been aware that their sons and daughters were thinking about tracing birth relatives, with the rest being either unaware or unsure. Almost a quarter did not learn about the search until after contact had been established. Those who said that they had always known, or at least had known before contact, were also more positive about the search/contact experience than those who had been told after contact.

The parents' initial reaction to the news that the adopted person was searching fell into two distinct patterns: anxiety and fear that their child might be hurt in the process, i.e., rejected by the birth family; and fear of loss, i.e. themselves losing the child to the birth family. Some of the parents whose sons and daughters were being sought had been annoyed initially, and one was angry, perceiving it as an 'intrusion'. On the whole, though, between half and three-quarters of them reported having been 'supportive' or 'pleased' about the search, largely viewing it as identity enhancing for their child, but between a quarter and a third had been either worried or nervous and a handful had felt hurt and upset. Those parents whose main initial reaction to the search/approach was to be frightened/worried/nervous, or other similar reactions, rated the overall experience of adoption as more positive than those reporting other reactions. This would suggest that their initial reaction was not unrealistic to the threat contact posed.

Many of the fears and worries anticipated at the start were realised in only a small number of cases. Possibly the biggest relief had been the discovery that the search had not affected the adoptive relationship and in a significant number of cases it was said to have 'enhanced' it. Around seven out of ten adopters also reported that the relationship with their sons and daughters remained unchanged, as a result of the search, with the rest mostly saying that it had been 'enhanced'. They were largely reassured that their sons and daughters could have more than one relationship without the one being at the expense of the other. They were also aware that, in the majority of cases, the new relationship had no strong parental overtones. Nine out of ten adopters reported ongoing direct or indirect forms of daily or weekly contact with their son or daughter, and for a quarter this was face-to-face. Hardly any had lost contact with the adopted person.

13 The adoptive parents' overall perspective on contact

Adoptive parent:

Concerns that he would leave us were groundless – he is even more sure he is 'ours' after the experience. We are happy that he has at last met his mother and made a friend of her.

This chapter largely provides an overview from the adoptive parents' perspective of the search and reunion process and its meaning and impact on them and their relationship with their sons and daughters.

Contact between adopters and members of the birth family

Two-thirds of adopters had established direct or indirect forms of contact with members of the adopted person's birth family, mostly the birth mother. Eight out of ten (80 per cent) of those who made contact had met face-to-face at least once. There was no difference between those adopters whose children searched and those who were sought by their birth mothers. Those parents who had met their son/daughter's birth relatives viewed the search and reunion experience more positively than the rest (p = 0.020). Where direct or indirect forms of contact took place, in two-thirds of cases it had been initiated by the adopted person, in a fifth by the adopters themselves, and in the remaining 14 per cent by the birth family. Adopters gave a number of reasons for wishing to meet members of the birth family. Apart from curiosity to see what the birth parent looked like, other reasons included wanting to say 'thank you' for what they considered to have been a "gift", understanding why their son or daughter was put up for adoption and 'showing' the birth parent how they had brought up their child. The possible development of a relationship was not at the forefront of their thoughts. As some explained: 'I needed to see her and say thank you'; 'Without the mother I would not have had a son';

and 'we wanted to thank his birth mother for all the joy and happiness S. had given us'. A number of them added that it would be only natural for the birth mother to want to meet the people who looked after her child, to see who they were and learn how they had brought up the child.

At the same time, many adopters stressed that they had agreed to meet members of the birth family only if their sons and daughters had asked them or wanted it, or if it was also the wish of the birth relative. In one case, only the adoptive mother had wanted to meet the birth mother, the father having declined. Some parents allowed time to pass before coming into the picture, not wanting to 'rush' it. It was also felt that they should give time to see how their son's or daughter's contact developed and perhaps let them decide when it was the right time: 'I would be hesitant,' said one, 'to rush into a contrived relationship'. A significant number saw contact with the birth family as a demonstration of their approval of and support for the adopted person as well as wanting to be part of what was going on. However, in several cases the adopted person had been insistent that his or her parents should not meet with the birth family. Equally, in a handful of other cases, it had been the birth family that did not want the contact. One adopter remarked: 'Our desire to meet them was not reciprocated by them'.

Around a third of adopters said they had not wished to meet members of the birth family. Many of them could not see what purpose contact would serve. There were also those who wanted to remain 'neutral', viewing it as an interference and serving no purpose, or as being a matter solely between the adopted person and the birth family. Some typical comments included: 'I never met or wanted to meet his mother'; 'nothing could be gained by such a meeting'; 'what good would it do them or me?'; or 'there would be no benefit in our having contact now our daughter was an adult'. Another referred to the promise they had made at the time of the adoption that they would make no contact with the birth family and they wanted to keep to it. Several others, possibly feeling threatened, had been fearful that contact might develop into a confrontation about which was the adopted person's "real" family and they wanted to avoid it. One of them stressed that they were the "real" family and not the birth relatives while another added:

Her relatives were brothers and sisters but I felt it was the brother and sister she had grown up with all those years who were her true family.

Initial feelings before contact with members of their sons and daughters' birth families included a mixture of anticipation and excitement along with apprehension and nervousness. Much of the nervousness came from not knowing what it would be like or how to manage it because of the unusualness of the situation. (An earlier chapter identified similar feelings among birth mothers prior to meeting with the people who had adopted their children.) In the absence of precedent, or of a script, on how to manage such encounters the anxiety was unsurprising. For example, some adoptive parents had wondered whether it would take the form of celebration or of bitter recriminations. While many adopters had come to view the child as a kind of gift from the birth mother, they were also aware that this might not be how the birth mother saw it. Notwithstanding the uncertainties, the majority of adopters had been pleased and glad that they did it because they had been made to feel welcomed. Again, as seen earlier, far from the birth mothers feeling hostile, as if their child had been 'stolen', they wanted to express their gratitude for the way the adopters brought up their child. A number of adopters added that the meeting had made them feel much more understanding and more empathic towards the birth mother for her own loss and pain over the years. Meeting the birth mother, said one adoptive mother, had helped her also understand her adopted son better. Others added that they had become more aware now of how much the birth mother or birth father had missed by not rearing their child. The following is a representative comment:

Pleased because if it hadn't been for the birth mother we wouldn't have had the happiness we had with our daughter.

A significant minority who were feeling more nervous and insecure, strange, apprehensive or even threatened by the forthcoming meeting mostly had their worries and apprehensions dissipated. There was reference to being 'more at ease' now; everything 'having gone well'; or having met birth family members they were 'now happy'; nervous at first 'but it wasn't long before we were all chatting naturally'; 'excited and relieved'; or 'all very amicable meeting at a motorway service station'. Overall, for these adopters, meeting the birth mother and coming to know her as a person had also greatly helped to reduce fears and anxieties associated with their son's and daughter's contact and they were equally glad to have had the birth mother's approval for the way they had brought up the adopted person.

Among those adopters who had established contact with birth relatives, in seven out of ten cases the relationship continued, but mostly indirectly. With the rest it lapsed altogether, mostly at the initiative of the adopted person and this reflected the state of his or her relationship with members of the birth family. Birth relatives and adoptive parents ceased contact in about equal proportions, mostly by allowing contact to wane, for example, birth relatives or adopters would fail to send a Christmas or holiday card. More often, indirect contact would follow after a one-off, face-to-face meeting, with several adopters describing it as contact 'at arms length'. In a minority of cases, face-to-face contact continued to take place once or twice a year, mostly with a birth mother, and sometimes a sibling. More unusually, some reported that their child's birth relative had become a distant friend or that enduring relationships had been forged with the adoptive and birth families taking holidays together, an adoptive mother developing a close relationship with the adopted person's half-sister, the two families meeting at Christmas or on birthdays or family members staying overnight at each other's homes. What mostly kept these relationships going were shared interests.

Contact, worry and stress

Similar to when they had first heard that the adopted person was searching or about to search for a birth relative, when contact became a reality, over half of adopters (55 per cent) reported a re-emergence of stronger feelings of worry and anxiety than before. The focus of the anxieties was the same but perhaps more pronounced, i.e. concern that their sons and daughters might be rejected by their birth family and suffer, or anxiety about the impact of contact on their relationship. While the majority wanted to be supportive and protective, they had also wondered if they were being marginalised gradually. A small number also thought that their sons and daughters had been particularly vulnerable at the time because they were going through a personal crisis such as a difficult relationship, a failed marriage, illness or generally being difficult to relate to. More pronounced concerns were expressed, particularly on behalf of those sought, because the adopted person had not been prepared for it beforehand and was not in control. For example, one parent reported that her daughter had become so upset that she gave up her job, went travelling and moved house. Another parent added that she had been afraid her son was going to have a breakdown after he was first contacted – because he was so upset. Some of the criticism was directed at the birth mother and some at the adoption society for not telling the adopters beforehand or even asking for their permission. There had also been some concern for sought birth mothers wondering how contact might affect their families. As will be shown later, and as with the earlier concerns, these worries mostly did not materialise, especially the impact of the search on the parents' relationship with their sons and daughters.

When asked to compare the amount of stress they had felt as a result of contact to other major life events, only six per cent of adoptive parents reported that the stress had been 'extreme' with another 34 per cent saying it was moderately so. This contrasted with over a quarter of birth mothers who reported that they had found contact 'extremely' stressful and over a third who found it 'moderately' so. One of these parents remarked that their other children had felt 'betrayed' by the adopted brother making contact, and in another case the siblings had been worried about having to 'share' their brother with his new family.

Closeness to the adopted person before and after contact

Around nine out of ten adoptive parents described very close or close relationships with their sons and daughters both before and after contact (Table 13.1). There were strong positive associations between the reported closeness to the adopted person during different stages from childhood to the present as well as the overall adoption experience. In other words, the higher the satisfaction with the overall adoption experience the closer also the reported relationship to the adopted person. (Early childhood $p = 0.042$; adolescence $p < 0.001$; before contact $p < 0.001$; currently p < 0.001.) Levels of closeness before contact were also highly predictive of post-contact closeness (p < 0.001). Equally, the closer the current relationship to the adopted person, the more positive the adoptive parents had been about the search and reunion experience (p = 0.004). Closeness was expressed in glowing terms such as: having always been 'very close and it continued like that'; 'a strong relationship always being present'; 'contact made no difference to our closeness'; 'a good loving family relationship' continuing; or a 'normal parent–child relationship continued'. As one of them explained: 'It's been deeply affectionate and continued so after his marriage and contact'. And another:

We have always been close and could talk about anything.

Only two parents said that closeness between them and their child had 'never developed'. One of them added that, over the years, the adopted person had shown her little affection and she came to see herself as being simply 'a provider'. A handful of others referred to mixed levels of closeness or that some distance had developed over the years. In one case, an adopted person had walked out because he was dissatisfied with his adoptive parents' lifestyle, while another had 'blamed' them for everything that had happened in her life.

Table 13.1
Levels of reported closeness before and after contact

Level of closeness	Before contact* %	Now[†] %
Very close, close	86	94
Mixed	10	4
Not very close or not at all close	4	2
Total	100	100

* Before contact N = 88 (missing 5)
[†] After contact N = 92 (missing 1)

Impact of contact on the relationship

Almost two-thirds of adopters (65 per cent) reported that contact had had no effect on the relationship they had with their sons and daughters, adding that the relationship had been good before contact and remained so afterwards. Over a fifth (22 per cent) claimed that it had been enhanced. The rest (13 per cent) said that it had deteriorated or come under strain (Figure 13.1). No differences in the effect of contact on the adoptive relationship were reported between searching and non-searching adopted people.

Figure 13.1
The effect of contact on the adoptive relationship

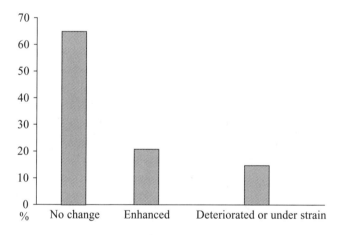

N = 82 (missing 11)

No change

The majority who said that there had been no change in the relationship after contact explained that the relationship had been good beforehand and remained so. One of them said that for their daughter 'contact was an enormous piece of happiness for her to share'; another that, 'his extra family has made no difference'. A number of parents commented on how contact helped them to better understand their sons and daughters and to develop more insight into their feelings of being adopted which, they added, brought them closer together. A significant number also described initial difficulties or doubts, although the relationship was reported to have reverted to previous levels. One adoptive mother remarked that initially contact had felt hurtful, but because they had built up so much affection for each other in the past, this had surmounted all difficulties. Another had felt 'pushed out' because the birth mother continually wanted to see their son and an adoptive father described his wife's early problems in 'reconciling' herself to the idea. Another referred to initial 'bitterness' but reported that the adoptive relationship had not been undermined. Possibly as a form of reassurance, a few parents stressed that the adopted person had related to his or her birth mother or father as a friend or as an aunt or uncle rather than as a parent. As one of them remarked:

Her birth mother has become a good friend to her and she has enjoyed also meeting her aunt and cousins.

Enhanced

Enhancement of the relationship was said to have occurred in over a fifth of cases. These parents claimed that contact had brought their relationship even closer referring to 'a happier adult relationship'; 'more open'; or 'more respect for each other'. Others reported that contact had made them feel more secure as a family or 'cemented' their relationship.

Strain and deterioration

Around one out of eight (12 per cent) parents said that the relationship had come under strain or had deteriorated as a result of contact. Some explained the strain as referring mainly to the initial stages when the uncertainty had generated anxiety and stress. Others, however, had different concerns, such as one parent who had felt 'continuously pushed out' by a demanding birth mother and one son who was reported to have left 'bitterness' behind him by leaving home and 'relegating them to the background'. Several other adopters had felt 'excluded' from the adopted person's new relationship, more so if the adopted person avoided talking about it. One adoptive mother described the aftermath of contact as a kind of 'bereavement' but with time it had healed. The views of this mother had some similarity with those of some birth mothers who said they had experienced the parting from their son or daughter as 'bereavement'. One of the two negative responses was from an adoptive mother who had felt 'diminished' because she viewed her daughter's contact with her birth mother as suggesting that her own parenting was inadequate. The other was that concerning an adopted person who became more private and far more distant after contact.

While most relationships were restored to previous levels before contact had taken place, this could disguise the amount of strain, doubts and anxieties a fair number of adoptive parents experienced. For these parents it had been possibly one of the most critical, if not the most critical, periods of the adoption experience because, as some put it, there was so much uncertainty about where contact would eventually lead. Being kept informed by the adopted person about what was happening had helped reduce the anxiety, but this did not always happen. Although the majority of adopted people had been concerned about the possible impact of their search and contact on their adoptive parents, a few had not kept them in the picture, mainly to protect them from being hurt. Their explanation did not differ much from that of a small number of adoptive parents who had experienced some difficulty in explaining the adoption and talking about the birth family from fear of hurting or upsetting the adopted person.

Counselling

While admitting to some concerns and anxieties, almost all adopters reported that they had not been worried to such an extent, or had such problems over the search and contact as to warrant seeking counselling. One of them characteristically said:

Worked them [anxieties] out during long walks and talking to my husband.

A handful of others had spoken to friends, or other adopters, specifically about the search. What possibly made most adopters come to feel that they did not need counselling had been the realisation soon after contact was established that there was nothing much to worry about because contact was not proving to be the Pandora's box they had anticipated – a reminder that the adoptive parents' score on the GHQ demonstrated high rates of emotional health. Only one parent in the sample had sought formal counselling from the adoption agency but a small number had met adoption counsellors as part of the search process, rather than for themselves. A handful would have welcomed more help from the adoption agency. These parents had felt betrayed and were critical of the adoption agency for paying so much attention to birth relatives, but offering them little support. One of them explained:

I did not get any support from the Society. It was all for birth mothers and adopted children. I felt very pushed out after his birth mother continually wanted to see S.

How contact turned out for the different parties

Almost seven out of ten adopters (68 per cent) evaluated the contact experience for themselves as having been very positive or positive, with almost a fifth saying that it had no effect either way. Only three per cent had found it negative (Table 13.2). The more pleased the adoptive parents had been that the adopted person had searched or had been sought out, the more positive also the overall ratings of the search/contact experience ($p < 0.001$). The more positive the adoption experience, the more likely also for adoptive parents to repeat that the search/contact had been positive ($p = 0.033$). Those who also thought that their son/daughter was 'just like

Table 13.2

The contact experience for each of the three parties as perceived by the adopters

Experience	Ad. parents* %	Ad. person %	Birth parent %
Very positive/positive	68	74	57
No effect	17	2	1
Not sure	12	18	32
Negative	3	6	10
Total	100	100	100

N = 87 (missing 6)

them' were more likely to be positive about the search/contact experience (p = 0.029).

Almost three out of five adopters (57 per cent) thought that the birth parents had benefited from contact, around a third (32 per cent) were uncertain and 10 per cent thought that the effect on them had been negative. Many showed considerable sympathy and understanding about the birth mother's position, with one of them summing it up by saying:

His birth mother must have wondered all those years where he was and what he was like. I am pleased for her sake that she now knows and sees him and his family from time to time. Equally, we know what she is like.

When it came to their son or daughter, almost three-quarters of adopters perceived the impact of contact on them as having been very positive or positive, with only six per cent describing it as negative. The positives for the adopters and the adopted person were said to have been the fulfilment of their wish to find answers to questions and in a number of cases to establish positive relationships with members of their families. For the birth parent, it was mainly to satisfy themselves about the well-being of the adopted person and again, in some cases, to establish relationships. On the whole, however, adopters placed less emphasis on the development of relationships than on other benefits. The few negative experiences for either the adopted person or the birth parent, were said to be due to upsets arising mainly from one party not wanting to see the other or terminating contact. In one case, the birth family was said to have become upset because they were hoping the adopted person would become part of their family and this had not transpired. A more disillusioned parent, whose two children had been 'rejected' by a birth parent, remarked that:

It had been an unnecessary experience that had not brought happiness to anyone.

Almost all adopters also said that the search had made no difference to their family life, with a handful adding that it had made them happier or brought them closer together. The most frequent answers, though, were 'no change', 'not at all changed', and 'no effect'. Like many others, one of them observed:

> No change at all. Just very pleased he has found his mother and continues to be happy with my wife and I.

A few qualified their answer by saying that there had been some initial worry or that the timing of contact had not been right, but the dust soon 'settled'.

What has been good or bad about contact

Irrespective of whether the adopted person had searched or had been sought, almost seven out of ten adoptive parents identified positives and benefits as having come out of it (Table 13.3). The "good" things identified by adopters were broadly, but not wholly, linked to the kind of expectations the adopted person had before the search.

Table 13.3
All the good things about the search/contact as perceived by the adopters

Good things	%
Establishing relationships	33
Obtaining information	23
Simply making contact	14
Impact on the adoption relationship	12
Mixed	7
No benefits	17
Other	4

N = 84 (missing 9)

The main benefits of contact came under three groupings: making contact and establishing relationships; obtaining information and satisfying curiosity; and the positive impact on the adopters themselves (Table 13.3).

Making contact and establishing relationships

Although the establishment of new relationships had not featured signifi-cantly in what the parents perceived as the adopted person's original expectations from the search, they now became more centre stage as the main good thing to have resulted from contact. These parents were pleased that their sons and daughters had found people with whom they could establish mutually productive relationships. Although not all contact had resulted in the development of such relationships, close ones did develop with birth mothers, then siblings, and often with a birth father. Like many others, one parent observed that her daughter traced her father and 'they now have a comfortable relationship'. Equally, there was recognition that the relationship with the birth relative did not often impinge upon theirs:

She found her birth mother and she has a good relationship with her, which does not impinge on our relationship.

Another parent remarked:

It enlarged our small family and my daughter loves all the extra family members – they also involve me and my son in family reunions.

Relationships had also been established with other birth relatives such as grandparents and siblings and many parents, far from feeling threatened, appeared glad on behalf of the adopted person that the latter had expanded their family circle. One referred to the extra grandparents in the family and how they themselves also became part of these relationships. Besides finding birth parents, adopted people were said to have found full and half-siblings, aunts and uncles and grandparents. The discovery of siblings, they said, gave the adopted person special pleasure. Several observed how their grandchildren now had four sets of grandparents: 'He has a relationship with his birth father and paternal grandmother and I feel this is a good situation for all of them'. There was also sadness if a birth parent or grandparent had died and the opportunity of meeting had been lost. One adopter remarked:

When his mother was dying I was glad she could see him for himself and see he was happy and to feel she did the right thing.

Obtaining information and satisfying curiosity

An earlier chapter showed that a major expectation on the part of the adopted person, as perceived by their parents, was to find out more about 'who' they were, i.e. to have background information about roots and origins and also to find out why they had been placed for adoption. In the parents' view, obtaining background information had been one of the key 'good' things to emerge from the search and it referred to two aspects of adoption: first, to genealogical and other background information, and second, to answers to the question '*why adoption*'. Adoptive parents showed considerable awareness about the importance of background information and the relevance of origins and genealogy in identity formation. There was reference to the adopted person finding or tracing their 'roots'; 'satisfying curiosity'; knowing their 'real parentage'; and firming or resolving 'identity' issues. 'Satisfaction for her having all her "unknowns" answered' was a common response. Some parents added that had they been in their child's position they would have done exactly the same, i.e. searched.

Adopters also reported that finding answers to the question of 'why placed for adoption' was another key gain from the search and/or contact. Overall, in the adopters' view, obtaining this information, learning the 'true' facts and seeing what a parent or relative looked like helped adopted people to understand themselves and their feelings better, put things in 'perspective' or simply 'complete' themselves and their identity. One of them reported that, having found an answer to the question 'why', her daughter had developed 'a clearer picture of herself' while another said that it had helped his daughter 'to understand her feelings better'. Some of the parents were aware that, behind the desire for an answer to the question 'why adoption', or 'why me', was the adopted person's hope of being told that they were not 'rejected' or 'unloved'. As some of them observed: 'it made her happy'; 'a more content person'; 'his confidence grew'; and 'it brought her much happiness'.

Enhancement of the relationship

Enhancement of the relationship between adopters and their son or daughter was highlighted in a significant number of cases (for more details see earlier comments on the impact of the search on the adoptive relationship).

What was 'not so good' about the search and contact?

About one-third of adopters identified moderate to serious problems (resulting from the search) affecting mainly the adopted person with fewer impacting on themselves. Some initial criticism centred on the timing of the contact, via the adoption agency, with some mothers saying that the adopted person and they themselves had been taken by surprise and were not ready for the approach. However, most of the disappointment had to do with the rejection of the adopted person by one or more members of the birth family, usually the mother; rejection by a birth relative was said to have occurred in 17 per cent of all cases. Rejection came mainly from the birth mother. More rarely, a father had not wanted to meet the adopted person. Typical comments included: 'birth mother's rejection'; 'she does not want to meet us'; 'not bothered'; 'her father is unwilling to meet her'; or 'disappointment that birth mother did not want any contact'. Another explained:

> Her birth mother, when traced, refused all contact between them – doesn't wish to meet her, and gives no reasonable explanation.

Adoptive parents were aware that such rejection would have been experienced as 'double' by the adopted person because of the original rejection. One adopted person had first found her birth mother who wanted to have nothing to do with her and later her father who also did not want to meet her. Another had found his father whom he did not like, and when he met his birth mother, her husband did not wish her to have any contact with him. Some adopted people could not understand why a half-brother or sister did not want to meet them. One adoptive parent explained that their daughter could not get a proper explanation as to why a birth parent kept another sibling but not herself, while another added:

> She could not understand why she was put up for adoption when hearing from other members of the family that they would have kept her.

Other 'not so good things' arising from the search and reunion had to do with communication problems with birth parents. This included the adopted person wanting more contact, which was not forthcoming, or not getting answers from the birth parents to questions, thus leading to frustration about the circumstances of the adoption. In a number of cases, it was the adopted person who was said to have either lost interest or been disappointed with what he or she found and they had then gradually withdrawn from contact. The explanations did not differ much from those offered by adopted people as to why contact had stopped. Parents made reference to the lack of common interests; 'the quality of birth relatives'; 'the birth mother having problems'; the birth family being 'mixed up'; or general disappointment 'with what he found'. In cases of adopted people who had been sought by their birth mothers, the adopters singled out the initial shock, adding that the adopted person had not been ready. In one case, the adopted person was married and it was said that, apart from experiencing the approach as 'overpowering', it had made his wife jealous. The approach had caused another adopted person 'a lot of stress' and she had declined contact, but after a few years she herself sought out her birth mother. A handful of adopters also referred to the 'emotional drain' that the search and its aftermath had caused in their lives and those of their children.

Perceived changes

Finally, adopters were asked to provide an overall evaluation of their son's or daughter's search and contact with his/her birth relative(s). The results are set out in Table 13.4.

A major characteristic of all the replies, which appear in Table 13.4, was the high levels of apparent satisfaction reported by adopters, irrespective of whether their sons and daughters had searched or had been sought. There were very few dissenting voices to allow for any wider conclusions to be made. The 19 statements could be separated into two groups: six of the statements refer directly to the perceived impact of the search and contact on the adopted person, and the rest on the adoptive parents themselves. Starting with the adopted person, almost half of adopters (47 per cent) said that their son or daughter's emotional outlook had improved since the search or contact, with only three per cent saying that it had worsened. A slightly lower proportion also said that the adopted person could now relate better to people because of his/her search or contact. Hardly anyone said that they wished their sons and daughters had not searched.

Table 13.4
Overall review of outcomes as perceived by adopters

Statement	Strongly agree/ agree %	Uncertain %	Strongly disagree or disagree %	All %
1. I am happy with my current level of contact with my son/ daughter	98	1	1	100
2. I would like more contact with my son/daughter	34	4	62	100
3. I am satisfied with my current relationship with my son/daughter	94	4	2	100
4. I feel my son/daughter can relate better to people because of his/her search or contact	44	43	12	99
5. I felt disappointed by my son/daughter's search or contact	9	9	82	100
6. I feel that my son/daughter's emotional outlook has improved since the search or contact	47	37	16	100
7. I feel that my son/daughter's emotional outlook has worsened since the search or contact	3	14	83	100
8. Overall I feel the search or contact has been a positive experience	79	16	6	101
9. My self-esteem has improved since my son/daughter's search or contact	21	19	60	100
10. My family's reaction to the search/contact has been positive	73	23	4	100
11. I wish my son/daughter had not met his/her birth relative(s)	4	5	91	100
12. I feel more relaxed since my son/daughter searched or had contact	55	8	37	100
13. I feel unchanged since the search or contact	77	5	18	100
14. I feel angrier since the search or contact	—	3	97	100
15. Overall I feel satisfied with the outcome of the search or contact	87	7	6	100
16. I feel a stranger to my son/daughter	1	1	98	100
17. My son/daughter is just like me	24	16	60	100
18. I feel confused about my feelings for my son or daughter	4	3	94	101
19. I found it hard to cope with the intensity of my feelings	11	3	86	100

Turning to themselves, over nine out of ten adopters (94 per cent) were satisfied with the current relationship they had with the adopted person and almost one hundred per cent were happy with the amount of contact they currently had, even though a third would have appreciated more. Over eight out of ten also reported that they were happy with their son's or daughter's search or contact, with only one out of ten saying they were disappointed. Almost eight out of ten evaluated the search or contact as having been a positive experience with only six per cent disagreeing. Only four per cent of parents wished the adopted person had not estab-lished contact and barely any felt angry with what had happened. The more positive the review of the search/contact experience, the less likely the adoptive parents were to wish that the adopted person had not met their birth relatives (p < 0.001). The 21 per cent who agreed or strongly agreed that their self-esteem had improved as a result of the search/contact were also likely to be more positive about the search/contact (p = 0.007).

Contact and the law

The Children Act 1975, which paved the way for access by adopted people to their birth records, was a landmark step at the time. To the best of our knowledge, however, there was no systematic collection of the adoptive parents' views to this change. In this study, nine out of ten adopters had known of the legal changes introduced by the Children Act 1975 which provided for access to birth records that could also lead to contact between adopted people and members of the birth family. Asked how they felt about it, three out of every five (61 per cent) were pleased, with another 14 per cent saying they were indifferent. However, 13 per cent felt either worried or angry about the changes (see Table 13.5).

Table 13.5
Reaction to the Act providing for access to the birth records

	Pleased	Worried	Angry	Indifferent	Not sure	All
%	61	8	5	14	13	101

N = 80 (missing 13)

The Adoption Contact Register and rights of access to birth relatives

Three-fifths (62 per cent) of adopters had heard about the Adoption Contact Register, but almost three out of ten (28 per cent) had not. The rest (10 per cent) were not sure. Asked whether birth relatives should have rights of access to the adopted person, the answers were split almost equally into three with 29 per cent being in favour, 39 per cent disagreeing and the remaining 33 per cent being uncertain. Adoptive parents who supported the view that birth relatives should have contact rights were also more likely to have better emotional health (p = 0.028). Those who were in favour of birth relatives having the right to obtain identifying information looked at it mainly from the birth mother's point of view, showing understanding and empathy towards her predicament. For example, they referred to the loss and grief arising from parting with a child, and the subsequent uncertainty about what happened to the child, and perhaps the mother being 'haunted' for the rest of her life. 'Because', one said, 'a mother never forgets the babies she bears and a healthy curiosity is present in most women'. Others recognised the social context within which the parting had taken place:

Often it wasn't the mother's choice because in years gone by there was no choice. For many mothers having to part with a baby must have been heart breaking.

Most of those who disagreed (39 per cent) said that the adopted person should be consulted first, or even that the initiative for the search should first come from him or her, once they were ready. It was felt that the age of 18 was too young for the adopted person to cope with the kind of emotions the approach might raise. The adopted person, it was argued, should preferably know beforehand what the birth relative wanted. On the whole this group wanted to stress the paramount importance of the adopted person's wish and their perceived right to be in control. One parent stated that although their son was aware of the existence of the Register, he did not want contact. There was a feeling that contact would be 'forced' on him adding: 'I think the adopted person should be allowed to contact but not the other way round'.

Drawing from their own experience, a handful of adopters were critical of the adoption society for not having let them know first that either their son or daughter or a birth relative was seeking contact, or even asking for their permission to proceed. They saw this as a 'failure' on the part of the society. No adopted person indicated that their adoptive parents' permission should be necessary for initiating contact, even though many of them informed them about their intentions beforehand.

Encouraging adopted people to have contact

Around three out of ten adopters (31 per cent) strongly agreed or agreed with the proposition that all adopted people should be encouraged to have contact with members of their birth family, with a fifth disagreeing. As many as half (49 per cent) expressed no opinion, suggesting some degree of uncertainty (Table 13.6). Whether adopters agreed, disagreed or remained neutral, they believed that the ultimate decision should be left to the adopted person. Only a handful of parents wanted to exercise a "veto" over it. There was no support for any pressure being exerted on adopted people to have contact. Parents were not opposed to openness but the initiative, they insisted, should come from the adopted person. Repeated comments included: 'leave it to the individual'; 'it should be a personal choice'; 'the exclusive right of the adopted person'; or 'it should always come from the adopted person'. In their view the role of others was to support and not to put pressure one way or the other, or as one of them put it, 'they should neither encourage nor hinder'. After all, some added, the adopted person may not wish to have contact or may not feel ready:

> It should be something the adopted person really wants to do. Not something they are persuaded to do.

A number of adopters also made the point that, for any one to put pressure on the adopted person to have contact, it pre-supposed that they knew when the adopted person was ready. It was not just a matter of age, some added, but also of overall emotional readiness. Some also commented on the "downside" of contact by making reference to the possible rejection and the pain that could result. One parent whose son was rejected by his

Table 13.6

Should all adopted people be encouraged to have contact with their birth families?

	Strongly agree/agree	*Neutral*	*Strongly disagree/ disagree*	*All*
%	31	49	20	100

N = 88 (missing 5)

birth mother commented that she would not encourage anyone to go through what her son had experienced.

The institution of adoption

Over nine out of ten adopters disagreed or disagreed strongly with the proposition that there should be no adoption in society. Adoptive parents who had more positive overall adoption experiences felt more strongly that there should be adoption in society (p < 0.001). Most adopters placed the emphasis on adoption being a child-centred activity that brought benefits to children adding that, without adoption, there would be many unhappy children. They also referred to children's need for 'a secure and loving home'; their 'right to have the love of a good family'; or the 'chance for a stable life'. One of many such comments was: 'There must be lots of children who need love and stability and lots of childless couples who could give them this'. There was also emphasis on the immense pleasure that adoption had brought to them as parents. Many were certain that, on the basis of their own experience, adoption had brought a lot of happiness and fulfilment to their children and otherwise, as one said, 'their lives would be empty'.

A large number of children and their adoptive parents/relatives have gained immeasurable happiness through the adoption system and it would be very wrong to stop it.

Some adopters recognised that in an "ideal world" it would not be necessary to have adoption, but that things being as they are, adoption offers a better solution than any of the alternatives. A significant number of adoptive parents pondered on what alternative provision could replace adoption and sending children to institutions or even placing them in long-term foster care were deemed unsatisfactory unless there were other reasons for doing so. As one of them pointed out:

Fostering? That can lead to dreadful insecurity. Children's homes? Adoption is the best answer.

Adoption, many added, achieves the double objective of providing a home for a needy child and also fulfilling the aspirations of those who have no children or wish to expand their families. The handful of adopters who were uncommitted or against the idea of adoption thought that all children should be brought up by their own families or that many single parents did a very good job in bringing up their children.

Recommending adoption to others

Nine out of ten adopters would recommend adoption to others, but the rest would not. Those who would did so on the basis of what it had meant to them and then to their children. Many explained that it had proved 'rewarding'; had 'enriched' their lives; had been 'a very positive experience'; or 'gave them a purpose in life'. A number of them said they would like others to experience the satisfaction they had experienced. Another typical comment:

It makes not only a home but also a family and the joy you have from seeing them grow up is indescribable.

The enthusiasm for adoption was occasionally tempered by some caution, thereby suggesting that adoption might not be for everybody or that there could also be pain, hurt and difficulties. Several added that, although they had no regrets, they would recommend fostering first, before moving to adoption. Several others added that, although not all adoption turns out well, parenting the child itself provides a lot of pleasure. A number were careful to also stress also that recommending adoption was not enough; the wish to parent someone else's child has to come from the individual and not be simply based on a recommendation.

Summary

With the exception of the period of adolescence, nine out of ten adopters described very close or close relationships between themselves and the adopted person during childhood, both before and after contact. During adolescence, the closeness of the relationship had decreased for 65 per cent of the sample, but recovered later. Levels of closeness between the adoptive parents and the adopted person before contact were highly predictive of current closeness between them. Distance proved to be a limiting factor for more direct contact. The closer the current relationship between adoptive parents and the adopted person, the more positive was the rating of the search/contact experience.

Before their son or daughter had contact, over half of adopters had been greatly worried about the possibility of their child being 'hurt' through rejection, or losing their child to the birth family. These fears proved mostly, though not always, unfounded. Two-thirds of adoptive parents themselves had some form of contact with members of the adopted person's birth family, and half of all adopters had had at least one face-to-face meeting with a member of the birth family, mostly the mother. Whether the relationship continued or not largely depended on what transpired between the adopted person and their birth family. Those parents who had met their son/daughter's birth relatives came to view the search/contact experience more positively than the rest. One-third of all adopters had not wanted to have any form of contact. Meeting the birth mother was mainly to say "thank you" for the "gift" she had made to them. Initial anxieties and worries about how to present themselves and/ or about the reaction of the birth family did not materialise and most experiences had turned out to be pleasant. Parents identified many benefits for themselves from having taken this step, with some claiming that it had heightened their understanding of their son or daughter and deepened their empathy for the birth mother.

Nine out of ten adopters were pleased that their son or daughter had searched or had been sought by a birth relative. Almost a similar proportion also said that the adopted person had benefited greatly, mainly in terms of strengthening their identity and knowing why they had been given up for adoption. It was also the view of two-fifths of adopters that contact had made their sons or daughters feel 'more settled' and 'happier'. For another two-fifths it had made no difference, as they were already well settled. Only a very small proportion of between three and nine per cent said that the adopted person had become unhappy or unsettled. A group of seven (or 8 per cent) adopters in the sample rated the contact experience of their sons and daughters as being negative or were not sure about it and this appears to have influenced their answers to other questions.

Two-thirds also reported that contact had made no difference to the relationship between themselves and their son or daughter, with another 22 per cent saying that it had in fact enhanced it. The remaining 13 per cent thought that it had affected it adversely. Finally, eight out of ten adopters felt that the search and contact had been a positive experience for themselves and 87 per cent felt satisfied with the outcome of the search and contact. Certainly contact did not appear to them to be as risky as many had originally feared. Nevertheless, this had not made the 'rejection' of their son or daughter by a birth relative, when it happened, any less painful, especially as the adoptive parents found themselves picking up some of the pieces. It could be argued that the very high levels of positive evaluation of the search and contact experience by adopters is a denial of the fears and worries that they went through, either about the adopted person or themselves.

14 Adopted people and their birth mothers – paired perspectives

Birth mother:
Having met my son I now feel more complete.

Son:
Now that I know more about the circumstances of my adoption I feel more complete.

Note: All examples in this chapter refer to members of the same dyad or pair.

Introduction

Previous chapters have detailed the separate perceptions of the two samples of adopted people and birth mothers. This chapter compares the perspectives on the search and reunion process of those in the samples who constituted *pairs* of birth mothers and their adopted sons or daughters. The group of adopted adults consisted of 49 females and 29 males. The sample is somewhat smaller than the main ones of birth mothers and adopted people who featured in previous chapters, because not all of those were matched. As a result, some variations could be expected in percentages between the main samples and this paired group.

Expectations of contact

The overall expectations of birth mothers and adopted people of contact had both similarities and differences (Table 14.1). Both wanted to have news of the other and to find about each other's well-being. Above all, birth mothers wanted to find out how well the adopted person was, while the latter wanted to learn why they had been adopted. Establishing a relationship was important, but at the pre-contact stage not paramount in their expectations. Although appearing to cherish the idea, some mothers said they did not want to hope for too much. Possibly highlighting the importance of physical identity, 90 per cent of adopted people placed greater emphasis, compared to their birth mothers, on wanting to see what the birth mother and other birth relatives looked like, but the difference did not amount to significance. Even so, the number of birth mothers who also wanted to see what their son or daughter looked like was high (79 per cent), in spite of the fact that the mother had more images of physical likeness through knowing other members of their biological family, and in around three-quarters of cases knowing also what the birth father looked like. This no doubt reflects a simple curiosity.

Table 14.1
The birth mothers' and adopted adults' *all* expectations of contact

Expectations	Birth mothers* %	Adopted people[†] %
Find out how well he/she is	94	63
Have news of him/her	86	66
Why adoption	79	72
See what he/she looks like	79	90
Establishing a relationship	59	58

*Birth mothers N = 71 (missing 7); [†]Adopted people N = 66 (missing 12)

Below are some typical examples of both congruence and difference in how pairs of birth mothers and their sons and daughters explained their expectations:

Birth mother: I wanted to say sorry and tell her how much I had loved her. I had hoped we could become good friends.

Daughter: I just wanted to know who I was and where I had come from and why put up for adoption.

Birth mother: To know she was well. From there on it would depend on what she wanted.

Daughter: Initially to know why given up where I came from. Now I wish we could have developed a proper relationship.

Birth mother: I wanted to know about his life and tell him anything he wanted to know.

Son: to see if I looked like my mother. Why I was adopted and if I had any siblings but mainly to get to know her.

Birth mother: I only had 'dread' rather than initial expectations. Only wanted indirect contact. It must seem I have disappointed and rejected her.

Daughter: I would have liked to have met my birth parents but they have both had reasons not to see me.

Birth mother: I wanted to know how he had grown up, lifestyle, etc., family likeness and to let him know that parting with him was the worst day of my life.

Son: I wanted to know everything at once and I hoped for an ongoing relationship. Wanted them [birth parents] to be healthy.

Birth mother: I wanted to know about her life and tell her anything she wanted to know.

Daughter: To see if I looked like her, why I was adopted and if I had any siblings. But mainly to get to know her.

Thinking about each other

Birth mothers were far more likely to say that they had thought of their child during his or her childhood compared to adopted people thinking about their mothers when they were children ($p = 0.003$). However, there were no significant differences between how often birth mothers and their daughters thought about each other; this difference was found only between the birth mothers and their sons ($p = 0.039$). These differences disappeared during adolescence and in adulthood. It seems to confirm other findings suggesting that awareness on the part of the adopted person about the full meaning of adoption is a gradual process and that full awareness is not reached until about adolescence.

The perceived reaction of their respective families to contact

Almost nine out of ten birth mothers (88 per cent) reported that their families (meaning husbands/partners and children) had reacted positively to the idea of contact. Only 12 per cent of them reported that their own families had either reacted negatively or been uncertain of their reaction. However, this could appear to be somewhat of an under-estimate when set alongside some of their comments which, in a number of cases, referred to disapproving husbands/partners and occasionally to siblings reacting negatively and viewing contact as detracting from the birth mother's current family. Significantly fewer adopted people (58 per cent) than birth mothers said that their adoptive families had reacted positively to the search and reunion event (p = 0.003). The rest were said to be either hostile or uncertain about their true feelings.

Satisfaction with the current level of contact

Nearly twice as many birth mothers as adopted people reported that they were happy with the current level of contact (p = 0.007) (Table 14.2). This difference was to be found more among seeker than sought birth mothers (p = 0.013) and in comparison to their daughters rather than sons (p = 0.004). Overall, there was little agreement within the pairs of adopted adults and birth mothers over who wanted or did not want more contact, which was not surprising. Presumably, if both in a pair wanted more contact, they would have arranged it.

Table 14.2
Would parties like more contact?

Level of agreement	Birth mothers* %	Adopted persons[†] %
Strongly agree/agree	60	33
Uncertain	20	30
Strongly disagree/disagree	20	37
Total	100	100

*Birth mothers N = 55 (missing 23); [†]Adopted people N = 63 (missing 15)

Perceived closeness of the relationship

Of those who continued to have contact, around seven out of ten from each group of birth mothers and adopted adults reported that the relationship was close or very close. The rest referred to it as distant or of mixed quality (Table 14.3). There was hardly any difference about the perceived closeness of the face-to-face relationship between the two groups. Their respective answers and descriptions overlapped extensively (p < 0.001). From their accounts, each side appeared to be aware of when the relationship was not going well even though some birth mothers played the differences down. However, adopted people seemed keener to highlight and explain differences.

Table 14.3
Perception of the closeness of the relationship in current face-to-face contact

Level of closeness	Ad. person's rating[†] %	Birth mother's rating* %
Very close	41	38
Close	27	35
Mixed	18	15
Not very close	10	7
Not close at all	4	5
Total	100	100

[†]Adopted people N = 78 *Birth mothers N = 78

When it came to satisfaction with the current quality of the relationship, again around seven out of ten birth mothers and adopted people said they were satisfied and there was significant congruence within the pairs over how satisfied they were (p = 0.003). However, around one out of ten would have liked closer relationships, while the rest were dissatisfied. It was not surprising to find some disillusionment among this small group, but they still had no regrets for searching or being sought because of benefits other than that of a continued relationship.

The nature of the continued face-to-face relationship

Only a quarter of birth mothers (28 per cent) and a broadly similar proportion of adopted people (27 per cent) perceived their relationship as parental/filial. The most common description was that of a friend, sometimes adding relative/friend or parent/friend (Table 14.4). Whether friends or parents, the experience was mostly described as very satisfactory or satisfactory. As one adopted person put it: 'it was the best thing that could happen to me' even though he did not look upon the relationship as that between a son and parent. In cases where birth mothers said they viewed the relationship as being more like that of a friend, the adopted person would at times describe it as distant or like meeting a stranger. When each group of respondents were more specifically asked to say whether they felt like a 'stranger' to each other, significantly more adopted people, than birth mothers, referred to the relationship as 'distant' or to their birth mother as a 'stranger' (p = 0.039). However, this difference was significant only in the pairs where the adopted person was male (p = 0.029). Adopted people, more males than females, would use words such as 'distant', 'nothing in common', 'discomfort', or 'she has too many problems'. Birth mothers, especially those searching, had obviously invested a lot in the search and it would possibly have been too much to acknowledge that the relationship was not at a higher level or 'distant' or that with a 'stranger'. Further, more of them tended to report finding similarities between themselves and their sons and daughters than would the latter. However, some of the mothers who did not think that their initial expectations had been met, also reported that there was "something missing", and a lack of "depth" in the relationship due to not having parented their child. Their expectation of making up for the "missed" years proved elusive.

Table 14.4
Description of continued face-to-face contact*

Description	Birth mothers* %	Adopted persons[†] %
Mostly like a parent	28	27
Friend/relative	51	45
Parent/friend	16	–
Distant/stranger/deceased	2	20
Uncertain	3	8
Total	100	100

*N = 71 (missing 21); [†]N = 71 (missing 7)

Below are examples of how pairs of birth mothers and their adopted sons and daughters described their current relationship. Because of their respective interests, there is a greater concentration on differences in perceptions than on similarities:

Birth mother: He is more of 'our' son now. The relationship is more comfortable, more loving, more laughter, more critical on our part. I could understand the story of the woman who fell in love with her own son.

Son: I have become more of a 'son'.

Birth mother: Mostly a friend.

Daughter: I am beginning to feel more like a daughter.

Birth mother: More like a friend than a stranger now and a lot more at ease now.

Daughter: I felt I ought to feel like a daughter but I didn't, that was artificial. A developing relationship like a friend.

Birth mother: I am unable to sort out the reality of the relationship because of my daughter's very defensive attitude.

Daughter: I know her better but she doesn't feel like a mother.

Birth mother: I do not feel like a mum as with my other children. He has a mum and dad who are his adoptive parents.

Son: Not changed, i.e. son and brother (to her other children).

Birth mother: We have got to know each other.

Son: I am having problems with my [adoptive] mother. She shows great jealousy of my life and relationships.

Birth mother: Still a friend.

Daughter: I now feel loneliness because her husband will not allow me into the family. This makes me revisit all my childhood feelings of anxiety, anguish and abandonment as I am seen as a problem and an outsider again.

Birth mother: The honeymoon period eventually wears off.

Daughter: It has been five years now. Obviously we feel closer, but not mother–daughter.

Birth mother: I felt like a stranger and very guilty.

Son: I expected to feel closer to my birth mother but really had little in common with her. Immediate rapport with my father, though.

Current views about having had contact

Over eight out of 10 adopted people (83 per cent) and almost all the birth mothers (92 per cent) were pleased that they had been sought or had set out to search. At the same time, some 16 per cent of adopted adults had mixed feelings about it compared to only seven per cent of their birth mothers. Overall, and when account is taken of the strength of the feeling, birth mothers had been significantly more pleased than their sons and daughters for having been sought or for having searched (p = 0.007). However, this difference was mainly found in relation to searching than sought mothers (p = 0.016). When asked whether, in retrospect, they would rather have not met each other, nine out of every ten adopted people, and all the birth mothers, said they had no regrets (Table 14.5). However, and though numbers were small, adopted people were significantly more likely to wish that they had not met their birth relatives than were the birth mothers (p = 0.018) The lower satisfaction on the part of adopted adults again concerned the fact that their expectations remained unmet or that more demands were being made on them in terms of the relationship. A handful were also disappointed to find that their mothers had problems. Nevertheless, the vast majority agreed or strongly agreed with their birth mothers that they were pleased they had met.

Although it was noted earlier that a significant proportion of birth

Table 14.5
Whether respondents would rather not have met each other

Level of agreement	Birth mother* %	Adopted person %
Strongly agree/agree	–	3
Uncertain	–	8
Strongly disagree/disagree	100	89
Total	100	100

*N = 62 (missing 16); †N61 (missing 17)

mothers would have liked more frequent contact, nevertheless they did not allow this to cloud their perceptions about the overall value of meeting their sons and daughters. The following are typical examples of what pairs of birth mothers and their sons and daughters had to say:

Birth mother: Life will never be the same again. He has unlocked my deep maternal feelings.

Son: My life has been transformed as a result of contact. All the people around me have been touched by the magic experience.

Birth mother: It has been a very positive experience. The circle is complete now. No missing parts.

Daughter: I have grown hugely as a person in the last seven years and have my identity now. I feel more sure of myself and who I am in a way I never did before I searched.

Birth mother: I regretted and would have always regretted not knowing what happened.

Daughter: Sometimes I feel guilty that I made the contact. At other times I am glad because it has made me a more settled person.

Whether contact was a positive experience overall

Nine out of ten respondents from each group agreed or strongly agreed that contact had been a positive experience overall (Table 14.6). However, the birth mothers reported that the contact had been significantly more positive than their sons did (p = 0.013). There were many examples of congruence in what the parties had to say and the following is one of them:

Table 14.6
Whether contact was a positive experience overall

Level of agreement	Birth mother* %	Adopted person[†] %
Strongly agree/agree	93	88
Uncertain	3	8
Strongly disagree/disagree	4	4
Total	100	100

*N = 72 (missing 6); [†]N = 72 (missing 6)

Birth mother: Because of contact I have a little bit of future now.
Daughter: I feel emotionally more secure and more complete. I can see where certain personality traits come from.

When respondents were asked to indicate how positive an experience the contact and reunion had been for themselves and each other, there were no differences in how birth mothers and adopted adults thought contact had been for the adopted person, but the adopted adults under-estimated how positive the experience had been for the birth mother in comparison with the mother's own rating (p = 0.005). However, it was adopted people who had searched (p = 0.015) and mainly female ones who had underestimated it (p = 0.041). Although a minority of around 10 per cent from each side reported that their lives had either deteriora-ted or become very strained as a result of contact, these reports were not always from the same pairs. The following are two examples:
Birth mother: I considered divorce after contact and I ran the risk of losing the love of my eldest son.
Son: I had a breakdown after contact. Contact has now stopped and I am a lot happier.

Birth mother: Very rewarding but there are difficulties with our relationship.
Daughter: She expected me to feel closer. We simply visit.

The impact of contact on emotional outlook and self-esteem

Between seven and nine out of every ten birth mothers and adopted people reported that, because of contact, their emotional outlook had improved, they felt more relaxed, could relate better to people and had changed for the better. They felt they had also reached higher levels of self-esteem, had a more positive outlook and were more at peace with themselves. However, a quarter of birth mothers and one out of every seven adopted adults did not think so. Birth mothers who had reported being pressurised into adoption were more likely to feel that their emotional outlook had improved since contact (p = 0.045). Each party identified many positives and typical examples of congruence included:

Birth mother: I feel much more settled inside, no longer wondering about her all the time.
Daughter: I feel more peaceful and relaxed. More supported and loved. I therefore have a greater capacity to love others.

Birth mother: I had the answers to all the worrying, thinking, imagining.
Son: Stronger as a person since tracing, as now I know where I come from and why I am adopted.

Birth mother: More complicated in regard to balancing relationships.
Son: I am a more psychologically stable individual.

Turning to self-esteem, 44 per cent of birth mothers and 44 per cent of adopted people agreed or agreed strongly with the statement that their self-esteem had improved. This was significantly lower than the improvements reported above in their emotional outlook (Table 14.7). They gave examples of having developed greater confidence, being more assured and having greater belief in themselves. Some added that the knowledge of 'who' they were and knowing why they had been adopted contributed to this.

A consistent group ranging from 10 to 20 per cent from each side

Table 14.7
Whether respondents thought that their self-esteem had improved as a result of contact*

	Birth mother* %	Adopted adults[†] %
Strongly agree	11	20
Agree	33	24
Uncertain	22	27
Disagree	30	28
Strongly disagree	3	1
Total	99	100

*Birth mothers N = 63 (missing 15); [†]Adopted people N = 71 (missing 7)
Note: The significance is the result of differences between 'strongly agree' and 'agree' and 'strongly disagree' or 'disagree'.

either had mixed feelings or were disappointed in all the above areas and were more likely to be seeker birth mothers and searching adopted people. Disappointments, sometimes distress, and occasionally anger, arose in a small number of respondents, mainly after one party had rejected the other by not wanting any more contact, or one party was making more demands, or because of pressures from their respective families or contact not having lived up to expectations. For example, one birth mother reported that her daughter wanted more than she could give while the daughter remarked how difficult it was to cope with the mother's depression. In another case, the birth mother was considering divorce because of the impact contact had had on her new family, while the adopted person found that the unsatisfactory experience of contact had drawn him much closer to his adoptive family. Another adopted person reported that he had had a breakdown as a result of the rejection while the birth mother reported that contact had made no difference to her general way of life because she had not come to feel as a mother to him.

Coping with the intensity of the feelings aroused by contact

It was to be expected, perhaps, that the search and contact would give rise to some very intense feelings in both the birth mothers and their sons and daughters, requiring adaptive and coping responses. While well over half from each group had not found it hard to cope with the intensity of the feelings experienced, a third from each group said they had (Table 14.8). Even though many of these were able to move on with their lives, about 20 per cent said they had been left feeling confused. Considering the

Table 14.8

Did respondents find it hard to cope with the intensity of the feelings aroused by contact?

Respondent	Agree/strongly %	Uncertain %	Disagree/strongly %	All %
Birth mother*	33	12	55	100
Adopted person[†]	29	13	58	100

*N = 66 (missing 12); [†]N = 72 (missing 6)

emotions and expectations built over the years, a greater number could have been expected to feel like that. The fact that they had not and the fact that so many relationships had worked out well could be attributed to the good will and sensitivity with which each party had approached the other.

Were expectations met?

Between three-quarters and 80 per cent of adopted people and birth mothers reported that their expectations had been met either 'well' or 'very well'. The rest were divided between those who had been left with mixed feelings or were uncertain (Table 14.9). There was considerable agreement, and no significant differences, between birth mothers and their sons and daughters about how well they thought their expectations had been met. However, this agreement was mainly found in cases where the adopted person had searched for the birth mother rather than when sought (p = 0.023). There was some uncertainty among both groups (18 per cent) rather than outright disagreement that their expectations had not been met. With regard to adopted people, the meeting of expectations had mainly to do with obtaining information, finding out why adopted, physical recognition and the establishment of new relationships. Those who said that their expectations had only been partly met reported issues concerning rejection by members of the birth family, the quality of the subsequent relationship, and were still looking for answers to the question

Table 14.9
Contact and the meeting of expectations as perceived by each group

How well met	Ad. person's rating %	Birth mother's rating %
Very well	52	59
Well	29	15
Mixed/not sure	18	19
Not very well	1	7
Not well at all	–	–
Total	100	100

'why adoption?'. For birth mothers the positives had to do mainly with the easing of the loss, learning that their sons and daughters were well and happy, and having the opportunity to explain 'why adoption' and the establishment of relationships. The birth mothers who said that their expectations had only been met partly or not very well spoke about not having enough contact or having no contact at all.

Illustrative examples of congruence and difference in the meeting of expectations

Birth mother: Like a dream come true – a fairy tale ending!
Son: Expectations more than met. I found a family I am now very close to.

Birth mother: Expectations exceptionally met. I need not worry.
Daughter: Not just met but they went beyond that. We got on so well from the minute we spoke on the phone.

Birth mother: Disappointed and upset that continuation of relationship was not successful.
Daughter: I feel more secure and less confused, but have mixed feelings about the contact.

Birth mother: Very satisfied. I know he had a good life.
Son: It hasn't totally worked out but it has healed my 'primal wound'.

Current physical and emotional health

On average, some 21 years in age separated birth mothers from their sons and daughters and therefore it could be argued that their health was not exactly comparable. Nevertheless, the answers to questions about their respective physical and emotional health were compared to identify similarities and differences. Eight out of ten birth mothers and adopted adults rated their physical health as 'good to very good', but unlike their sons and daughters, birth mothers were more likely to say that their health was 'good', rather than 'excellent' or 'very good'. Further, one out of ten of the latter rated their physical health as poor compared to only three per cent of their sons and daughters. Overall, the birth mothers' current physical health was significantly poorer than that of their adopted sons and daughters' (p = 0.001). However, when it came to frequency of visits to their doctor in the last six months, there was hardly any difference between the two groups.

The emotional health of the two sample groups at the time of the study as scored on the GHQ showed no significant differences between them (Table 14.10). The expectation, suggested by some studies, that birth mothers might be more emotionally stressed was not sustained. Previously, birth mothers have been portrayed as deeply bereaved and adopted people as mostly well adjusted, so a significant difference would have been expected. Over 70 per cent of adopted adults (72 per cent) and three-quarters of mothers (76 per cent) had low scores, i.e. from 0–3, suggesting good emotional health. Fourteen per cent of each group scored 4–9 points, suggesting that they were experiencing moderate difficulties at the time. When it came to severe emotional problems, 13 per cent of adopted people and nine per cent of birth mothers scored in this category. Overall, birth mothers scored a somewhat better emotional health than their sons and daughters, but the difference did not amount to statistical significance. Irrespective of the past distress that many birth mothers had gone through as a result of the parting, and any stresses adopted people may have experienced from being adopted, it could not be said that their current emotional health was unusual. However, as we say elsewhere, both parties reported that their emotional outlook had improved significantly after

Table 14.10

The current emotional health of adopted people and their birth mothers based on the GHQ

GHQ Score	Birth mothers* %	Ad. people† %
0	58	58
1–3	18	14
4–9	14	14
10–15	9	13
Total	99	99

*N = 77 (missing 1); †N = 77 (missing 1)

273

contact and the scores were possibly reflecting the positive impact of contact on the subjects' emotional health.

When this paired sample was also asked if any of their health problems, physical or emotional, could be attributed to adoption, around three-quarters in each group did not think so. However, 15 per cent of adopted adults and eight per cent of birth mothers thought that it could, with the rest being uncertain. Although adopted adults were somewhat more likely than their birth mothers to ascribe health problems to their adoption, it did not amount to significance. There was considerable congruence between birth mothers and their sons and daughters over whether their physical and emotional problems were or were not related to the adoption. However, this congruence was found predominantly in the pairs where the adopted adult had searched for the birth mother (Kappa = .43, p = 0.001) but not in those who had been sought.

Why sought birth mothers and sought adopted people did not initiate a search

The majority of searching adopted people knew about the Adoption Contact Register but only a fraction of non-searchers did. Of adopted people who knew about the Register, 30 per cent had entered their names compared to 50 per cent of birth mothers. The difference between them is not surprising because most adopted people knew that the law gave them more rights, and offered them more ways to go about establishing contact than simply through the Register. For birth mothers, the Register was the main avenue to contact. The main explanation for more of them not registering was that they did not want to intrude, they were apprehensive of the kind of reception they might have or wanted to leave the initiative to the adopted person. In an earlier chapter it was noted that far more seeker mothers (80 per cent) knew about the Register compared to only half (40 per cent) of sought ones. Of those who knew about it, seeker mothers were far more likely again to enter their names for a match than sought ones (44 to 15 per cent). The suggestion is that birth mothers who enter their names are not only more likely to become seekers, but that non-seeker ones do not appear to register in the same proportions either as seeker mothers or as searching adopted people do.

Table 14.11 presents the reasons that sought birth mothers and sought adopted people did not take the initiative to search. The majority of mothers did not think they could interfere because they had signed their rights away when their child was adopted and any move had to come from the adopted person first. A significant proportion also said that they did not know how to search. Adopted people placed the emphasis on the adoptive parents being their "real" parents and not wishing to upset them. While birth mothers also expressed fears of being 'rejected' and 'blamed', adopted people were afraid of finding something 'unpleasant' or upsetting their adoptive parents. A sizeable proportion of birth mothers (38 per cent) were also concerned about their secret coming out, mainly among members of their new family. Comments included: 'it wasn't my right';

Table 14.11

All reasons why sought birth mothers and sought adopted people did not search themselves

Sought birth mothers*	%	Sought adopted people[†]	%
Not my right	71	Felt my adoptive parents are my real parents	47
Did not know how to search	46	Did not want to upset adoptive parents	44
Fear of rejection	38	Scared of finding something nasty	31
Close people not aware of adoption	38	Not emotionally strong to search	30
Blocked it out	23	Never thought much about birth father	26
Inhibited by legal reasons	21	No point. Felt birth parents already rejected me by placing me for adoption	23
Afraid of finding something nasty	15	No desire to learn more	22
Did not want complications	15	No knowledge of how to search	22
Wait until time was right	10	Never thought much about birth mother	21
Not enough time or money	8	People close to me might feel upset	13
		Not enough money to start a search	8

*Sought birth mothers N = 60 [†]From first part of the study N = 78 (Howe and Feast, 2000) 'not aware that I could'; 'I didn't know how to go about it'; 'afraid of rejection'; or 'anxious about my secret coming out'. However, sought adopted people seemed content with how things were going, saying that they were not particularly motivated to search, with some of them reporting that either they never thought of their birth mother or were not interested to learn more about their background. A few others added: 'I had parents'; 'didn't want to upset my parents'; 'was scared of finding something unpleasant'; or 'not feeling emotionally strong'.

Summary

This chapter compared and contrasted the views of birth mothers with those of their sons and daughters on a range of variables about the search and reunion process and outcome. Searching and non-searching adopted people knew about the Adoption Contact Register in almost similar proportions, but it was more likely for searchers than non-searchers to enter their names. When it came to birth mothers, double the percentage of seeker birth mothers knew about the Register, compared to sought ones, and seeker mothers were also far more likely to enter their name in the Register hoping for a match with their sons and daughters.

The current emotional health of both birth mothers and their sons and daughters was surprisingly found to be broadly within the norm so it could not be concluded that parting with a child for adoption, or being adopted, carried higher levels of stress. However, the scoring took place some eight years after contact had been established and with most respondents reporting on its positive impact on themselves. Besides high levels of satisfaction being reported on a range of items, and high levels of agreement found between the two groups, there were also some significant differences, mainly between adopted people and seeker mothers, and occasionally more so between male adopted adults and their seeker mothers.

Around three-quarters from each group were satisfied with the level of contact, but searching mothers were likely to want more. Dissatisfaction was mainly ascribed to incompatibility, lack of closeness or the perception of the birth parent as a needy person. Seven out of ten from each group were satisfied with the closeness of the relationship, but agreement was more likely if the adopted person had initiated the search than if he/she had been sought. Similarly, the expectations of the adopted person were more likely to be met if he/she had initiated the search. Adopted adults who were sought, particularly males, were also more likely to refer to the relationship with their birth mothers as 'distant', or to the birth mother as a 'stranger', instead of a friend or parent.

Each party also expressed very high levels of satisfaction about the overall outcome of contact, with many of their comments suggesting that 'they had found themselves again'. Possibly having invested a fair amount of effort, and taken the initiative to search, seeker mothers tended to overrate the positives. Overall, and compared to adopted adults, birth mothers:

- wanted more contact and more closeness, particularly seeker mothers;
- tended to minimise differences;
- had fewer regrets than adopted adults about searching or being sought;
- were more positive about the contact experience, more so sought than seeker mothers;
- evaluated the overall satisfaction with the outcome of contact higher than their son/daughters did, more so seeker mothers in relation to their sons;
- were more likely to see similarities between themselves and their sons or daughters than the latter did.

In spite of wanting more contact and more closeness, it was a characteristic of both sought and seeker mothers to want to fit in with the adopted person and to appear to be more easily satisfied with the frequency and outcome of contact arrangements, as if they did not deserve better. On the whole, birth mothers who had been sought were more likely to be satisfied with than searching mothers, such as on the frequency of contact. In contrast, adopted people were more likely to be satisfied with the closeness of the relationships, have their expectations met, and be satisfied with the overall contact experience if they had initiated the search than if they had been sought. Adopted people who were sought were also less likely to agree with their birth mothers about the closeness of their relationship, tending to rate it lower; to describe the relationship with their birth mother as 'distant' or like that with a 'stranger', more so males than females; and were less likely than their birth mothers to find positives in the overall contact experience, again more males than females. Disappointments were far more likely when the parties entered contact with greatly differing expectations.

15 Adopted people and their adoptive parents – paired perspectives

Adoptive mother:
Adoption was a greatly rewarding experience.

Daughter:
I was given love and opportunities but sad for my birth mother who had to give me up.

Note: All examples in this chapter refer to members of the same pair or dyad.

Introduction

The separate perceptions of the two samples of adopted people and their adoptive parents were described in earlier chapters. This chapter compares the perspectives on the adoption, search and reunion process of those in the samples who constituted pairs of adoptive parents and their adopted sons and daughters. The emphasis is again on identifying similarities and differences in perception. From the total sample, 86 pairs of adopted people and adoptive parents were identified and matched. The group of adopted people consisted of 55 females and 31 males. Because the number of non-searchers was small (N = 15) no attempt is made to separate them. Reference to them is only made if and when a robust finding was suggested. Turning to the adoptive parents, three-quarters of the questionnaires were completed by adoptive mothers and the rest either by the adoptive father or jointly. This sample is somewhat smaller than the main sample of adoptive parents and adopted people because that sample had not been fully matched. As a result some variations in percentages could be expected between the main and this matched sample.

Telling and sharing background information

It is acknowledged that caution is required when referring to when and how adoption was disclosed and background information shared because both the adopted people and their parents were relying on memory about events that happened a long time ago. The proportion of adoptive parents who thought that the adopted person had been told about the adoption before the age of five, was significantly higher than the proportion of adopted people who said so (p = 0.003). This difference predominantly occurred with those who had searched or where the adopted person was male. Over three-quarters of adoptive parents (78 per cent) also said that they had shared as much background information as the adoption society had given them. Two-thirds of adopted people supported their parents' statement but a third, compared to only 14 per cent of their parents, said that they had been given none or very little. Overall, the proportion of adopted adults who thought that they had been given no or little background information was significantly higher than the proportion of adoptive parents who thought that they had given no or little information to the adopted person (p = 0.002). This difference was again mostly found in the searchers but this time mainly among female adopted adults. Compared to adopted people, adoptive parents were also far more likely to say that the adoption had been discussed openly within the household (p < 0.001).

A minority of adopted people reported that they had sensed that discussing the adoption within the household was not acceptable. Several commented on not having had the opportunity to discuss something that was so integral to their lives. Similarly, the proportion of adopted adults who said that they had thought about their birth relatives a lot during childhood, adolescence and adulthood, was significantly higher than the proportion of adoptive parents who reported that their adopted child talked about their birth relatives in childhood and adolescence (childhood and adolescence p < 0.001; adulthood p = 0.001). In other words, adopted people might not have talked openly much about their birth families within the household, but this did not mean that they were not thinking about them a lot, particularly the women. Overall, adopters reported greater openness on their part than adopted people could remember – a clear difference in perceptions.

Whether happy about having adopted or been adopted

Almost all the adoptive parents (93 per cent) were very positive or positive about their adoption experience, a few were mixed, and only one felt negatively about it. This contrasted with only 69 per cent of adopted people who were positive or very positive about their adoption. The most significant difference was between the 72 per cent of parents who described the experience as 'very positive' compared with only 34 per cent of adopted people (p < 0.001). Just over a quarter of adopted people (26 per cent) opted for 'mixed' (Table 15.1). Overall, adoptive parents, especially of searchers, were significantly happier about having adopted than these adopted people. The differences in perception were confined more to female searchers than male ones (p < 0.001). There was far more congruence between parents and non-searchers than parents and searchers. Although our numbers were small, the findings confirmed those of the first part of the study, i.e. that adopted people who had initiated contact with a birth relative were somewhat less likely to feel as happy about being adopted as those who had not, and more so women than men. The mixed or negative reactions came mainly from those who said they had failed to connect emotionally with their adoptive parents, or their parents were either too strict or not appreciative enough. The group included some of those who were from minority ethnic backgrounds.

In spite of the differences noted above, the majority of both adopted people (70 per cent) and most adoptive parents (93 per cent) had happy memories of their adoption experience. The following two examples of

Table 15.1
Overall adoption experience

Levels	Adopted people %	Adoptive parents %
Very positive	35	72
Positive	35	21
Mixed feelings	26	6
Negative	4	1
Very negative	1	–
All	101	100

Adopted people N = 84 (missing 2); adoptive parents N = 86

pairs of adoptive parents and adopted people are one of many conveying mutually satisfactory experiences:

Adoptive parents: With adoption our lives were complete.

Sought son: I have had a very happy adoption and never thought of looking for birth relatives, they came looking for me. I am happy now they did. I feel part of a huge happy family.

Adoptive parent: If we had not adopted, we would not have experienced the joys and sadness of having a family.

Son: I was given to the best possible adoptive parents.

The following are two more mixed examples, with the adoption experience being qualified by both sides:

Adoptive mother: In retrospect, I do wonder whether it was a good thing to take one adopted child into a large established family. Blood is thicker than water.

Daughter: Even though I knew I was loved, it just wasn't the same. It was and still is a strain not to be the same.

Adoptive parent: Our relationship has grown continuously stronger. My son was willing to listen and be pointed in the right direction.

Son: I have never been able to do the right thing. Depressed about the uncertainty of their reaction.

In spite of how well the adoption had worked out, a continued thought with some adopted people had to do with not having experienced living with the birth parent. The following is one of a number of examples:

Adoptive parents: I can't imagine what our life would have been like without the children.

Daughter: I felt loved and wanted but I will never know what it would be like being brought up by my own.

Adoptive mother: Quite simply a joy [the adoption].

Daughter: I did not want for love or indeed anything else but having met my birth mother, I think I would be much more emotionally stable having someone who understood me and could relate to me while I was growing up.

Being loved and having a sense of belonging

Almost nine out of ten adopted people (87 per cent) agreed with a statement that their parents loved them and over nine out of ten (93 per cent) adopters agreed that they felt loved by their respective children. When account is taken of the difference between 'strongly agree' and 'agree', significantly more adoptive parents felt they loved their son/ daughter, than the adopted adults felt they loved their adoptive parents (p = 0.013). In other words, parents somewhat overestimated how much they were loved by their searching children, especially daughters, but were more accurate with regard to those who were sought. The same pattern was repeated when it came to a sense of belonging (Figure 15.1). A greater proportion of adoptive parents (93 per cent) felt that their son or daughter belonged in the adoptive family than the adopted adults (74 per cent), but again the difference was more likely to be found among searching than non-searching adopted people (p<0.001) and confined more to women than men (p = 0.005).

Overall, adoptive parents overestimated how happy their sons or daughters were with their adoption, how much they were loved by them and the extent to which the adopted person felt he or she belonged to the family. However, these observations were more likely to be in relation to searchers than non-searchers and to daughters rather than sons.

Figure 15.1
Sense of belonging

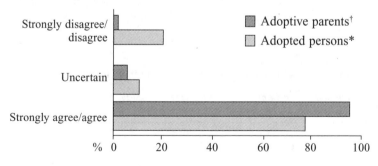

*N = 84 (missing 2); †N = 85 (missing 1)

Similar or different treatment from birth children?

Of 38 adopted people who were reared in households in which parents had one or more birth children, almost half (47 per cent) reported that they came to feel that they were treated differently by their parents in comparison with birth children (Table 15.2). Furthermore, far more adopted people felt like this than their parents realised (47 to 14 per cent, $p = 0.019$). This was especially true again of the female adopted adults ($p = 0.007$). It was mainly those adopted adults, more females than males, who felt that they had been treated differently from birth children and the views of those from minority ethnic background that somewhat depressed the overall satisfaction with adoption.

Examples of congruence and mis-perceptions:

Adoptive parent: It is different having a birth child. The circumstances were uneasy. Had I known I would have a child I wouldn't have adopted.

Daughter: Felt the odd one out – didn't feel any common ground.

Adoptive parent: Have always tried to treat them all alike but different characters create different relationships.

Daughter: Felt that they treated the boys differently – more privileges, let out more.

While some adopted people felt that they had definitely been treated differently, others came to feel like this not so much because they were negatively discriminated against, but simply because of an awareness that they were different from the rest of the family and did not 'fully belong' like the birth children. Although this was a minority response, neverthe-

Table 15.2
Whether treated the same or differently from birth children

Respondent	Same %	Different %	Don't know %	All %
Ad. Persons*	50	47	3	100
Ad. Parents[†]	81	14	5	100

*N = 38; [†]N = 38

less it conveyed the view that the presence of birth children made continued comparisons inevitable, acting, perhaps, as a kind of repository for other feelings.

The extended family

When it came to members of the extended family, almost nine out of ten adopters (88 per cent) reported that the wider family had treated their son or daughter the same, but only three-quarters of adopted people (74 per cent) felt the same way. While only two per cent of parents reported that their child had been treated differently, 14 per cent of the latter felt so. In effect, the proportion of adoptive parents who thought that the adopted person had been treated the same by the extended family was significantly higher than the proportion of adopted adults who thought so ($p = 0.017$). Again, this was especially true for adoptive daughters rather than sons ($p = 0.002$). Although parents had been aware at times that the extended family treated their adopted child differently, this was not always the case, especially in relation to children from minority ethnic backgrounds. The following two examples of acceptance and non-acceptance presented in pairs of adopters and their sons or daughters are typical:

Adoptive mother: Grandparents, brothers, sisters (ours) were brilliant.
Daughter: I don't know, I just feel that they don't love me as much as they would if I was a "blood" grandchild. I don't think the bond is very strong. (This person also felt she didn't "belong" in the household.)

Adoptive mother: They [extended family] gave love and support to us and our adopted son.
Son: They [extended family] seemed to distance themselves.

Ethnicity

The number of adopted people in the matched sample whose ethnic background was different from that of their adoptive parents was small ($N = 10$). As a result, no firm conclusions can be drawn, except to highlight similarities and differences in perceptions. Parenting the transracially and/or transculturally placed child or growing up as such a child proved far from easy for both the parents and the adopted person. The two central issues that emerged were the experience of being the butt of racist remarks and of identity issues faced by the adopted person. Both parents and children were partly agreed on the racist remarks, but the parents appeared to underestimate their son or daughter's struggle to establish their identity. At times, the struggle on the part of the adopted person overshadowed their feelings for their parents, generating anxiety and guilt arising from feelings of disloyalty. In spite of their struggle for cultural identity and a sense of self-worth, there was some lack of positive feelings for their adoptive parents. Several parents did show understanding of how difficult it must have been for their child to grow up in an all white community, but it was not surprising that their sons and daughters emphasised what this meant for their racial awareness and identity:

I wanted to find out more about my identity and culture, but the opportunities were not available.

Some parents attributed the racism of the occasional misguided comment either by a member of the extended family or an outsider to ignorance, or as being related to the adoption rather than to their ethnicity as such. By contrast, adopted persons commented mainly on the failure of their parents to either protect them from racism or acknowledge its presence both within the extended family and elsewhere. The parents of one adopted person stressed that "ethnicity" as a factor made no difference to them, but their daughter felt differently. She said:

I didn't belong because of my background. Lack of confidence, self-respect and bullying affected my education and social skills.

Some parents had not also fully appreciated how members of the extended family, including two grandparents, appeared to find it as difficult as outsiders to accept a person from a different ethnic background as a member of their family. In one of a number of cases, the adoptive mother observed that:

Adoptive mother: There was never any difference made between the children and our daughter was made very welcome.

But the daughter commented:

Daughter: I rarely have had privileges the other children had. I was treated in a patronising way. Relatives of my adoptive parents seem to always be looking askance at me. I was an easy scapegoat.

Another adopted person, while feeling very protective towards her adoptive family, also said that throughout she had felt "racially apart", and experienced racism and an identity crisis which contributed to her lack of self-esteem. While her parents acknowledged that there had been some problems at school, the daughter recalled how desperate she had been to identify with someone who was visibly different from her white environment. Another family said that their daughter was 'a complete part of the family', whereas the daughter referred to them 'as a very British white family and I couldn't be like them'. Several adopted people of minority ethnic background, while appreciating the love of their parents, observed with some irony how "fashionable" it seemed to be in the 1960s to adopt transracially, perhaps enhancing the family's prestige in some eyes or making them feel 'how wonderful they were'. The following example shows that while the parents were glad the adoption had taken place, and were proud of their daughter, this was not so for their daughter:

I struggled a lot growing up and felt like a freak – dirty and not belonging to any group. My immediate family felt the effect of this most. My identity confusion was a factor.

Perceptions of closeness between adopted people and their parents

With one exception, all adopters said that they had felt 'very close' or 'close' to the adopted person when they were children and 83 per cent of adopted adults said they had felt the same (Table 15.3). The rest had either not felt like this or had mixed feelings about it. The parents perceived the relationship with the adopted child as having been significantly closer than reported by the adopted person (p = 0.001) but more so in relation to searchers than non-searchers and daughters than sons. Both groups agreed that the closeness of the relationship had decreased significantly during adolescence to 65 per cent as reported by the parents and to

51 per cent as reported by the adopted adults. Adoptive parents reported a significantly closer relationship with the adopted person in adolescence than did the adopted adults (p = 0.005) and again, this was more likely in relation to searchers than non-searchers and daughters rather than sons. Adolescence proved to be a more unsettling experience for females than males. In adulthood the closeness of the relationship had increased in comparison to that reported in adolescence. According to 86 per cent of the parents, the relationship was 'very close' or 'close', but this was supported by only 72 per cent of adopted people. Overall, parents tended to overestimate the level of closeness they had with their sons or daughters during different stages, but more so in relation to searchers than non-searchers and daughters rather than sons.

Table 15.3
Closeness between adopted people and their parents at different stages

Levels of closeness	Adopted persons' rating[†]			Adoptive parents' rating[*]		
	Child-hood	Adolescence	Before contact	Child-hood	Adolescence	Before contact
	%	%	%	%	%	%
Very close/close	83	51	72	99	65	86
Mixed	10	27	16	–	26	10
Not close/ Not at all close	7	22	12	1	9	4
Total	100	100	100	100	100	100

[†]Adopted persons: childhood N = 84 (missing 2); adolescence N = 86; before contact 82 (missing 4).
[*]Adoptive parents: childhood N = 83 (missing 3); adolescence N = 85 (missing 1); before contact 72 (missing 14).

There were many examples of considerable congruence between the perceptions of parents and their adopted sons and daughters as shown by the following typical examples:
Adoptive parent: We grew to have a strong relationship.
Son: I have always regarded my adoptive parents as my rightful parents who loved and cared for me.

Adoptive parent: We've always felt close.

Daughter: I have never felt that I was not part of the family. My adoptive mother to me is my birth mother.

There were also a few examples of difference:

Adoptive parent: We've always been very close and we loved her from the first day.

Daughter: We are very different. My mother does not make any attempts to understand anyone emotionally, she is closed up. My father is more honest and understanding.

There were also a handful of examples of parents and children being aware of the distance between them. For example, one mother said that although they had done their best for their daughter, there was not much closeness between them. The daughter described the relationship as 'OK' adding that she had never felt close to her parents. Another mother's feeling that her daughter had shown little affection towards her either as a child or as an adolescent was confirmed by the daughter who added that her mother had supported her and encouraged her in her search and contact.

The adoptive parents' reaction to contact

Around three-quarters of adoptive parents (76 per cent) reported that they had been supportive of their son or daughter's contact and about an equal proportion of adopted people said they had found their parents supportive (Table 15.4). As expected, there was significant association and agreement within the pairs ($p<0.001$). However, the proportion of adopted people who thought that their adoptive parents had at the same time been worried about contact was significantly higher than the proportion of parents who said so ($p = 0.016$). A much higher proportion of adopted people (26 per cent) perceived their parents as also having been upset about contact whereas only five per cent of parents said so ($p < 0.001$), this difference coming predominantly from the searching dyads. Although numbers were small, the proportion of adopted people who said that their parents had been angry about the contact at the time was also significantly higher than the proportion of adoptive parents who reported feeling this way (p = 0.039).

Table 15.4

How adoptive parents said they had reacted initially to contact and what adopted adults had to say about their parents' reaction

Respondent	Adopted persons* %	Adoptive parents† %
Supportive, pleased, etc	83	76
Nervous/worried	39	27
Upset	26	5
Angry/hostile	12	1

*N = 77 (missing 9); †N = 82 (missing 4)

Satisfaction with the overall outcome of the search/ contact

When reflecting on the overall outcome of the search and contact, almost three-quarters of adopted people (73 per cent) and 86 per cent of their parents were satisfied about the outcome (Table 15.5). Typical examples included:

Adoptive parent: He needed to know his origins and he did.
Son: Doubt and wonder removed.

Adoptive parent: She now has the answers to all the questions.
Daughter: I feel more secure knowing my roots and the family history of my children.

A quarter (27 per cent), though, of adopted people were either uncertain or perceived the outcome in more negative terms. There was a high level of agreement within the pairs about how satisfactory the contact experience had been (p = 0.0002) although parents once again somewhat overestimated how satisfactory the experience had been for their sons and daughters. The adopted adult's disappointment arose mainly from rejection by members of the birth family, not having had sufficient information about the birth father and, in some cases, their emotional outlook having deteriorated since contact mainly as a result of what they found. In spite of this, only one in ten adopted people and adoptive parents said that they wished the adopted person had never met members of their birth family or were uncertain about the value of contact and reunion. At the same time, it appeared that adopted people underestimated how positive their parents believed the search and contact had been for them, often unnecessarily thinking that they were being disloyal.

Table 15.5
Overall satisfaction with the outcome of the search/contact

Levels of satisfaction	Adopted persons* %	Adoptive parents[†] %
Strongly agree/agree	73	86
Uncertain	15	8
Strongly disagree/disagree	12	6
Total	100	100

*N = 73 (missing 13); [†]N = 80 (missing 6)

Whether pleased now that the adopted person had searched or had been sought

The next table shows that the great majority of adopted people (79 per cent) and adoptive parents (87 per cent) reported and cited many examples of benefits from contact and their views were mostly in agreement (Table 15.6). The following are some typical examples:

Adoptive parent: His birth mother must have wondered all those years where he was and what he was like.
Son: It's been good. I have found out more information regarding why I was placed for adoption, nice to meet up with nice people.

Adoptive parent: She now knows the answers to all the questions she asked us when she was growing up.
Daughter: I feel more secure knowing my roots and the family history for my children, especially the medical side.

A minority of both parents and children had some doubts about the value of contact because the outcomes for them were not viewed as exactly satisfactory. The main reasons were the lessening of contact or a parent refusing to have or continue contact. There were also a handful of cases where the parents viewed the experience as not very positive for their son or daughter, but the adopted person explained it away, saying that their parents 'had not fully come to terms with it'.

Table 15.6
Retrospective reactions to the search and contact

	Adopted persons*	Adoptive parents†
Views now	%	%
Very pleased/pleased	79	87
Mixed	19	12
Not pleased	2	1
Total	100	100

*N = 85 (missing 1); †N = 84 (missing 2)

Contact and its impact on the relationship

For the majority of adopters and adopted people, the relationship was reported to have remained the same after contact, mostly meaning that it was already good or very good to start with (Table 15.7). About equal proportions reported that it was enhanced because of contact, but although no parent said it had deteriorated, around one in ten adopted people said it had. In two to three other cases, both parents and the adopted person acknowledged that their relationship had badly deteriorated as a result of contact, but the qualitative comments suggest that contact appeared to define more sharply an already strained relationship.

Typical examples of congruence included:

Adoptive parent: The bonds are closer now because she feels she belongs truly in our family and felt no ties to her birth family.

Daughter: It has really made me appreciate mum and dad and I'm so thankful and grateful to have been placed with them and brought up by them. I'm sure my life would not have been enriched otherwise.

Table 15.7

Whether the relationship between parents and children changed because of the search and contact

Impact	Adopted persons* %	Adoptive parents† %
Enhanced	35	30
No change	53	70
Deteriorated	12	–
Total	100	100

*N = 84 (missing 2); †N = 85 (missing 1)

Adoptive parent: My family and children are very upset because they thought it [contact] was very bad.

Son: My adoptive mother still cannot really understand how I would want to be in touch with my mother 'who gave me up'.

And some differences in perception:

Adoptive parent: Always close.

Daughter: A great strain initially being torn between two families.

Although three-quarters of adoptive parents said that contact had been a positive experience for them, only 43 per cent of adopted people had thought that it had been so for their adoptive parents. It is hard to explain why so many adopted people came to think that their parents did not benefit from contact, except that perhaps this is how they perceived their parents' general response to the search and contact. Elsewhere it was noted that birth mothers too, possibly for different reasons, underestimated the extent to which adopters had benefited from contact.

Other impacts of contact

Compared to what their parents said, significantly more adopted people reported that their self-esteem had improved as a result of contact (p < 0.001). Mainly because of rejection by a birth relative experienced by a minority of adopted people, significantly more adoptive parents felt

293

that the adopted adults' emotional outlook had worsened since contact (p < 0.001). Compared to their parents, adopted people were far more likely to say that they had found it difficult to cope with the intensity of the feelings arising from contact (46 to 12 per cent or p < 0.001). Although perhaps not surprising, the biggest difference between the parties was that almost eight out of ten adopters (78 per cent), but only 14 per cent of adopted people, said that they had felt unchanged since the search/contact (p < 0.001). In fact, three-quarters of adopted people said that they had felt changed mainly because of the benefits that had resulted from contact such as higher self-esteem, better emotional outlook, satisfaction on receiving sufficient background information, a more secure sense of self and the forming of new relationships with members of their birth family. At the same time, a fifth came also to feel angrier after contact; this arose from rejection by members of the birth family or disappointment over aspects of the relationship with them. Overall, it could be surmised that, although adoptive parents went through a period of anxiety and worry because of contact and reunion, it did not reach the levels of intensity as experienced by their sons and daughters. Neither did the former appear to recognise this high level of intensity. It is also possible that the adopted person did not reveal much of this, possibly to protect his or her parents from worrying about them.

The current closeness of the relationship

Eight out of ten adopted people reported 'very close' or 'close' current relationships with their parents and over nine out of ten adoptive parents (93 per cent) reported the same (Table 15.8). Where differences occurred, this was mainly in female dyads. Even though adoptive parents somewhat overestimated the level of closeness, especially to their daughters, there was considerable agreement among the dyads about the positive nature of the current relationship (p = 0.0003). Both adopted people and parents rated the relationship as somewhat closer than before contact had occurred. Therefore it could not be said that contact had a negative effect and in actual fact, it had a positive impact in most cases.

Table 15. 8
Current closeness of the relationship

Level of closeness	Adopted persons' rating %	Adoptive parents' rating %
Very close	57	59
Close	24	34
Mixed	14	5
Not very close	4	2
Not close at all	2	–
Total	101	100

Adopted people N = 85 (missing 1); adoptive parents N = 85 (missing 1)

Congruence between the parties was extensive and the following are typical examples:

Adoptive parent: The relationship has not changed at all. It was always close.

Son: Dad and my brother were fully supportive of contact and did not take it to be a reflection of how I felt about them.

Adoptive mother: Contact has brought us closer together as we were able to discuss it openly.

Daughter: I feel more 'whole' as a person. I am much happier and more content with my relationship with my adoptive mother.

Misperceptions were few but the following are examples:

Adoptive parent: No change. Contact made no difference to our relationship.

Daughter: I have come to feel more insecure and unsure of myself.

Adoptive parent: No change since contact.

Daughter: I now have two families neither of which gives me the feeling of love and acceptance I crave.

Current physical and emotional health

It is recognised that the physical and emotional health of adopted people and of their adoptive parents may not exactly be comparable because of the significant age differences between them. With this in mind, similar questions were still asked of both parties about their respective general physical health, frequency of visits to their family doctor and their scores on the GHQ (General Health Questionnaire) on emotional health were compared. Almost three-quarters of adopters, and just over three-quarters of adopted people, reported 'very good' or 'good' physical health, with another 14 per cent of adopters and 17 per cent of adopted people describing it as 'excellent'. At the other end of the spectrum, 12 per cent of adoptive parents and six per cent of adopted people described their health as 'very poor' or 'poor'. In spite of the big differences in age, no significant differences were found in physical health between parents and children or in the number of visits to their doctor in the last six months.

The parties' emotional health at the time of participating in the study as scored on the GHQ showed significant differences between them. Almost four-fifths of adopted adults (77 per cent) and over eight out of ten adoptive parents (86 per cent) had low scores, i.e. from 0–3 suggesting good emotional health (Table 15.9). Broadly a similar proportion of each group scored 4–9 points, suggesting that they were experiencing moderate emotional problems at the time. When it came to severe emotional problems, 13 per cent of adopted people, but only 4 per cent of adopters scored in this category. Overall, adopted adults scored a poorer emotional health compared to their adoptive parents ($p = 0.013$). However, this difference was only found in relation to searching female adopted adults. It is difficult to explain why female adopted people had a poorer emotional health than males or their adoptive parents. We also know that females rated several aspects of their adoption experience lower than males, e.g. feeling less loved and less close to their adoptive parents and having a lesser sense of belonging, again raising the question of whether adoption is more stressful for females than males. We also do not know how adopted people would have fared on emotional health if they had been scored before contact had been established. It has already been noted, however, that contact had a positive impact on many adopted people's self-esteem and general emotional outlook, so it should only have improved their emotional health.

When this paired sample were also asked if any of their health problems, physical or emotional, could be attributed to adoption, around three-fifths of adopted people and over nine out of every ten of adoptive parents did not think so. However, almost a fifth (18 per cent) of adopted adults and five per cent of adoptive parents did. In effect, adopted adults were more likely than their adoptive parents to ascribe any health problems to their adoption ($p = 0.02$), but this time there were no significant differences between female and male adopted people.

Table 15.9

The current emotional health of adopted people and their adoptive parents as scored on the GHQ

GHQ score	Adopted people*	Adoptive parents†
0	62	73
1–3	15	13
4–9	11	11
10–15	13	4
Total	101	101

*N = 86; †N = 86

Summary

By the very nature of the exercise, this chapter has concentrated more on differences, so it must be stressed that the great majority from both groups were both pleased about having been adopted and having adopted and about the contact and search experience. In spite of the big differences in age, no significant differences were found with regard to the physical health of adoptive parents and their adopted children, now adults. Adoptive parents, however, scored a better current emotional health compared to their sons or daughters. Unlike their parents, adopted adults were also more likely to ascribe health problems to their adoption. Overall, adoptive parents appeared to be a physically and emotionally robust group of people. If adopting was stressful, it did not reflect negatively on their physical and emotional health. Compared to their adopted sons and daughters, adoptive parents were more likely also to say that they:

- shared background information with the adopted person;
- disclosed the adoption before the age of five;
- discussed adoption more openly within the household;
- treated their adopted children the same as birth children or that the extended family treated them the same.

Around seven out of ten adopted people, but over nine out of ten adoptive parents reported very close or close relationships during different stages of the adopted person's life and were also 'very positive' or 'positive' about the overall adoption experience. Broadly similar proportions from each group also reported that the adopted person had felt loved by their parents and that they came to develop a sense of belonging. Although there was considerable agreement between parents and children, on the whole, adoptive parents overestimated the adopted person's satisfaction in all these areas, more so in relation to searchers than non-searchers and more so in relation to their daughters than sons. Even though the level of reported closeness to their adoptive parents was 80 per cent, overall satisfaction with the adoption experience was 'mixed' for around 25 per cent of adopted people with another seven per cent describing the experience as unsatisfactory. The mixed feelings and dissatisfaction were mostly expressed by those who either felt that they and their parents had not properly attached and/or that they had been treated differently compared to birth children and/or by the extended family, or simply that they did not fit. These were also mostly found among searching women and those from minority ethnic backgrounds.

Three-quarters of adoptive parents also said that they were supportive of their sons and daughters' contact, and this was largely echoed by their children. However, adopted people reported that their parents had been more worried, upset and angry because of contact than their parents reported. Equally, adopted people did not agree with their parents that for a proportion of them their emotional outlook had worsened since contact. Although the majority of parents had been supportive of their children's quest, and they could identify many benefits, a minority were more likely than their sons and daughters to report that their children had suffered emotionally through rejection by a birth parent or birth relative. Nevertheless, almost three-quarters of adopted people (73 per cent) and 86 per cent of adoptive parents had been satisfied with the outcome of contact. However, over a quarter of adopted people and 14 per cent of parents were either uncertain or negative about it. Many parents also appeared, on the whole, to underestimate the inner struggle that their sons and daughters of minority ethnic background were going through to establish who they were and forge an identity and a sense of belonging. Their undoubted love did not appear to make up for their children's lack of a positive ethnic identity.

A persistent theme permeating the findings was of parents significantly overestimating their closeness to the adopted person, or how happy the adopted person was about being adopted, or how much they had developed a sense of belonging to the immediate and extended family. This was mostly in respect of searchers than non-searchers and more so in relation to their daughters than sons. On the whole, and compared to what their parents said, adopted females, mainly searching ones:

- thought they were given less background information by their parents;
- disagreed that their adoption was openly discussed within the family;
- scored a poorer emotional health;
- felt differently treated by their parents in comparison to birth children;
- reported being less close to their parents now;
- felt differently treated by the extended adoptive family;
- felt less happy about being adopted;
- felt less loved by their parents; and
- reported a weaker sense of belonging to the immediate or extended family.

16 The triangle

Birth mother:
I needed to know if she was well and happy and to explain why the adoption.

Adoptive mother:
She wanted to fill in the gaps herself as a person. She once described it as a hole that she felt she had to fill in.

Adopted person:
I feel more sure of myself and who I am in a way I never did before I searched. I also felt very strongly that I wanted her to know I was alright.

Note: All examples in this chapter refer to members of the same triad.

Introduction

The two previous chapters have contrasted the views and perspectives of adopted people with those of their birth mothers and with those of their adoptive parents on a number of similar questions asked of each. This chapter continues to do the same, but this time in the light of the perspective of all three parties on similar questions. Out of the total sample of 312 birth mothers, adopted people and adoptive parents, the study identified and matched 38 triads. Of the 38 adopted people matched to their birth mothers and adoptive parents, 23 were female and 15 male. The female–male ratio in the pairs and triads remained constant at around 60 to 40 per cent. Twenty-seven of the triads were formed with adopted people who had initiated the search and the other 11 triads were with sought adopted people (where the birth mother had initiated the search). In 28 of the triads, the adoptive parent was the adoptive mother. Seven of the other triads contained an adoptive father and the remaining three triads contained both adoptive parents.

Impact of contact on family relationships

When it came to the impact of contact on their respective family relationships, a third from each group reported that these had been enhanced. No adoptive parent indicated deterioration, but around one out of eight birth mothers (13 per cent) and adopted people (13 per cent) did. Even though family relationships did not appear to suffer unduly as a result of contact, at the same time there was no significant agreement within the triads over whether they thought that the search and contact had had an effect on the relationship with their respective families.

Table 16.1
How had contact affected family relationships?

	Adopted persons %	Birth mothers %	Adoptive parents %
Enhanced	32	29	34
Deteriorated or under strain	13	15	–
No change or not applicable	55	56	66
Total	100	100	100

Adopted people N = 38; birth mothers N = 34 (missing 4); adoptive parents N = 38

Contact and self-esteem

Around half of adopted people and birth parents agreed or strongly agreed that their self-esteem had improved as a result of contact, whereas only a quarter of adoptive parents thought it had (Table 16.2). In effect, adoptive parents were less likely to say that their self-esteem had improved since contact (p = 0.007). The views of all three members of the triad were not congruent. In other words, adopted people, birth parents and adoptive parents who reported that their self-esteem had improved did not come from the same triads, thereby suggesting that the impact of contact affected parties in same relationships differently. Unsurprisingly, perhaps, contact and reunion had a lesser impact on the self-esteem of adoptive parents than that of birth mothers and adopted people. Many of them reported that they had no problem over their self-esteem before contact and it remained like that afterwards.

301

Table 16.2

Whether respondents' self-esteem improved as a result of contact

Level of agreement	Adopted persons %	Birth mothers %	Adoptive parents %
Agree/strongly agree	45	52	25
Uncertain	21	17	16
Disagree/strongly disagree	33	31	59
Total	99	100	100

Adopted people N = 33 (missing 5); birth mothers N = 29 (missing 9); adoptive parent(s) N = 32 (missing 6)

Contact and feeling more relaxed

Between half and two-thirds of members of all the triads said they felt more relaxed after contact, with more birth mothers saying so but the difference was not statistically significant (Table 16.3). We saw in an earlier chapter that there was close congruence between birth mothers and adopted people about how relaxed they came to feel after contact (p = 0.004), and this was echoed in the triads as there was also significant congruence between all three parties (p = 0.012).

Table 16.3

Whether feeling more relaxed after contact

Level of agreement	Adopted persons %	Birth mothers %	Adoptive parents %
Agree/strongly agree	49	67	54
Uncertain	24	17	11
Disagree/strongly disagree	27	17	34
Total	100	101	99

Adopted people N = 33 (missing 3); birth mothers N = 35 (missing 3); adoptive parent(s) 35 N = (missing 3)

Contact and change

The most likely person to have felt unchanged from the impact of contact were the adoptive parents, with 81 per cent of them saying so (p < 0.001). At the same time, seven out of ten birth parents and adopted people reported that they did feel changed (Table 16.4). With such big differences between the adoptive parents and the other two members of the triad, no agreement could be expected between all three parties of the triad. While birth parents and adopted people recounted the mostly beneficial impact of contact, as described in other chapters, adoptive parents viewed themselves as having been contented before contact and that there was no change following contact. They might have gone through some anxious and worrying moments because of contact but this did not necessarily change them as people. Some of those who had met members of the birth family referred to the development of a better understanding of them and also of their sons and daughters.

Table 16.4
Did respondents feel unchanged since contact?

Level of agreement	Adopted persons %	Birth mothers %	Adoptive parents %
Agree/strongly agree	12	19	81
Uncertain	12	10	6
Disagree/strongly agree	76	71	14
Total	100	100	101

Adopted people N = 33 (missing 5); birth mothers N = 31 (missing 7); adoptive parent(s) N = 36 (missing 2)

Contact and anger

The most likely person to report feeling angry after contact was the adopted person, and the least likely the adoptive parents. Almost a quarter of adopted people, and one out of ten birth mothers felt angry, but no adoptive parent said they felt this way. These differences did not reach statistical significance however. As said in previous chapters, most of the adopted persons' anger had to do with how contact had developed or failed to develop and the same explanation applied to birth mothers. Much of it arose from entering contact with very specific expectations that did not materialise.

Coping with the intensity of the feelings involved

All three members of the triad had experienced some intense feelings prior to and after contact, but adoptive parents claimed to have been the least affected. Over a third of adopted adults and birth parents said they found it difficult to cope with the intensity of their feelings compared to only 8 per cent of adoptive parents (Table 16.5). All three parties of the triad were significantly different from each other (p = 0.011). The findings suggest that the search and reunion process is a more intense emotional experience for adopted people and birth parents because of strong feelings, thoughts and expectations built up over many years. In spite of their initial concerns, fears and worries, adoptive parents appeared to cope well with the uncertainty that surrounded contact. As a result, compared to the other two parties, they disagreed most strongly that they had found it hard to cope with the intensity of their feelings.

Table 16.5
Coping with the intensity of the feelings aroused by contact

Level of agreement	Adopted persons %	Birth mothers %	Adoptive parents %
Agree/strongly agree	34	34	8
Uncertain	9	13	6
Disagree/strongly disagree	57	53	86
Total	100	100	100

Adopted people N = 35 (missing 3); birth mothers N = 32 (missing 6); adoptive parent(s) N = 36 (missing 2)

Views on the search

Whether pleased the search occurred

Eighty-four per cent of adopted people and 92 per cent of birth mothers were pleased that they had searched, but only three-quarters (76 per cent) of adoptive parents were pleased that their sons and daughters had done so (Table 16.6). Birth mothers were significantly more pleased than the adoptive parents and the adopted people, that the search had occurred (p = 0.011). The birth mothers' response was in line with their general attitude of reflecting on the positives that came out of contact, while the adoptive parents' displeasure reflected the new rejection suffered by a small number of adopted people and, in a handful of cases, from strained relations developing between them and the adopted person.

Table 16.6
How pleased are you now that you searched or were sought?

	Adopted persons %	Birth mothers %	Adoptive parents %
Very pleased/pleased	84	92	76
Mixed	16	8	21
Not pleased/not at all pleased	–		3
Total	100	100	100

Adopted people N = 37 (missing 1); birth mothers N = 36 (missing 2); adoptive parent(s) N = 38

Typical examples of congruence and non-congruence between the parties:

Adopted person: It's all been good for me and doesn't seem to have done any lasting damage to anyone else. I got a great deal of everything I was looking for and enjoy the enhancement of my life in every way.
Adoptive parent: I am pleased that it has been a happy event.
Birth mother: It is important to me that he has sought me and wanted to know who his mother was. Unbelievable gift.

An example of differing views:

Adopted person: Pleased to find them but they do not seem to understand the feelings I had to go through to get to see them.

Adoptive parent: I have always felt a child should, if possible, know about his origins and the reasons for his adoption. Also that the birth parents should know of his well-being.

Birth mother: It was a shock, but perhaps a good one. I am pleased to be able to talk about him with my children and husband now.

Although a high proportion of adopted people and adoptive parents did not wish that contact had not taken place, it was again the birth mothers who disagreed most strongly with this statement with all of them indicating their support for the contact (p = 0.023).

Table 16.7
Whether respondents from each group wished contact had not occurred

Level of agreement	Adopted persons %	Birth mothers %	Adoptive parents %
Agree/strongly agree	4	–	9
Uncertain	8	–	9
Disagree/strongly disagree	89	100	83
Total	101	100	101

Adopted people N= 27 (missing 11); birth mothers N=30 (missing 8); adoptive parent(s) N = 35 (missing 3)

How positive was the outcome?

About nine out of ten adopted people and birth mothers said that the contact experience had been positive compared with only 72 per cent of adoptive parents (p = 0.016) (Table 16.8). There was significant agreement within the three parties over how positive the contact had been (p = 0.0002). Typical examples of congruence between the triad:

Birth mother: I wanted to know that he had been happy in his adoptive home and had been successful in his work.

Adopters: My son is happy that we are supportive and in a small way we can share this experience with him.

Adopted son: It has been a positive experience all round.

Birth mother: I regretted and would have always regretted not knowing what had happened.

Adoptive mother: If it were me, I would want to know my background and have all the answers.

Daughter: Sometimes I feel guilty that I have contacted my birth parents, other times I feel that it made me a more settled person because of it.

Birth mother: It is important to me that he has sought me and wanted to know who his mother was. Unbelievable gift.

Adoptive parent: I am pleased that it has been a happy event.

Adopted person: It's all been good and doesn't seem to have done any lasting damage to anyone else. I got a great deal of everything I was looking for from this new set of relatives and enjoy their enhancement of my life in every way.

Table 16.8
How positive was the overall contact experience?

Level of agreement	Adopted persons %	Birth mothers %	Adoptive parents %
Agree/strongly agree	89	94	72
Uncertain	6	6	19
Disagree/strongly disagree	6	–	8
Total	101	100	99

Adopted people N = 35 (missing 3); birth mothers N = 35 (missing 3); adoptive parents N = 36 (missing 2)

Overall satisfaction with the contact experience

Self-reported satisfaction with the outcome of contact was about the same between birth mothers and adoptive parents, but lower among adopted people. This time, around eight out of 10 birth mothers (85 per cent) and adoptive parents (84 per cent), in contrast to 69 per cent of adopted people, had been satisfied with the outcome of contact (Table 16.9). However, these differences did not reach statistical significance. Nevertheless, there was agreement within the triads over how satisfied they felt with the overall outcome of the contact (p = 0.007).

Table 16.9
Overall satisfaction with the outcome of contact

Level of agreement	Adopted persons %	Birth mothers %	Adoptive parents %
Agree/strongly agree	69	85	84
Uncertain	17	9	16
Disagree/strongly disagree	14	6	–
Total	100	100	100

Adopted people N = 35 (missing 3); birth mothers N = 32 (missing 6); adoptive parent(s) N = 36 (missing 2)

Adopted people seemed to make a distinction between contact being positive (89 per cent) and level of satisfaction with contact (69 per cent). As said elsewhere, their misgivings had mainly to do with how contact had developed, i.e. levels of contact or their perception of the birth relative. Although a number of birth mothers had broadly similar experiences, that is, of contact not going well for them or problems developing within their new family, there was a tendency on their part to deny difficulties, concentrating instead on the gains made by contact.

Current closeness of the relationship between the parties

The next table sets out side by side how adopted people rated their closeness to their birth and adoptive mothers respectively and how birth and adoptive mothers rated their closeness to the adopted person. Over seven out of ten adopted people (72 per cent) felt close or very close to their birth mother compared to 78 per cent who felt like this about their adoptive parent. However, while only 32 per cent of adopted people reported feeling 'very close' to their birth mothers, 51 per cent felt like this about their adoptive parents. In other words, adopted people reported a significantly closer relationship to their adoptive parent than to their birth mother (p = 0.027). Compared to birth mothers, adoptive mothers somewhat overestimated their closeness to the adopted person.

Table 16.10
Perception of the current closeness of the relationship in current face-to-face contact

	Adopted persons' rating of closeness to birth mother	*Birth mothers' rating of closeness to adopted person*	*Adopted persons' rating of closeness to adoptive parent*	*Adoptive parents' rating of closeness to adopted person*
Very close	32	32	51	60
Close	40	36	27	38
Mixed	12	12	16	3
Not very close	8	8	5	–
Not close at all	8	12	–	–
Total	100	100	99	101

Physical and emotional health

Adopted adults reported significantly better physical health than their birth mothers (p = 0.005) but in spite of the age differentials, not significantly different to that of their adoptive parents. Turning to the emotional health of the parties as scored on the GHQ, between 76 and 87 per cent in each group scored good emotional health, with between 14–24 per cent scoring moderate to severe problems (Table 16.11). Adoptive parents scored the least severe problems and adopted people the most moderate and severe problems, especially when compared to the emotional health of their adoptive parents. Differences between the three groups were not significant. The expectation that birth mothers would score worst of all three groups was not borne out. However, as the scores were obtained well after contact took place, they were possibly measuring the beneficial effects of contact for both birth mothers and adopted people as set out in earlier chapters. The somewhat poorer emotional health of adopted people could suggest that being adopted is perhaps more stressful than parting with a child for adoption, but other factors were present which could explain this, such as the level of closeness to their adoptive parents, how much they felt they were loved, the sense of belonging and being a person from a minority ethnic background.

Table 16.11
Results of the GHQ concerning current emotional health

	Adopted persons	Birth mothers	Adoptive parents
Frequency	*%*	*%*	*%*
0	71	61	73
1–3	5	18	14
4–9	13	11	11
10+	11	11	3
Total	100	101	101

Adopted people N = 38; birth mothers N = 38; adoptive parent(s) N = 37 (missing 1)

When respondents were asked whether any health problems, physical or emotional, they had had over the years could be attributed to adoption, significantly more birth mothers and adopted people than adoptive parents thought this was the case (p = 0.015). The adoptive parents were the least likely to attribute any ailments or emotional problems to having parented the adopted child.

Contact, the law and adoption as an institution

The Adoption Contact Register

In this triadic and matched sample, knowledge about the existence of the Adoption Contact Register did not differ significantly between the parties. Around six out of ten birth mothers and adopted people and a slightly higher proportion of adoptive parents (65 per cent) knew about its existence.

Birth relatives and rights of access

Only a quarter to a third of birth mothers, adopted people and adoptive parents supported the view that birth relatives should have the right to obtain identifying information about the adopted person (Table 16.12). Any differences between the three parties were not significant. The expectation that an overwhelming proportion of birth mothers, compared to adoptive parents, and perhaps adopted people, would support the right to access did not materialise. However, compared to birth mothers, double the proportion of adopted people and adoptive parents were definitely against the idea. On the whole, birth mothers were more likely to opt for 'unsure' on the proposal.

All three groups tended to stress the right of adopted people to give their consent to the arrangement. Adopted people who supported the idea saw it as a kind of 'healing' experience for the birth relatives (mainly the mother) and as a reassurance about the well-being of the adopted person. Those who opposed it wanted to spare the adopted person from experiencing surprises and wanted them to be in control. Birth mothers who supported it felt very strongly, stressing it as a right and as one of them put it: 'I feel it is a monstrous situation that a woman who has brought a child into the world should be left without any further knowledge of that child – all she has is a big hole'. Those who opposed it wanted to leave the decision to the adopted person. Adoptive parents placed emphasis on the adopted person and themselves having more control.

Table 16.12
Views of whether birth relatives should have access rights

Answers	Adopted persons %	Birth mothers %	Adoptive parents %
Yes	24	34	26
No	41	21	42
Unsure	35	45	32
Total	100	100	100

Adopted people N = 37 (missing 1); birth mothers N = 38; adoptive parent(s) N = 38

311

The following were typical examples of congruence and non-congruence between the parties.

Congruence between all three:

Adopted person: It should be up to the adoptee to initiate contact. Birth relatives give up their rights in that person's life when they gave them away so that they have no right to suddenly get involved again when it suits them.

Adoptive parents: It should be left to the child to make contact. The child should have the choice.

Birth mother: No right, because the child in question is probably very happy with their adoptive parents.

Congruence between adopted person and adoptive parent only:

Adopted person: No right, because it could be distressing for the adopted person. It should be up to them to make contact, if desired.

Adoptive parent: It should not be a right but should have the consent of the adopted person.

Birth mother: I think the right should be there if they wish to find or see the adopted person.

The institution of adoption

Because of the occasional call for the abolition of the institution of adoption, respondents were asked for their views and these are set out in Table 16.13. Only one adopted person supported the idea, while one other remained neutral. The rest opposed it. Adoptive parents gave broadly similar answers. Although it was thought that, because of their experiences, a great number of birth mothers would support the proposal, this was not the case. However, just under a fifth (19 per cent) of them did support it, which was significantly higher than the adoptive parents and adopted people ($p = 0.001$). Those who opposed the proposal stressed the positives of adoption and how it offers a family to children who may otherwise grow up in institutions with no family to call their own. Birth mothers who supported the abolition of adoption referred mainly to their personal experience of 'pain' and 'anguish' over the years, while others qualified their opposition by saying that adoption should be allowed only 'in certain circumstances'.

Table 16.13
Whether the institution of adoption should be abolished

Level of agreement	Adopted persons %	Birth mothers %	Adoptive parents %
Agree/strongly agree	3	19	3
Neutral	3	11	–
Disagree/strongly disagree	95	70	97
Total	101	100	100

Adopted people N = 38; birth mothers N = 36 (missing 2); adoptive parent(s) N = 38

Examples of congruence between the parties:
Birth mother: Adoption is a good thing provided the adopters are fully investigated. P. speaks very well of his parents.
Adoptive mother: Adopting our three children brought us happiness beyond description. We like to think it has brought them happiness too!
Adopted person: I have never heard this view. It is obviously bonkers.

A minority of birth mothers took a different view but the adoptive parents or the adopted person did not support it:
Birth mother: I do not think that adoption is a good idea. It causes too many problems and is not good for anyone.
Adoptive father: No child should be raised in an institution.
Adopted person: Adoption gives a person a good chance of having a better life. Often it is a positive experience for the adopted person and the adopters.

Summary

It was perhaps too optimistic to expect significant agreement about the impact of the contact and reunion experience between members of the adoption triad. Although the reported positive impact of contact on their lives was high and specific benefits were identified such as improved self-esteem, feeling more relaxed and better emotional outlook, agreement about the different levels or value of contact proved more elusive. What mostly led to the lack of congruence between the parties was that adoptive parents, as members of the triangle, were somewhat of an outsider or onlooker. Although they shared many common feelings with the other two members, they did not share with them the kind of expectations built up over many years with the intensity of feelings that surrounded them.

When it came to satisfaction with the overall outcome of contact, there was considerable agreement among the parties about its positive outcomes. Any differences were not significant. In contrast to their birth mothers, adopted people were more likely to single out difficulties that arose, while birth mothers appeared to ignore or minimise problems, concentrating instead on the positives for everyone and also on themselves. As said elsewhere, birth mothers were, on the whole, simply glad for having had the opportunity to meet, explain and see for themselves that the adopted person was well. A significant minority of adoptive parents were more likely to have some doubts about contact having taken place at all, by reporting that their sons and daughters had been hurt in the process or that contact had given rise to strains within the family. Considering, though, that the former were seen as the neglected or ignored party, they came to look upon contact in a mostly positive and constructive way with few regrets. They also came to feel reassured that they remained the primary parental figures, something confirmed by the adopted persons' ratings, including the higher levels of closeness to them compared to their birth mothers. However, the closeness of relationships developed with birth "siblings" were reported as being higher than with adoptive siblings.

Although the positions taken by the three members of the adoption triangle in respect of rights of access for birth relatives and the continued existence of adoption as an institution were fairly congruent, unlike adopted people and adoptive parents, birth mothers were more likely to support the proposal for the abolition of adoption.

17 **Birth fathers**

Introduction

The study made efforts to obtain the perspectives of birth fathers who had either been sought by their sons and daughters or those who had taken the initiative to search. Of the 33 birth fathers with whom adopted people had established contact, only 15 (or 45 per cent) responded to our approach to take part. Fourteen of these had been sought by their sons and daughters and in only one case had the birth father taken the initiative to search. Besides being too small a number for reliable analysis, it could not be considered as representative as the rest of the study. Because of this, the analysis undertaken was mainly qualitative. Even though the findings mostly confirm what birth mothers had to say on the same issues, nevertheless they need to be treated with great caution. The experiences of these fathers were real for them but they cannot be generalised. The main reason it was decided to publish them was because, with the exception of Clapton (2003) and Witney (2004), there is no other British research known to us on the subject. Where applicable, the experiences of the birth fathers are compared with those of the birth mothers in the study.

To put the current material in context, it is useful to briefly review what some other studies have had to say about birth fathers. A US study (Deykin *et al*, 1988) reported that approximately half of the fathers interviewed had some involvement with the adoption procedure and most of them said that the adoption was due to their own un-readiness for fatherhood or that they felt that adoption was in the best interests of the child. These respondents were approving of adoption. However, the birth fathers who were excluded from the adoption procedures and who said that the adoption took place because of external pressures, were opposed to adoption. For this second group of fathers, exclusion appeared to be long lasting. The study went on to claim that the older a birth father had been at the child's birth, the more likely he was to hold a negative view of adoption. Relatively few reported that having been a birth father had an impact on their current parenting function, but apparently those who felt excluded from the adoption process were two and a half times as likely to have fathered additional children as those who had participated in the adoption. Two recent British studies, which explored the experiences of 30 fathers, reported evidence of feelings of loss, and in some cases of grief, along with curiosity and concern about what happened to the child. The fathers' exclusion from the decision-making process, and in some cases from seeing the mother and child, added to feelings of powerlessness. Many also said that the detrimental effects of adoption had contributed to disrupted relationships in their lives in the years following the adoption. The main motive of those seeking contact was for news about the child and his or her welfare and well-being. Most contacts were reported as having been happy occasions for both parties (Clapton, 2003; Witney, 2004). In contrast to the Deykin *et al* (1988) study, Clapton found that there was some reluctance on the part of fathers to seek out sons or daughters to avoid 'rocking the boat' for the child and their adoptive family.

Characteristics of birth fathers

With the exception of two birth fathers in this study, the remaining 13 were now either married or living with partners. A number of them had been separated and had started new relationships. The great majority (N = 12) were white of European background and the remaining three from other ethnic groups. With three exceptions, all the others were in non-manual occupations. Half of the total could be described as now holding middle-class-type jobs including managers, civil and local government officers, a teacher and a consultant engineer. Like birth mothers, the very low representation of birth fathers holding manual, semi-skilled and unskilled jobs was largely a reflection of adoption policy and practice at the time. The mean age of fathers at the time of contact was 53, broadly similar to that of birth mothers. The mean age of adopted people at contact was 32. On average, seven years had elapsed between being contacted and participating in this study.

From birth to contact

With one exception, all the birth fathers featuring in the sample said that they had been aware that the mother was expecting their child. Just over half described the relationship as having been steady, again dispelling the myth that many of the pregnancies were the result of "one-night stands". Over a third (36 per cent) said that they saw the child soon after the actual birth. (It was most unusual at the time for a father to be allowed to be present at the birth.) More than half reported that they had seen the child before the adoption. Three of these fathers later married the mother of their child. Equally, well over half had told their families about the pregnancy. Like birth mothers, birth fathers too reported that, when told, their parents had been shocked, upset or did not understand. They attributed it to the prevailing stigma of the period and to their parents' fear that their family's image would be tarnished in the eyes of others. From the birth fathers' accounts, it could not be said that, compared to the reactions of the birth mothers' parents, their parents were any less critical or more understanding.

My parents were concerned what everyone would think about it and they would not let us keep the baby.

The child's birth mother said in respect of her parents:
My parents wanted to send me away to a mother and baby home. My baby's father was very upset about this, as he wanted us to be together.

Emotional support and understanding were approximately equally split between fathers who said their families had been supportive and understanding and those who had not. There was a suggestion that perhaps birth fathers, compared to birth mothers, had received slightly more support from their families but with small numbers it cannot be certain. Some parents who had wanted to be supportive were said not to know what to do. As one father explained, he could understand his parents' dilemma 'because they didn't know how to handle it'. Nevertheless, there was pressure from within the family to keep the pregnancy secret and for the matter to not be talked about. One father remarked: 'It seemed that if we didn't talk about it, it would go away'.

It may be recalled that birth mothers (whose views were outlined in Chapter 4) had reported that birth fathers were the least supportive during the pregnancy and after confinement. The explanations from some of the respective birth fathers here suggest that either because of fear about their parents' reaction, their youth or ignorance about what to do, they had panicked, with some of them saying that they had been unable to offer support to the mother of their child. The following are the respective accounts of the father and mother of a child:

Birth father: Because of the social stigma about unmarried pregnancies, I felt I could not tell my parents or family.

Birth mother: The father of my child was only 18 at the time and returning to college. He did not want his parents to know. I found a new partner during the pregnancy who I later married; he was supportive.

The adoption decision and the parting

Half of those fathers who knew about the pregnancy said that they had taken an active part in the adoption decision, but others had not. The reasons given for the adoption decision, starting with the most important, were parental pressure; the decision being the mother's preference; social pressure; lack of provision; being too young and/or not yet ready for parenthood. A quarter conveyed the view that the decision had been a joint one, with one of them saying:

We thought that by placing the child for adoption we were doing the best thing for him. Once the decision had been made I decided to get on with life.

The birth mother supported this birth father's statement saying, 'I felt this was the best option for my child and myself'. Another birth father said that once the 'wheels' of adoption had been set in motion, it seemed to follow its own momentum and could not be stopped. The corresponding birth mother suggested that her family had planned her future and she had little choice over it. There were also other cases where both the birth father and birth mother reported that adoption became inevitable because it was what their parents wanted.

Birth father: Parents told us we had to.

Birth mother: My parents said I had to 'have my baby adopted' and in those days you had to do as your parents said.

Two-thirds of the fathers (10 out of the 15) retrospectively said that they would have liked to have kept the child, which was more than the proportion of birth mothers who said the same, but it is very likely this was again a reflection of the sample's bias. With one exception, these fathers added that they could have brought up the child either jointly with the birth mother or within their own family. One of them, who was married to someone else at the time, said that he and his wife could have brought up the child. Another one said that he could find no support for his wish to keep the baby, and the child's mother supported his view saying that he had been very upset as he had wanted the baby. Nevertheless, her parents had insisted that she move away to have the baby and have it adopted before she returned. A third of birth fathers reported that they had definitely been pressurised into adoption, compared to 68 per cent of birth mothers.

As with birth mothers, birth fathers experienced a range of emotions before the parting, with the most prominent ones being sadness, powerlessness about what to do, and worry about the child's future. These reactions were later followed by grief, anger, confusion and bewilderment. As one father and the respective mother explained:

Birth father: Very upset but I could do nothing.

Birth mother: Very upset, angry and wondered what and where she was going and would the adoptive parents really love her.

Three fathers reported feeling very angry at the time but a similar number admitted to feeling relieved that it was all over. The main feelings that remained after the adoption were sadness and powerlessness followed by relief and worry about the child's well-being. One of those who had wanted to keep the baby said that he felt 'resigned', but equally 'sad' because he loved his daughter. The birth mother's comment was that she had realised she had 'lost' her daughter and she had concerns about her future, while also asking of herself: 'what would she think of me in the future?'

The few fathers in the sample who found out later about the adoption tended to be angry and even more powerless. They implied that they would have liked to know about and to be involved with their child's future from the start. One of them added that he had been so devastated when he found out that it took him many years before he could trust himself to have a relationship with a woman. Another one remarked that he had felt 'extremely angry' that he was not informed or given a chance to do anything, more so because he had had no other children subsequently. The mother of the child explained that she had felt so sad at the parting that it was as if their son had died. Even though she had accepted that she could not keep her son, her request to meet the adopters was not granted, which only added to her worry of whether he was 'safe, happy and well'.

Irrespective of their feelings, six of the 15 birth fathers thought that on the whole adoption had been the right decision, but more birth mothers reported similar views. Birth fathers were somewhat more optimistic, implying that if they had kept the child, either with the birth mother or other relatives, they could have managed. It is hard to say how far this was meant to assuage guilt arising from the decision or perhaps their failure to offer more support to the mother at the time. One of them remarked that neither he nor the mother had wanted the adoption to take place. Another said how the adoption decision might have been good for his daughter, but he had spent 37 years looking for her. In contrast, one father observed that adoption had enabled him and his girlfriend to 'create' their own lives.

After adoption and before contact

Following the adoption, a sense of loss and guilt was conveyed by the majority of the birth fathers, with some of them saying that they had been unable to get over it. In addition, and like birth mothers, they had been wondering how the child was doing and whether he or she was happy and well. The following are typical comments by the respective birth fathers and birth mothers:

Birth father: A sense of loss through no contact or not seeing her grow up.
Birth mother: The memories are always there with a great sense of loss – the tears still come and there is no one who understands.

A sadder note came from one father who said:
Sad that this was the case – my only true son adopted. I was later married twice without children.

Birth mother: A great sense of loss. It caused so much personal distress and took a long while to establish some cause to my life again.

Some said that wondering what had happened to the child and what it could have been like had they kept him or her, or the guilt they felt, never went away. Others would add that it was still hurting, or that they felt 'guilty and bitter that the adoption went ahead':
Birth father: Maybe the adoption could have been avoided and other options considered. I was never interviewed by a social worker about my feelings about the adoption.
Birth mother: I still miss her. If I close my eyes I can still feel her on my shoulder snuggling against my neck. I have two other children now – I can't remember them as babies – only her.

There was also some guilt that their feelings over the adoption were perhaps affecting their new relationship. As with birth mothers, comfort mainly came after they had met the adopted person and found that the adoption had mostly worked out well and that their sons and daughters had done well in life and were not feeling resentful about the rejection. However, one of these fathers said that even with continued contact 'it still hurt'. This was in contrast to another one who remarked that, although pleased he had met his son, he did not regret the decision to place him for adoption. Most of these fathers said that they often thought about the child after the parting, but more so during the first than subsequent years. Birthdays and Christmas were the most likely times. The thoughts that dominated over the years had to do with what the child looked like, their personality, whether alive, well and happy, whether he or she felt rejected by their birth family, whether he or she would like to hear from them or wanted to develop a relationship.

Only two birth fathers reported that they had experienced some depressive feelings over the years, in contrast to a higher proportion of birth mothers. Nobody reported that his or her self-esteem had been damaged as a result of the adoption. A different picture could have emerged if a sizeable sample in the study had sought their sons and daughters. The birth fathers' score on the GHQ (self-administered at the time of reporting to the study) suggested good emotional health, broadly similar to that of the birth mothers in the sample. Only one of the 15 fathers said that adoption had affected his capacity to make relationships. However, five reported other negative effects of one kind or another such as problems in their marriage or with their careers. Asked whether parting with their child had affected their relationship with their other children, most of them did not think so, but three of the 15 said that it had. With one exception, all had told their other children about the adopted son or daughter. While some told them from early on, others had left it until after the adopted person had contacted them. They denied, however, that adoption had affected the relationship with their other children. One father thought that in fact it had helped, while another added that the loss enabled him to develop a closer relationship with his other children. A birth father and a birth mother (not a couple) made similar points on the subject:

Birth father: I have loved all my children and brought them up to the best of my ability.

Birth mother: As each of my other children came along I loved them, but I did miss my daughter.

Contact and the legal position

Compared to birth mothers, few birth fathers had known about the 1975 Children Act and its provision for access to their birth records by adopted people (birth fathers 20 per cent; birth mothers 68 per cent). The three who knew said that they were pleased but one of them had some worries. Only two of the 15 birth fathers had heard about the Adoption Contact Register compared to 54 per cent of birth mothers; both had placed their name on it. In comparison, well over half the birth fathers in Clapton's (2003) sample had placed their names on the Contact Register. The differences between this and Clapton's study are possibly the result of sample biases in both. If this study was heavily biased towards fathers who were sought, Clapton's was biased towards seeker birth fathers. As we have demonstrated from the sample of birth mothers, which included

both searchers and those who were sought, there are significant differences between the two groups. It is likely that the same would apply to
birth fathers.

When it came to the question of whether birth relatives should have
rights of access, the birth fathers' views were not too dissimilar from
those of birth mothers: 40 per cent were in favour, 20 per cent said 'no'
and the remaining 40 per cent were uncertain. Those who said 'no' or
were uncertain wanted to leave the initiative to the adopted person.
Equally, birth fathers strongly supported the presence and practice of
adoption in society, giving examples similar to those of birth mothers,
adopted people and adoptive parents.

Contact and reunions

Except for one birth father, all the remaining 14 had been sought by their
sons and daughters. Contact had been continuing for an average of seven
years, with the shortest being 18 months and the longest 15 years. This
was slightly less than the average that the birth mothers had, suggesting
that adopted people were more likely to have contact with their birth
mothers first and then with their birth fathers. Most contact had been
negotiated by intermediaries who approached other relatives first and then
told the birth father. In three cases, the approach had been made directly
by the adopted person. Birth fathers reported surprise but also excitement,
pleasure and happiness at the news and the prospect of meeting their sons
and daughters. One birth father reported how very happy and pleased he
had been to hear from his son, while another said he had always wanted to
meet his daughter to tell her he loved her and say how sorry he had been
for not being there for her, but he hoped she had a happy life. Yet another
one added that his daughter 'had always been in his heart' and he always
hoped she would make contact. Below are examples of initial reactions
expressed by the birth fathers and birth mothers of the same adopted
person when they separately heard that she was seeking them:

Birth father: Pleased that questions were going to be answered, such as
what does she look like, what she has been doing.

Birth mother: I wanted to see her, but was afraid she wouldn't like me and
would blame me for giving her away. Wouldn't know what to talk about.

While one birth father stated that he was indifferent to the approach, no other negative response was reported. With two exceptions, they had agreed from the start to have contact. However, they found, like birth mothers, that the happiness and pleasure felt at the news was moderated by some worry, concern and even fear about what to expect about the effect of contact on other members of their own or the adopted person's family:

Birth father: Totally mixed emotions and not knowing what to expect. Something I had really wanted – I was not at all surprised – wanted to see her right away.

Birth mother: I was worried about my husband's reaction, as he had wanted to pretend that the pregnancy never happened.

Most of the anxieties were said to disappear after contact, with one father saying how happy he now was about the contact because he had no other children. Another had been initially worried that the person who presented as his daughter might not have been her. The first people birth fathers told about the contact were their partners, children, then parents and later friends and colleagues. Apart from some surprise, almost everybody was said to have been pleased on his or her behalf and their families were said to have been curious, pleased and supportive. However, one birth father reported his second wife as having been difficult and another said of his wife:

My wife was not happy. Now she accepts the situation but she still does not like to meet my daughter. My other two daughters are happy. They always write letters and telephone.

In a third case it was the other children of the family who had taken some time to accept the adopted person.

Birth fathers gave a variety of explanations as to why they had not searched instead of waiting for the adopted person to contact them. Similar to what birth mothers had said, their main reason was that they did not think they had a right to do so or that they were not legally entitled to. There was also concern amongst them about upsetting the adopted person, their family or their own, or not having enough information or not knowing how to go about it. For three of them, contact had posed problems in that close family members had not known about the adoption. Two others had been afraid of being rejected by the adopted person. One birth father remembered being told at the time of the adoption that he had no rights and he would not receive any help in tracing his son.

Birth father: I didn't know where to start.

Birth mother: I did not think that I had a legal right and was a little afraid she would not want to know me.

The only father featuring in the study who had searched for his child said that he felt he owed it to his child to do so.

The birth fathers' main expectations had to do with the establishment of a relationship, to see what the adopted person looked like, to explain the parting and ask if he or she was well and happy. Compared to birth mothers, birth fathers appeared to give greater importance to the possibility of developing a relationship with their sons and daughters. Birth mothers had placed the emphasis on knowing whether the adopted person was happy and less so on the development of a relationship as their main expectation. As some birth mothers put it, they did not want to expect too much. However, when it came to *all* expectations rather than *main* ones, differences between them were small. Similar to those of birth mothers, the birth fathers' initial fears had to do with anxiety that they might not get on well, followed by the possibility of finding out that their child had been unhappy, that contact might create problems with their families or the adopted person might be angry with them. However, they did not want to look upon these as fears but simply as concerns about the impact on their relationship with their families with one also stressing concern for the adoptive parents' feelings. The following is an example of how the birth father and birth mother of the same adopted person expressed their concerns:

Birth father: My concern is for both his new family [adoptive] and my other children.

Birth mother: I had no fears really as my daughter said: 'Mum, he must be like us!' and this was so true.

Concerns about their own families' reaction proved largely unfounded and only two reported that it put the relationship with their partner or their children under strain. Almost half said that contact had in fact enhanced the relationship with their partner and a couple of them added that it had enhanced their relationship with their children.

Face-to-face contact

Fourteen of the 15 birth fathers in the sample had had face-to-face contact during the first year. The most frequent contact during this period was monthly contact or contact every 1–4 months and the same applied to indirect forms of contact. It was somewhat less frequent in subsequent years and while four of the 14 had lost face-to-face contact, three of them had maintained indirect forms such as by phone, letters or cards. A couple of them had moved to a distant part of the country or abroad. Descriptive comments made by fathers and sons and daughters conveyed pleasure and satisfaction from most of the encounters such as the following:

Birth father: Feels so normal and natural – we are just part of each other's lives.

Daughter: I feel close to my birth father now. He does not feel like a stranger.

Birth fathers and adopted people gave descriptions of visiting each other and it was not unusual for a son or daughter to stay overnight or longer. The following are the respective accounts of the birth father and birth mother about one contact:

Birth father: Shortly after we met, he stayed with me for several weeks. We also went on holiday together. We saw a lot of one another over the first 18 months.

Birth mother: When I first had contact with my son, he was living in the same town and I saw him regularly. When he moved, contact was less frequent.

Unusually, one daughter brought together both her birth mother and birth father and they met 'as a trio' several times. One father implied that his first reaction to his daughter had erotic elements about it, but the daughter had not seen it like that.

Of those who continued to have contact, over half were happy with its frequency but the rest would have liked more. There was a general view amongst the first group that taking account of distance and other commitments, contact had reached its own balance. There was the feeling that the parties also had their own lives to be getting on with. For example, one father who felt content with the frequency described the relationship as 'a loving friendship' while the daughter felt that the frequency had reached its own level. It was the birth mother who had wanted more contact. The main obstacle to more frequent contact proved to be distance, shortage of time and family commitments. A father who would have liked more contact was living abroad and his daughter confirmed that with him being so far away she could not visit as much as she would like. In another case the daughter came to England from the southern hemisphere and two years later, the birth father and his family had visited her in her country.

The nature of the relationship

The initial nature of the relationship between fathers and daughters was approximately equally split between being described as parental or as friendship. Two fathers, though, referred to it as like two strangers meeting. Sometimes the adopted person agreed with the father's description but not always. The following cases illustrate both agreement and differences in perceptions between birth fathers and their sons and daughters:

Birth father: We got on well immediately and it seemed natural. It seems like a natural father–daughter relationship.

His daughter: Felt like a daughter and friend instantly. I was very excited. My father has been somewhat overwhelming and I am finding it difficult to handle.

Birth father: Totally natural father–daughter relationship as if we had never been parted.

His daughter: My father felt like a stranger.

In one instance, the birth father reported that he felt like a 'loving parent', but the daughter reported that she felt her father was 'playing' the father role and there was 'no bonding' as a birth relative. Others also agreed that the relationship was more like friendship, or as one adopted person put it, more like an uncle or distant relative rather than a father but one father reported:

> I felt a little between a parent and boyfriend. It was a very strange experience. She so reminded me of her mother. It was very emotionally loaded.
> *Daughter*: I felt like I ought to feel like a daughter, but I didn't – that was artificial. I feel far more comfortable developing the relationship as a friend.

Over time the majority of birth fathers came to describe the relationship as friendship rather than as parental, and they were at ease and comfortable with it. There was reference to feeling more relaxed, a deepening of feeling, liking spending time together and increasingly getting fonder of each other. Many of them added that the main reason they were continuing contact (direct or indirect) was because it felt comfortable, even though one-third said that they did not have much in common. Sensing that the adopted person understood why they were adopted gave additional pleasure and insight. In the view of the majority, the relationship, whether as a friend or a parent, was going well. The following is another example of the two parties agreeing:

> *Birth father*: A father–daughter relationship.
> *Daughter*: He feels like a father. His ways are very similar to my adopted father. I felt close from the first meeting. We are able to speak very openly.

The parties reported similar and different perspectives about the nature of the relationship over time. While one birth father described the relationship as father–daughter – 'as if she had never been adopted' – the daughter referred to it as a 'close friendship'. In another case the birth father continued to refer to the relationship as like that of a father, while the adopted person remarked:

> *It is difficult and disappointing – but not his fault. I have trouble forming a close relationship. He is a lonely old man and is a bit overwhelming.*

One father referred to the adopted person as 'a lovely friend' and the daughter reported good and immediate rapport with him, but found she had little in common with her birth mother. The birth mother herself said that she felt like a stranger towards her daughter, which made her feel very guilty. In another family, the birth father and birth mother of the same adopted person described their relationship over time:

Birth father: My feelings have deepened. I feel warm and loving towards her and want to protect her just like I do with my other children.

Birth mother: Something went wrong. Her initial actions of sending me cards such as on Mother's Day stopped and she didn't seem as enthusiastic. Maybe I wanted too much . . . I couldn't cope with not being someone special so I retreated. We are both very similar in character.

Contact between birth fathers and adoptive parents

A third of birth fathers had had direct contact with the adoptive parents and another two by phone. Only two, however, continued contact. Somewhat more birth fathers than birth mothers had direct contact with the adoptive parents (33 to 20 per cent) but this could be because of a bias in the small sample of birth fathers. The adopted person initiated much of the contact.

The overall experience

More than half of the birth fathers reported that contact had helped them to cope better with their feelings about the adoption. Only one said it had no effect, while the rest were uncertain. Most of them also said that their life had been enhanced as a result of contact. Only one was left feeling disappointed. All 14 fathers who answered this question said they had found contact either very positive (N = 11) or positive (N = 3). A broadly similar proportion thought it was also positive for the adopted person but less so for the adoptive parents implying, like birth mothers did, that it must have been more worrying or unsettling for the adoptive parents. Nine of the 11 who had continued ongoing direct contact described the relationship with their sons and daughters as very close or close. Only one described it as of mixed quality or as not close. Of those who had established contact, only one birth father had lost both direct and indirect contact with the adopted person.

One father reported that contact had enhanced his life and his daughter commented that she was pleased when told that 'not a day had gone by without him thinking of her'. Another father recalled how meeting his daughter had changed his life because he now had someone who gave him a purpose in life. The daughter, who had not yet found her mother, remarked that contact with her father had:

> ... made me feel a better person. It has answered so many unanswered questions which have been nagging in my mind and upsetting me all my life. My mind is nearly at rest on the subject.

One birth father felt that after meeting and getting to know his son they had now become a united family. The son's comment was that he felt he could now tell his children all about his past and let them meet all his family, both adoptive and birth.

Even though contact was largely perceived as being positive, nevertheless a couple of fathers conveyed rather mixed attitudes about it and so did the adopted people involved. One father, who had subsequently married the birth mother, felt that contact was of greater benefit to his wife, while the daughter reported that she was glad her children had both a grandpa and a grandma. Another expressed mixed feelings by saying that he was busy looking after his *own* family, while the adopted person was left feeling rather disillusioned, and saying:

> In some ways I feel more confused re: my identity, but in other ways it has been helpful to put myself in context. My anger towards my circumstances, however, seems to get greater as time goes on.

With one exception, all the other birth fathers who had contact reported that they were very pleased that they had been contacted and one was simply pleased. They made comments such as: 'a dream come true'; 'what more can I say about the pleasure it gave me'; having 'a sense of completeness', feeling 'fulfilled' or 'meeting the daughter I never thought I would see again'. The following example gives the reaction of all three related parties to contact:

> *Birth father*: I did not think she would ever want to know who I was.

Birth mother: I always hoped we would meet one day.
Daughter: Questions have been answered. I have an extended family.
My children have extended grandparents.

Well over half of birth fathers said that their expectations had been very
well or well met, mostly very well, and they gave examples, which were
supported by their sons and daughters. The following is typical:

Birth father: I couldn't have wished for more.

Adopted person: I have found out enough to help me emotionally to
stop thinking about my adoption on a regular basis, with loose ends
tied up, and unfinished work for me.

The few fathers who expressed disappointment, even though they were
pleased that contact had been established, included two fathers who later
married the birth mother and somehow did not feel that contact had much
in it for them. Two others needed more contact or 'more of a relationship'.
In one of these cases the adopted person said that the relationship had
depth in it but it felt 'overwhelming and difficult to cope with'.

Review of outcomes

A key area of interest in this study was whether contact had helped birth
fathers to cope better with past feelings of loss, guilt and worry connected
with the adoption decision and the parting with the child. Although,
admittedly, the numbers were small, and possibly biased, they provide an
overall picture of how these fathers who had mostly been sought, came to
feel after an average of seven years of contact. The 11 items that appear
in the Table 17.1 address the issue and are contrasted with what birth
mothers had said. The great majority of birth fathers (71 per cent) said
that they were very happy or happy with the present level of contact. The
rest would have liked more, but distance or family commitments on either
side, did not allow for this. Had they had the choice, two-thirds would
have liked more contact. The rest were happy with things as they were.
Only one birth father was disappointed with his relationship with the
adopted person and another was uncertain.

When it came to personal benefits a third felt that, as a result of contact, they could now relate better to other people, and an even higher proportion reported that their emotional outlook had improved since contact. Two-thirds believed that their self-esteem had improved as a result of contact and only one out of those who established contact did not think that contact was a positive experience. Of the 13 who answered this question, nobody said that they wished they had not met their sons and daughters, a similar proportion as birth mothers. The great majority felt more relaxed following contact with the adopted person, more than half felt changed and no one reported feeling angry. When reporting on their overall satisfaction with the outcome of contact, 87 per cent were either very satisfied or satisfied, one was uncertain and the other dissatisfied. While one birth father continued to feel like a stranger to the adopted

Table 17.1

An overview on contact provided by birth mothers and birth fathers

Statement	*Birth mothers* Strongly agree/agree %	*Birth fathers* Strongly agree/agree %
My emotional outlook has improved since the contact	60	67
Overall I feel the contact has been a positive experience	94	93
My self-esteem has improved since contact	45	64
I feel more relaxed since I have had contact with my son/daughter	63	86
I feel changed since the contact	70	66
Overall I feel satisfied with the outcome of the contact	86	87
I do not feel confused about my feelings for my son/daughter	69	85
Contact helped cope with main feelings of loss, guilt and worry	79	85
Expectations met	74	71
Glad I met my son or daughter	93	100
Life enhanced since contact	64	67
Average	**72**	**79**

person, 80 per cent reported affinity with their sons and daughters. Just over half described the experience as being only moderately stressful. However, two felt confused about their feelings towards the adopted person and three said that they found it hard to cope with the intensity of their feelings. In comparison with the birth mothers in the sample, a higher proportion of birth fathers reported better outcomes but not much should be read into this because their numbers were small, and possibly biased in that direction.

Summary

What birth fathers and birth mothers reported in the current study does not support the stereotype current at the time of the adoption that most births out of wedlock were either the result of one-night stands or had been fleeting relationships. The majority of the relationships had been ongoing and steady, and this was supported by the views expressed by both parties. Birth fathers also reported broadly similar experiences as those expressed by the birth mothers concerning their families' attitude to the pregnancy. For example, their families had reacted to the news of the pregnancy with equal shock and upset, wanting to keep the pregnancy secret and not wishing to talk about the event within the family. Birth fathers did not appear to receive more support and understanding from their parents than birth mothers did, thereby debunking the myth that parents would be more indulgent towards birth fathers.

Similar to birth mothers, birth fathers also perceived the adoption decision as having been imposed on them by their parents or by other factors beyond their control. Their sadness and sense of reported power-lessness were also similar to what was reported by birth mothers. On the whole, however, birth fathers appeared more optimistic than birth mothers that they could have coped had they kept the child, even though the reality of their plans appeared somewhat questionable.

As expected, the parting with the child had caused sadness, guilt and the wish to know how he or she was faring. There was a suggestion that, unlike birth mothers, birth fathers tended to think less intensely about the child during the years between the parting and contact. Although a number of them said that their marriage and careers had suffered as a result of the adoption, most of them did not think that the experience had stopped them from being good fathers to their other children. Their reported general emotional health appeared good and, unlike birth mothers, there was little history of mental ill-health after the adoption. This was very likely due to the absence in the sample of a significant number of birth fathers who had searched for their sons and daughters, rather than having been sought. Like birth mothers, and in spite of what these fathers said they felt about the adoption, most of them were supportive of the existence of adoption in society. A big difference from birth mothers was the high proportion of birth fathers who were largely ignorant about the provisions of the Children Act 1975 and the subsequent existence of the Adoption Contact Register.

There was considerable agreement also between birth fathers and their sons and daughters about the process of contact and its long-term outcome. This was reported from both sides as having been a mostly pleasurable experience and the main reason for there not being more frequent contact was distance, time or family commitments. A few birth fathers would have liked more frequent contact and a closer relationship than adopted people could respond to. Compared to birth mothers, hardly any of these birth fathers had lost contact altogether, but this may reflect the nature of the sample. Nevertheless, two birth fathers who had married the birth mother were rather off-putting towards the adopted person. Whether this arose out of guilt or rivalry it is hard to say.

Based on their accounts the great majority of these birth fathers reported that contact, and the subsequent relationships that they developed with their sons and daughters, had helped them to cope better and come to terms with their feelings about the adoption. Furthermore, and again like birth mothers, they said that contact had enhanced their outlook and their self-esteem and they were very glad they had been sought out. There was no evidence that these fathers' mental health had been damaged as a result of their loss, and on the more objective GHQ test they came across as an emotionally well-balanced group.

The overall pattern to emerge was of mostly satisfied birth fathers whose experiences were largely supported by the comments of their sons and daughters; three or four fathers either had no contact, refused contact or found contact less satisfying than expected. Compared to their sons

and daughters, birth fathers tended to place more emphasis on the relationship, while the priority for adopted people was to obtain more background
information and then develop a relationship.

18 Shared fate

We borrow the title of this chapter from the late Professor Kirk (1964) in recognition of the way he used the term "shared fate" to crystallise the fact that many of the issues faced by adopted people, birth parents and adoptive parents are similar. Shared fate here is meant to refer to the many shared feelings and thoughts experienced by all three members of the adoption triangle arising from the situations each find themselves in. These have included shame and stigma, frustration and powerlessness, loss, sadness and depression, rejection, anxiety and worry, fears, pleasure, happiness, dissatisfaction and, in a few cases, disillusionment. An attempt is made here to bring together these feelings and thoughts from the pregnancy stage up to an average of some eight years after the search and reunion event took place. Four stages have been singled out: early feelings; from adoption to the search; seeking and being sought; and finally the post-contact stage.

Early feelings

The initial feelings that were prominent with birth mothers were shock on finding themselves pregnant followed by shame and its accompanying stigma, isolation, frustration and powerlessness after the pregnancy became known. During the same period, the would-be adopted child was either in the uterus or experiencing life as a newly-born infant. There is an increasingly held view that a child's emotional life in the uterus can be affected as much by the state of the mother's health and disposition at the time as by their physical health, but how exactly this operates is far from clear. We have seen the turmoil of strong feelings experienced by most mothers and their distress during the pregnancy and before the parting, but it is hard to estimate the impact of such intense feelings on the unborn child or very young infant (Schore, 2003). It is unlikely, however, that whether in the uterus or during the few weeks or months before the adoptive placement, these children had an optimum start in life.

For the childless adopters it was a period of hopelessness about never having a birth child, accompanied by sadness and feelings of loss for the child they could not have. Leaving aside possible feelings of stigma arising from not having a genetic child in a society that highly values children, waiting to be approved to adopt appeared to touch some basic feelings about the adopters' self-worth. As shown earlier, adopters described not being able to have a birth child as a great deprivation, using words and phrases such as: 'a heavy blow'; 'squashing'; 'sad'; 'devastated'; 'deeply upset'; 'very disappointed'; 'grief and sadness'; 'unhappy' or 'absolutely heartbroken'.

The birth mother's feelings during the pregnancy period were compounded after confinement by lack of control and powerlessness, a decision that the great majority did not feel they owned. This was in addition to the sadness and grief arising from the expected loss of the child. As most of the children were placed with their adoptive families when still babies, their feelings could not be known except that they now had to make psychological attachments to people who were not their biological parents. During the same period, adopters experienced the anxiety, and sometimes frustration, that set in from the unavoidable assessment processes and delays before they could experience the excitement, anticipation and pleasure following from the child's placement.

From adoption to the search

The main feelings and thoughts that pre-occupied the majority of birth mothers in the sample following the parting continued over the many years that followed, at least up to the stage of being sought. In addition to the sadness, there was now a much stronger sense of loss, along with guilt and worry. If, by becoming pregnant outside marriage, they had transgressed social norms, the parting appeared to have had a more personal and deeper meaning, that of appearing to reject or abandon their own child. It is perhaps easier for a birth parent to explain away the adoption when it is a matter of life and death, as some of the intercountry adoptions can be, rather than the kind of adoptions we are concerned with here. Added to the strong sense of guilt was the continued worry and anxiety of whether their child was well and happy. This was made worse by ignorance of the child's progress because even indirect forms of contact were not considered at the time. Equally, the secrecy that had to be maintained within the family prevented the sharing of the feelings and thoughts she had about the child. Other thoughts had to do with what the adopted person looked like and whether they would like to meet. Anniversaries and key periods such as Christmas were particularly painful. The dominant feelings and thoughts of that period were graphically expressed in words and phrases such as: 'overwhelming sense of loss'; 'never a day went by without thinking about her'; 'could not run away from it'; 'relentless sense of loss'; 'sadness and depression'; 'did I do the right thing?'; 'wondering if happy and well cared for'; 'is he happy?'; 'do they love him?'; 'is she alive or dead?'; 'does he feel rejected?'; 'does she hate me?'.

Getting married and having other children, along with making new relationships, were events singled out by the majority of birth mothers as having had a big positive impact on their later lives and going some way to neutralise the negative impact of parting. The non-display of anger, except by a few, was a significant characteristic of this and the other periods and it is hard to explain this other than that they perhaps came to perceive themselves as blameworthy.

For the adopted person, the feelings and thoughts between adoption and the search, had many similarities, but also differences, to those of their birth mothers, but were different from those of their adoptive parents. The work of Brodzinsky (1984) has more clearly documented how children do not begin to understand the meaning of adoption until about the age of five or so, with increasing understanding gradually developing in the subsequent years. However, full understanding does not usually develop until the adolescent years. An earlier chapter showed how the adopted persons' closeness to their adoptive parents dipped during the adolescent years, but picked up again after that period was over, though not reaching the heights of the childhood period. The sense of loss, curiosity about origins, and 'why adoption', or indirectly 'why the rejection', far from disappearing after adolescence, continued for many in forms of various intensity until the contact stage. If the birth mother wanted to meet her son or daughter to relieve her sense of loss and expiate her guilt, and also explain that adoption was not a rejection, the adopted person also wanted answers to the same question to enable him or her to develop a coherent account of themselves and who they were, including the knowledge that they had not been rejected and hoping that they had been loved. Typical pre-occupations during this pre-contact period included: 'feeling of not being wanted'; 'of being rejected'; 'the sheer thought of being given up as unwanted'; 'being unworthy to keep'; 'the sense of loss is like a hole'; 'like a void'; 'a gap'; 'something missing'; 'what I thought I never had'; 'why adoption'; 'to know about my heritage'; 'know where I came from'.

What most adopted people reported as providing solace and comfort during this period was the love of their adoptive parents and the sense of belonging to and being wanted by them: 'affection from my parents'; 'the experience of being nurtured'; 'wanted'; 'loved'; 'feeling safe in my adoptive family'; 'time and attention from adoptive parents'; or 'good relationships'. The close association found by the study between closeness to the adoptive parents and the lowering of feelings of loss and rejection, suggested that adoption went a long way to provide a healing experience or did not allow these feelings to develop. A greater satisfaction for some was reached following contact and having found answers to their questions.

For the adoptive parents, the pre-contact period was one of consolidating their family, with almost eight out of ten of those who had not given birth to children saying that previous feelings surrounding their "infertility" did not persist. Similar to adopted people who found that the love and affection of their adoptive parents helped to reduce their feelings of loss and rejection, adoptive parents now said that having adopted one or more children largely dealt with their sadness and feelings of loss; a minority (21%) continued to experience some sadness arising from not having given birth to a child. However, the study found no significant differences between the emotional health of those adoptive parents who gave birth to children and the rest, thereby suggesting that by the time of the study, adoption provided, perhaps, a healing experience. Typical comments from them included: 'adoption totally taken the regret away'; 'having adopted two lovely boys'; 'over the moon'; 'delightful'; 'wonderful'; 'a real gift'; or 'having a family through adoption'.

Adoption could not be said to have provided the same kind of healing experience for the birth mother during the in-between years as that identified for many adopted people and adoptive parents, except for those birth mothers for whom adoption had been their choice.

Seeking and being sought

Although for most birth mothers and many adopted people feelings about the adoption in the pre-contact period, but not necessarily throughout their lives, had been dominated by loss, sadness, rejection and guilt accompanied with thoughts about the welfare of the other and what the other looked like, a shift in thoughts and feelings occurred at the information that a son or daughter or a birth mother was seeking news and possibly contact. For birth mothers, the emerging possibility that she was about to meet her child gave rise to mixed feelings that worries might be eased or confirmed. There was certainly excitement, happiness and pleasure at the prospect of a meeting, mingled with apprehension, anxiety, nervousness, worry and some fear about its outcome. While the possibility of a meeting and the prospect of a relationship were too good to be missed, a dominant thought was the opportunity to explain the adoption and satisfy curiosity. At the same time, there was the worry, anxiety, and even fear, that their child might dislike them, reject them, be angry or relate that he or she had had an unhappy life and was hurt or be hurt in the process. This mixture of anticipation and anxiety was expressed in typical comments such as: 'over the moon'; 'elated, thrilled'; 'longing for it'; 'would she blame me?'; 'would he feel rejected?'; 'afraid he might not like me'; 'I might be intruding in her life'; 'finding he had an unhappy life'; or 'my family know nothing about it'. A handful were angry feeling that their privacy had been 'invaded'.

Many of the birth mothers' feelings and thoughts were also experienced and shared by adopted people. Alongside anticipation and excitement and the need to know 'why?' was also the anxiety or worry of being hurt or fear of causing hurt because of the birth parent not wanting to see them and thereby experiencing a second rejection. They also feared hurting their adoptive parents and the birth parent's new family. Even though many knew that their adoptive parents supported them, or would support them when told, it did not stop them from feeling concerned about the possibility of upsetting them. It proved difficult for some to not view their move to establish contact as a sign of disloyalty towards their adoptive parents, even if they knew they had their support. The parents' more active support went a long way to reduce some of the guilt, but they also had to tread carefully so as not to take over from the adopted person. For adopted people, alongside the fear of causing hurt or being hurt was that of finding out things they might not like.

Although a significant proportion of adoptive parents had not known about the search or the establishment of contact until later, it had not come as a surprise to most when they were told or when they found out. This was something they had often thought might happen. Although most adoptive parents had not been surprised or shocked at the news, the reality of contact gave rise to both pleasure and apprehension, but mostly the latter. There was pleasure that contact could be of benefit to their son or daughter, mainly for genealogical and identity reasons, along with apprehension that contact might not work out and their child would get hurt through rejection. In a smaller proportion of cases, there was a fear that this was the start of the slippery slope leading to the loss of their child. In contrast to birth mothers and adopted people who were finding each other to resolve feelings of loss and rejection, some adoptive parents were beginning to lose confidence in the quality of the relationship they had with their son or daughter and anticipate their possible rejection, and therefore a possible loss.

Overall, while each member of the triangle was mostly concerned about not hurting the others, the others did not know this and were suspicious and fearful about the possibility of being hurt. In a minority of cases, there was some suspicion of the motives of the person who had initiated the search. The anticipation by each party of the possibility of being hurt was perhaps a protective psychological mechanism.

After contact

Feelings of separation, loss and rejection generally appear inherent to all members of the adoption triad, although it does not mean that these will actually develop or develop with the same intensity for each. As seen in previous chapters, whether or not these feelings develop appears to be

341

ameliorated by a number of factors, some of which we may never know. For the birth mother it could be new relationships and a new family, for the adopted person and the adoptive parents the adoption experience per se. These feelings appeared to resurface at the time of reconnection with a delayed opportunity to alleviate or exacerbate the associated feelings. Having outlined the kinds of feelings and thoughts that prevailed over the three previous stages, including those that surrounded the prospect of contact, attention now shifts to what actually happened to all these feelings and pre-occupations after contact was established.

For the birth mother the three previous stages witnessed a progression, and sometimes a change, in feelings and thoughts, moving from initial isolation and stigma, to loss and sadness, along with guilt and concern that the child might have had an unhappy adoption. It culminated in anticipatory pleasure at the prospect of meeting with a son or daughter, but tempered by fear and anxiety that her child might not like her, might have felt rejected, or that he or she had had an unhappy adoption. For some it was also the fear of the adoption secret being revealed within their family. The great majority of mothers now said, in more ways than one, that contact had helped to erase most of the former unpleasant feelings and thoughts, replacing them now with: satisfaction, pleasure, relief, feeling at peace with oneself, no more guilt and sadness, improved emotional outlook and self-esteem, and the establishment of new relationships. Overall, there were few emotional upsets, which were mainly over not having enough or more contact, but no regrets. Some typical comments included: 'eased the feelings of loss'; 'a huge burden was lifted'; 'overjoyed'; 'no more sadness and depression'; 'I need not have worried'; 'laid the guilt to rest'; 'final chapter in 18 years of worry and upset'; 'no more secrets'; 'my family are very pleased for me'.

Like their birth mothers, most adopted people had entered contact seeking answers to many questions, with around two out of five being troubled by feelings of rejection and loss. They had also shared their birth mothers' and adoptive parents' fears of a possible new rejection and of being hurt. Alongside that was the fear of hurting others, mainly their adoptive parents, or disturbing their birth mothers' new family. Following the establishment of contact, and again like their birth mothers, hardly anyone had regrets about seeking or being sought, even though a small proportion had felt hurt in the process. The latter had found other benefits, they said, that went some way to compensate. Most of the satisfaction experienced came from a new sense of completeness in the form of genealogical and identity gains and the knowledge that the act of parting was not because they had not been wanted. Besides these, the majority (although more so the searchers than those sought) established new relationships, reported an improved emotional outlook, made gains in self-esteem, and felt more relaxed in the knowledge that they mostly had the support of their adoptive parents. There was no doubt about the pleasure and satisfaction the great majority of them had experienced after contact: 'the emotional and psychological satisfaction of finding being wanted and loved'; 'knowing she cared'; 'knowing why I was adopted'; 'lovely to find out who I am'; 'completing my self'; 'piece of puzzle found'; 'feeling complete and secure'; 'discovering my identity'; 'feel whole'; 'knowing my roots'; 'a chapter of my life that can now be closed'; 'recognising myself'; and 'knowing they are well'.

While acknowledging that members of the triad with the worst experiences may have not participated in the study, for adoptive parents in the sample the biggest relief was finding that most of their worst fears did not materialise, i.e. the fear of their son or daughter being hurt or losing their child to the birth family. There was also the added satisfaction (for the great majority) that the adopted person had benefited from contact; a significant number found that the relationship with their son or daughter had even been enhanced. Their levels of satisfaction, both with the overall adoption experience and the contact experience, were nearly always very high. Most of them were pleased on behalf of their son or daughter because contact had worked out well. They talked about: 'untold joy and happiness on his behalf'; and that their son or daughter 'came to feel more complete'; 'more satisfied for having answers to questions'; 'found an identity'; 'came to value friendships and relationships more'; 'felt happier because no more unanswered questions' or 'satisfied that all loose ends had been tied up'.

Referring to themselves, they added that contact had: 'brought us closer together'; 'made us more secure as a family'; and that they now had 'a happier adult relationship'; 'more open relationship'; 'more respect for each other' or 'she has come to appreciate us more'.

Summary

This chapter has explored the evolution of each party's main feelings and thoughts at four different stages of the adoption process, and discussed what happened to these feelings well after contact had been established. Based on self-reporting, and although coming from different experiences, all parties shared many similar and some different feelings and thoughts. The three key feelings that had most powerfully affected all three members of the triad were those of sadness/loss, rejection and finally relief for most of them. There was evidence to suggest that contact had contributed significantly towards greater peace of mind, improved outlook, enhanced self-esteem, fewer worries and greater contentment overall. Contact offered birth mothers the opportunity to explain to their son or daughter 'why adoption'; offered adoptive parents a chance to thank the birth mother for the "gift"; and offered an opportunity for adopted people to find answers to their many questions and broaden their relationships, but not at the expense of their adoptive family. To call the experience a healing and enhancing one may sound exaggerated, but it should not disguise the fact that a small number from each group, albeit fewer amongst adopters, were now left with new feelings, mainly of disappointment, frustration and some anger from not having had all their expectations met.

19 **Summary and conclusions**

Introduction

Based on information obtained from the perspective of all three members of the so-called adoption triangle, this study reported predominantly on two specific stages of adoption. First, the experiences of giving up a child for adoption some 40 to 50 years ago, rearing an adopted child and growing up as an adopted person. Second, the more recent experiences of all three groups surrounding the search and reunion process and its outcome for each after an average of eight years. The birth mother's feelings and thoughts were charted from the time of the pregnancy to the post-reunion period, and those of the adopted child from being raised as an adopted person to the aftermath of the contact and reunion experience. Finally, the adoptive parents shared their views, feelings and thoughts about raising the adopted child and the impact on themselves and the adopted person of the search, contact and reunion. Besides eliciting and recording each group's separate experiences, it was also possible to contrast them in matched dyads and triads. A key focal point was a study of the outcomes of what Hill (1991) described as 'the shift in adoption paradigm from previous ideas based on secrecy and unitary identity to one embodying greater honesty and recognition of the continuing duality of adoptive parenthood and identity. That double nature occurs whenever genetic and social parenthood are partially or wholly separated, whether through adoption, assisted reproduction techniques or widowhood' (p. 21).

Previous studies have looked at some of these issues from the perspective of a particular group but rarely from that of all three. Furthermore, no study known to us has included sizeable samples of people in the same adoption triad. In addition, this study has included both mothers who were sought by their sons and daughters and those who sought their child. Like the preceding study (Howe and Feast, 2000), this one too covered searching and non-searching adopted people, but the sample of those not searching was small. As a result, levels of significance referring to them

were only quoted when these were robust and where there was descriptive material to support them. To summarise, the main sample consisted of:
93 birth mothers, of whom 61 were sought and 32 were seekers;
126 adopted people, of whom 104 were searchers and 22 non-searchers;
93 adoptive parents, 77 of whose children were searchers and 16 sought.

Included within the sample were:
78 birth mother dyads (adopted person, birth mother);
86 adoptive parent dyads (adopted person, adoptive parent(s);
38 triads (adopted person, adoptive parent(s) and birth mother).

The study elicited both retrospective and more recent experiences and took a longitudinal perspective that allowed for contrasts to be made before, between and after experiences. Retrospective and self-reporting accounts are inevitably, perhaps, influenced and coloured by time and the changing social context, but by asking a number of related questions it was possible to look at the data from different angles. As far as the more recent events were concerned, that is, since the search began and the subsequent reunions, the fact that the sample had included many who were related, that is, birth mother, adopted people and adoptive parent(s), offered additional safeguards through cross-checking. As has been shown in earlier chapters, considerable congruence was found, especially within the dyads of birth mothers and adopted adults and of adoptive parents and adopted adults. Overall, significant agreements were found between the groups on a range of variables, but also some important differences such as between birth mothers and adopted people, adopted people and adoptive parents, searchers and non-searchers or males and females. Fewer contrasts were possible within the triads because many of their experiences as triads were not exactly comparable. In addition, the views of a small and rather unrepresentative sample of birth fathers have been included.

Birth mothers and adoption

Policy and practice in the UK, and in many other Western countries, have come a long way since the opening of the birth records to adopted people after the mid-1970s. Leaving aside the compelling moral arguments for doing so, what mostly persuaded legislators then to open the sealed records was research-based evidence demonstrating the value and benefits of such a step to adopted people. Since the original study, *In Search of Origins* (Triseliotis, 1973), which contributed to the opening of the records, there have been over a hundred other studies in the UK and elsewhere reaching broadly similar conclusions and confirming the positive impact of the opening of the records on adopted people's lives. The new studies also provided further insights on the search and reunion process and outcome. What has held back equivalent provision for access to birth relatives, mainly parents, has been the absence of similar studies, identifying what benefits such a step might bring to them without causing undue distress or harm to either the adopted person or their family. In spite of this limitation, changes have been made in the recent past, culminating in the provisions of the Adoption and Children Act 2002, which were discussed in Chapter 1. Provisional findings from this study contributed to the debate at the time.

Research available on birth mothers until recently was mostly of a qualitative type which, even though valuable, lacked proper sampling approaches (see Chapter 2). Their main weakness was a reliance on samples of birth mothers who had mainly approached an agency, were self-selected or who had been recruited through the media. Although the reported experiences of these mothers were real to them, this study has shown that they were not representative of the experiences, attitudes and outlook of all mothers, i.e. those who had not approached agencies and had not sought the adopted person. The differences found between searching and sought birth mothers were equivalent to those identified by the first part of the study in respect of searching and non-searching adopted people (Howe and Feast, 2000). It must be remembered that we still do not know the perspectives of those birth parents who refused contact altogether when approached directly by or on behalf of the adopted person.

In this study the views, thoughts and feelings of birth mothers were sought in respect of four different stages of their lives that were linked to the adoption decision and its aftermath. It covered the pregnancy; the child's birth and the parting; from parting to the stage of being sought or starting to search; and finally from contact up to an average of eight years later.

From the pregnancy to the parting with the child

The amount of shame, stigma and secrecy that surrounded non-marital births for some decades up to about the late 1960s is now history, but most of those mothers who suffered from the exclusion, condemnation and pressures are still around, trying to come to terms with the adoption decision and the way it has impacted on them and their child. It would be too easy to condemn the birth mothers' parents for the way they reacted, including the withholding, by the majority, of emotional and practical support and the eventual pressure on their daughters to part with their children. They too were largely both the products and perhaps the victims of the same prevailing ethos and harsh moral code of the period. Similarly, the social and institutional structures of the period had almost no place for women giving birth to a child outside of marriage. Adoption was seen as freeing the child born outside of marriage from the stigma, and as Howe *et al* (1992) point out, it was the women who bore its negative effects. The high proportion of women who said that their self-esteem had been affected (40 per cent) confirms Goffman's (1969) studies suggesting that 'a spoiled identity' usually develops from the receipt of consistently negative messages from those around us.

Mander (1995) interviewed birth mothers, mainly from a medical perspective, and reported that the attitudes of various professionals with whom the mothers had contact did not differ much from the censorious views of many parents. She added that the feelings and thoughts that dominated the lives of many mothers in her study were shame, isolation, lack of control and guilt (see also Winkler and Keppel, 1984; Bouchier *et al*, 1991; Howe *et al*, 1992; Modell, 1994). What was found from the present study was that resistance to pressures to have the child adopted required strong personal resources and sufficient external emotional and practical support which were mostly unavailable to many birth mothers who found themselves largely isolated. Not being able to make decisions based on choice increased their sense of frustration and powerlessness, even though they hardly expressed any anger about what happened to them. Birth mothers who said that the adoption decision was largely theirs were less likely to report either poor mental health or be seekers. The same mothers also said that they felt more 'vindicated' in their decision after seeing how well their child had been brought up and how well he or she had done as a result. It could be argued that, under the prevailing conditions of the period, far from these mothers being 'selfish' for parting with their child, they were probably well adjusted because they could anticipate the difficulties ahead. A father or mother who surrenders his or her child today would possibly feel, or be made to feel, more guilt because of the different social conditions.

Apart from the actual parting with the child, what pained most of these mothers was the pretence on the part of their families that nothing had happened, rather than recognising a major loss equivalent to bereavement, and therefore having to keep their sorrow private without being able to grieve more openly for the loss of their child. Witney (2004) quotes Sprang and MacNeil (1995) as saying that 'normal grief is sanctioned by society but stigmatised grief is disenfranchised, isolates the bereaved and denies them expression. Their sorrow remains hidden and unrecognised' (p. 56). Friends and siblings, especially friends, proved at the time to be the most supportive, possibly because they were of a new generation and more ready to look at things differently. Even during these early stages, significant differences were found between sought and seeker birth mothers, with the latter having had more censorious parents who were more prepared to withhold their support from their daughter and also pressurise her towards adoption. Because of the mainly censorious attitudes towards the pregnancy, there were hardly any accounts of mothers enjoying their pregnancy.

Although only around one out of five of the relationships with the child's father were described as 'casual', after the pregnancy or the child's birth, three-quarters of the relationships came to an end. Mothers and fathers decided in about equal proportions to terminate the relationship and in the rest it was a mutual decision. Based on the mothers' accounts, some birth fathers panicked and disappeared from the mothers' lives. The low level of support provided by birth fathers largely mirrored that of the mothers' parents, and it was well below that provided by siblings and especially friends. However, as we found from the few fathers we recruited, many were themselves young and inexperienced, and felt as confused as the mothers. In contrast to the negative perception of the child born outside marriage in Western-type societies in the recent past, Washington (1982) wrote that African cultural mores valued any infant as being of fundamental importance for the community. 'In this context', he wrote, 'procreative activities which insured the survival of the group were held in high regard and those couples who conceived offspring as a result of the valued sexual liaisons were able to claim increased status and prestige in the community' (p 298).

Unsurprisingly, perhaps, many mothers referred with some envy to current conditions that offer far more choices to single parents but little anger was expressed about what happened to them then. We can only speculate that any anger may have been turned inwards in the form of guilt about parting with their child in a society that valued the bearing and rearing of children, albeit within marriage. It is also possible that, because the study took place some eight years after contact had been established, any harboured anger had given way to the satisfaction derived from the mostly positive outcomes of the contact and reunion experience. Since the 1950s and 1960s, when most of these mothers had parted with their children, there has been a revolution in public attitudes and a decisive shift away from strict codes of sexual behaviour towards freer express-iveness and to different types of relationships and partnerships. The emphasis has shifted from fidelity to the quality of relationships and self-fulfilment. The shame and guilt usually experienced by those who failed in the past to observe the sexual moral code have little or no place in a post-modernist Western society. More than a third of children are now born within partnerships, not marriage, and single mothers head a high proportion of households with children. Introducing a series of articles on the family in the 21st century, Roseneil and Budgeon (2004) observed, 'At the start of the 21st century, "the family" is a sociological concept under severe strain. Processes of individualization are rendering the romantic dyad and the modern family formation it has supported increas-ingly unstable, and the normative grip of the gender and sexual order that has underpinned the modern family is ever weakening. As a result more and more people are spending longer periods of their lives outside the conventional family unit'. Later, in the same journal, the authors make the point that 'the heterosexual couple, and particularly the married, co-resident heterosexual couple with children, no longer occupy the centre-ground of Western societies and cannot be taken for granted as the basic unit in society' (Roseneil and Budgeon, 2004, p 140). The apparent current emphasis on individual expression and choice were not available to many mothers expecting a non-marital child at the time. It is also a far cry from the predominant theoretical explanation of thirty to forty years ago, which came from psychoanalysis, that mothers giving birth to a non-marital child suffered mostly from psychopathology, with the pregnancy being the acting out of conflict and unmet need within the mother (e.g. Young, 1954).

The years before contact

If the pregnancy and parting were a difficult and upsetting stage, the majority of mothers experienced the period between the parting and the search as equally distressing and sad, with the loss weighing heavy on their minds. Although distressed, the majority still enjoyed good emotional health. For 40 per cent of them, the dominant effect of the parting during this stage was the sense of loss, with its accompanying sadness and depression. Professional writings discussed by Brodzinksy (1990, p 309) are in agreement with the idea that, when given the opportunity to grieve openly and fully in a supportive environment, human beings will experience a reasonably satisfactory resolution to their feelings about loss. Parkes (1975), too, noted that a satisfactory resolution assumed the availability of opportunities to mourn and grieve with the support of others. The importance of support was further highlighted by Brown and Harris (1978), whose study showed that women who had a confidante as a form of support were less likely to develop depression. Grief theory also suggests a range of different stages which those who experience loss, such as death, normally go through: from initial denial or isolation, to confusion or anger, bargaining, depression and acceptance (Kubler-Ross, 1970). Others have noted that the realisation of the magnitude of the loss can lead to the onset of 'despair' and depression (Bowlby, 1980; Parkes, 1975). Although some mothers in this study likened the loss of their child to bereavement, one difference was that they could not share their grief because those around them mostly failed to acknowledge the loss. Equally, the view of professionals then was that the parting with the child was an altruistic activity on the part of the mother who could see that it was for the good of her child. Such attitudes could again have inhibited mourning for the child. For example, Mander (1995, p 191) noted from her study that the way the various professionals communicated with the mother limited her scope for the expression of her grief.

For many of the rest in this study, as several described it, it was a 'limbo' period because the child was neither dead nor had they contact with him or her. Above all, what many of them found was that they could not forget or "block off" what had happened and a persistent, and for some unrelenting, thought was wondering whether their child was well, had a happy life and would like to meet them one day. Reporting on the same theme, Fravel et al (2000) explained the "not forgetting" by saying that although the child is physically absent from the birth mother's life he or she remains psychologically present in her mind. Others have pointed out that the possibility of the reappearance of the 'relinquished one' serves to impede, by delaying or prolonging, the mother's grief (Mander, 1995). This study found that it was different for those mothers who said that it had been their own decision to part with their child. These mothers mostly reported being able to get on with their lives, believing that they had done the right thing and adding that they had few regrets and were not consumed by guilt.

Besides feelings of loss and grief, 79 per cent of mothers in this study reported guilt as one of a number of lasting impacts arising from the parting decision; almost a fifth (17 per cent) reported it as the main impact. The guilt arose mainly from the realisation that, irrespective of the circumstances, they had rejected their child. Although no mother reported low self-esteem as a main impact arising from the adoption decision, 40 per cent quoted it as one of a number. Lewis (1971) has suggested that parents who cannot keep their infants have a sense of worthlessness and much guilt. The anxiety arising also from the pressure and felt need to keep both the birth and the adoption secret impacted equally heavily on many mothers, with almost a fifth (19 per cent) reporting it as a main impact and 64 per cent as one of a number. The fact that many still felt they could not talk about it increased both their sense of isolation and the anxiety of being found out. In fact, half of them had not told their other children or husbands/partners about the adoption until shortly before, or after contact, was established. As some explained, they were caught between the desire to have news of their child, and perhaps meet one day, and apprehension that the secret would come out and, perhaps, shock their new family. Telling and explaining to their other children appeared to cause a greater sense of guilt than telling husbands and partners. Except for a small number, for the majority it was a relief to find that, when told, their new family's response was on the whole understanding and far from condemnatory. Difficulties did arise, however, especially for sought mothers, but in the end they had no regrets, they said, because of the relief at having shed the secret and shared the feelings associated with it.

During the same period, i.e. between the parting with the child and contact, almost all mothers (98 per cent) said that one of their thoughts was about whether their child was well and happy. Their main wish was to know what had happened to their son or daughter. Over half (52 per cent) singled this out as their main preoccupation. The main coping mechanism most mothers developed was holding on to the belief that the child went to a "good" home as promised by the adoption agency. Having news of the child could have gone further, some said, to alleviate doubts about the parting, and the anxiety and guilt they felt. Compared to sought mothers, seeker ones were more likely to report being more anxious and worried about their child. Significantly, more of them also reported poorer physical and mental health, a lower self-esteem, taking more alcohol and attributing all this to the adoption. However, there was no significant association between being pressurised to consent to the adoption and being a searching mother.

Other studies have also suggested a relationship between parting with a child for adoption and impairment in psychological functioning, but there is no agreement about its extent (see Rynearson, 1982; Winkler and Keppel, 1984; Bouchier et al, 1991; Logan, 1996). Only a tiny number of birth mothers in this study reported having been diagnosed with a mental health problem before the adoption (3 out of 93). However, almost a quarter reported having been diagnosed with such problems, mostly for depression, between the parting with the child and contact, and almost all were from the seeker group of mothers. It cannot, of course, be inferred with certainty that the poorer mental health reported could be attributed to the loss of the child, because other factors may have intervened. Poor mental health, however, was less likely to be reported by mothers who said that adoption had been their personal choice. Previous studies which found significantly higher levels of mental health problems amongst birth mothers had relied heavily on mothers who took the initiative to enquire or search, were self-selected or were recruited through the media (see Winkler and Keppel, 1984; Bouchier et al, 1991; Modell, 1994; Logan, 1996). By including both searching and non-searching mothers in this study, it was possible to obtain a more balanced view about the mental health of both. With the exception of seeker mothers, half of whom had been diagnosed at some point with poor mental health, birth mothers, on the whole, were not found to be significantly different from the average in the population before contact took place. Although parting was experienced as a sad and guilt-ridden experience by many mothers, and significantly more so by those who later set out to seek their child, the great majority were able to get on with their lives and with their new families, although many said that what had happened had changed them for life and left its scars. Overall, seeker mothers had been affected more severely by the loss of the child and possibly felt the need to repair the loss more than non-seekers. Lazarus and Folkman (quoted by Brodzinsky, 1990 p 306) have suggested that adaptational outcomes in response to a stressful situation are the result of an interaction between the individual's perception of the event, their repertoire of coping behaviours, personality characteristics, and the social realities which surround the situation. The combination of family, institutional and social disapproval experienced by these mothers from pregnancy to confinement and beyond, and the lack of choice for most, could also have led to learned or imposed helplessness described by some writers such as Seligman (1975).

Being sought or seeking

The great majority of birth mothers were both excited and elated at the news that their son or daughter was trying to establish contact with them. The study, however, from the outset had not included mothers who might have rejected any form of contact. Of those who initially responded and featured in the study, there was no evidence that most of them were inconvenienced, except for a handful of sought mothers who were annoyed or angry that control had been taken out of their hands and their privacy 'invaded'. These were mostly mothers who had made a conscious decision from the start that adoption was the right thing to do. However, following an average of eight years after contact was established, hardly any birth mother regretted the event. Although a minority of sought mothers had previously initiated unsuccessful searches themselves, the majority had held back, feeling they had no right to do so, afraid that their sons or daughters might reject them or that they might upset the adoptive family. Seeker mothers entertained similar concerns but eventually their strong desire to establish contact overcame their other considerations.

The dominant expectation had to do with the wish to find out whether their sons and daughters were well and had a good adoption. Seeker mothers were more likely to express heightened fears of their child not having been happy, whereas sought ones were more concerned with whether they would get on with their son or daughter and be liked by them. This was followed by a kind of expiating wish, that is, to explain why the adoption had occurred and tell them how much they loved them and that they were not forgotten or rejected. Knowing that their child was well and had a good adoption, along with being able to explain to them why the parting, appeared to do away with some of the guilt arising from the parting. Although forming a relationship was part of their expectations, it did not hold centrestage before contact took place, but seeker mothers stressed it more than sought ones. For both groups of sought and seeker mothers, the excitement and pleasure of seeing their sons and daughters was also tempered by considerable anxiety, worry, and sometimes fear, that they might hear that he or she did not have a good adoption, that they might be blamed for the parting or that their son or daughter might not like them. A minority were worried about how a husband or their other children might react, because some of them did not know about the adoption. These fears largely did not materialise.

Contact and its outcome

Although not consciously planned by many, it was not unusual for the two phases of searching and contact to become part of the same process. For that reason, searching and contact became at times inextricably mixed.

355

In the end, some form of contact was nearly always established and in the majority of cases sustained. Contact and reunion stood the test of time over an average of eight years, even though almost a third of mothers did not currently have face-to-face contact. Seeker mothers were more likely to lose contact at the initiative of the adopted person, who tended to find faults of incompatibility or make reference to the birth mother's emotional state or her making too many demands. Losing contact was disappointing and painful but many of these mothers took the view that they had already gained a lot and been relieved of much of the guilt by having the opportunity to explain. However, even most of those who lost contact still felt the value of the experience and had no regrets. For the majority, contact continued to take place at least once every three to four months, but again more frequently for sought than seeker mothers. While sought mothers were likely to cite distance as the main obstacle, seekers were more likely to report that the adopted person was not always too keen to see them.

Looking at the overall picture, almost all birth mothers said that they were pleased that their sons and daughters had established contact or that they had searched for them, and 94 per cent added that the experience was positive. Only eight per cent reported that their expectations of contact had not been met, mostly amongst seekers, but no birth mother said she wished that she had not met her son or daughter. Those who had reported experiencing intense feelings of loss between the adoption and contact appeared to benefit most from contact and reunion. Other key benefits identified for themselves included:

No more:
- guilt (79%);
- sadness or grief (79%);
- confused feelings about their son or daughter (69%).

Improved:
- emotional outlook (60%);
- self-esteem (45%);

And:
- an enhanced life (64%);
- changed for the better (70%).

One of the less expected benefits, seldom openly declared as a main expectation prior to contact, was the establishment of new and durable relationships between birth mothers and their sons or daughters, frequently also involving other members of the family such as half-siblings and grandparents. On the whole, birth mothers looked at what they got out of contact without dwelling too much on experiences of rejection or of reduced contact. As will be seen later, they retained this outlook on other matters relating to the contact and reunion, tending, at times, to exaggerate the positives. A handful of mothers also expressed guilt arising from the contact and reunion experience, saying that they could not respond to their adopted son or daughter with the same love they felt for their other children. There were also a few who admitted to feeling 'envious' and 'jealous' of the adoptive parents for having watched their child grow up, something that they had missed and which was irreplaceable. However, when one looks at their responses, almost all birth mothers were contented and happy with what they got out of contact. Even when disappointed by not having face-to-face contact or only infrequent contact, they felt that having had news of their sons and daughters was a kind of bonus. Where a relationship was established, it was 'the icing on the cake' as one of them put it. Because of such acceptance, it might be suggested that these mothers did not, perhaps, feel that they deserved better and that contact was an expiation experience, especially as so little anger was shown against the conditions of the period that led to the adoption of the child. Their ready acceptance could be interpreted as a kind of apology to their sons and daughters.

On the more objective GHQ score, which measured current emotional health, birth mothers came out well. The finding of no unusually high levels of emotional problems amongst all birth mothers, and of no significant differences between seekers and sought some eight years after contact, could suggest the positive impact of contact on all birth mothers, but more so on seekers. This is in contrast to the mental health problems reported by almost a quarter of birth mothers, mostly seekers, which developed between the parting and contact. We could not, of course, be certain that other factors did not intervene in the lives of these mothers, who currently appeared to function no differently from the rest of the population.

Finally, a progression was identified for birth mothers from high levels of distress, grief and isolation from the pregnancy to the parting, to worry, fear and guilt during the period between the parting and contact, to little evidence being found for the continued presence or continued intensity of these feelings and thoughts after contact was established. It is a matter of conjecture whether, if they had been involved from the start in open forms of adoption, much of the pain and distress would have been avoided. For that we have to wait for the eventual publication of longitudinal studies in the USA (see Grotevant and McRoy, 1998 for an early account). However, for a minority of mothers, ranging from 10 to 20 per cent of cases, some of these feelings and thoughts persisted, mainly among the seeker group. Some of these mothers reported that, irrespective of the happy outcome, they still felt guilt for having given their child away. As one of them said:

The feeling of guilt never left me and probably never will, but I separate it from all the love I have had since we found each other.

Overall, for almost nine out of ten birth mothers (89 per cent), contact and reunion was said to have been a happy and satisfying experience. The rest either felt disappointed or wanted more contact or said that they found it hard to cope with the intensity of their feelings aroused by contact. Half of these were unhappy with contact, dissatisfied with the relationship with their sons or daughters, wanted more contact, found it hard to cope with the intensity of the feelings aroused by contact, and were not satisfied with the overall outcome. We have no explanation for why this small group came to feel like this, neither were they predominantly from the group of seekers. The small numbers did not allow for tests of significance to be conducted. Others have also reported that birth mothers who had contact with the adoptive family and the child, either ongoing, partly or fully disclosed, showed better resolution of their feelings than did mothers who never had such contact or had less open contact (Dominick, 1988; Keppel, 1991; Cushman et al, 1997; Neil, 2000; Grotevant, 2000). In the birth mothers' view, contact was more likely to continue if it felt comfortable; if there was compatibility or they had a lot in common; if there was depth in the emotional connection; if the son or daughter showed that they were glad to meet the parent; if the birth parent was sensitive to their son or daughter's feelings; or if the birth parent was not making too many demands.

Birth fathers

The accounts of the small number of birth fathers who featured in the study suggested hardly any differences from those of birth mothers. Although the possibly biased nature of such a small sample is recognised, nevertheless they confirmed that their experiences, feelings and thoughts over the years, their reaction when told that their sons and daughters were seeking them, and the subsequent contact and relationships had many similarities with those reported by birth mothers. Compared to the latter, however, birth fathers hardly reported poor mental health during the period from the parting to contact, but this could be because 14 of the 15 fathers had been sought by their sons and daughters. Recent accounts of birth fathers make no reference to their emotional or mental health (Clapton, 2003; Witney, 2004). In the case of birth mothers, it was those searching for their sons and daughters who mostly reported much of the poor mental health during that period. Like the birth mothers, the great majority of these birth fathers reported that contact, and the subsequent relationships that developed with their sons and daughters, helped them to cope better and come to terms with their feelings about the adoption. Most of them were very positive or positive and satisfied about the outcome. Furthermore, and again like birth mothers, they said that contact enhanced their outlook; and changed them for the better, almost half said their self-esteem had improved; and with one exception, the rest reported they were very glad they had been sought out. There was no evidence that the emotional health of these fathers had been damaged as a result of their loss and, on the more objective GHQ test, they came across as an emotionally well-balanced group. But again they may not have been representative of all birth fathers.

Overall, the birth fathers' description of the type of relationship they had developed with the adopted person did not differ significantly from those developed by birth mothers. In the majority of cases, their sons and daughters agreed with these perceptions but in a minority of cases there were differences such as whether the relationship was like that with a parent or friend. Occasionally, birth fathers tended to see more in the relationship than the adopted person did.

Growing up adopted

It was pointed out at the start that it was not the intention to repeat the first part of the study, which was published in 2000, but mainly to reflect on the adopted person's past and current experiences and circumstances in the light of those of their birth mothers and adoptive parents and to address areas that had not been explored in the same detail before. However, a number of overlaps were inevitable. In their book, Brodzinsky *et al* (1992) acknowledge that being adopted is something that colours a person's relationship with his or her adoptive parents, his or her emergent sense of self, and the intimate relationships he or she forges for the rest of their life. 'If you are adopted', they add, 'you will think about that fact of your life now and again – maybe when a question arises about your genetic background, maybe when you encounter a particularly rough spot in your life, maybe every single day' (p 1). To aid adoptive parenting, they set out in their book a model of 'normal adjustment to being adopted as it occurs throughout the life span'. The first part of this study (Howe and Feast, 2000) showed that the majority of adopted people who had searched or had been sought, had adjusted well to their adoptive status and the search and reunion experience had benefited them significantly in a number of ways, but mostly in terms of genealogy and identity.

In this study, around 80 per cent of adopted people said that they felt happy about being adopted, felt loved by their parents and had developed a sense of belonging. A broadly similar proportion reported having developed very close or close relationships with their adoptive parents during childhood. There were no differences in reported closeness between mother and father. Although this was a retrospective reporting, closeness fell sharply during adolescence and it partly recovered by adulthood, but it never reached the closeness achieved during early childhood. Some eight years after contact, closeness stood at around 70 per cent. Those who were either feeling not close or distant were around one in seven, while the rest fell in between. The fall during adolescence, and the fact that it never regained the childhood levels later, may not be surprising. Adulthood implies a move to greater independence and a loosening of attachments from familiar figures and the seeking of relationships and intimacy outside the parental home. However, as this study has found, almost everyone kept the links with their adoptive family. The closer adopted people felt to their parents, the more openly was their adoption discussed within the family, the happier they felt about being adopted, the more they felt they belonged, the higher their self-esteem as found on a standardised scale and the better their emotional health as scored on the GHQ. Although closeness was not significantly affected by the presence of biological children within the adoptive family, significantly more of those brought up in such families said that they came to feel 'different'. Overall, the findings suggested that self-esteem and emotional health were related to the quality of the adoptive relationship.

Two feelings and thoughts that had dominated much of the lives of half the adopted people were those of rejection and loss experienced in relation to the parting from their birth family. Some experienced these feelings very strongly. Most of those who felt rejected were broadly the same as those who felt the sense of loss. For the adopted person, as Brodzinsky et al (1992) put it, 'the experience of loss is usually felt in the context of the search for self' (p.12). In their view, for early placed children, the sense of loss is not consciously experienced until the age of five or so. In this study, the presence of strong feelings of rejection and loss increased also the motivation to search. Searchers were more likely than non-searchers to report such feelings. These feelings appeared to act as a strong motivating force for the search and wanting especially to find out 'why put up for adoption', and indirectly whether wanted or not. Why only half of them, though, came to feel the sense of rejection and loss is possibly explained by the findings suggesting that the closer their reported relationship to the adoptive parents, the less likely they were to have experienced these feelings and thoughts. As many of them explained, 'it was the love of my parents that did it' (meaning adoptive parents), suggesting again that close relationships and feeling loved by a parent acted as a protective shield against the development of such feelings. However, where such feelings persisted, it was contact this time that was reported as having helped to extinguish or lessen their impact. As an example, 55 per cent of those who had felt rejected had reported that any feelings of rejection disappeared after contact and 68 per cent said the same about feelings of loss. Those who reported the disappearance or lessening of feelings of rejection and loss were also more likely to report closer relationships to their adoptive parents. These findings raise again the question of whether more open forms of adoption from the start could have prevented such feelings from developing in the first place. For example, one writer maintains that, when a disruption such as this occurs in the biological link, the emotions associated with the break remain buried pending a reunion with the birth mother (Robinson, 2004). In this writer's view, both birth mothers and adopted people need to address their feelings of loss and grief through counselling. However, as this study found, such feelings are not inevitable nor are they experienced with the same intensity. As shown earlier, other factors appear to mediate, leading to the absence, decrease or increase of such feelings.

The search and contact

The wish to search and make contact with birth relatives appears to be heightened from adolescence onwards and the majority of those searching in Britain are women with an average age of around 30. There is no shortage of studies and writings explaining why adopted people search and what they expect from it. There is agreement that much of the search is for genealogical connectedness having mainly to do with establishing roots and identity. It could also be part of the move to independence and the search for new intimacies without necessarily discarding old ones. Some writers refer also to the search as the wish 'to undo the trauma of separation' (Anderson, 1988 p19) and/or for an explanation of why the 'rejection' or 'loss' (Triseliotis, 1973; Weiss, 1988). Not surprisingly, perhaps, adopted people in our study who took the initiative to search were more likely than non-searchers to have felt rejection and loss in relation to their birth family. Other expectations had to do with physical appearance and the recognition of oneself in others, or to find out about the circumstances and well-being of members of the birth family.

In this study, and as with birth mothers, a face-to-face meeting with a birth relative was usually viewed as desirable, but the possibility of a relationship did not initially appear as central to the search. It mostly evolved over a period of time and after the parties came to know each other. Along with excitement about the prospect of meeting a birth parent or relative, there was also uncertainty, nervousness and the fear of hurting or of being hurt. Uncertainty was mainly to do with what they might find, nervousness was to do with how to handle a face-to-face meeting in particular, and the fear was to do with hurting their adoptive parents, their birth relative or themselves. After an average of eight years following contact, eight out of ten were still in some form of direct or indirect contact, with around 70 per cent having face-to-face contact. The frequency of contact varied a lot, but most typical was a few times a year. Two-thirds of those in contact also described close to very close relationships with their birth mother, thus only slightly lower compared to current relationships with their adoptive parents. For around 25 to 30 per cent, direct contact had ceased at the initiative of the adopted person or the parent/relative. Who rejected whom was not always easy to establish, but the most common explanations were incompatible interests, the birth mother's alleged problems and rejection by a birth parent. Many of the relationships described appeared strong and rewarding, but they mainly acted as an extension, rather than a substitute, for other relationships such as with the adoptive parents. Around a third had established contact with a birth father, three-quarters with at least one sibling and almost half with a grandparent. Although these relationships were fluid and their strength variable, finding a half-brother, half-sister or grandparent gave great pleasure to many adopted people.

Around half of adopted people featuring in the study identified many benefits from the search and contact and almost a similar proportion identified some; only five per cent said they derived no benefit at all from contact. The benefits were similar to those identified by previous studies, such as that of Howe and Feast (2000). These mainly included receiving background information, finding answers to many questions such as knowing 'why they were given up', 'physical recognition', 'knowing their birth relatives were mostly well', 'developing new relationships' and much practical information such as about medical history. Much of this, they reported, improved their sense of identity and of who they were; they came to feel more secure and more complete; they achieved higher levels of self-esteem and of emotional functioning; and their feelings of loss and rejection decreased or disappeared. There was also considerable relief in finding that the birth parent was well. A psychoanalytic explanation could be that the relief was from finding that their anger over the adoption had not damaged the birth parent.

All these benefits were more likely to be reported by those who had declared close relationships with their adoptive parents and an equally close one with the birth mother. It looked as if the good start given to them within the adoptive family was an important factor that contributed to these outcomes, but we cannot be certain. There were indications that non-searchers were more likely to report benefits than those who searched, but many of those who searched also reported many benefits. Contact having been terminated by the adopted person or the birth mother did not mean that there were no rewards or gains. Around eight out of ten were glad they had searched or had been contacted and a similar proportion felt that their original expectations had been well or very well met. Overall, and though it is recognised that other factors may have intervened, there were indications that a close relationship with the adoptive parents, including feeling loved and developing a sense of belonging, acted as protective factors and also impacted positively on other areas of the adopted adults' life, including on the contact and reunion experience. Although not exactly comparable, a study of children in adoptive families that included birth children found that greater mutuality (closeness) between mother and child was associated with lower levels of child behaviour problems. The authors concluded that mother–child mutuality is child-specific within families and that there was no evidence of passive gene-environment correlation, suggesting that the link between lower levels of mutuality and higher levels of child behaviour problems is not only reflecting overlapping genetic influences on parent and child behaviour (Deater-Deckard and Petrill, 2004).

A consistent proportion of between 10 to 20 per cent of adopted people, found more amongst searchers than non-searchers, reported that feelings of rejection and loss persisted and that being adopted had affected their marriage, well-being, education, career and relationships. Broadly, the same group reported lower self-esteem and poorer emotional health and they were also less likely to be satisfied with the outcome of contact, saying that their expectations of contact had not been met. For this group, it was hard to separate that which related to the adoption from other factors in their lives. There were indications that non-searchers were less likely to report such feelings. However, there was no significant overlap between this small group of adopted people and a similar proportion of birth mothers, who felt equally dissatisfied over a number of issues concerning the outcome. A lower proportion of seven per cent of adopted people had both low self-esteem and poor emotional health as scored on more standardised tests. The same group was also more likely to give negative answers to outcome questions about being adopted or about the contact and reunion experience. For example, adopted people who entertained strong feelings of rejection and loss were more likely to rate the contact and reunion experience as less positive.

Although numbers of those from a black or minority ethnic background were small, their comments suggested that the main experience that stood out for many of them was the racism they had experienced, mostly at school, their awareness that they were different, not fitting in with those around them or of not being fully accepted by members of their wider adoptive family. This was also confirmed by the first study, which covered a larger sample (Howe and Feast, 2000). Ethnicity and "race" issues appeared to matter to this group and the few who moved within a more ethnically diverse environment were more positive. Although there are no easy answers, inevitably the tension between the need to provide for the cultural and racial identity of children and also provide a secure social base in their lives can only be met if a sufficient number of matching and suitable placements can be found. Failing that, an ethnically diverse environment, good preparation and ongoing support could go some way to make up for other shortcomings (see also McRoy et al, 1984).

Like earlier studies, the majority of adopted people responding to this and the first part of the study (Howe and Feast, 2000) reported on how identity-enhancing they found the reunion, including the information gained through it and the relationships established. There was also evidence that the contact and reunion was experienced as even more positive by those who were already feeling well settled. The accounts from adopted people suggested that aspects of the new information gained, including answers to the central questions 'why' and 'who am I', appeared to be integrated with other aspects of the adopted person's identity to contribute towards a more whole self. In other words, the biological

365

heritage and psychosocial rearing were blended in a kind of duality that left the majority of adopted people satisfied. Although the circumstances are not exactly similar, Tizard and Phoenix (1993) reported from their study that children of dual heritage and ethnicity raised by their families appeared to successfully integrate in themselves both aspects of their background. Yet post-modernist language would suggest that 'identity' is a dated concept with 'diminishing' returns. On the whole, post-modernism questions the authenticity and desirability of fused, unitary identities. On the other hand, Giddens (1992, p 53), writing not long ago, captured the importance of continuity in life by saying that 'it is the reflexively understood by the person in terms of her or his biography. Identity here still presumes continuity across time and space; to be a "person" is not just to be a reflexive actor, but to have a concept of a person as applied both to self and others.'

Birth mothers and their sons and daughters

The views and perspective on the reunion experience of 78 birth mothers were compared and contrasted with those of their sons and daughters. A key purpose for doing so was to establish how congruent their answers were to similar questions, such as their perception of contact and its outcome. The comparisons identified both high levels of congruence and also important differences. Significant differences were again found between seeker and non-seeker birth mothers and searching and non-searching adopted people, confirming that those who take the initiative to search, be it birth parents or adopted people, are perhaps motivated differently from non-searchers.

Birth mothers and adopted people were in agreement on many aspects of the search and reunion process and outcome, including how helpful contact had been to them and giving credit to the other party for making it turn out like that. High percentages of both birth mothers and their sons and daughters were pleased that they had searched or had been contacted, but seeker mothers were significantly more pleased than the adopted person who had been sought. As said elsewhere, adopted people preferred to be in control of when to search or make contact. Seven out of ten birth mothers and adopted people also agreed that their relationship was 'close' or 'very close' but the agreement between them as dyads was mainly congruent in cases where contact had been initiated by the adopted person rather than the other way round. Not unexpectedly, perhaps, the physical health of birth mothers was found to be poorer than that of their sons and daughters, who were on average 21 years younger. However, when it came to emotional health, there was no significant difference between mother and offspring. The birth mothers' family were said to have reacted significantly more positively to the idea of contact compared to the adopted person's family. However, around one in ten from each group also reported some strains developing between themselves and their families. A greater number of birth mothers than adopted people, especially seeker mothers, wanted more contact and more closeness. Those who wanted more contact from each group did not often match, i.e. were not from the same pair. On the whole, reunions seemed more lasting when instigated by the adopted person.

Although high percentages from both groups were glad that they had met, adopted people were more likely to wish that they had not, but few recriminations were voiced. When it came to satisfaction with the overall contact and reunion experience, there was again considerable agreement between the parties about the high level of satisfaction. Adopted people's expectations, especially those of males, were more likely to be met if they had searched, rather than been sought by their birth mothers. There was also a high level of agreement between both that because of contact they could also relate better to other people. A slightly greater number of adopted people than birth parents reported that their self-esteem had improved after contact (55 to 44 per cent) with sought mothers appearing to have gained more than seeker ones in self-esteem. However, about an equal proportion of birth mothers and adopted people (a third) had found it hard to cope with the intensity of their feelings aroused by contact, but these were not from the same dyads.

The most common description of the relationship given by both mothers and adopted people was that of friendship, with just over a quarter describing it as filial or parental. Many adopted people distinguished between looking for and welcoming a relationship with a birth parent and seeking a parental-type relationship. The latter was mostly reserved for their adopters. Nor did the majority of birth mothers expect a parent–

child relationship, with many of them likening the relationship to that with a friend or an aunt. In other words, when it came to "parent", the blood relationship was important but only relative. Broadly similar findings were reported by Kennard (1991), Sachdev (1992) and March (1995). Unlike a number of adopted people, almost no birth mother described the relationship as distant, or thought of herself as a stranger after continuing contact. What the various findings as a whole suggest is that, in spite of high levels of agreements between the two groups on a range of issues, disagreement was more likely between seeker mothers and sought adopted people, especially a small number of males who, on the whole, did not see things the way their birth mothers did; their birth mothers tended to somewhat exaggerate the positives and minimise the negatives. Two factors appeared to bring this about: the adopted adults' apparent desire to be in control of when to search and the greater loyalty displayed, especially by males, to their adoptive families. In spite of wanting more contact and more closeness, it was a characteristic of both sought and seeker mothers to want to fit in with the adopted person and to appear to be more easily satisfied with the frequency and outcome of contact arrangements, as if they did not deserve better.

Being an adoptive parent

The generation of adopters featuring in this study came into adoption at a time when they were urged to treat the adopted child as their own, as if there was no difference between adoptive and biological parenthood. The secrecy that was almost guaranteed by legislation helped to reinforce this message, leading perhaps to a "denial" of the difference that was high-lighted by studies later on. Writing about US law, which is not very different from British law, Modell (1994) said that 'a made relationship, American law claims, can be exactly like a natural relationship: the child is *as-if-begotten*, the parent *as-if-genealogical*' (p 2). Eventually, by initiating searches and establishing contact with birth family members, adopted people came to challenge the non-recognition of the biological connection. Besides offering optimum parenting, adoptive parents are expected also to acknowledge the difference between adoptive and bio-logical parenting (Kirk, 1964). In a later book, Kirk (1981) reinforced this theme by saying that: 'given that the adoptive situation at the inter-personal level is objectively different from the situation of the family based on consanguinity, the solidarity of the adoptive family's membership is enhanced when their atypical reality is acknowledged in their daily relationship' (xv).

Based on his early study, Triseliotis (1973) suggested that the acknow-ledgement of the genealogical connection and the sharing of background information could help the child to accommodate in his or her developing personality the concept of two families – a biological and a psychosocial family. Couples who happen to be infertile or childless, as the majority of them are, are also expected to mourn and come to terms with any sadness arising from their position. Infertility implies a big loss and although many of those affected apparently cope well without resorting to outside help, for others it may become a continuing preoccupation that could affect the parenting of the adopted child. Brinich (1990) argues that if the adoptive parents 'are to be able to see their adopted child for whom he is, and if the adopted child is to be able to see his adoptive parents for whom they are, they must mourn the loss of their respective fantasised biological child and fantasised biological parents. The lost (fantasised) relationships must be mourned before the new (real, adoptive) relationships can flourish' (p 47). Mann (1998) gave the example of how few adoptive parents, unlike adopted people (and perhaps birth mothers), have written their accounts and went on to add that 'the shame and guilt that was so much part of the birth mother's experience in earlier studies is now appearing to be transferred to adoptive parents' (p 50). The pressures and extra tasks would suggest that adoption can be a stressful process, both for the adopted child and the adoptive parents. However, and as far as those adopted as infants are concerned, outcome studies suggest that they hardly differ from the general population, suggesting that the presumed problems of adoptive parenthood are not too challenging (e.g. Bohman, 1970; Brodzinsky, 1990).

Almost all the adopters in this study found the experience of raising the adopted child rewarding and satisfying and were prepared to recom-mend it to others. They mostly used superlatives to describe the pleasure that adoption had brought to their lives, believing that it was also good for the child. They reported high levels of closeness and attachment between themselves and their adopted son or daughter during different stages, except for adolescence when a significant proportion of relationships became strained. At the same time, a number of them also reported an element of guilt, wondering if they could have done better. Some difficulties did arise, especially for the small group who had adopted a black or mixed heritage child. A number of them became aware, they said, that they could not fully understand or enter the world and experiences of their child and therefore empathise sufficiently with their pain when at the receiving end of racial abuse and discrimination.

With regard to disclosing and talking about adoption, between 10 and 20 per cent of all adopters delayed the telling or sharing of background information. This small minority still expected the child to take the initiative to ask. A broadly similar percentage was found by Craig (1991) who talked to parents who had been specially prepared some 20 years earlier about how to approach this subject. In this study, those parents who said that their child never spoke about their birth family during adolescence were also more likely to score a poorer emotional health on the GHQ. Grotevant and McRoy (1998) reported from their longitudinal study that open styles of communication about adoption were found to produce significantly higher identity scores among adopted adolescents.

The expectation, from some of the literature, that those who adopted to create rather than to expand their family would report lower levels of emotional health was not borne out. The great majority reported that the adoption experience had 'eclipsed' any continuing feelings of disappointment surrounding their infertility. However, a significant minority (21 per cent) reported that these feelings still lingered. The latter were also more likely to report that they felt less close to the child in infancy, early childhood and adolescence. However, no differences in closeness were reported when their sons and daughters became adults or before or after contact or in current relationships.

Access to information and contact with birth relatives

Considering that the message at the time these parents adopted was that there was no difference between adoptive and biological parenthood, and that they had been reassured about maintaining secrecy, it was perhaps surprising that the majority in this study reported that they had reacted positively to the legislation that provided for the opening of birth records to adopted people and that they were equally supportive of their son or daughter's search and contact. At the same time, a significant minority reported feeling like spectators or as having been sidelined in much of the discussions and arrangements surrounding contact. It was their view that the focus of adoption had shifted to birth parents and to the adopted person, or as one of them put it:

> It appears that the rights of the child and the birth mother rub out all the loving care and devotion to the unwanted infant and the adoptive parents are pushed out into the background.

If a greater number of parents felt like this, they did not say so, appearing to want to act in a way that was supportive of the adopted person. There was a general view, however, that they could have been consulted more or perhaps their contribution in raising the adopted person given more recognition. While around three-quarters of them reported that they had supported their sons and daughters' search, and a significant number had welcomed it, at the same time almost half could not also help entertaining concerns and fears about their child or themselves being hurt in the process. Around a quarter of them came to learn about the contact only after the event, which hurt, but was explained, or rationalised, as a protective measure on the part of the adopted person. Those parents who knew about the search and contact beforehand were also more likely to look upon it more favourably. Even though most adopters were certain of the strength of their relationship with their sons and daughters, nevertheless, when it came to actual face-to-face meetings with the birth parent(s), some could not avoid wondering whether they might not in the end be rejected. Their certainty wavered progressively as each step taken by the adopted person led to greater involvement with the birth family. The gradual evolution from enquiry to contact and then to the development of relationships began to shake the certainty of many adoptive parents.

As it turned out, most of the fears either about themselves or of the adopted person being hurt in the process did not materialise. In contrast to the earlier fears and anxieties, the majority of parents came to identify many benefits for their sons and daughters, and some for themselves. For the adopted person, they particularly singled out background information, identity enhancement and the establishment of new relationships. It was surprising to find how many articulated identity issues as a key benefit to the adopted person and were very approving of the outcome. A significant proportion also referred with warmth and approval to the new relationships forged by the adopted person. The main benefits of contact they reported for themselves were a better understanding of the adopted person and, frequently, a strengthening of their relationship. The reported levels of closeness between them and the adopted person before and after contact and reunion with the birth family hardly changed. Almost nine out of ten reported very close or close relationships both before and after contact. Any criticisms they had about the outcome of contact was mainly about its impact on the adopted person. No adoptive parent had lost contact altogether with the adopted person, with almost nine out of ten saying that they had some form of direct or indirect contact at least once a week. In fact, our figures suggested that adoptive parents are more frequently in touch with their children than, perhaps, the general population (see McLone, 1996).

Those adoptive parents who had met the birth mother and/or other birth relatives were likely to come to view the search and contact more positively than the rest. In addition, they were pleased to have the birth mother's approval about the way they had brought up her child. Overall, eight out of ten said they were pleased about their sons and daughters' search and contact, even suggesting having benefited more from contact than the birth mother. The very positive evaluation of their relationship with the adopted person, and equally the good approval rates given to the outcome of contact overall, could raise questions about whether they were denying the fears, worries, anxieties, concerns and doubts they went through at the start, either on behalf of the adopted person or of themselves. As an example, in answer to a different question, around a quarter expressed a fair amount of dissatisfaction and concern, believing that their son or daughter was hurt, or had become unhappy or unsettled mainly as a result of rejection, but this was in relation to the adopted person and not themselves. A handful of them stood out from the rest by having rated the contact experience of their sons and daughters as being negative or being unsure about its value altogether. The great majority, however, were relieved that they were still viewed as "parents" by their sons and daughters and that the relationships that had developed with a birth parent were not on the whole of a parental nature.

Adoptive parents and their adopted sons and daughters

As with birth mothers and their sons and daughters, the perspective of 86 pairs of adoptive parents and adopted people were similarly compared and contrasted. The two groups reached high levels of agreement on a range of variables concerning the experience of growing up and with the search and reunion process, but significant differences also emerged. Almost half the adopted people who grew up in families with biological children said that they had been treated differently from birth children, but only 14 per cent of their parents confirmed this. In spite of this, no significant differences were found in terms of closeness to the adoptive parents, being loved, the overall adoptive experience or sense of belonging. One study that reported on children placed for adoption between the ages of five and nine found that children placed in families where there were already biological children tended to do worse on their measures of stability (Quinton et al, 1998).

More females than males in the present study disagreed with their parents and came to feel:

- less close to their adoptive parents;
- less happy about being adopted;
- a lesser sense of belonging;
- less positive about the overall experience of adoption;
- less included by the extended family;
- and scored higher emotional problems on the GHQ.

Sachdev (1992) and Pacheco and Eme (1993) too found that females in their studies were more likely to report an unhappy adoption experience and more identity problems. Interestingly, males in this study came to feel less positive in relation to their birth mothers while females felt less positive in relation to their adoption. The males' descriptive accounts confirmed greater loyalty to their adoptive parents and less to their birth mother, while the opposite appeared true in respect of females. We can only speculate whether females attach less well to substitute parents, and have a greater need, perhaps, to experience the birth parent–child relationship.

There were other areas where significant differences emerged between adopted people and their adoptive parents such as: the timing of the disclosure of the adoption, how openly adoption was discussed, and whether the extended family treated them the same. On the other hand, three-quarters of adopted people confirmed their parents' view that they had been supportive and pleased when contact was initiated. This was much more than the 36 per cent reported by Pacheco and Eme (1993) from their US study. Adopted people usually said that they got more out of contact than their parents, but a significantly higher proportion of the parents reported that they too benefited from it. Equally, parents did not agree with their sons and daughters that they were more worried, upset and angry about the contact. Significantly more adopted people did not agree with their parents' view that the contact experience had proved unsettling for them. Almost all adoptive parents described their current relationship with their sons and daughters as 'close' or 'very close', but only around three-quarters of adopted people agreed. Overall, levels of agreement between parents and children in many areas were high, but adoptive parents tended either to somewhat exaggerate their past and current closeness to the adopted person or, in the case of a minority, tended to exaggerate the negatives of contact. In the eyes of their sons and daughters, they minimised their own upset and worries arising from contact and stressed setbacks arising from their sons and daughters' relationship with a birth relative. Only exceptionally, however, did an adoptive parent criticise the adopted person directly, such as for not telling them beforehand about the contact, or for having acted disloyally or for not seeing more of them.

The adoption triangle

The impact of contact and reunion on each of the three groups has been a matter for speculation over the last thirty or so years following the opening of the records making contact possible. The general view so far has been that adoptive parents get the least out of contact, having been largely sidestepped (Post-Adoption Social Workers Group of New South Wales, 1988; McMillan and Hamilton, 1992; Mann, 1998). The final part of this analysis was to compare the views of adopted people, their birth mothers and adoptive parents in the 38 families where all three perspectives were available. Depending on who was being asked, the great majority of respondents from each group were pleased that the search and contact had taken place, though this ranged from three-quarters of adoptive parents to nearly all birth mothers. When asked if they wished contact had never happened, hardly anyone agreed: none of the birth mothers wished contact had not happened and only four per cent of adopted people and eight per cent of adoptive parents felt this way. When it came to how positive the overall experience had been, the levels were over 90 per cent for birth mothers and adopted people, but only 72 per cent for adoptive parents, confirming again that adoptive parents had more misgivings. Although their sons and daughters did not always share the negatives perceived by their parents, a minority of parents wanted to stress that their concerns arose from 'watching their child suffer', as some of them put it. On the whole, birth mothers did not appear to want to report negatives, expressing the highest levels of satisfaction compared to the other two groups. In the view of many birth mothers, they had already got a lot out of contact, often against all expectations. Relationships which consequently developed were looked upon as a kind of desired, but unexpected, bonus.

Around half of adopted people and birth parents, but only a quarter of adoptive parents, said that their self-esteem had improved as a result of contact. It is not surprising that significantly fewer adoptive parents reported an increase in self-esteem, as the main issue was between the birth mother and the adopted person. Around half of adoptive parents and adopted people, but two-thirds of birth mothers, also reported feeling more relaxed after contact. Our explanation for this is that birth mothers were more fearful, worried and anxious from the start and the mostly positive results reflected a relief. Members of each group who felt strained by the process were unconnected with each other. Possibly the biggest difference found between the three groups was that around three-quarters of adopted people and birth parents said they felt changed after contact, but only 14 per cent of adoptive parents said the same, suggesting again that the emotional stakes were not, perhaps, as high for them. Although most adoptive parents went through a period of doubt and anxiety about the adopted person's continued loyalty, only a few reported having found it difficult to cope with the intensity of the feelings aroused by contact. This contrasted with a third of adopted people and birth parents. Many of the adopters suggested that, although there were anxieties and worries, and sometimes concerns, they felt they could cope. Considering the good emotional health they scored on the GHQ, perhaps this should not come as a surprise.

All three groups emerged well with regard to their current emotional health. Adoptive parents scored the fewest severe emotional problems and adopted adults the most, but the difference was not significant. There was no congruence between the triads regarding the presence of severe emotional problems. In other words, it could not be said that if adopted people scored high on emotional problems they reflected the emotional health of either their adoptive parents or birth mothers. Compared also to adoptive parents, adopted people and birth mothers were more likely to ascribe any physical or emotional problems to the adoption. None of the three groups came to view contact as fraught with danger, even though, as seen elsewhere, for a minority of between 10 and 20 per cent of birth parents and adopted people, there was also rejection, disappointment and some disillusionment. Each group concentrated predominantly on the benefits they got out of contact rather than the disappointments. For adopted people, the benefits mainly concerned identity enhancement, the knowledge that they had not been rejected and the establishment of new and productive relationships. For birth mothers, it was the satisfaction that their child had a happy adoption and did not harbour anger towards them, thus allowing them to shed their guilt, as well as a relationship that they had hoped for but which was not central in their expectations. Even though between a quarter and a third of adoptive parents continued to have some misgivings, the main positives for them were the knowledge that, on the whole, their adopted sons and daughters were not hurt as they had feared and that they were still high in their children's estimation and love. They also acknowledged that, in a proportion of cases, the relationship between the adopted person and their newly-discovered birth family was working well and they were glad for them.

The law, contact and the future of adoption

A broadly similar proportion of all birth mothers, adopted people and adoptive parents knew about the Adoption Contact Register. However, seeker mothers were more likely to know about the Register than non-seeker ones, even though they did not enter their names in greater proportions. Seeker mothers were also less likely to worry about the provision of the Children Act 1975 for access on the part of the adopted person and more likely to support the idea of birth relatives having a right of access to the adopted person. Overall, the majority of these mothers' responses (60 per cent) suggested feeling mainly a lack of entitlement and fear about the reaction of their son or daughter, preferring to leave the initiative to the adopted person. Seeker mothers were also more likely to support the view that there should be no adoption in society. A small number of them were still carrying a fair amount of anger and bitterness about the "loss" of their child and thus wanted to redress the balance by supporting a right of access by birth relatives.

Of adopted people who knew about the Register, significantly more searching than non-searching ones entered their name, but then a greater number of the latter did not know about the Register. The wish of the majority of adopted people to be in control and have the initiative about who contacted them and when to search, found support from around two-thirds of both birth mothers and adoptive parents. Only a handful of adoptive parents wanted to be asked for their permission first.

In view of questions being raised, mostly outside Britain, about the continuation of adoption as an institution in a modern society, it was interesting to note that hardly any adopted person or adoptive parent subscribed to the idea of abolishing it. Almost all adoptive parents were in favour of continued adoption, as were nine out of every ten adopted people. It would be understandable that the birth mothers, mostly seekers, would support abolition, but in fact over two-thirds supported adoption (73 per cent). Many respondents from each group, including birth mothers, gave graphic examples of why they thought adoption should be preserved. Not only did they think that the alternatives were unattractive, but they claimed that the need for child care of this kind would always exist.

377

Final comments

What emerged from this study was that before contact all three members of the triangle, more so birth parents and adopted people, shared feelings and troubling thoughts that had mainly to do with loss, rejection, grief, sadness, guilt, fear and worry. Writing over ten years ago, Jane Rowe (1991, p7) made the comment that 'adoption grows out of grief and is never accomplished without pain'. Nothing found in this study would contradict that statement. Despite the additional tasks that both adoptive parents and adopted people had to accomplish, the outcomes found here about the quality of relationships between the two groups do not appear to differ from those in the general population. Furthermore, their almost total endorsement of adoption also gives additional credence to these findings. However, these findings hold true only for adopted people joining their adoptive families when mostly under the age of 18 months and who searched for or were sought by their birth mothers.

The approach for contact and reunion introduced both excitement and anticipation along with new fears, worries and suspicion, mainly about the other party's motives and expectations. At the same time, each party displayed mostly sensitivity and care to avoid hurting or upsetting the other or their respective families. All three parties were aware that the idea of contact was largely an uncharted area with no script to follow, except perhaps for what they had seen on television, read in newspapers or heard on the radio about contact and reunions. At the end, sufficient evidence was found by the study to suggest that contact contributed significantly to greater peace of mind for most members of the triangle. The new reported feelings, that mostly replaced the earlier ones, now included satisfaction and contentment, no more worry or fear, less or no guilt, feeling more relaxed, enhanced self-esteem, better emotional health, and no more or reduced feelings of loss and rejection.

Contact offered birth mothers the opportunity to satisfy themselves that the adopted person was well and mostly happy and to explain why they had been adopted. For the adopted people it was the satisfaction of finding answers to the many questions that had been troubling them for years and the subsequent linking of the information gained to various parts of their identity. New relationships were formed without it being at the expense of existing or parental ones, but relationships with siblings were particularly valued. Although it would appear that contact and reunion benefited mostly birth mothers and adopted people, adoptive parents insisted that they too got a lot out of it, mostly the satisfaction that many of their anticipated fears about the adopted person or themselves being hurt did not materialise. Even more satisfying for them was the knowledge that their sons and daughters' new relationships were not at their own expense. Considering the assumptions under which they adopted, the majority demonstrated remarkable adaptations, such as coming to recognise the place of the blood relationship in their child's life and their own.

We have no explanations for the finding that males were more likely than females to be loyal to their adoptive families and somewhat more critical of their birth mother. It could, however, explain the fact that fewer appear to search compared to females. Equally, it is a matter for speculation why females in the study came to feel less close to their adoptive parents, less happy about being adopted, conveyed a lesser sense of belonging, were less positive about the overall experience of adoption, felt less included by the extended family and scored higher emotional problems on the GHQ. Whether women have a greater need than men to experience the birth parent–child relationship remains an open question. It could reflect the comment made by about a fifth of birth mothers that something was missing from their relationship with the adopted person, probably because they had not parented him or her.

All the gains reported from contact and reunion should not detract from the intensity of the feelings experienced by many members of the triangle, the complications that at times arose, the anxieties many went through and the continued fluidity and changing nature of relationships giving rise to new anxieties and to a fair amount of stress. A small number from each group were still left with some disappointment or disillusionment. On the whole, the more disappointed the adopted adult or birth mother was, the more likely it was that they would be found amongst searchers than amongst non-searchers, but it should not detract from the fact that most searchers were positive or very positive about the contact and its outcome.

Considering the reported benefits of contact and reunion for all parties, the question could be asked whether forms of adoption that are open from the start could have prevented much of the anguish and pain. Since then, changes have been noted in the increasing number of mostly older children who now have contact with members of their birth families after adoption (see Lowe *et al*, 1999; Smith and Logan, 2004). With attention in Britain being focused on the adoption of older children, open adoption for very young children has hardly been debated. Speaking in the early 1990s, Hill (1991) referred to 'the continuing tendency to deal separately with just two periods in an adopted child's life – early childhood and early adulthood'. The reasons for this could be found in Modell's (1994) comment that 'open adoption is disturbing because it does not allow adoptive kinship to be just like biological kinship' (p 231). Although open adoption is not for everybody, it is perhaps the ultimate in acknowledging the "difference" that the blood connection makes in adoption, with adoption coming eventually to be seen, perhaps, as part of the "gift" relationship.

Finally, adoption touches the lives of millions in Britain either as adopted people, those related by blood to the adopted person and those related by adoption. The present study has explored the connections between experiences across several life stages from the viewpoint of birth parents, adopters and adopted people. Inevitably, such long-term follow-up reflects on circumstances and social conditions now well in the past. Besides demonstrating once again the importance of the blood relationship, the study also showed that psychosocial parenting worked well. The study has also identified the persisting interconnectedness of the three main parties in adoption even after years of total separation and, for the most part, the positive and reparative effects of searching and reunion. The issues will continue to be relevant for children who are reared by those other than their biological families and this includes those who are now adopted when older or from overseas.

Bibliography

Andersen R S (1988) 'Why adoptees search: motives and more', *Child Welfare*, 67:1, Jan–Feb, pp 15–19.

Aumend S A and Barrett M C (1984) 'Self-concepts and attitudes toward adoption: a comparison of searching and nonsearching adult adoptees', *Child Welfare:* LXIII (3), May/June, 1984, pp 251–259.

Betrocci D and Schechter D (1991) 'Adopted adults' perception of their need to search: implications for clinical practice', Smith Collection of Studies in Social Work, 61:2, pp 179–96.

Bohman M (1970) *Adopted Children and Their Families*, Stockholm: Proprius.

Bouchier P, Lambert L and Triseliotis J (1991) *Parting With a Child for Adoption*, London: BAAF.

Bowlby J (1980) *Attachment and Loss Vol. 3, Loss, Sadness and Despair*, New York: Basic Books.

Brinich M P (1990) 'Adoption from the inside-out: a psychoanalytic perspective', in Brodzinsky D M and Schechter M D (eds) *The Psychology of Adoption*, Oxford: Oxford University Press.

Brodzinsky A (1984) 'New perspectives on adoption revelation', *Adoption & Fostering*, 8:2, pp 27–32.

Brodzinsky A (1990) 'Surrendering an infant for adoption: the birth mother experience', in Brodzinsky D and Schecter M D (eds) *The Psychology of Adoption*, Oxford: OUP.

Brodzinsky D M, Schechter M D and Henig M P (1992) *Being Adopted*, New York: Doubleday.

Brown G W and Harris T (1978), *The Social Origins of Depression*, Tavistock: London.

Campbell L, Silverman P and Patti P (1991) 'Reunions between adoptees and birth parents: the adoptees' experiences', *Social Work*, 3, pp 329–35.

Clapton G (2003) *Birth Fathers and Their Adoption Experience*, London: Jessica Kingsley.

Cowell J, Crow K and Wilson A (1996) *Understanding Reunion: Connection and complexity*, New South Wales Post Adoption Centre.

Craig M (1991) 'Adoption: not a big deal', Unpublished report, Edinburgh: Scottish Adoption Society.

Cushman L T R, Kalmuss D and Namerow P B (1997) 'Openness in adoption: experiences and social psychological outcomes among birth mothers', in Gross H E and Sussman M B (eds), *Families and Adoption*, (pp 7–18). New York: The Haworth Press, Inc.

Deater-Deckard K and Petrill S A (2004) 'Parent–child dyadic mutuality and child behavior problems: an investigation of gene-environment processes', *Journal of Child Psychology and Psychiatry*, 45:6, pp 1171–1179.

Department of Health and Welsh Office (1992) *Review of Adoption Law: Report to the Ministers of an Independent Working Group: A consultation document*, London: Department of Health.

Department of Health (2000) *Intermediary Services for Birth Relatives: Practice guidelines*, London: Department of Health.

Depp C H (1982) 'After reunion: perception of adult adoptees, adoptive parents and birth parents', *Child Welfare*, 61, pp 115–119.

Deykin Y E, Pratti P and Ryan J (1988) 'Fathers of adopted children: a study of the impact of child surrender on birthfathers', *American Journal of Ortho-psychiatry* 58:2, pp 240–48.

Dominick C (1988) *Early Contact in Adoption*, Research Series 10, Dept of Social Welfare: Wellington, New Zealand.

Fratter J (1995) *Perspectives on Adoption With Contact: implications for policy and practice*, PhD Thesis, University of Cranfield.

Fravel D, McRoy R and Grotevant H (2000) 'Birth mother perceptions of the psychologically present adopted child: adoption openness and boundary ambiguity', *Family Relations*, 49, pp 425–33.

Garfinkel H (1967) *Studies in Ethnography*, New Jersey: Prentice Hall.

Giddens A (1992) *Modernity and Self Identity*, Cambridge: Polity.

Gladstone J and Westhues A (1998) 'Adoption reunions. A new side to intergenerational family relationships', *Family Relations*, 47, pp 177–184.

Glendinning R, Buchanan T and Rose N (2002) *A National Scottish Survey of Public Attitudes to Mental Health, Well Being and Mental Health Problems*, Edinburgh: Scottish Executive Social Research. (Unpublished information on the physical health of women by age group was also supplied to the writers privately.)

Goffman E (1969) *The Presentation of Self in Everyday Life*, Harmondsworth: Penguin.

Goldberg D (1972) *The Detection of Psychiatric Illness by Questionnaire*, Oxford: OUP.

Goldberg D and Williams P (1988) *User's Guide to the General Health Questionnaire*, Nelson: NFER.

Gonyo B and Watson K W (1988) 'Searching in adoption', *Public Welfare*, Winter, pp 14–22.

Greenwood S and Foster S (2000) *Tell Me Who I Am: Young people talk about adoption*, Manchester: TalkAdoption.

Grotevant H D and McRoy R (1998) *Openness in Adoption: Exploring family connections*, Thousand Oaks, CA: Sage.

Grotevant H D (2000) 'Openness in adoption: research with the adoption kinship network', *Adoption Quarterly*, 4, pp 45–65.

Haimes E and Timms N (1985) *Adoption, Identity and Social Policy*, London: Gower.

Hill M, Lambert L and Triseliotis J (1989) *Achieving Adoption With Love and Money*, London: National Children's Bureau.

Hill M (1991) 'Concepts of parenthood and their application to adoption', *Adoption & Fostering*, 15:4, pp 16–23.

Howe D (1996) *Adopters on Adoption*, London: BAAF.

Howe D, Sawbridge P and Hinnings D (1992) *Half a Million Women*, London: Penguin.

Howe D and Feast J (2000) *Adoption, Search and Reunion*, London: The Children's Society.

Howe D and Feast J (2001) 'The long-term outcome of reunions between adult adopted people and their birth mothers', *British Journal of Social Work*, 31, pp 351–368.

Houghton Committee Report (1972) *Report of the Departmental Committee on the Adoption of Children*, Home Office and Scottish Education Department.

Hughes B and Logan J (1993) *Birth Parents: The hidden dimension*, University of Manchester: Department of Social Policy and Social Work.

Hurst Report (1954) *Report of the Departmental Committee on the Adoption of Children*, London: HMSO.

Jaffee B and Fansell D (1970) *How They Fared in Adoption*, New York: Child Welfare League of America.

Keppel M (1991) 'Birth parents and negotiated adoption arrangements', *Adoption & Fostering*, 15:4, pp 81–90.

Kennard J (1991) *Adoption Information: The repossession of identity*, Wellington: Victoria University.

Kirk H D (1964) *Shared Fate: A theory of adoption and mental health*, New York: The Free Press.

Kirk H D (1981) *Adoptive Kinship*, Toronto: Butterworths.

Kornitzer M (1952) *Adoption in the Modern World*, London: Putman, 2nd edition 1959.

Kornitzer M (1968) *Adoption and Family Life*, London: Putman.

Kowal K A and Schilling K M (1985) 'Adoption through the eyes of adult adoptees', *American Journal of Orthopsychiatry*, 55, July, pp 354–62.

Kubler-Ross E (1970) *On Death and Dying*, London: Tavistock.

Lazarus R S and Folkman S (1984) *Stress, Appraisal, and Coping*, New York: Springer.

Lewis H D (1971) 'The psychiatric aspects of adoption', in Howells J A (ed) *Modern Perspective of Child Psychiatry*, New York: Brunner/Mazel.

Lichtenstein T (1996) 'To tell or not to tell: telling their adoptive parents about their search', *Child Welfare*, LXXIV (1) Jan–Feb, pp 61–72.

Lifton B J (1979) *Lost and Found: The adoption experience*, New York: Dial.

Logan J (1996) 'Birth mothers and their mental health: unchartered territory', *British Journal of Social Work*, 26, pp 609–625.

Love A (1990) *Adoption Reunion Study*, Children's Aid Society of Metropolitan Toronto.

Lowe N, Murch M, Borkowski M, Weaver A, Beckford V and Thomas C (1999) *Supporting Adoption*, London: BAAF.

Mander R (1995) *The Care of the Mother Grieving a Baby Relinquished for Adoption*, Aldershot: Avebury.

Mann S (1998) 'Adoptive parents: a practice perspective', *Adoption & Fostering*, 22:3, pp 42–52.

March K (1995) 'Perception of adoption as a social stigma: motivation for search and reunion', *Journal of Marriage and the Family*, 57, pp 653–60.

Marshall A and McDonald M (2001) *The Many-sided Triangle: Adoption in Australia*, Melbourne: University Press.

McLone M F, Park A and Roberts C (1996) *British Social Attitudes the 13th Report: Relative values: kinship and friendship*, Dartmouth: Darmouth Publishing Co Ltd.

McMillan R and Hamilton F (1992) 'Initiating contact with adoptive families and adopted people on behalf of birth parents and relatives', in *Conference Proceedings, Adult Counselling and Adoption*, Essex: Barnardos Post-Adoption Centre.

McRoy R, Zurcher L, Lauderdale M and Anderson R (1984) 'The identity of transracial adoptees', *Social Casework*, 65:1, pp 34–9.

McWhinnie A M (1967) *Adopted Children: How they grow up*, London: Routledge & Kegan Paul.

Midford S (1987) 'A measure of adoptee identity', *Uniview*, 6:1, pp 8–9.

Millen L and Roll S (1985) 'Solomon's mothers: a special case of pathological bereavement', *American Journal of Orthopsychiatry*, 55, pp 411–418.

Modell J S (1994) *Kinship With Strangers: Adoption and interpretations of kinship in American culture*, Berkeley: University of California.

Muller U and Perry B (2001) 'Adopted persons' search for and contact with their birth parents II: Adoptee-birth parent contact', *Adoption Quarterly*, 4:3, pp 5–37.

Neil E (2000) 'Contact with birth families after adoption', Paper given at the BAAF Research Group Meeting on 20/01/00.

Network 2:1 (1987) Wellington, New Zealand.

Pacheco F and Eme R (1993) 'An outcome study of the reunion between adoptees and biological parents', *Child Welfare*: LXXII, pp 53–64.

Pannor R, Massarik F and Evans B (1971) *The Unmarried Father: New helping approaches for unmarried young parents*, New York: Springer Publishing.

Parkes C M (1986) *Bereavement: Studies in adult grief*, 2nd edition, London: Tavistock.

Post-Adoption Social Workers Group of New South Wales (1988) *Experiences of Reunion After Adoption*, Sydney: The Post-Adoption Social Workers Group of New South Wales.

Quinton D, Rushton A, Dance C and Mayes D (1998) *Joining New Families: A study of adoption and fostering in middle childhood*, Chichester: John Wiley & Sons.

Raynor L (1980) *The Adopted Child Comes of Age*, London: Allen and Unwin.

Robinson E B (2000) *Adoption and Loss: The hidden grief*, South Australia: Clova Publications.

Robinson E B (2004) *Adoption and Recovery: Solving the mystery of reunion*, Clova Publications.

Roche H and Perlesz A (2000) 'A legitimate choice and voice: the experience of adult adoptees who have chosen not to search for their biological families', *Adoption & Fostering*, 4:2, pp 8–19.

Rockel J and Ryburn M (1988) *Adoption Today: Change and choice in New Zealand*, Auckland: Heinemann/Reed.

Rosenberg M (1965) *Society and the Adolescent Self-image*, New Jersey: Princeton Universtiy Press.

Rosenberg M (1979) *Conceiving the Self*, New York: Basic Books.

Roseneil S and Budgeon S (2004) 'Cultures of intimacy and care beyond 'the family': personal life and social change in the early 21st century', *Journal of Current Sociology*, 52:2, pp 135–159.

Rosenzweig-Smith J (1988) 'Factors associated with successful reunions of adult adoptees and biological parents', *Child Welfare*, 67, pp 411–422.

Rowe J (1991) 'Perspectives on adoption', in Hibbs E D (ed) *Adoption: International Perspectives*, Madison: International University Press.

Rozenberg, K F and Groze V (1997) 'The impact of secrecy and denial in adoption: practice and treatment issues', *Families in Society*, 78:5, pp 522–30.

Rynearson E K (1982) 'Relinquishment and its maternal complications: a preliminary study', *American Journal of Psychiatry*, 139, pp 338–40.

Sachdev P (1989) *Unlocking the Adoption Files*, Toronto: Lexington Books.

Sachdev P (1992) 'Adoption reunion and after: a study of the search process and experience of adoptees', *Child Welfare:* LXXI:1, pp 53–68.

Sants H J (1964) 'Genealogical bewilderment in children with substitute parents', *British Journal of Medical Psychology*, 37, pp 133–41.

Schechter M D (1960) 'Observations of adopted children', *Archives of General Psychiatry*, 3, July 1960, pp 21–23.

Schore A N (2003) *Affect Dysregulation and Disorder of the Self*, Norton & Company.

Seligman M E P (1975) *Helplessness*, San Francisco: Freeman.

Selwyn J and Sturges W (2001) *International Overview of Adoption – Policy and practice*, University of Bristol, School for Policy Studies.

Smith C and Logan J (2004) *After Adoption: Direct contact and relationships*, London: Routledge.

Sobol M and Cardiff J (1983) 'A sociopsychological investigation of adult adoptees' searching for their birth parents', *Family Relations*, 32, pp 477–483.

Sprang G and McNeil J (1995) *The Many Faces of Bereavement: The nature and treatment of natural traumatic and stigmatised grief*, New York: Brunner/Mazel.

Stanway, E (1996/97) 'Birth parent initiated contact: views and feelings of adult adoptees', *Adoption and Fostering*, 20:4, pp 22–28.

Stein L M and Hoopes J L (1985) *Identity Formation in the Adopted Adolescent*, New York: Child Welfare League of America.

Stoneman L, Thompson J and Webber J (1980) *Adoption Reunion: The study of the effect of reunion upon members of the adoption triad and their families*, Toronto: Children's Aid Society.

Stroebe W and Stroebe M S (1987) *Bereavement and Health: The psychological and physical consequences of partner loss*, Cambridge: University Press.

Tizard B and Phoenix A (1993) *Black, White or Mixed Race*, London: Routledge.

Triseliotis J (1970) *Adoption Policy and Practice*, University of Edinburgh: Department of Social Administration.

Triseliotis J (1973) *In Search of Origins*, London: Routledge & Kegan Paul.

Triseliotis J (1985) 'Adoption with contact', *Adoption & Fostering*, 9:4, pp 19–24.

Triseliotis J (1991) 'Maintaining the links in adoption', *British Journal of Social Work*, 21, pp 401–14.

Triseliotis J and Russell J (1984) *Hard to Place: Contrasting adoption and residential care*, London: Gower.

Triseliotis J, Shireman J and Hundleby M (1997) *Adoption: Theory, policy and practice*, London: Cassell.

Valley S, Bass B and Speirs C C (1999) 'A professionally led adoption trial group: an evolving approach to search and reunion', *Child Welfare*, LXXX, pp 363–379.

Velrhurst F C (2001) 'The development of internationally adopted children', in Selman P (ed) *Intercountry Adoption*, London: BAAF.

Warman A and Roberts C (2003) *Adoption and Looked After Children: An international comparison*, University of Oxford: Working paper 2003/1, Oxford Centre for Family Law and Policy and Department of Social Policy and Social Work.

Washington A (1982) 'A cultural and historical perspective on pregnancy-related activity among US teenagers', *Journal of Black Psychology*, 9, pp 1–28.

Wegan K (1997) *Adoption, Identity & Kinship*, London: Yale University Press.

Weinreb M and Murphy C (1988) 'The birth mother: a feminist perspective for the helping professional', *Woman and Therapy*, 7, pp 23–26.

Weinstein E A (1960) *The Self-image of the Child*, New York: Russell Sage Foundation.

Weiss R (1988) 'Loss and recovery', *Journal of Social Issues*, 44:3, pp 37–52.

Wells S (1993) 'What do birth mothers want?', *Adoption & Fostering*, 17:4, pp 22–26.

Winkler R and Van Keppel M (1984) *Relinquishing Mothers in Adoption*, Melbourne: Institute for Family Studies.

Witney C (2004) 'Original fathers: an exploration into the experiences of birth fathers involved in adoption in the mid-20th century', *Adoption & Fostering*, 28:3, pp 52–61.

Wrobel Ayers-Lope S, Grotevant H D, McRoy R and Friedrick (1996) 'Openness in adoption and the level of child participation', *Child Development*, 67:5, pp 2358–2374.

Young L (1954) *Out of Wedlock*, New York: McGraw-Hill.

Yelloly M (1965) 'Factors relating to an adoption decision by the mothers of illegitimate infants', *The Sociological Review*, 13:1, pp 5–14.

Index

Compiled by Elisabeth Pickard